'I SHALL NOT DIE'

'I SHALL NOT DIE'

Titokowaru's War
New Zealand, 1868-9

James Belich

The author gratefully acknowledges the assistance of the New Zealand Literary Fund and the Victoria University of Wellington Research Committee.

First published in 1989 by Allen & Unwin New Zealand Limited in association with the Port Nicholson Press, Wellington, New Zealand.

Reprinted in 1993 by Bridget Williams Books Limited, PO Box 11-294, Wellington, New Zealand.

ISBN 0 04614 022 0

The author gratefully acknowledges the assistance of the New Zealand Literary Fund and the Victoria University of Wellington Research Committee.

Typeset by Saba Graphics, Christchurch.
Printed by GP Print, Wellington.

CONTENTS

MAPS AND PLANS

Chapter One

TITOKOWARU'S PEACE

In 1845, after three years of missionary labour in South Taranaki, the Reverend John Skevington felt the need to refresh himself amongst his Methodist brethren. In September of that year, he travelled to Auckland to participate in the District Synod. He took with him the most promising of his young acolytes from the Ngati Ruanui tribe. On 21 September, Skevington and his party attended the Methodist church in High Street to hear James Wallis, 'a prince of preachers'. Perhaps overcome by Wallis's oratory, Skevington had a seizure and died on the spot. His grieving Maori disciples were left to wander around Auckland for a few days before beginning the long journey home. Among them was a young man of about twenty-two, baptised Joseph Orton, after another Wesleyan missionary.

Auckland would have made a profound impact on the young man. In a mere five years, it had grown to a township of 3,000 people, the largest community he had ever seen. As New Zealand's capital, it already had a few substantial buildings, and Orton may have seen Governor Robert FitzRoy and his entourage riding through the streets. In 1845, Auckland was also a major military base, the point where troops and cannon disembarked from Australia before going north to fight the Ngapuhi chiefs, Hone Heke and Kawiti. Joseph Orton could have watched the splendid 96th Regiment parade at Fort Britomart and the tall ships sail in and out of the Waitemata Harbour.

But he would not have gone away totally impressed with British power and the splendour of its works. He may have walked in awe up Queen Street, but he would have done so up to his knees in mud, fording a stream where the Town Hall now stands. Auckland in 1845 was 'a beggarly collection of poverty stricken huts and wooden houses'; 'the whole town had a slatternly and neglected look'. Another visitor, Constantine Dillon, found it 'a horrid place, always raining . . . everything dirty and shabby, the people all Jews or people from N.S. [New South] Wales'. The local Maori, Ngati Whatua, lounged in the streets in groups, smoking pipes, still pleased with themselves for having obtained so many valuable Pakeha (Europeans). But there was room for cultural misunderstanding. One Pakeha patronisingly admired the facial moko of a passing Maori while walking up Queen Street. The Maori turned his back and exposed his even more richly tattooed buttocks, saying, 'That's nothing, look at this' – the traditional whakopohane insult, recently revived in New Zealand.

The talk of the town in September 1845 was all bad, for the Northern War had so far been an unbroken series of British disasters. In March, Ngapuhi had taken and sacked the important settlement of Kororareka, and a punitive expedition against Heke in May had failed. On 1 July, the brilliant old general Kawiti had thrashed a British force six times his own strength at his pa of Ohaeawai, perhaps the most advanced earthwork fortification built anywhere up to then. Auckland had panicked, and some townspeople had sold off their goods for token prices and shipped out. When an Auckland property developer sells three houses for fifteen pounds, the situation must be dire indeed. Blockhouses were built and the barracks fortified. Its trench was dug the same size as the Duke of Wellington's at Torres Vedras, on the assumption that what had stopped Napoleon's armies would certainly stop Hone Heke's. And, on the very day of Skevington's death, Governor FitzRoy received notice of his dismissal and Auckland was 'all in a bustle' at the news.

Joseph Orton was a highly intelligent young man, with keen eyes and a retentive memory. He would have learned a lot from the Auckland of September 1845 – about British military might and its limitations, about British politics and the way it could effect the conduct of war, about British thinking, its peculiarities, strengths, and weaknesses. Had the Aucklanders been able to see into the future, they would have deeply begrudged him this knowledge. For Joseph Orton was also Riwha Titokowaru, perhaps the greatest war leader either of New Zealand's peoples has ever produced.

Titokowaru was born about 1823 near the southern slopes of the lone mountain, Taranaki. He traced his descent from the legendary ancestor Turi, captain of the *Aotea* canoe, and his lineage embraced the Ngarauru tribe and two of Ngati Ruanui's three subtribes, Tangahoe and Ngaruahine. Ngaruahine was his primary subtribe and Ngati Manuhiakai was his hapu, or clan. His father, the elder Titokowaru, was one of the leaders of Ngaruahine at the great victory of Waimate about 1834, when they and their allies of the Taranaki tribe finally repulsed the invasions of the Waikato confederation – an achievement sometimes credited to his eleven-year-old son. The elder Titokowaru became Christian around 1845, but his 'conversion' was not the sort of which missionary tales are made. He seems to have been baptised simultaneously into the Anglican and Methodist churches, the former as Teira (Taylor, honouring the influential missionary Richard Taylor), the latter as Hori Kingi (George King). Hori Kingi Titokowaru died in 1848, as one of the leading chiefs of the whole Ngati Ruanui tribe.

The inheritance of leadership was by no means automatic, and Titokowaru did not equal his father's mana, or prestige, until his mid-forties. He spent his life until then as an important but secondary chief and spokesman, and as a student of Maori and Pakeha knowledge. He joined John Skevington at his Heretoa mission station in 1842, was baptised Hohepa Otene (Joseph Orton), mastered the Christian Bible, and learned to write superbly in Maori by 27 September 1845, the date of his first known letter. 'Had Mr Skevington not settled among us,' he wrote, 'my people [would have] all gone over to the church of outward shows' – the Church of England. After visits to Auckland and other towns, and ten years as a Methodist teacher, his knowledge of Pakeha was much deeper than that of most Maori. There are one or two signs that he may even have been able to read English. But ultimately his immense Maori learning contributed most to his mana. How he came by it we do not know, though we may guess he was formally trained as a tohunga, or priest, perhaps by or with the renowned Ngaruahine priest-historian, Tauke Te Hapimana.

Titokowaru's life must also have included a great deal of learning about war. 'In his youth', it was said, 'he was an unusually plucky, dare-devil kind of young man, ready for any mischief, and perfectly fearless.' No doubt he absorbed the lessons of the tribal 'Musket Wars' of his childhood, together with the vast knowledge of war in Maori tradition. But aspects of his military art could only have come through experience. At about the age of seventeen he probably fought in skirmishing against the Whanganui and Ngati Tuwharetoa tribes during which his father spared the life of a captured Whanganui chief – an act of mercy that was to stand him in good stead. His first sustained military experience, however, could not have come until his early thirties.

In August 1854, Ngati Ruanui, staunch land holders, marched north to aid Wiremu Kingi Te Rangitake of Te Atiawa against the land-selling faction of his tribe. The fighting was somewhat restrained, as befitted a quarrel between relatives, but it flared anew in 1856 and 1858, and most Ngati Ruanui warriors were involved in it. The

tribe backed Wiremu Kingi again in the Taranaki War of 1860-1,
first of the Anglo-Maori conflicts of the 1860s. The Maori army mass-
produced modern pa of the Ohaeawai type, and it was presumably
here that Titokowaru acquired his great practical mastery of field
engineering. Titokowaru himself may be the 'Hohepa' who killed
Captain William King near New Plymouth on 8 February 1861. Ngati
Ruanui were less prominent in the Waikato War of 1863-4, when
the British sought to crush the great Maori nationalist organisation,
the King Movement. But they were involved in renewed fighting
in Taranaki on 30 April 1864, when they and other adherents of
the new Pai Marire religion rashly assaulted a redoubt at Sentry
Hill. Titokowaru was badly wounded when a glancing blow on the
brow from a rifle bullet cost him the sight of his right eye. He
carried the terrible scar for the rest of his life, an enduring reminder
of the folly of frontal attack.

   Peace and war were always the competing halves of Titokowaru's
life. After the tribal fighting of 1840, he was converted to peace
by Jesus Christ. If he is the Hohepa identified by Taranaki historian
Ian Church, he was preaching peace in Christian terms in 1850: 'Give
over war. Do not say I am laying down the law, it is Christ who
is doing so.' But by 1854 both tone and message had changed. In
May that year, Ngati Ruanui hosted a great land-holding meeting
at Manawapou, a seminal event in the history of Maori nationalism.
Here Hohepa said: 'My mother is dead and I was nourished by her
milk and thus let our land be kept by us as milk for our children.'
He was the first to sign the land-holding oath – 'The man first,
the land afterward' – and for the next decade he walked the paths
of war. But in 1866 he was again converted to peace by a great
prophet: this time Te Ua Haumene, founder of Pai Marire.

   Te Ua, a man of Taranaki and Atiawa, evolved his creed between
1862 and 1864. Like previous prophetic movements, Pai Marire
amalgamated Maori and European beliefs with the innovations of
its founder. The contribution of ancient Maori religion was less overt
than in some earlier and later cults, but Te Ua still functioned as
a traditional tohunga, mouthpiece of his special gods. The 'Christian'
element actually emphasised the Old Testament, with Jehovah as the
main deity and the Maori associated with the Jews. Te Ua also
emphasised Rura and Riki, twin gods of peace and war. The Pakeha
always associated Pai Marire with Riki; 'Hauhau' became a synonym
for hostile Maori, and it is true that subordinate prophets sometimes
used it as a militant creed, as at Sentry Hill. But in Te Ua's own

Te Ua Haumene
Auckland Institute and Museum

thinking, Rura always dominated Riki. Indeed, Te Ua can be seen as the founder of a great Maori movement of non-violent resistance of which the Maori King, Tawhiao or Matutaera, the prophet Te Whiti O Rongomai of Parihaka, and Titokowaru himself became branches.

Te Ua's career was influential but short. When he died in October 1866, it was Titokowaru who took up his mantle. Whether Titokowaru was simply the new priest of Pai Marire is another matter. Maori religion did not work that way; each in a succession of prophets struck his own balance between old and new. Pai Marire was certainly an element in Titokowaru's religion, but so was Christianity and an increased emphasis on selected traditional Maori beliefs. We know most about this in the context of war, when Titokowaru revived fearsome ancient ceremonies and invoked the gods Tu, Maru, and Uenuku, all of whom had warlike aspects. But the original syncresis, like Te Ua's, was one of peace and reconciliation. Uenuku,

Titokowaru's special deity, whose divine breath was the north-west wind, was the Rainbow God, of many aspects. The ancient carving representing him can still evoke awe. Uenuku was also the enemy of Turi in legendary Hawaiki. Titokowaru healed rifts in the spiritual world and, partly through this, in the temporal. Like Te Ua's before him and Te Whiti's after him, Titokowaru's religion was originally pacifist.

The physical picture of Titokowaru left us by the historical record is one-dimensional and often hostile. The sketches taken of him in later life, showing a hunched old man with a long black beard, are little more than caricatures, and around this time a colonial soldier described him as 'the ugliest and most villainous looking Maori I ever saw, and his blind eye added much to his lack of favours in looks'. This scar did leave him a 'disfigured countenance', but he was also 'a stern and commanding man', 'strongly-built', of 'medium height', with no moko and a 'commanding and determined aspect'. 'He was about five feet nine in height and somewhat spare and muscular, with fine bone, an alert active man, but by no means good-looking. His skin was rather darker than the general run of Maoris, and his nose low in the bridge, with wide nostrils.' Even in old age, the most unusual thing about him was his voice.

His voice was particularly striking. In ordinary speech even, it was arresting in its depth and fulness, overwhelming all other voices in the vicinity, and without any effort, filling the room. It was a remarkably clear, full, deep-toned voice . . . awe inspiring in its power and tremendous effect upon his hearers.

In 1867, it was said that 'when roused he had a voice like a roaring lion'.

Titokowaru impressed others effortlessly, and his subsequent achievements as well as his voice inspired awe amongst his friends and fear amongst his enemies. But Titokowaru had other facets, hints of which poke through the documentary record. He enjoyed liquor and friendly banter, and probably played draughts. He made strong friendships with both men and women, and may have been very active sexually with the latter. That he was capable of great kindness and sensitivity is abundantly clear from his treatment of his friend and servant, the renegade Kimble Bent. And, in the context of his bush village in war-torn South Taranaki, he was given to dressing in a manner that can only be described as eccentric: 'he frequently appeared in a black "hard-hitter" hat and a full suit of European clothing'.

Imperial troops crossing the Tangahoe River during Cameron's invasion *From a watercolour by E. A. Williams, Alexander Turnbull Library*

So we find Titokowaru at the beginning of 1867, the point at which his story merges with that of this book.

For the Maori people of South Taranaki, that year opened like the aftermath of some natural disaster, a new stillness marred by the echoes of terrible strife. Despite their involvement in the wars of 1860-4, Ngati Ruanui and Ngarauru had always fought away from home and so emerged almost unscathed – even at Sentry Hill they lost only eight dead. But in 1865-6, their invulnerability collapsed in fire and blood as the British mounted three campaigns against them. In January–March 1865, an Imperial army under General Duncan Cameron invaded them from the south. With 3,000 men to their 500, Cameron pushed through Ngarauru, Pakakohe (the third Ngati Ruanui subtribe), and Tangahoe coastal territory, bypassing the strong modern pa of Weraroa, and tempting them into brave but disastrous open battles at Nukumaru and Te Ngaio. Cameron was much maligned for his slowness in the colonial press. In fact, his methodical invasion ripped open South Taranaki like a tin-opener, leaving it vulnerable to the tender mercies of his ruthless successors.

Ngarauru prisoners taken at Weraroa during Cameron's invasion   *R. Parsons Album, Alexander Turnbull Library*

In January–February 1866, the Imperial General Trevor Chute mounted a lightning campaign further inland with a mixed light column of Imperials, colonials, and Whanganui 'kupapa' – Maori fighting on the British side. His eventual march around the mountain to New Plymouth became undeservedly famous, but before this he destroyed a score of Ngati Ruanui settlements. Not all the pa stormed were hostile, not all the villages burned were fortified, and not all the Maori slain were armed, but the devastation was just the same. This was the terrible strategy known as 'bush-scouring' – sudden attacks on soft targets, even deep in the bush. Later that year, from August to November, colonial troops under Major Thomas McDonnell took over active operations from the Imperials in a campaign sparked off by McDonnell's treacherous attack on the village of Pokaikai. With fewer resources than Chute, McDonnell had a harder time of it, but he too killed and burned his share.

By the end of 1866, South Taranaki had been disembowelled. The surviving Ngati Ruanui and Ngarauru had fled the coastal lowland for their ancient fastnesses in the mountainous inland forest. But the notion that Maori could easily pluck a living from the bush was always nonsense: these refuges could not feed them for long, and soon some had to trickle back to the arable areas, under the shadow of British redoubts. This was the classic lever by which Maori groups were prised into some sort of submission: concede, become 'insiders' and lose some of your best land, or remain 'outsiders', independent in your bush fastnesses, and lose the lot. So the people emerged from their hideouts and set about picking up the pieces of their lives, renewing cultivations, building new villages, and rebuilding some of the old. The mere cessation of violence was not enough to allow this process of reconstruction. The tensions between tribe and subtribe, born of desperate and sometimes selfish resistance and collaboration, had yet to be repaired. There were still more than 1,000 troops in the district, Imperial, colonial, and kupapa, and the situation was always ready to explode like an unstable bomb. Until peace was formalised and given some prospect of permanence, the situation remained hopelessly insecure. It was in this context that Titokowaru began his great campaign of peace and reconciliation.

This peace campaign and Titokowaru's leadership of Ngaruahine begin together; it made him just as he made it. His own rise was paralleled by the increasing significance of his village, Te Ngutu o te Manu, The Beak of the Bird. Indelibly associated, like its chief, with later, bloodier events, it too first came to prominence as a focus of peace, comparable to Te Whiti's Parihaka. Around the New Year 1867, it was rebuilt from the ashes of McDonnell's campaign as the headquarters of Ngaruahine. The new village had fifty-eight houses, a large marae, and a great meeting house, Wharekura or House of Knowledge, variously reported as being seventy and ninety feet long and made of dressed planks described by one Pakeha as 'weatherboard'. It was 'beautifully carved and lined with ornamental flaxwork' in the traditional style, and had a raised platform at one end from which the chief addressed his people. It was erected in six days, in obedience to the Scriptural command 'Six days shalt thou labour'. Archaeologists sometimes assess a ruler's power by the resources he could command for building. In terms of the war-torn South Taranaki of 1867, Wharekura and the new village of Te Ngutu are solid evidence of Titokowaru's ascension to a role of subtribal and even tribal leadership. The previous chief, Tamati Hone Oraukawa, lived at Te Ngutu in respected semi-retirement. Titokowaru's lieutenants included Haowhenua, Toi Whakataka, Kokiri, and Tauke Te Hapimana.

Te Ngutu o te Manu was the scene of a series of tribal and inter-tribal meetings, the basis of Titokowaru's peace campaign, held throughout 1867 and early 1868. The first known peace hui at Te Ngutu was held around 4 January. Titokowaru hosted a delegation from the King Movement, led by the chief More, who was henceforth

to act as the Kingite ambassador to Taranaki. More represented the
organisation which had been the backbone of Maori military resistance,
but his mission was now one of peace. Ngaruahine told him that
they too wished for peace, and More announced this to the Pakeha,
their first intimation of Ngaruahine's change of heart. In mid-February,
another, larger meeting was held at Te Ngutu of all the Ngati Ruanui
resisters. As a result of this, a formal letter was sent to the Pakeha
commanders, announcing a desire for peace on the basis of the status
quo: 'The reason of our meeting is we wish to return to our former
position and live in peace with the Pakehas.' Ngaruahine would 'not
molest anybody if nobody molested them'. But things were not that
simple. To be acceptable to the Pakeha, peace had somehow to
accommodate one great problem: creeping confiscation.

In 1865, Governor George Grey had proclaimed the whole South
Taranaki coast, from the Stony River to the Waitotara, a belt twenty
miles broad, to be confiscated. Some was to be sold to help pay
for the war, and some allocated to the 'Military Settlers' recruited
to fight it. On this basis, Ngati Ruanui and Ngarauru returning to
their coastal lowland in 1867 were all squatting on government land.
But the Maori treated confiscation by proclamation as meaningless,
and, in practice, so did the government. It had neither the foresight
nor the resources to implement confiscation wholesale. Actual
surveying and occupation depended on short-term, pragmatic factors:
the need to acquire land for a particular purpose, such as finding
farms for a military settler unit whose term of service had expired;
the availability of funds and troops for surveying and covering parties,
and the extent to which it seemed a given group of Maori could
be pushed before they began to resist. So real confiscation was sporadic,
piecemeal, and unpredictable; an insidious, seeping, nibbling process,
a slow cancer.

There were two ways in which the Maori could seek remission.
One was to negotiate with the government for formal recognition
of ownership through the establishment of 'Native Reserves'. The
other was to gain informal recognition of ownership through persistent
'passive' resistance. The colonial government no longer had much
Imperial help, and it was reluctant to renew expensive warfare if
it could get what it wanted without it. If it seemed that peaceful
obstruction might turn violent, the government might hesitate. But,
after Cameron, Chute, and McDonnell had done their work, South
Taranaki Maori military power was at a low ebb. Passive resistance
became a deadly dangerous game of bluff.

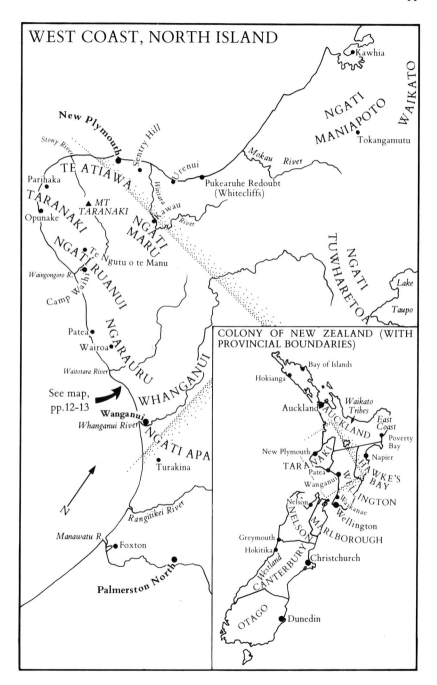

WEST COAST, NORTH ISLAND

Kawhia

NGATI MANIAPOTO

WAIKATO

New Plymouth

Stony River

Sentry Hill

Urenui

Mokau River

Tokangamutu

TE ATIAWA

Waitara

Parihaka

▲ MT TARANAKI

Kawau River

Pukearuhe Redoubt
(Whitecliffs)

TARANAKI

Opunake

NGATI MARU

Te Ngutu o te Manu

NGATI TUWHARETOA

Waingongoro R.

NGATI RUANUI

Camp Waihi

Lake

Taupo

Patea

Wairoa

NGARAURU

COLONY OF NEW ZEALAND (WITH
PROVINCIAL BOUNDARIES)

Waitotara River

WHANGANUI

Bay of Islands

Hokianga

See map,
pp.12-13

Waikato
Tribes

Auckland

AUCKLAND

Wanganui

Whanganui River

East
Coast

NGATI APA

New Plymouth

Poverty
Bay

Turakina

TARANAKI

Napier

Patea

HAWKE'S
BAY

Wanganui

WELLINGTON

N

Nelson

Waikanae

Rangitikei River

Wellington

NELSON

MARLBOROUGH

Manawatu R.

Foxton

Greymouth

Hokitika

Christchurch

Westland

Palmerston North

CANTERBURY

OTAGO

Dunedin

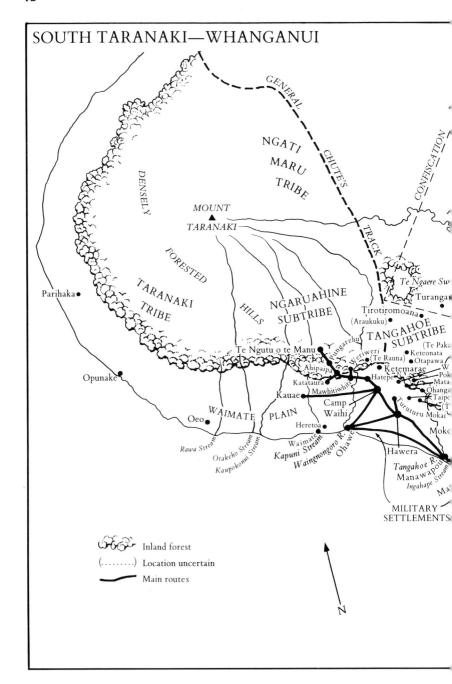

SOUTH TARANAKI—WHANGANUI

GENERAL CHUTE'S TRACK

CONFISCATION

NGATI MARU TRIBE

DENSELY

MOUNT ▲ TARANAKI

FORESTED

Parihaka●

TARANAKI TRIBE

HILLS

NGARUAHINE SUBTRIBE

Te Ngaere Sw

Turanga

Tirotiromoana● (Araukuku)●

TANGAHOE SUBTRIBE

(Te Paka

Te Ngutu o te Manu●

Wiriweri (Te Rauna)

Keteonata● Otapawa●

Ahipaipa

Ketemarae●

W Po Mata

Opunake●

Katataura● Hatepe●

Ohanga Taipo (T

Kauae● Mawhitiwhiti

Camp Waihi

Turuturu Mokai Moko

Oeo● WAIMATE PLAIN

Heretoa●

Rawa Stream

Otakeho Stream

Kaupokonui Stream

Waimate Kapuni Stream

Waingnongoro R. Ohawe

Hawera

Tangahoe R. Manawapou Ingahape Stream Ma

MILITARY SETTLEMENTS

Inland forest

(........) Location uncertain

—— Main routes

N

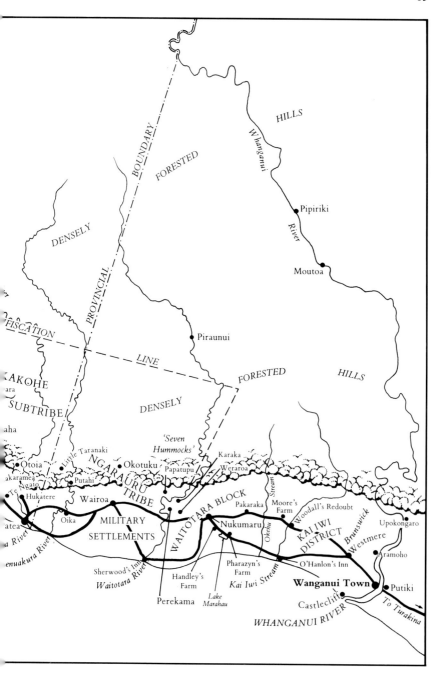

The first solution to creeping confiscation was practised most successfully by 'insider' chiefs, who had opened good channels of communication with Taranaki Civil Commissioner Robert Reid Parris, his subordinate James Booth, Resident Magistrate of Patea, and his superior James Richmond, *de facto* Minister of Native Affairs – all three of whom were sometimes humane but always land hungry. Most Ngarauru and Tangahoe chiefs were now insiders, and they did least badly from the Native Reserves. The officials also negotiated with Ngaruahine and Pakakohe, mainly 'outsiders', who were prepared to sacrifice some land in return for peace. But the reserves planned for them were small and ill defined, and included insufficient good land for their needs. The government had 'called them to come . . . [and] live peaceably', they told Parris, 'and now are going to starve them'. They reoccupied empty land anyway, assuming the Pakeha had taken their share, but were periodically pushed off by fresh nibbles of creeping confiscation. 'Parris', they said, 'went eating up the land as cattle did grass.'

On 20 March 1867 Ngaruahine and Pakakohe faced this crisis at meetings at Te Ngutu and its Pakakohe equivalent, Whakamara. The decision for peace was unanimous, but the meetings also decided passively to resist the further extension of confiscation. As it happened, the government was not yet ready to encroach into Ngaruahine territory, and it was Pakakohe who bore the brunt. The term of service of two companies of military settlers had just expired, and the government decided to locate these around Manutahi, in the economic heart of Pakakohe country. The surveyors were soon hard at work here, but they found that Pakakohe 'seemed determined not to allow the survey to go on'. The Manutahi surveys were stopped several times before the end of March, and an attempt to survey the Whenuakura block, south of the Patea River, met similar obstruction. During April, both sides persisted in their efforts. The surveyors made some progress in the immediate vicinity of Manutahi, but could not proceed further inland. On 25 April one surveyor reported that 'the surveys have again been stopped for the fifth time by the Natives of Te Whakamara', this time led by an armed warrior, Tutere. 'He told me that the surveys must stop at the Mokoia track as no sword had ever been drawn upon the inland side of that place therefore the land belonged to them.'

On 15 May James Booth met the two leading Pakakohe chiefs, Te Wharematangi and Ngawaka Taurua, at Hukatere. Te Wharematangi told Booth,

*I speak on behalf of my tribe the Pakakohi. The surveyors shall not cross
the Patea. You are a bad man, you come amongst this people professing to
bring peace and goodwill, we agree to peace and now you want to steal our
land. If the Governor wanted to take our land why did he not take it at
the time fighting was going on, and not first make peace with us, and afterwards
take our land.*

Booth replied, 'Your lands were confiscated in 1865 and you have
all along been aware of the fact.'

'The Governor has no land whatever in this district,' said
Wharematangi.

Booth turned to the practicalities. 'If I persist and send the surveyors
tomorrow what course will you take?'

'Listen, we will not strike the first blow,' he was told, 'but we
will send off anyone who may attempt to make any survey on our
lands.'

Taurua supported Wharematangi. They were, he said, 'one and
all determined to resist any attempt at surveying beyond the Patea'.
Folding his arms across his chest, he declared, 'We mean to resist
in this fashion, but if you the government after our passive resistance
determine that the work shall go on, we are quite agreeable that
it shall be so. Do not think that this is a new word, all this was
arranged during the meeting at Whakamara.'

At this clear evidence of Pakokohe determination, Booth called
off the survey for the moment, and referred the problem to Wellington,
now the capital. But Wharematangi believed that it was only a matter
of time before the government called his bluff, and he began to consider
military resistance. In this frame of mind, he travelled north to attend
another meeting at Te Ngutu, long scheduled by Titokowaru for
25 May. Here he proposed a resort to arms, 'but Tito Kouru the
Chief who called the meeting was opposed to this', and he managed
to dissuade Wharematangi and renew the tribe's determination for
peace. By 2 June, a colonial officer could already see the effects:
'The Natives in this district from the favourable result of the meeting
. . . of the 25th of last month have assumed a much more peaceful
attitude.'

Titokowaru probably did not disagree with Wharematangi's belief
that creeping confiscation had been postponed, not defeated. He felt,
rather, that even this loss had to be minimised then accepted as
preferable to a hopeless war. But to persuade others to this view,
to reduce Pakeha aggression through formal reconciliation, and so

prevent a recurrence of the May crisis, required more than peace meetings alone. So in June 1867, he set off on a hikoi, a march of peace and reconciliation, accompanied by virtually his whole following – fifty or sixty men and eighty women and children. They came first to the colonist military base at Camp Waihi, where on 10 June a remarkable ceremony took place, of which Captain William Newland left this account:

Titoko Waru . . . sent word . . . he wished to pay a compliment by marching around the Position three times to show his great respect for the Queen. Col. McDonnell was in Wanganui . . . so I had to do the entertaining . . . seeing them coming all the men were ordered inside the Redoubt till they had marched three times round, about 50 of them in the procession, Titoko Waru with his other head men walking in the rear. After performing this piece of foolery, they walked to the enclosure provided for them and sat down . . . The food that had been in course of preparation was brought to them and they looked as if a good feed would do them no harm. They waited till Titoko Waru came in front and looked at the food and then broke a piece of bread and tasted it.

Newland later invited Titokowaru and his leading subordinates to the officers' mess:

Titoko Waru looked at me with his one eye and said 'why invite us and leave out all my Tamariki' meaning his followers. I told him the Officers were inviting him and only Rangatiras [chiefs] would be present . . . He remained undecided for a short time then said he would come . . . We all adjourned to the Mess-room and had a long talk, but old Waru was too cunning to say much, and time soon passed. I said 'Before you go I want to propose health and long life to Queen Victoria . . . all stood but Waru and his followers. I said stand up and drink the health. He muttered something [about] not caring [for] it . . . I said . . . I am surprised after your being allowed to march around the Redoubt, in compliment to the Queen, that you should refuse to drink her health.' After a little more talk I suppose his heart softened for he and his followers stood up and drank the health.

The following day, the expedition proceeded to the next colonist post, Turuturu Mokai, where the ceremony was repeated. Again 'they were given plenty to eat. Titoko Waru as before came forward, broke a piece off one of the loaves, put it in his mouth and made a signal with his hand that it was all right.' Again Nguruahine participated in the Pakeha ceremony of a toast in rum: 'Strange to say there were no abstainers and they took the medicine very kindly.' The hikoi then continued south.

McDonnell, now a lieutenant-colonel, returned from Wanganui to Patea on 12 June and rode immediately to Camp Waihi, where Newland told him he had missed Titokowaru's hikoi by two days. Determined to get in on the act, McDonnell wrote to Titokowaru about 15 June requesting a meeting at Manutahi. By this time, Titokowaru had already visited the district and was scheduled to move on to Hukatere. He sent McDonnell 'a very cool and dignified answer' to the effect that they should meet there instead. McDonnell would have none of this native bounce, and he replied that it would be Manutahi or nowhere. So Titokowaru turned about, with his entourage of men, women, and children, and returned to Manutahi. Here, on Wednesday 19 June 1867, the two leaders met face to face.

A tall, well-built man of thirty-four years, with soldierly whiskers and a dashing air, Thomas McDonnell was a Pakeha New Zealander, born in the Philippines by a travelling accident but bred since early childhood at the Hokianga, north of Auckland, with his three younger soldier-brothers, William, George, and Edward. His father, Thomas senior, had been a naval officer: a captain in conversation, a commander in writing, and a lieutenant in fact. In the wild Hokianga of the 1830s he became a merchant prince, and his sons grew up self-confident and tough. Thomas senior was wealthy, but he was sometimes known as 'McDiddle', and young Tom claimed he 'never received a penny . . . to commence life upon'. After spending his twenties drifting around Australasia, Tom joined the colonial forces in 1863, during the Waikato War, and found his niche in life. He crammed a great deal of experience into four years' warfare, and his rise was swift. By 1866, 'Fighting Mac' was the colony's favourite soldier, 'regarded as the embodiment of Pakeha prowess and determination' and rivalled only by his friend Gustavus Von Tempsky. 'McDonnell is the man to go out with!,' enthused one subordinate, 'he is "all there" as the saying goes.'

In fact, McDonnell was not quite 'all there'. His mastery of Maori metaphor was a self-delusion, and he believed that force was the only argument which natives respected. There was a touch of paranoia about his jealousy of rivals such as Robert Parris, his desire for acclaim, and his readiness to detect treachery everywhere. But McDonnell was a physically and mentally formidable fighting man, with some real knowledge of Maoridom, and his volatility made him all the

Thomas McDonnell
Alexander Turnbull Library

more dangerous. Handling him would be a stern test of Titokowaru's diplomacy.

The two exchanged greetings and 'Titokowaru then sang a few songs expressive of his wish for peace.' Of the disputed lands he said: 'As for the lands let them go I wish to leave in peace.' McDonnell congratulated him on his enlightenment, and invited the whole hikoi to Patea. It came, and the Waihi reconciliation ceremony was again repeated. But this time all did not go smoothly. 'In the evening they gave us some songs and Hakas,' wrote McDonnell, 'and Titokowaru presented me with a small earring of greenstone, towards the finish

they had some prayers, and at last began to pray for the Maori King.'
For McDonnell, as for most Pakeha, the King was still the symbol
of Maori intransigence at its worst. The fact that peace was now
the Kingite policy had simply passed them by. With still less tact
than his subordinate Newland, McDonnell did not even bother to
remonstrate but opted for instant confrontation. 'We all rose up and
left the House', giving three cheers for the governor. He returned
Titokowaru's gift, and reversed his decision to accompany the hikoi
on the next leg of its journey. This was potential disaster, for a
furious McDonnell was no joke. He observed the Maori reaction
with some satisfaction. 'I never saw Natives in a greater fright.'

Next morning, Titokowaru set about the delicate task of appeasing
McDonnell with a foray into mysterious Pakeha ritual. McDonnell
was parading his men in an intimidating display of power when the
Maori joined the parade and gave three cheers for the Queen. This
was enough to defuse McDonnell, who then accompanied the hikoi
to Putahi. Here, on 21 June, it received a very warm welcome from
the assembled Pakakohe, who presented McDonnell with a taiaha
as a gift for the governor and reiterated their desire for peace –
'but the survey was not mentioned by them'. All three groups –
colonists, Ngaruahine, and Pakakohe – then moved on to Okotuku,
where the Ngarauru of Waitotara had gathered to meet them. Here,
at a hui on 23 June, they accepted the current losses of land in return
for peace.

Now Titokowaru took stock of his peace campaign. McDonnell
was concerned that Pakakohe were still 'silent on the subject of the
surveys' though 'otherwise exceedingly polite and civil' and 'anxious
for peace'. Titokowaru advised him not to hurry them, and there seemed
reason to hope that his advice would be heeded. The only remaining
'outsiders' were Ngati Tupaea, who 'refused to give in against the
repeated wishes and advice of Titokowaru and the other Chiefs'.
But they could wait, and the time seemed ripe to take the message
of reconciliation to North Taranaki and Whanganui. Wharematangi
and the important Tangahoe chief, Tito Hanataua, were delegated
to go north, and Titokowaru himself went south. Wharematangi and
Tito reached Opunake before 13 July, intending to go as far as Mokau,
which they probably did. They went as representatives of Titokowaru,
and carried word that he intended 'to splice, to stick together the
whiteman and the Maori, that they may become one skin. Pokaikai
was the Sabbath of the evil and the appearance of good. The mission
of this journey is to trample down evil that good may come forth.'

In the south, Titokowaru reached the major Pakeha settlement of Wanganui Town on 4 July and conferred with the kupapa chiefs at neighbouring Putiki next day, reaffirming his peaceful intent. He and his entourage, now 230 people, continued on up the Whanganui River for several days, meeting with the Whanganui Kingite minority. He told them 'not to fight, it was up to God to give back their lands'. Then, at last, the hikoi turned for home.

Meanwhile McDonnell had not been idle. Far from responding to the hikoi's efforts with some concession of their own, he and his superiors decided to recommence the survey of the Whenuakura Block, beginning on 16 July. That day, a survey party under Charles Wray went to work near Oika, a small village on the Whenuakura River. Wharematangi was absent on his peace mission, but his brother Te One Kura came to support the local chief, Rurangi. Three men and a woman were sent out, and they politely but firmly told Wray to pack up and go. Noting that some one hundred Pakakohe had assembled at Oika, Wray obeyed, sending word of what had happened to McDonnell at Patea. McDonnell had been expecting this. He had mustered a hundred men, and on receiving Wray's message marched immediately, crossing the Whenuakura by 2.30 am on 17 July. He quietly distributed his force to command the village and, unarmed rode in with Booth and two others, after arranging for the rest to charge in at a given signal. The colonist party found Oika asleep, never suspecting that McDonnell could react so quickly. The colonel woke the leading men and asked them why they had stopped the surveyors. They replied that 'no survey would be permitted by them from the south bank of the Patea River to the Waitotara'. It was time to call in the hidden troops.

But now McDonnell discovered a hiccup in his plans. Camped just across the river, so close that his troops might have bumped into them on the march, was Titokowaru and the whole homeward-bound hikoi. McDonnell left Booth at Oika 'to talk to the Natives and keep them engaged during our absence' – a task for which the resident magistrate was well qualified – and recrossed the river. 'I had a long conversation with Titokowaru,' wrote McDonnell, 'and I told [him] how vexed I was at the conduct of the Pakakohi in sending the surveyors back, and that I had returned with them, accompanied by one hundred men, to enforce the work if required.' Titokowaru replied, 'I have advised them (as you and Mr Booth know) to allow the survey to proceed without hindrance, but they would not listen to me; however, as you return, do not forget they sent the surveyors back in daylight, and did not hurt any one or seize any thing.'

Titokowaru had proved himself the most determined pacifist in South Taranaki, but his warriors were armed. McDonnell 'promised to think of it as I went back', and told Titokowaru that 'the Pakakohi might thank him [that] I had not taken them all prisoners for their temerity in sending the surveyors back'. Thwarted of a full-scale Pokaikai, but still determined the survey should proceed, the colonel again recrossed the river to Oika, where he found Booth still talking. Te One Kura and Rurangi remained firmly opposed to the survey and McDonnell's further attempt to 'convince them of their folly' failed. McDonnell then left, saying he would bring the surveyors in the morning. Rurangi insisted on accompanying him. About 250 yards from the village, McDonnell wrote, 'our force started up to receive us, and as the moon was shining brightly, the sudden appearance of so many men had a most startling effect on Rurangi'.

Pakakohe and the colonists met again about 8 am. The iron fist in McDonnell's glove was now exposed, and this, combined with Titokowaru's persuasion, led them to give up their determined resistance. Rurangi said, 'I, for one, give up; I have finished; I oppose the survey no more after this; I see it is useless.' The rest of the people agreed, although Te One Kura could scarcely bring himself to participate, and all registered their protest. 'Do not ask us to give our consent to the surveys, as we protest against them; on that point we are silent, but we promise not to interfere or further molest the work.'

So, in late July, the hikoi finally returned home after a journey of six weeks. It had achieved its purpose. Even the determined Ngati Tupaea eventually took Titokowaru's advice. Despite a reflexive threat from McDonnell 'that if they give any more insolence, I would pay them a visit when they least expected', they sent him messages of peace in early October. On 13 November, Ngati Tuapaea came to Waihi and formally made peace, 'the last of the natives in this district who have until now been hostile to us' to do so.

The summer of 1867-8 saw the successful conclusion of the peace campaign with two more great hui at Te Ngutu o te Manu on 28-29 November 1867, and in late March 1868. Booth attended both. At the November meeting, he was accompanied by the Whanganui kupapa – or rather, he accompanied them. He noted that Ngaruahine seemed impoverished, which was hardly surprising, and that the ritual distribution of food to guests was made possible only by a gift of

a ton of flour from Whanganui. Titokowaru began the main speeches
by firing a double-barrelled shotgun, or tupara, in the air, and throwing
it at the feet of his visitors.

*He said that the evil weapon which had caused so much mischief and ill-
will, and which had been loaded with the blood of men, was now thrown
down and trodden under foot (he now kicked the gun), and should never hereafter
be taken up again. This he would promise, that this laying down of the evil
weapon should be for all time, and not only as regarded himself and his immediate
followers, but it should also be buried by all the tribes with whom he had
any influence.*

At the large March meeting attended by 600 people from all over
Taranaki, Titokowaru completed the process begun at Patea and
Putiki. However mistakenly, the Maori King was inseparable in the
Pakeha mind from Maori military resistance, and now Titokowaru
formally sacrificed his connection with the King Movement in the
cause of peace. Standing outside Wharekura and gesturing to it, he
said:

*Many years ago, two houses were built for the land councils, and named
Taiporohenui and Kumeamai, afterwards two houses were built for the Maori
king, and named Aotearoa and Rangiatea. These houses are no longer in existence
and I wish to direct your attention to the house we have lately built, and
the purpose for which it is intended. This house was built for the King of
Peace; there is no longer a Maori king in this district.*

Between January 1867 and March 1868, Riwha Titokowaru had
performed remarkable deeds for his people – deeds which should
have made him famous had he done nothing else. He had taken a
knot of great suspicion, and danger, and patiently untangled it. He
had spared no effort in the cause of peace and reconciliation, stretching
his subtribe's resources to the very limits to host at least five great
inter-tribal hui, taking the whole of his people, men, women, and
children, on a long and dangerous journey, eventually renouncing
King Matutaera, and meeting and converting the most hostile of his
enemies. Indeed, the final assessment of Titokowaru's Peace can safely
be left to one of these, James Booth:

*I may state, in conclusion, that ever since Titokowaru made the first overtures
towards establishing friendly relations with us, he has shown the most untiring
energy in his efforts to bring other tribes to make peace. He has visited all
the hapus between Taranaki and Wanganui, and has now succeeded in bringing
them in.*

Chapter Two

THE YEAR OF THE DAUGHTERS

Titokowaru symbolised his great peace campaign with the proclamation 'Hearken, hearken all ye people! This is the year of the daughters, this is the year of the lamb.' His 'year of the daughters' actually stretched from early 1867 to mid-1868, and it brought hope and reconciliation to the Maori people of South Taranaki–Whanganui. But it was among the Pakeha of the region that both lambs and daughters really began to increase.

The new prosperity was most apparent in Wanganui Town, founded at the mouth of the river by the New Zealand Company in 1841. For years the population had languished at around 200, the people given to 'drinking and sabbath-breaking' and 'the lowest debauchery'. But by 1868 it had 2,120 inhabitants, with another 2,000 Europeans in the surrounding districts. There were fifteen general stores, eleven carters, six bakers, five auctioneers, and three each of photographers, undertakers, and newspapers – the *Chronicle*, *Times*, and *Evening Herald*. There was an Oyster Saloon, a Bowling Saloon, and a small theatre in occasional use, featuring such delights as a 'somersault thrower, clown and Shakespearean Jester', assisted by a 'Posture Master and Modern Samson'. The retailers advertised 'A fresh supply of superior leeches' and 'No inferior sausages manufactured. God Save the Queen.'

Wanganui's zone of influence was also expanding. Though technically part of Wellington Province, it was as populous as the New Plymouth region, a province in itself. Geography meant that the Pakeha settlements of South Taranaki looked to Wanganui, not New Plymouth, as their centre – the polar opposite, as it were, of Te Ngutu o te Manu. It was run by a small group of officials and richer citizens, such as Resident Magistrate Walter Buller and the shippers Thomas Taylor and William Watt. Anglican missionary Richard Taylor, for whose 'church of outward shows' the young Titokowaru had had so little time, was an important figure but was then on a protracted visit to England, leaving his spiritual and secular affairs in the hands of his son, Basil. The town had once been represented in the Colonial House of Representatives by William Fox, a clever and sarcastic lawyer who was soon to become Leader of the Opposition as Member for Rangitikei. Wanganui's Parliamentary interests were now in the hands of Henry Harrison, 'A Yorkshire

gentleman of considerable means', who left us the Harrison Hack
Handicap and disliked 'swinelike' Maori. The Superintendent of
Wellington Province, Dr Isaac Featherston, also exerted some sway.
Featherston had marched with Chute as a civilian adviser, going into
battle, Churchill-like, in a dressing gown and with a black cigar
clenched between his teeth. He had accompanied Chute on the march
around the mountain and nearly starved because he could not bring
himself to eat horse. He was forced to forgo the entry into New
Plymouth, where a triumphal arch had been built and the band played
'See the Conquering Hero Comes', because he had lost his trousers.
But 'Old Feathery' was an influential figure, a friend and adviser
of Fox and McDonnell.

Wanganui faced its river. 'The Beach' or river bank, also known
as Taupo Quay, was in effect the main street, noted for bustling
activity, mud, and blown sand. From its jetties, the town communicated
by water with its Maori hinterland upriver and the rest of the colony
downriver, where it was four miles to the sea past Castlecliff. Water
transport could be dangerous, cumbersome, and slow. Three ships
were wrecked on the bar in 1863, cattle were still swum out to
the ships and hoisted aboard by 'donkey-engine', and a criminal escaped
Wanganui by steamer only to be intercepted at the Heads by the
bailiff who had run overland. In 1866, reported the *Wanganui Herald*,
four travellers had been drowned coming through the Heads in a
boat 'totally unfit for the purpose'. They had been forced to do so
by a ship captain, William 'Bully' Hayes, who did not want to 'lose
time'. Captain Hayes and his lady companion spent the next night
in town anyway, 'but made no report . . . of the loss of his passengers.'

Even by steamer, communication with Wellington could take
anything from twelve to forty-eight hours. But there was no telegraph,
the overland mail service had been discontinued, and the forlorn piles
of an abortive bridge bore witness to the failure of attempts to span
the Whanganui. Sea transport was the best of a bad job. The overland
journey 150 miles south to Wellington could take four days on
horseback. It began by wire-ferry, a large boat drawn across the
river along a fixed wire. 'It is a common thing to wait for an hour
to take a horse across.' The only other dry way over was in a
wheelbarrow pushed across the ferry-wire by a tightrope walker.
This method was offered in October 1867 by Monsieur Vertelli, the
self-proclaimed 'Great Australian Blondin', whose 'performances had
earned him everlasting renown'. No one took him up, although Vertelli
did walk the wire over and back by himself.

Wanganui Town, circa 1868 *Wanganui Museum*

In one respect at least, Wanganui had remained true to its early traditions. A speaker at an 1867 temperance meeting maintained that 'of all the places he had ever seen, Wanganui was the most drunken'. Alcohol was still a major industry and provided much of the Customs revenue. There were some sixteen hotels, ranging from Yankee Smith's Hotel where the carpenters had drunk their pay before finishing the building, through Honest John Gotty's Rutland Hotel where 'a sandwich and a pint of Colonial beer can be had for sixpence', to Mr Dunleavy's Wanganui Hotel complete with 'two charming daughters'. The publicans had more than each other to compete with. In 1867 Joseph Sole began business as a winemaker – he later gained 'several international awards' – and illicit stills dotted the district. Bootleg whisky could be had for three shillings and sixpence the bottle, a type of 'liquid that had a kick in it not to be met with in these degenerate days'.

Until October 1867, an integral element of Wanganui Town, almost as important as drink, was the British army. From 1847 the town had a garrison of Imperial troops, and in 1865 the arrival of Cameron's army in its thousands created a tremendous boom in business, trebling the population at a stroke. Supply contractors like David Peat, James Alexander, and George Lethbridge made small fortunes. Now the thousands had gone, but the York and Rutland Stockades still stood, ghostly sentinels flanking the town, as did the married men's huts known as 'The Rookery', a place of ill repute. Here, prostitutes like Harriet Waters (alias 'the Alpacha') were occasionally arrested for having 'no lawful means of support'. Many old soldiers had taken their discharges in Wanganui, where the British army had a demographic impact matched only by the New Zealand Company. If, in March 1868, you had visited Wanganui your board and private hotel room would have cost you one pound five shillings per week. If you tired of hotel fare you might have tried Jacques James' Ferry Restaurant, although the Crimean War, in which the chef claimed to have been trained, was not notable for its cuisine. On the way, you might have been almost run down by a young hooligan. 'John Igoe, a lad of about 14, was brought up for furious riding on Taupo Quay, cautioned and discharged.' If, at the restaurant, you had met Maria Booth, wife of the magistrate, she might have complained of the cost of keeping her four girls at school (thirty pounds a quarter) and given you the gossip: Mrs Potto's 'Tuscan Bonnets' are no such thing; Rose McDonnell, the colonel's wife, is ill again, and Viscount Avonmore, an officer in the Wanganui garrison in the 1840s, has been tried for bigamy in England. Mrs Booth might also have recommended a canoe trip up the river and a sight-seeing ride to the north. Let us imagine, for the rest of this chapter, that you took her advice.

Next day, you cross by ferry to Putiki, Wanganui's Maori other half, to hire your canoe. Here live the leading Lower Whanganui chiefs with many of their followers, though some have other residences upriver. The Lower Whanganui are kupapa, 'pro-British', but this does not mean they woke up one morning brimful of loyalty to Queen Victoria. They sold Wanganui Town site and its surrounds for a list of goods including umbrellas, Jews' harps, and red nightcaps but the real price for the town was its existence as an outlet for Maori products, a source of European goods, and the ultimate status symbol. The Maori would probably have paid to have it, and both sides must have left the sale laughing at having duped the other. Lower Whanganui consider the town to be their property, Pakeha and all. They defended it against their upriver kin in 1847 and 1864. Some Pakeha are grateful; others, such as Harrison, resent their dependence. Wanganui and Putiki are twin settlements, but which is an adjunct of the other is a matter of perspective.

You are fortunate enough to see the great chief, Hori Kingi, now old and ailing, and his competing heirs-apparent: Mete Kingi Paetahi and Kepa Te Rangihiwhinui. The former, in his mid-fifties, is the senior, and currently has the inside running. Though popularly known as 'General' Mete Kingi, 'he never aspired to be a warrior'. Instead, he is a politician of great ability, soon to take up one of the four

Mete Kingi Paetahi
*R. Parsons Album, Alexander
Turnbull Library*

seats allocated kupapa tribes in the House of Representatives. Kepa
holds real military rank – as a captain in the colonial forces. His
mother, Rere Omaki, one of the few women to sign the Treaty of
Waitangi, was sister to Hori Kingi. Kepa, a masterful man, quarrelled
with his uncle and, although now reconciled, his tribal mana is still
less than that of his older rival, Mete Kingi. But among the Pakeha,
to whom he is known as Kemp, it is far higher, and Kepa skilfully
uses the one to lever up the other. He is an excellent commander.
Later portraits show him bewhiskered, in full regalia, uniform, medals,
and sword of honour, a brown Lord Kitchener. An earlier photograph
shows a hard, ruthless face. Kepa Te Rangihiwhinui is a good friend
and a deadly enemy. Governor George Bowen, the Oxford-trained
classicist who has just replaced Grey, describes Kepa as the Whanganui
Achilles and Mete Kingi as their Ulysses. Bowen is sometimes too
free with such analogies – he once compared colonial Queensland
to classical Greece – but this one is apt enough.

Pakeha and Maori meet at Putiki, outside Mete Kingi's house   *Danbury Album,*
Auckland Institute and Museum

Two men whom you do not see at Putiki are said to have great
influence over Whanganui. One, Kawana Hunia Te Hakeke, actually
does. Chief of the associated Ngati Apa tribe living south of the
river, he is boastful but able. He seems younger than Kepa's forty-
four from contemporary photographs, and he too is a soldier, though
more in the traditional, tribal sense than as a Pakeha auxiliary. The
other leader's influence is partly mythical. Superintendent Featherston
is one of those colonists the envious describe as 'Maori Doctors',
supposedly so influential among kupapa tribes that they can muster
hundreds of faithful sepoys at a click of the fingers. Whanganui are
Featherston's special tribe, and he does have some influence. But
there are contexts in which, as far as they are concerned, he can
click his fingers to stumps.

Evening falls as you talk with and of those dignitaries, and you
are invited to stay the night – not by Mete Kingi, 'often accused
of parsimony', but by yet another chief, Kawana Paipai, 'much
esteemed for his hospitality to strangers'. You are amazed and delighted
to find that in his youth he hunted moa, the giant birds you had
hitherto thought extinct for several centuries. Kawana Paipai is an
exponent of a widespread genre of Maori humour practised upon
credulous Pakeha, which gives rise to all sorts of wonderful legends,
some of which are still with us. But he does not go quite so far

The official Kepa
From T. W. Gudgeon,
The Defenders of New Zealand

as some 'old Waikenae natives', who told H.C. Field that their grandfathers had 'tamed the birds and kept them as pets'.

Next day, say, you arrange with Mete Kingi to hire a canoe and four paddlers to take you up the beautiful Whanganui River. The Heads and the sea are one lifeline of Wanganui Town; the river is the other, an important highway. Downriver in canoes and barges come pigs for Wanganui's well-known ham and bacon, dressed flax, timber, flour, potatoes, and other produce. Upriver go clothing, liquor, sugar, tools, and ammunition to the long string of Ngati Hau villages – thirty of them, containing 1,400 people. Four miles from Putiki you pass Aramoho, home of Wirihana Puna, Kepa's formidable lieutenant; four miles further is Upokongaro, around which are villages of the Whanganui Kingite minority led by the Turoa family, Pehi, Topia, and Tahana. They are now peaceful, but still adhere to the King Movement.

The real Kepa
Alexander Turnbull Library

    Your paddlers take you slowly up the peaceful river, singing a
canoe chant addressed to their own reflections in the water:

> *I am a bird, I fly in the sky.*
> *I am a spirit! I have escaped*
> *I have escaped to heaven*
> *Oh, bird of the clouds.*

You stop at a village, say Koratia, where Pakeha are still something
of a novelty among the children. They mimic your speech. 'The letter
s is apparently an outstanding feature of the English language and
sis sis sis . . . whispered from one to the other would be their way
of speaking English amongst themselves, punctuated by gales of
laughter.' On the second day, you pass the little island of Moutoa
where, your paddlers tell you, kupapa and Pai Marire factions of
their tribe fought a fierce but ritualised battle four years before.
You then reach Pipiriki, fifty-five miles upriver, the furthest limit
of kupapa and government influence. Beyond this, the river winds

on for 140 miles into the Kingite heart of the island. The upper Whanganui chiefs, notably the 1847 resistance leader Topine Te Mamaku, are no longer hostile, but you prefer not to test their forbearance and turn back after a night at Pipiriki. Now helped by the current, you reach Upokongaro in one day and go to the hotel where William Caines brews his own well-regarded beer. But you find that your paddlers expect five shillings a day each, not five shillings the lot, and you exhaust your cash paying them. They leave you, you cannot pay Caines, and you spend the next day digging his drains with the shovel he keeps behind the bar for precisely this purpose. It is a stiff, weary walk to Mr W. F. Russell at the Bank of New Zealand in Wanganui Town. Pakeha rarely get the better of a bargain with Mete Kingi.

Wanganui Town's Maori hinterland is still vital to it, but its relative importance is diminishing with the growth of Pakeha agriculture. In 1867, European farmers owned or leased 120,000 acres in the Wanganui Electoral District, pasturing 3,000 horses, 12,000 cattle, 138,000 sheep, and 10 mules and donkeys. Meat for the new goldfields on the west coast of the South Island is a major export, as is wool. Part of this hinterland has grown up south of the river, around Turakina, which is linked with Wanganui by a daily six-seater Cobb coach service, despite a bad accident in February owing to the poor road. Further south still, Fox's Rangitikei district also ships its products through Wanganui. But it is in the north that the most exciting progress is occurring.

In mid-March, resupplied with cash, you leave Wanganui Town to explore these northern districts. On a horse hired from J. Brown and Co., you ride up Victoria Avenue, once known as 'Victoria Canal' but now gravelled, and out to St John's Hill. Perhaps you stop at James Cathro's hotel for a morning draught before proceeding on to Lake Westmere, four miles from town, and then fives miles on to the mouth of the Kai Iwi Stream. The district you have just traversed has been Pakeha for twenty years, and now it is closely settled in substantial and productive farms. The yield of wheat and oats is 'highly prolific', and every paddock is 'well-stocked with well-bred sheep, horses, or cattle', supported by 'the richest possible clover' – 'the meat is of the best quality'. Farmers such as John Bryce of Brunswick, a part of the district settled by Nova Scotians in 1852, and the enterprising James Alexander are doing very well here. You pass an abandoned Imperial redoubt on Alexander's farm above Mowhanau Beach, perhaps pausing again to refresh yourself at C.P. O'Hanlon's

Brighton Hotel, before crossing the Kai Iwi and entering the real
frontier districts.

From Kai Iwi the road angles inland a little through the sand hills
towards another recently abandoned Imperial redoubt, eleven miles
away on the Waitotara River. This road was made in 1864 by
impoverished diggers, brought from an abortive South Island gold
rush, after the purchase of the large Waitotara Block for £2,500 from
a Ngarauru man 'who had no right to sell'. The deal was struck
by the colony's master land buyer, Donald McLean, an extremely
clever Scotsman who hates sweat. 'White . . . sweats too much to
please me. He mops and mops and is in a perpetual stinking condition.
I never sweat, Domett does, awfully.' McLean has now built himself
an empire in Hawke's Bay, on the opposite coast, but the tentacles
of his influence still penetrate Taranaki. Since the government
considered it had bought, rather than confiscated, the Waitotara Block,
it had been sold off in quite large estates, not given over to military
settlement as with the land further north. Partners named Moore
and Currie already have buildings worth £3,000, and the wealthy
Wellingtonian, Robert Pharazyn, has an absentee holding of 5,000
acres at Lake Marahau.

Pharazyn has just sent up a manager from Wellington, young Harry
Lomax, and with a frontier hospitality almost as generous as the
Maori kind, he invites you to stay the night in his half-built house.
Lomax had been to a party in Wanganui yesterday: 'I enjoyed myself
very much, and danced 6 or 7 times with one girl and then took
her home. I do not feel seedy this morning.' This is just as well,
for 'there are such a devil of a lot of things to do the first year
on a new place' – building, fencing, acquiring stock, and, above all,
clearing land to plant oats and cocksfoot grass seed. Lomax has some
hired help, but he himself works a thirteen-hour day: 'I am working
like a nigger and have a pair of hands like a sailor more than a
gentleman.' But he is quite proud of the problem this causes with
some flannel shirts his mother sent him: 'Tell Mama they are first
rate only my biceps are rather too large for the sleeves.'

Next day, you ride with your host over to Perekama on the
Waitotara River, where Lomax hires a Ngarauru stockman named
Jacob. Ngarauru have rebuilt Perekama since Cameron's time, and
it and the cluster of smaller villages around Weraroa, together with
the large village of Papatupu across the river, is again their agricultural
headquarters. In return for a measure of security here, they have
been forced to accept the loss of the rest of their coastal lowland,

The Waitotara River *From an E. Wearing watercolour, Wanganui Museum*

except for a few pathetically small reserves. But, like Ngati Ruanui, Ngarauru are excellent farmers and they are beginning painstakingly to rebuild their wealth. They keep horses, cattle, pigs, sheep, poultry, and honey bees. In cultivations strung up the Waitotara they grow maize, potatoes, pumpkin, water melon, kumara, taro, and tobacco. There are about 450 Ngarauru, led by Hare Tipane, Pehimana, and Aperahama Tamaiparea, and they try to keep on good terms with invaders like Lomax; indeed, they still speak of the settlers around Weraroa as 'their ' Pakeha. Yet they carefully maintain their refuges up the Waitotara, especially Piraunui.

You return to Marahau for dinner round noon, and then bid farewell to Lomax and continue north. (It is actually north-west, but we will follow convention by disregarding the finer points of the compass.) Instead of crossing the Waitotara by the inland road, via Perekama, you take the coastal route. A couple of miles from Marahau, you pass Nukumaru, a succession of pretty little lakes and the Handley family's model farm. It was here that Ngarauru and Ngati Ruanui rashly attacked Cameron in 1865. You cross the Waitotara at its mouth by punt-ferry, pausing at Sherwood's Inn. By late afternoon, after turning inland again, you reach Wairoa (later Waverley), thirty miles from Wanganui and the most southerly of the military settlements. Wairoa is the centre of a Pakeha population of about 200 and has a post office and general store run by military settler lieutenant Albert Fookes. But you are unable to take advantage of the bar, two parlours, and seven bedrooms of Palmer's Hotel because it opens next month, and instead spend an uncomfortable night in a surveyor's tent. The surveyors are hard at work on the Okotuku block, inland of Wairoa, and their diaries record gradual progress, together with such useful information as a cure for flatulence: '¼ ounce of Carbonate of Soda in ½ pint of water take two table spoonsfull three times a day'. Early next morning, you watch the Wairoa men at work building a redoubt, supervised by Robert Hawes, the leading settler. They sweat to dig the ditch broad and deep. Another onlooker is a seventeen-stone Ngarauru warrior, 'the locally celebrated Big Kereopa'. A 'herculean savage', he is said to have been shot through the head in 1866, but survived 'as hearty as he ever was' and with his sense of humour unaffected. After waiting for the ditch to be finished, Kereopa bets Hawes a bottle of rum he can jump it. This he does, from a standing start, and the ditch has to be redug.

You then resume your journey along the rich coastal lowland, not flat but very fertile, especially where it intersects with river valleys. The great inland forests loom a few miles to your right. You take the inland track to Oika on the Whenuakura River. Here, Ngarauru territory ends, Ngati Ruanui begins, and Wellington Province theoretically turns into Taranaki. Rurangi's Oika, saved from McDonnell by Titokowaru last July, and Putahi, further up the Whenuakura, make up the southernmost agricultural area of the Pakakohe subtribe. Both were destroyed by Chute in January 1866. Like Ngarauru, the surviving inhabitants fled upriver, and then returned to their old homes. The weather is fine, the wind north-west, and you can clearly see the mountain.

From Oika, you ride seaward, crossing the Whenuakura and Patea Rivers by ferry to Patea Town, the capital, port and military centre of the whole district. Originally another of Cameron's redoubts, the township is on the north bank about a mile upriver, mostly on a natural terrace up a steep sand hill from the beach, forty miles from Wanganui. A different town site on more fertile land further upriver has been surveyed and named Carlyle. Describing Patea as a 'port' is a little generous. Vessels of up to nine feet draught can cross the bar at the river mouth, but it is a dangerous business. The *Alpha* and *Shamrock* were wrecked in 1865, and the government paddle-steamer *Gundagai* met the same fate the next year. Some vessels now stand off and land their cargo and passengers 'on a sort of pontoon raft, composed of empty cases and timber'. The *Gundagai* was not a total write-off. Imperial troops used its mast as a greased pole, climbing it for a sovereign donated by the officers. Private Harry Autridge always won – he cheated by filling his jersey with sand to improve his grip. You dine at John Casey's Shamrock Hotel on the beach, where 'the accommodation is good and the charges are moderate', then stagger up the steep sand hill to view the rest of the town. There are eighty buildings, including seventy houses, most little more than shacks and some in ruins. There is a day-school run by Mrs Morrison, an Anglican Sunday school, and a general store run by John Gibson for the Wanganui auctioneers Edward Lewis and Co. There are two other hotels, R. Campbell's Royal and Alex Summers' Patea, but no church.

In 1866, with thousands of Imperial troops to supply, Patea had been a bustling place, with three general stores and a 'large building used occasionally as a theatre' in which a ball was once held. The Imperial regiments have long gone and even the colonial troops now use Camp Waihi to the north as their field base, though Patea is still the administrative headquarters. In 1867, the military settler units were disbanded; the men either left the district, took up their confiscated farms, or joined the small new colonial regular army misleadingly known as a police force – the armed constabulary, organised into five 'divisions', each around seventy strong. The change is not popular – the men dislike their new 'Billy-cocked hats' and the officers refuse to use their police ranks of 'Inspector' and 'Sub-Inspector' – but the force is efficient. 'Inspector' Thomas McDonnell has remained in command of the two divisions stationed in the district, apart from a brief absence in 1867 fighting the prophet Hakaraia at Rotorua. McDonnell was temporarily replaced at Patea by Colonel Mathew Lepper, one of an unfortunately named class of colonial officers which also includes Ensign Louis Von Rotter and Captain Arthur Crapp. McDonnell, the government's troubleshooter, returned last June in time to meet Titokowaru's hikoi, but now he is about to go off again to deal with another crisis.

You return to the Shamrock, where you meet George O'Halloran, a cheerful twenty-four-year-old ex-military settler from Antrim who now runs a pack-horse line from Patea to the various military settlements to the north. He tells you that the settlers are 'now pretty well established and do not anticipate any further trouble with the natives'. Most are enrolled in the militia, however, and keep their Enfields clean and drill a few times a year. O'Halloran himself is captain of the Patea Light Horse Volunteers, and Tom McDonnell is his patron – a good one. He has pushed O'Halloran from private to captain in a few months, just as he made his own brother William a lieutenant on one day and a captain the next. 'Fighting Mac' is the man to deal with the Fenian troubles at Hokitika, says O'Halloran, but you are not sure what he is talking about. He tells you to beware of sharks if you take the beach route north – he recently killed a six-foot one trapped in a pool by the tide – finishes his whisky and leaves.

Sitting at the bar, you decide to catch up on the news from a copy of the *Taranaki Herald* just in from New Plymouth. There is a story about an American crossed in love who attempted suicide with a dose of yeast powder: 'He immediately rose above his troubles.' But the main news of the day is the 'Fenian trouble', to which O'Halloran referred. In Sydney, on 12 March, a Fenian sympathiser wounded the touring Duke of Edinburgh, Queen Victoria's son, in an assassination attempt. This has further inflamed feeling at Hokitika and elsewhere on the west coast of the South Island, where Irish Catholic gold miners have already clashed with their Protestant compatriots and the authorities, to the point where armed rebellion seems possible. It is this situation that McDonnell is being sent to deal with. You gloomily close your paper, fearing, like the government, that a Maori war is about to be replaced by an Irish one.

Leaving Patea next day, you follow the road a few miles along the Patea towards Kakaramea, close to the Te Ngaio battlefield. The Patea River is the second of the main Pakakohe agricultural areas, land able to produce potatoes weighing four pounds each. But Pakakohe have lost land on the north bank to military settlers based at Patea Town and Kakaramea and have built a new village on the south bank at Hukatere, where they met Booth last May. Kakaramea was more recently the scene of an equine tragedy. The colonial forces held a fifty-eight-mile horse race, from Patea to the Waingongoro and back. On the return trip, Trooper Crichton, well in the lead on a fine bright bay, stopped at either William Aikman's Black Bull or William Sergeant's Royal Tiger and gave his horse a bottle of stout. The horse fell dead a few miles from the finish line, 'slaughtered by the ignorance and neglect of its rider'. Captain A.M.A. Page won the race by default on a humble cream cob.

From Kakaramea, you ride on along the coastal lowland, more broken than south of Patea but still very fertile. Since the Waitotara the roads have been 'just cleared tracks . . . dusty in summertime but in winter potholed and seas of mud'. Ahead of you lies the area generally known as Manutahi – Manutahi itself, Manawapou, and Mokoia. Once comprising the third and greatest of the Pakakohe agricultural areas, all are now military settlements. On the road, you meet one of these settlers – Diston Ginger, who farms with his two brothers at Manutahi. Ginger has been visiting his sister Sophia, 'a woman of wonderful personality', at Kakaramea. You tell him of your travels and he observes that you have been taking it very easy. It is possible to ride from Wanganui to Patea in well under twelve hours if you have a good horse and are lucky with the rivers. Ginger hunts, for food and sport, and he tells you of the 457-pound, seven-foot four-inch boar shot by James Atkinson in 1866. There are still some pigs, but big black bulls are now the main game, sprung from thoroughbred New Plymouth stock confiscated by Ngati Ruanui during the Taranaki War. They ran wild in 1865, after Cameron's commissariat gathered up the cows, and now these bachelor bulls roam the coastal lowland and its bush islands and fringes in groups of three to five for company. There is just a chance of more exotic game. In 1867, the Wanganui Acclimatisation Society released eight kangaroos, and some are still alive.

Ginger feeds you soda bread and bull beef at Manutahi, eight and a half miles from Patea. You then ride inland a short distance to Taumaha, a village newly built by Pakakohe in a beautiful grove of ngaio trees to replace the lost centres. Here you meet Ngawaka Taurua, one of the two principal Pakakohe chiefs, said to be 'one of the finest men the Maori race ever produced'. He is busy but courtesy itself, and with the 'somewhat sad expression' now habitual to him, he tells you of the bitter defeat of Te Ngaio, where Ngati Ruanui lost perhaps a quarter of their 300 warriors – a much more grievous loss than that sustained on the occasion of Chute's better-known victory at Otapawa, when nine men were killed. Taurua, a superb Christian theologian, is a man of peace, but if he has to fight he does so well.

Curiosity leads you to ask Taurua about Kimble Bent, the renegade, and after some hesitation he tells you. An American serving in the British army until his desertion in 1865, Bent now lives with his chief, Rupe of Tangahoe, in the forest hamlet of Te Paka, and is married to his 'handsome' and 'very gentle' daughter, Rihi. The Pakeha

conviction that he killed his old colonel, J. Hassard, at Otapawa is
not true. 'Bent is a man of easy disposition, rather sensitive, and
without any indication of viciousness, strong passion, or boldness.'
But he is not the only British deserter in the area, and some are
more formidable. Michael O'Connor, Charles Kane, Jack Hennessy,
and Humphrey Murphy – all Irishmen – are the four whose names
are known. Murphy lives with Te One Kura at Putahi on the
Whenuakura, and is soon to be killed by him for attempting reverse
desertion. Te One Kura's brother, Te Wharematangi, is the second
of the leading Pakakohe chiefs. More warlike than Taurua, but less
so than Te One Kura, he is chief of Whakamara, the forest capital
and refuge of Pakakohe. Wharematangi is a Pai Marire priest, and
Taurua, despite his Methodism, tells you proudly of the great niu
at Whakamara, a flagpole eighty feet high, with cross-yards like
a ship's mast and many flags, which acts as a focus for Pai Marire
services; a lofty altar.

  From Taumaha, on the fringe of the great forest, you ride down
the Ingahape Stream, ford it opposite Mokoia, and continue to
Manawapou on the coast down a notoriously steep and difficult side
cutting. For the first time on your journey rain comes, and you decide
to stay the night here, at one of the river-ferry hotels. This one
is run by Charles Hirtzell, another one-time colonial officer. You
have to listen again to the story of the Kakaramea horse race, in
which Hirtzell also rode. It is fine again next morning, and riding
out of Manawapou you soon leave Pakakohe territory, crossing the
Tangahoe River into the land of the subtribe of the same name. Over
the river, the road forks, with the coast route ascending a sand hill
so steep that carts need double teams to get up it. But you take
the inland track towards the villages of Tangahoe: Taiporohenui,
once their capital, beautiful Ohangai, tragic Pokaikai, Te Ruaki,
Matangarara, Whareroa, Otapawa. Most were sacked by Cameron,
Chute, or McDonnell and the people fled further inland – to
Tirotiromoana and Turangarere, and even to their legendary ultimate
fastness, the great Te Ngaere Swamp. Like Ngarauru and Pakakohe,
they have had to come back. Tito Hanataua, an uneasy insider, lives
at Taiporohenui, or what is left of it. His august relative, Patohe,
once leader of the allied forces at Nukumaru, lives with him in
retirement. Deeper inland, the Ngati Tupaea hapu, the last to come
in the previous year, live at Keteonata and Tirotiromoana under their
chief, Ahitana.

  You visit Matangarara, where you meet Eruini Tukino, Natanahira

Ngahina, and his wife Maata Moerewarewa, all insider chiefs who once lived in Pokaikai. They have just returned from giving evidence at Wanganui to a Parliamentary inquiry into McDonnell's attack on their village two years previously. Natanahira was in New Plymouth making peace with Parris at the time, but Tukino and Maata were present, and they tell you the tale.

On the night of 1 August, Pokaikai slept secure. Though peace was being formalised through Parris, the villagers had repeatedly agreed to it with McDonnell as well and were perfectly convinced of his good faith. Tukino had letters and symbols of peace 'from your friend McDonnell', and Maata had that day prepared a gift of potatoes for the colonial troops. They lay beside her in her house in three flax kits while she slept with her children. 'The sleep,' she says, 'was the sleep of fools.' About 1 am, they were 'roused by a yell almost enough to raise the dead and by firing through and through their whares [houses]'. McDonnell and 200 men burst into the village. Some were drunk and the attack came a little prematurely. Tukino, not fully asleep, was up and out in an instant – 'on hearing the rush of the men', as he puts it. He saw the troops 'fire at a child . . . but miss it'. Seeing there was no chance of resistance, he called to his people to flee and flung himself down a nearby gully, 'naked as I was'. In the dark, most were able to follow him and escape shocked and frozen into the bush with nothing but their lives. Maata and her family were not so lucky.

At the first shots, one of Maata's daughters, aged ten, panicked and ran to the nearby house of Maata's elderly parents. It was surrounded soon after she entered, and riddled with bullets. Her grandparents just had time to throw her into 'a kind of loft' before they were both killed. The troops also killed one of their own men, in mistake for Kimble Bent, but this was small comfort to Maata as she emerged from her house to find her parents laid out dead on their doorstep. Her ten-year-old was safe, but she did not know this. 'I remained standing at my own door with a second child in my arms.' Most of the troops rushed on, but one, Zecheriah Bezer, came up to her. Her shark's tooth earring caught his eye, and he pulled at it, ripping the cartilage, but the ornament did not come free. 'Do not rob me whilst I am alive,' Maata said to him, 'you had better shoot me with your rifle.' Instead, Bezer drew a knife and cut the earring free, also cutting her hand as she tried to protect herself with one arm while holding her child with the other. An officer arrested Bezer, but he was soon released.

Maata shows you her scars, but notes that her fate was nothing to that of another woman, Mereana Matau, whom she suspects was raped while wounded by several colonists. Maata herself confronted McDonnell, the village still burning around her, and demanded he wrap her parents' bodies before burial. He agreed, but she later found that 'the dogs scratched up and consumed a portion of the body of my father, which was naked'.

Maata upbraided the colonist commander for his night's work. 'It was very wrong to attack the village while my husband Natanahira was absent, having gone to . . . Mr Parris to make peace.'

McDonnell replied, 'Who is Mr Parris? I am the person with whom peace should be made.'

Despite that night in August 1866, or perhaps because of it, Tukino, Natanahira, and Maata still hold to a policy of non-resistance. They are not kupapa – they would not fight for the Pakeha – but they co-operate quite actively. Pokaikai rankles, but peace now seems the only path, and their friend Robert Parris has brought about the current inquiry. They laugh about McDonnell's refusal to give evidence. He claimed to be suffering from 'concussion of the brain' as a result of a fall from a horse, and persuaded a doctor to state that conversation with Parris 'might ruin him for life'. Knowing the attitude of most colonists, you suspect they will be less amused by the results of the inquiry, and time will prove you right. All this makes you a little uncomfortable, and you are not reluctant to leave Matangarara.

The coastal lowland broadens here, and you ride to Hawera through 'a most beautiful country, covered with light fern, flax and tutu, amidst which natural grasses and white clover grow luxuriantly. The country is well-watered, but there is rather a scarcity of bush.' Hawera, site of an abandoned redoubt known as Round Bush, is a tiny hamlet whose leading settler is Daniel Bradshaw and whose publican is a man named Sweeney. Hawera is one of the last three foci of military settlement; the others are nearby Ohawe, at the mouth of the Waingongoro, and Ketemarae, inland of Camp Waihi, where settlement is only now beginning.

From Hawera, you turn your tired horse seaward towards Ohawe. You pass the new farm of James Livingston, who has 1,200 sheep. Huge, resourceful, and indomitable, Livingston is one of the few settlers actually to live up to the pioneer ideal. Ohawe is another tiny hamlet, made up of the farms of Chubbin, Lambert, and Edward McDonnell, brother of the colonel, and perhaps one or two others, together with the ramshackle little White Hart Hotel run by a Mr

The Waingongoro River *From an E. Wearing watercolour, Wanganui Museum*

Smith. But Ohawe is a significant place, for here, from the ruined redoubt which marks the furthest point of Cameron's advance, you gaze across the Waingongoro River, up the high cliffs and black iron sand of the grim Taranaki coast, into independent Maoridom.

You venture across, to find that Maori independence is maintained in more ways than one. The first village is Kauae, whose Ngaruahine inhabitants were insiders well before Titokowaru's peace campaign. Their chief, 'the old gentleman' Wiremu Hukanui Manaia, is 'very hospitable', and he tells you proudly of his co-operation with the government. Last year he even allowed Commissioner Parris to try an adultery case at Kauae, and the offender was fined five pounds. He declined to pay, of course, but British law is welcome at Kauae.

You now ride north to Oeo, across the Waimate Plain, five miles broad between beach cliffs and forest, over which land buyers longingly licked their lips. Like Arthur Atkinson the previous year, you find that 'coming across the plains was a great treat. The great expanse of open land and herds of wild cattle, a large number of them huge buffalo like bulls was something quite new, and seemed . . . worth the journey to see.' To your left, on the coast, are the twin Waimate pa, where Waikato were repulsed in 1834, and the

Hone Pihama
Taranaki Museum

ruins of poor Skevington's mission station. You ford the Kapuni,
Kaupokonui, Otakeho, and Rawa rivers and streams, fortunate that
the weather is still fine, and reach Oeo, fifteen miles from Ohawe.
Here you stay for the first time at a Maori hotel, the accommodation
house run by Hone Pihama Te Rei Hanataua, brother of Patohe.
Edward McDonnell warned that you would be fleeced here – his
brother hates Pihama, a friend of Parris. But you are not, for Pihama
is a man of 'great natural ability and intelligence and unquestioned
integrity'. He is, by descent, the senior chief of the whole of Ngati
Ruanui, but he and his followers live apart from the rest of his Tangahoe

people, and his very close links with Parris and Richmond have cost him some influence. He and Hukanui maintain their independence by diplomacy, not arms.

Oeo is the limit of Ngati Ruanui territory. Eight miles north, at Opunake, Wiremu Kingi Matakatea and his co-chief Arama Karaka maintain the independence of the Taranaki tribe with tactics similar to Pihama's. Fourteen miles beyond that, at Parihaka, Te Whiti and his co-chief Tohu Kakahi are rising in influence as prophets of peace, though they do not yet rival Titokowaru. This, with the Atiawa and Ngati Maru territory directly inland, up to and beyond the great mountain, is Maori Central Taranaki. Twenty-six miles from Parihaka, 107 miles from Wanganui, is New Plymouth and Pakeha North Taranaki. You do not visit these regions, and turn your horse for home. But there is one more side trip you intend to make.

After taking leave of Pihama, you ride back across the plain, recross the Waingongoro, and ride up it to Camp Waihi. Here, No. 2 Division Armed Constabulary garrison a substantial fort, built partly on the remains of the ancient pa Mangamanga on the banks of the Waihi Stream. Apart from the constabulary there are fifty-five Whanganui kupapa based here, the last vestiges of a failed experiment in Maori military settlement. They are commanded by Ensign Poma and occasionally visited by Kepa and Wirihana, but soon they too will go home. Waihi is an important place, strategically sited to control the Waingongoro frontier and threaten Ngaruahine territory. Some Ngaruahine land at Ketemarae has been confiscated, but there is still a village of that subtribe south of the Waingongoro, at Hatepe, close by Waihi, under the chief Hane Wiremu. There are two major fords over the Waingongoro, the Upper and Lower, north and south of Te Whenuku Bush, a mile or so from Camp Waihi. The Lower ford leads to Kauae, the Upper to other insider Ngaruahine villages, or at least their ruins: Wereweri, Katautara, Ahipaipai, and, most important, Mawhitiwhiti, whose chief is Paramena Te Rangihekeiho. These fringe villages, amidst copses of bush, form a thin transition zone between the coastal lowland and the inland forest. Eastwards, another section of Ngaruahine live at Araukuku with their chief, Kaake. From Mawhitiwhiti, a track runs into the forest through a string of clearings, including ruined Pungarehu, to Te Ngutu o te Manu, twelve miles from Waihi, home of the renowned peacemaker, Titokowaru.

You could visit Te Ngutu – James Booth is being feasted there at this moment – but you have been promised a meeting with an

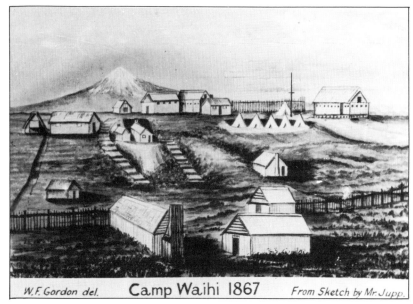

W.F. Gordon del.   Camp Waihi 1867   From Sketch by Mr. Jupp.

Wanganui Museum

ex-Hauhau right here in camp. You have met Lieutenant Walter
Gudgeon, one of the kupapa's superfluous European officers. Like
William Newland, who has been detached temporarily to garrison
Sentry Hill in North Taranaki, Gudgeon is not a great soldier. But
he is a kindly man – he later helped his impoverished father Thomas
to write two books on the New Zealand Wars, and allowed him
to take the credit and the royalties. The warrior you are about to
meet is a friend of his: Wiremu Katene Tuwhakaruru, trusted
lieutenant of both Riwha Titokowaru and Thomas McDonnell.
    If he had thought of it, Governor Bowen might have described
Katene as the Maori Alcibiades. The son of Korere of Ngaruahine
and Pinuia of Ngati Awa, he was taken prisoner by Waikato as a
child in the early 1830s. Until October 1866, he was a leading
Ngaruahine warrior, eventually accumulating eight bullet wounds
and a great reputation as a war leader, master of bushcraft, and
'a real fire-eater'. Then, after McDonnell attacked Pungarehu in
October 1866, he suddenly turned his coat, explaining the action as
follows:
    'I have tried to do my best for the tribe. When I lead them into
fight they do not back me up; and when I told them that Pungarehu

would one day be surprised, they laughed at me, and now these men are dead. I am sick of the whole thing. I shall stay with the Pakeha.'

He then became chief guide to the colonial forces. Immensely active, an excellent shot and horseman, you find he has a wry wit and real military knowledge. Booth does not like him, but McDonnell, whose distrust of the Maori is otherwise universal, has great faith in his advice and believes that as a scout he 'could not be excelled'. But Katene is a man in two minds. As your conversation draws to its close, Katene asks Gudgeon: 'Do you trust me?'

Gudgeon replies that he does and Katene says, 'You are right and you are wrong; you are right to trust me now, for I mean you well, but never trust a Maori. Some day I may remember that I have lost my land, and that the power and influence of my tribe has departed, and that you are the cause; at that moment I shall be your enemy; do not forget what I say.'

Your journey is over.

Chapter Three

'I SHALL NOT DIE'

At the end of March of 1868, as the Taranaki summer faded into autumn, the time came for bush-clearing: for burning a little more bush off one's farm and sewing grass seed in the ashes. If the bush was heavy, the major trees had to be felled beforehand and the stumps left to dry before the burn. As Harry Lomax was learning the hard way, this was the major cost, in work or money, of setting up a farm. The heavier the bush, the harder it was. This made the military settler allotments on the forest fringe the least attractive, and it was only now that they were being taken up. For the first time, a trickle of Pakeha settlers moved on to marginal farms inland of Wairoa, Kakaramea, Mokoia, and Camp Waihi and began work. Their sections had been proclaimed confiscated in 1865; they had been surveyed in large blocks in 1866, and cut up into individual farms in 1867; they had been selected, sometimes sold as land-orders, and perhaps even resold. But they had not been occupied until now.

At the same late-March meeting at Te Ngutu at which Titokowaru renounced the Maori King, and with him military resistance, the assembled tribes of Taranaki faced this problem. The slow cancer had begun again and would shortly leave them without enough fertile land to feed themselves. Soon, in North Taranaki, a meeting of the Taranaki tribe and sixty Ngati Ruanui visitors was telling Parris that they agreed to 'the land taken for military settlement remaining with the white man, but that they would not assent to any extension of the system of taking land'. And in the south, referring to the troubled area inland of Mokoia, Pakakohe stated that: 'We never gave our consent to the confiscation of *this* land.' But the gradualism of Pakeha confiscation had never been based on a spirit of compromise. Despite the great peace effort of Titokowaru and his followers, despite reconciliation and the renunciation of the King, despite concession after concession after concession, confiscation crept on.

At the Te Ngutu meeting, Ngati Ruanui decided again to try passive resistance, but this time with an added refinement. They decided to apply the ancient law of muru to the disputed farms. Muru, the exaction, without war, of compensation for an offence, was ideally carried out with the acquiescence of the offender, and there were even cases where the victims had urged the taua muru to take more of their property. No one expected the Pakeha to be so reasonable, but if the exactions were made with caution there seemed a slim hope that the new settlers would be harassed off their land. Slim hopes were the only kind available. So began a wave of what the Pakeha described as petty thefts, though some realised there was method in them. In James Richmond's words, 'a really systematic scheme had been devised for expelling the settlers from the district by acts of robbery and other annoyances'. The scheme extended as far south as Ngarauru country. At Wairoa, the first major growth of which stemmed from this phase of creeping confiscation, the settlers were harassed by small thefts. Further north, at Oika and inland of Kakaramea, Pakakohe did the same thing. 'Mr' E. Bayley suffered most, probably because his property was larger and further inland. Muru did not necessarily involve personal antagonism. Booth noted that apart from the thefts 'the natives were perfectly civil and obliging everywhere, and the settlers, one and all, speak very highly of the kind treatment they receive personally from their Maori neighbours, with the single exception of Mr Bayley'.

The initial government reaction to all this was a little muted by its one great principle: pragmatism. McDonnell left Patea for Hokitika on 30 March, taking most of the district's constabulary with him. During McDonnell's absence, Major William Magee Hunter held command in Patea. About the same age as his commander, Hunter had joined the Waikato Militia in 1863, and became 'a most efficient and valuable officer' with 'a great aptitude for military organisation and drill'. He was more stable and less active than McDonnell and it was this, together with the absence of so many troops, that moderated the government reaction. But not for long, or by much.

The double act of McDonnell and James Booth had long been castigated by the Wanganui settlers for following 'a dual policy of blister and ointment', with McDonnell the hard-liner and Booth the soft. Hunter was much more amenable to Booth's influence than the colonel, but Booth took the opportunity to show that his softness was only relative, that he too was capable of a little blister. No sooner was McDonnell on the way to Hokitika than Booth asked Hunter to send parties of constables against the two southern muru centres, Wairoa and Kakaramea, 'to apprehend any natives who are determined to oppose the settlers in the occupation of their land'. This move passed off quietly enough, with the local Maori again accepting that the government had the whip-hand. A more serious problem arose further north, again among the sorely tried Pakakohe of the area inland of Mokoia.

On 10 April, two farmers named Henderson and Luxford began work on land they had bought from military settlers at a place called Matakara, so far inland of Mokoia that it was closer to Whakamara. They had a bag of grass seed taken from them and were turned back. They complained to Booth, and next day he accompanied them to their farm, only to meet 'with the usual arguments of the Hauhau, that we had first made peace with them and after lulling them into security, were now, in time of peace, trying to steal the land'. Pakakohe, wrote Booth, 'requested me to return and locate the settlers seaward of the Hingahape [Ingahape] Stream, but that the Maoris would never consent to settlers occupying land near the bush'. Booth asked Hunter to call out fifteen militia and station them at the Mokoia redoubt, but despite this Henderson and Luxford were again turned back on 13 April. A week later, Booth organised a night expedition à la McDonnell. He, Hunter, and thirty militia and constabulary marched secretly to Matakara and seized two Pakakohe 'ringleaders', Tokorangi and the old chief Paraone Tutere of Manutahi. This was more hostage-taking than arrest, for when Wharematangi hurried up from Putahi and, fearing for the two men's safety, promised to stop the obstruction of Henderson and Luxford, Tokorangi and Paraone were released. Wharematangi kept his word, and Booth withdrew the troops, having shown he could play McDonnell's game as well as the man himself.

But it was in the north, in Titokowaru's sphere of influence, that the autumn muru was most persistent, and it was led by his chief active lieutenants, Toi and Haowhenua. 'Petty thefts' began here in late March, and on 7 April Andrew Hiscox, lately a military settler sergeant and now settled on his selection inland of Ketemarae, was robbed. The same day Katene Tuwhakaruru broke into a house and took goods valued at fourteen pounds. Katene, struggling to live with two loyalties, evidently saw no contradiction in assisting the muru and being a kupapa. But, in the absence of his patron McDonnell, Booth promptly tried him and sentenced him to six months' prison with hard labour. A few days later, a man named Waru, visiting Te Ngutu from Warea, broke into the whare of storekeeper Richard Lennon at Turuturu Mokai. Both Waru and Lennon were rather vain men; Lennon must have been the only Patea pioneer with three mirrors in his rough hut, and these were all that Waru took. Lennon may have broken a fourth, because within four months he was to have more had luck. Another Ketemarae settler, Cameron, lost all his household goods on 11 April, and Gordon Gilfillan, farming near Turuturu Mokai, had a revolver stolen.

Booth was fully aware that Titokowaru's people were responsible for these muru incidents. But Te Ngutu was deep in the bush, outside the Pakeha zone of control, and was less vulnerable to Pokaikai-style policing, at least while most of the constabulary were at Hokitika. Booth contented himself with writing a letter demanding the return of the goods. In late April, the pilfering was extended outside the Ketemarae district, to Ohawe at the mouth of the Waingongoro. Titokowaru had consistently conceded this fertile district to the government – 'To the south (or seaward) of Turuturu are the houses of gentlemen.' But the law of muru always applied not to individual offenders but to the group responsible for them. At Ohawe, the publican Smith had two horses taken, together with one belonging to his neighbour, Edward McDonnell. One of these horses had actually been looted from Kokiri, a lieutenant of Titokowaru's, in 1866. A week later, Smith received information that the three horses were at Te Ngutu, and on 3 May he rode into Patea and told Booth.

McDonnell had returned from Hokitika with most of his men five days before. While there, he and his troops had kept close guard on six Fenians imprisoned for rioting – there were rumours that the local gaolers were not to be trusted – and had remained sober in the face of 'much temptation'. But there had been no fighting, and the Irish threat had died down. Now that the troops were back, Booth decided it was time to try his luck at Te Ngutu. He wanted troops as a background threat rather than for security, for he was still convinced of Titokowaru's pacifism. On 4 May, with an escort of only three constables, he rode from Patea to Te Ngutu.

Titokowaru was ill, and Booth was received by Toi Whakataka. Booth demanded the horses and other goods.

Toi replied, 'We have the horses you have come in search of, I have them and I do not intend to give them up; one, a mare, was mine originally, the others are the property of Europeans; I intend to take the horses and other property of Europeans wherever I can.'

'What is the cause of this change?' asked Booth. 'I have kept my word; we Europeans have not molested you in any way. Why have you committed this great wrong, and gone about like rats to a potato pit to steal away property by night; you dare not attempt, like men, to take away anything by daylight.'

'You are doing a great wrong to us, so great that you do not see it,' Toi replied.

Disregarding Toi's parting plea, 'Do not go in anger', Booth rode off. He returned to Waihi, and there issued McDonnell with a warrant to arrest 'Toi, Hau Whenua, and other Aboriginal Natives of New Zealand of the Ngaruahine hapu, of the Ngati Ruanui tribe, and now residing at Ngutu-o-te-Manu'. At 8.30 pm on Monday 11 May, McDonnell set out to execute the warrant, using his favourite tactic of a surprise night visit. He took a large force: fifty-five constabulary, seventeen of O'Halloran's 'Light Horse Volunteers', thirty-four local militia, and a few others – a total of 110 men. McDonnell, on principle, did not share Booth's confidence in the Maori. There was one exception. After a long argument with Booth he secured Katene's release, standing surety himself for the fourteen pounds, so as to have the services of an expert guide. This was McDonnell's first visit to Te Ngutu. It was not to be his last.

McDonnell crossed the Waingongoro and marched to the insider village of Mawhitiwhiti, where he had been informed Toi was staying. He found Toi had left that day and, friendly status notwithstanding, he seized two leading villagers, Wairau and Hakopa Te Matauawa, as hostages. Wairau was an important Pai Marire priest, and Hakopa was an old warrior of great courage and resource. McDonnell intended silently to surround Te Ngutu, then demand the return of property and thieves. But, as he approached at 3 am, Hakopa broke free of his guards and ran to warn the sleeping village, pursued by Katene. Few men moved faster through bush than Katene, but the renegade's family was in Te Ngutu, and purposely or not he did not catch his quarry. Thus, groaned McDonnell, 'all my plans were frustrated by the desertion of the Mawhitiwhiti Native, and I felt certain that all the inhabitants were now awake and on the alert, and that if I took the men on I was sure to get a volley, so I determined to go into the pa alone, to reassure the Natives if possible.' McDonnell lacked many virtues but courage was not one of them.

Hakopa's warning enabled Toi and Haowhenua to flee and Tauke Te Hapimana to come out, alone like McDonnell, and meet the colonial troops. Tauke led McDonnell on to the marae and asked him to bring in his men, which he did. Though it was only 4 am, the people began cooking food for their guests, and gave over Wharekura for them to sleep in. 'Having placed a sufficient guard,' wrote McDonnell, 'we lay down till daylight.' At 8 am, the villagers assembled; Titokowaru was still sick and Tauke and Kokiri spoke for him.

McDonnell demanded Toi, Haowhenua, and the horses, only to be
told that none was present. He then threatened to take the whole
village prisoner unless Tauke and Kokiri returned with him. Eventually
Tauke agreed to go as, in McDonnell's own words, 'a sort of hostage',
and the force returned to Waihi.

Throughout their passive resistance, Ngati Ruanui had always gone
only so far as they reasonably could in the hope of outbluffing the
Pakeha. Whenever this failed, they had stopped short of violence
and made the minimum concession necessary to avert war. The autumn
muru had now clearly reached this point, with the beloved Tauke,
the living repository of Ngaruahine history, in Pakeha hands. They
could stand no more surprise visits, each a potential Pokaikai. It was
time to concede. So when Booth, probably on Tauke's advice, sent
Natanahira Ngahina to Te Ngutu with a final demand on 12 May,
Ngaruahine sent the three horses, including Kokiri's, back with him.

Natanahira arrived back at Waihi with the horses at 11 am on
13 May, naturally assuming that another dangerous crisis had been
defused. But he found Booth enraged: he himself had played no part
in resolving the crisis, the 'thieves' had not been caught, and in
Natanahira's absence the magistrate received word that two more
stolen horses, hitherto mentioned by no one, were still at Te Ngutu.
Booth immediately told McDonnell, Natanahira, and Tauke of the
extra horses.

'Perhaps so, but I am not aware of it,' said Tauke, 'let me return
and I will bring them to you, Colonel, if they have been taken;
or I will remain and let Natanahira go.'

Booth said, 'No, I will go with a dozen men and bring the horses
and the thieves.'

Even McDonnell tried to dissuade him, to no avail, although he
at least prevailed on him to take Tauke. Without telling Tauke, the
colonel also arranged to follow a couple of miles behind Booth's
party with his main force of infantry. At 2 pm, while McDonnell
was busy with these arrangements, Booth set out with Major Hunter
and twenty mounted men, including Katene and Davis Canning, a
gentleman visiting from Hawke's Bay, whose liking for adventure
was to get him killed on the other side of the North Island within
three months. But the party did not include Tauke; Booth had
reluctantly agreed to take him, but neglected to provide him with
a horse. The old chief, a man of about fifty-seven years, desperately
followed Booth on foot, until McDonnell and the infantry caught
him up. McDonnell professed 'great astonishment' at finding him,

but Tauke 'stared at me and said, "I have been deceived".' McDonnell gave Tauke his own horse and urged him to gallop after Booth 'and prevent evil with your people'.

Booth reached Te Ngutu at dusk, seizing two horses which someone 'recognised' on the way in. He marched straight to Wharekura without ceremony, and demanded to talk to all the villagers. They 'seemed very much alarmed at our appearance, and ran off into the bush as fast as possible'. Canning wrote, 'they appeared to me to be frightened lest they should be taken prisoners'. But some stayed, mostly armed. Booth then had three men seized, probably at random. He later alleged that one, Ihaka, had had 'an information' laid against him 'that he had broken into a settler's house at Waingongoro', but even he conceded that the other two were innocent. Booth then ordered the seizure of a fourth man, Kokiri, 'one of their principal and most influential chiefs'. The tension tightened to breaking point. 'Kokiri was resisting all in his power,' wrote Canning, 'endeavouring to escape by means of slipping through his blanket.' Ngaruahine, who had almost run out of chiefs and were now led by old Tamati Oraukawa, cocked their guns. One man levelled his weapon at Canning and Corporal William Crichton, who were still struggling with Kokiri. Katene emphatically told Booth that Ngaruahine would fire if Kokiri was not released, and Booth reluctantly acquiesced. But he insisted on taking the other three prisoners and the two horses. The situation remained desperately tense, and Hunter sent an urgent message to McDonnell to come up at the double, 'there being every probability of shots being exchanged'. The messenger added, 'For God's sake come on quickly, the natives have taken to their arms, and Booth and his party will be killed.' At some stage in this long moment Tauke raced into the village on McDonnell's horse. His influence, and the fact that he was alive and well, apparently saved the situation. McDonnell wrote, 'I firmly believe that his presence saved bloodshed.' Booth was allowed to withdraw with his prisoners, and this parting remark: 'I also warned them that if the rest of the stolen property was not sent into Waihi they must not be surprised if we went again to look for it.'

A certain ambiguity could be read into Titokowaru's own part in these events. He was genuinely sick, victim of a minor epidemic which had killed several Ngaruahine, including Tauke's wife. This prevented him from attending the important hui held in North Taranaki about 19 May. But he may also have been unwilling to talk any more to Pakeha officials, and he did not. This probably stemmed from deep anger, not from any hesitations about the conduct of his people. The autumn muru had been his doing, initiated at his hui in March and implemented by his chief lieutenants. He later listed the 'horse stealing' as one of 'his laws'. It had been forced on him by renewed Pakeha encroachment, throwing back in his face his efforts in the peace campaign, which even Booth recognised were unequalled. And the government reaction to the muru threatened not only the land but also Ngaruahine independence. Te Ngutu o te Manu, even Wharekura itself, had three times been violated by Pakeha police actions, and his people had been repeatedly hauled off to Waihi like the horses that went with them. Even the sacrifice of Kokiri's own horse had not been enough. During the hikoi and the numerous hui of the peace campaign, Titokowaru's patience had seemed infinite. But it had its limits.

On returning from Te Ngutu, Booth examined his three prisoners. For all his faults, he had some sense of justice, and he released the two against whom he had no evidence. But Ihaka was remanded for a week in Waihi gaol until, in Booth's words, 'further evidence can be produced'. The week passed. Ihaka remained in prison; Tauke, grieving for his wife who had died on 14 May, wrote in moving terms begging for Ihaka's release, but to no avail. Believing his firmness had resolved the situation, Booth reported complacently to Richmond on 26 May that there had been 'no further cases of horse-stealing in this district'. Then, on 7 June, Ihaka somehow broke out of Waihi gaol and escaped to Te Ngutu. Ngaruahine could have no doubt that Booth and McDonnell would soon be coming for him. The question was, would they give him up? The answer came on Tuesday 9 June 1868.

About noon of that day, at a clearing called Te Rauna in the Ketemarae area, a little more than two miles from Camp Waihi, three men sweated as they worked in the dull winter sun. One was David Cahill, an ex-sergeant of the military settlers. His brother Patrick was a lance-corporal in the mounted constabulary at Waihi. 'Old Cahill' was popular amongst his neighbours, and one of them, Thomas Squires, an old military settler comrade, was helping him build his house. The third man, William Clark, late of the Wanganui Rangers, had been hired by Cahill to help with the work. The present rough whare was sparsely equipped with 'sawing tools, some axes and papers, a few blankets, and cooking utensils', but there was a fire burning in the hearth. The men were pit-sawing – back-breaking work which involved dragging a log to a pit, heaving it on to skids laid across, and cutting it into planks with an eight-foot, two-man saw. A large wooden mallet was used to adjust the skids as work progressed. All three men were needed to drag up logs, but while two sawed the third cut more trees in the nearby forest with an axe.

About a mile away, across the wooded gully of the Waingongoro River, Katene and his young comrade Moko Te Katu were visiting Mawhitiwhiti. As they were sitting on the small marae, twelve more visitors walked in, men of Te Ngutu o te Manu. All were armed with tomahawks and guns, at least two of which were tupara, the double-barrelled shotguns favoured by the Maori. They included Ngana, Te Iki, and the escaped prisoner Ihaka, and they were led by Haowhenua, short, stout, and nearly seventy, but one of the few Ngaruahine warriors whose reputation exceeded even Katene's. After exchanging greetings, Haowhenua casually 'remarked that they were going to shoot cattle, and asked if there were any Pakehas about, saying they did not want to alarm them by the firing'. Katene suspected there was more to it. 'There are no Pakehas about,' he replied, 'they are too frightened to work on their farms, as they believe you intend murder.' Just then, the sound of an axe came through the still, cold air from Te Rauna. Haowhenua rose and said, 'If we are going to shoot cattle, the sooner we begin the better.' The party moved off, and Katene prepared to sprint to warn the tree-fellers. But two of Haowhenua's men 'sauntered back and sat down by Katene, remarking that they were too tired to run after cattle, and preferred to rest until their comrades returned'.

Cahill, Squires, and Clark were struggling to haul a large log to the sawpit when a shot rang out from the nearby bush, followed by another, then eight more in a volley. Haowhenua and his men charged out. Cahill himself immediately fell mortally wounded, hit twice, in the right arm and left side. Squires also fell with a broken thigh, but Clark, unhit, sprinted for his life. Before he had got ten yards, a man with a tupara fired his second barrel and the ball passed through Clark's left arm, chest, and heart, killing him instantly. By now, the Maori were at the sawpit. One struck the dying Cahill in the chest with a tomahawk. Another picked up the wooden mallet and hit him a fearsome blow on the back of the head, fracturing both his skull and his spine. Only Squires, wounded in the leg, was able to put up some kind of fight – 'the deceased appeared to have struggled in death'. But the man with Cahill's mallet struck him down too, and another tupara-armed warrior dealt the *coup de grâce* with a bullet in the left side. Dropping the mallet, Haowhenua and his men left the bloody scene.

Soon afterwards, at Mawhitiwhiti, Katene saw them emerge from the Waingongoro gully and come towards him. Haowhenua was blunt.

'Go,' he told Katene, 'and tell the camp to bury their dead.'

'Yes,' replied the irrepressible renegade, 'and be accused of having done it myself: go you and tell them.'

With wry smiles, Haowhenua's party left Katene unharmed and moved off towards Te Ngutu, running with their blankets thrown over their shoulders to keep them out of the way. Titokowaru's Peace was over. Titokowaru's War had begun.

There can be little doubt that Titokowaru himself ordered these killings, but it must have been a bitter moment for him. His peace campaign, for which he had sacrificed so much, had been robbed of fruition after seeming success, and his few Ngaruahine warriors now faced a war against impossible odds. They were fairly well armed, and many were veterans, but military experience had its price. A disproportionate number of Te Ngutu's warriors were very young or very old, and they were pitifully few – so few, in fact, that most can be named. Some other Ngaruahine joined up immediately – Wairau, Hakopa, and Kaake, with his Araukuku warriors. Rupe of Tangahoe, with the renegades Bent and Kane, did likewise, as did the young priest Tihirua of Ngati Maru, the Central Taranaki tribe most sympathetic to Titokowaru. But this made no more than sixty fighting men. The Ngaruahine of Kauae, Mawhitiwhiti, and Hatepe remained neutral. So did Pakakohe, Tangahoe, and Ngarauru. These people remembered the campaigns of 1865-6 all too vividly, and feared a repetition. 'I came out of the fire,' said Tamati Kahukaha of Ngarauru, 'now I have no wish to return.' Without a chance of victory, Titokowaru could get no more warriors. Without more warriors, victory seemed impossible. He had done his work of peace too well.

For three days after Te Rauna, Ngaruahine's actions reflected Titokowaru's doubts. On 9 June itself, when Haowhenua was already on the way to Te Rauna, another Ngaruahine party caught James Booth as he was going to visit Araukuku. Booth had done as much as any man to bring about the war, but they let him go his way unharmed. Next day, fifteen armed Ngaruahine went to the house of Cahill's neighbour, Andrew Hiscox, which he happened to have left in the care of an old employee named Griffiths while visiting

Waihi. The Maori asked Griffiths if he held any land at Ketemarae. Griffiths replied, 'No, I am a poor man and have no land.'

Ngaruahine said, 'You are the same as the Maoris, they are poor men too and have no land.'

They told Griffiths to warn Hiscox to stay away, and to go away himself, but they did not harm him. It was a curiously merciful way for men soon to be described in the colonist press as 'fiends in human shape' to fight a desperate war.

But on 12 June this changed. At 3 pm that day, Tom Smith of the mounted constabulary at Waihi discovered that his horse had strayed from the picket lines. Disregarding standing orders, he went to look for it. A party of Ngaruahine were hidden about a mile from Waihi, lying in wait for just such an occurrence. The unfortunate Smith walked straight into their arms, his last mistake. When his comrades came up, they found only the lower half of his body and had to identify it by 'a peculiar lump on his toe'. His killers took his upper half to Te Ngutu, where two ancient ceremonies were performed on it. The heart was cut out and singed, the smoke an offering to Tu, God of War. And, in a ritual sometimes associated with Uenuku, parts of the flesh were cooked for eating. Titokowaru never ate human flesh himself, and one of his warriors later strongly denied that anyone did. But Kimble Bent and others recalled that a few selected warriors did eat of it, on this and subsequent occasions. It was no item of diet, but a traditional religious ritual, arguably more akin to the Christian communion than to lurid visions of cannibal feasts, and in cold reality it did Tom Smith no more harm than death itself. But Titokowaru would not have thanked us for excusing an act which his forebears saw as no crime, invoking the old gods in this hour of crisis. And this cannibalism was intended to strike fear and rage into Pakeha.

Titokowaru was no grim bush chieftain, an isolated traditionalist ignorant of European ways. He was a student of Europeans in general, and he knew his particular enemies quite well. He had had many hours of conversation with Booth and McDonnell, and he had lived through the terrible campaigns of 1865-6. He guessed McDonnell would await reinforcements, train them, then use his huge superiority in numbers to reapply the bush-scouring strategy and repeat the campaigns of 1865-6. The only way to pre-empt the inevitable was to provoke a premature attack, ideally on a place of Titokowaru's choosing, carefully prepared in advance. The place, Titokowaru decided, would be Te Ngutu itself, already well known to the colonists as his headquarters. In a letter passed on to McDonnell through the insider Ngaruahine, Titokowaru threw down his gauntlet in the most defiant terms:

Although a thousand should go he will be found at Te-Ngutu-o-te-Manu; should even the whole island rise against him, he will stay at Te-Ngutu-o-te-Manu, with his women and his children.

On 14 June his warriors raided Ohawe, which had been evacuated after the death of Smith. They burned the hotel, and drove off Lambert and Chubbins' cattle, but more importantly they burned Edward McDonnell's house to the ground and slaughtered his stock. The colonel now had a destitute brother to avenge, as well as Tom Smith. For, knowing of the Pakeha dread of cannibalism, Titokowaru took care to publicise Smith's fate. On 25 June, he sent another letter to the colonists:

A word for you. Cease travelling on the roads; stop forever the going on the roads which lead to Mangamanga [Waihi], lest you be left on the roads as food for the birds of the air and for the beasts of the field, or for me, because I have eaten the European, as beef, he was cooked in a pot; the women and children partook of the food. I have begun to eat human flesh, and my throat is constantly open for the flesh of man. I shall not die; I shall not die. When death itself is dead I shall be alive.

Chapter Four

THE PATEA FIELD FORCE

News of the 9 June killings reached McDonnell next day at Wanganui, where he was attending a sitting of the Pokaikai Commission. He raced north through the night, arriving at Waihi on the morning of 11 June. Here he found Hunter had the defensive situation in hand, but the prospects of an offensive seemed less promising. Booth asserted, wrongly but confidently, that Titokowaru had 200 warriors. McDonnell had one hundred constabulary – Newland and forty had been detached to Sentry Hill – and he could expect as many as 200 local militia and volunteers, but he wanted enough men to be certain of success. He decided the best way to get them was to confront the government in person. By 12 June he was back at Wanganui taking ship for Wellington, having ridden 150 miles in two days.

He arrived in the capital on Sunday 14 June, and had a private meeting with Premier Stafford and Defence Minister Haultain. Edward William Stafford is the forgotten man of New Zealand political history, perhaps because of 'an entire want of social magnetism'. But, in purely political terms, he was one of New Zealand's most successful prime ministers, running the colony for ten of its most volatile years. A hard and able man, and a retrenching premier, economy was his watchword. He could appreciate McDonnell's recent hard riding. Stafford was certainly the best jockey ever to have ridden New Zealand, having won the Canterbury Cup on Ultima at the age of forty-three. But he did not appreciate much else about the colonel, or his Patea district. 'The Colony is tired of that district and its belongings,' Stafford had once written, 'and from North and South there is but one expressed opinion – that the country has had enough of it.'

Now he responded to McDonnell's demand for money and troops 'in rather an unpleasant manner': 'I won't give you a man; you must abandon all your posts in advance off the Patea redoubt, and concentrate your force there.'

McDonnell pointed out, with calm dignity in his own recollection, that this would mean the ruin of a promising region.

Stafford replied, 'The sooner the better; I don't care, the Assembly would not vote the money.'

Theodore Minet Haultain
Alexander Turnbull Library

But events had already moved beyond Stafford's control. After McDonnell's departure, Haultain was able to talk him into a more realistic frame of mind, something the defence minister was good at. A fifty-year-old, Sandhurst-trained Imperial veteran, he had settled in New Zealand in 1849, becoming colonel commandant of the Waikato militia in 1863 and defence minister in 1865. His predecessor, Harry Atkinson, considered him 'quite unfit' – 'of course no words can now hide Haultain's incompetency' – and it is true that he was stolid and stereotypical. But he was also patient and honourable within his limits, and he ran the colony's rudimentary military machine with surprising success. Haultain now prevailed upon Stafford to initiate the mobilisation that, within two months, would produce 'the largest colonial force that has ever yet taken the field' – the Patea Field Force.

So when McDonnell and Haultain met again next day, without Stafford, they made more progress. McDonnell was in a powerful position as man of the moment. He blamed the outbreak of war on his not having authority over Parris and Booth, and demanded

full powers and at least 400 additional men. Haultain mildly replied
that this was placing the impoverished government 'in a fix', but
offered to return Newland's subdivision from Sentry Hill, transfer
a whole division from Waikato, and allow McDonnell to raise a
'Native Contingent' of Whanganui kupapa and a new corps of
government volunteers in Wellington. After threats to resign, with
which Haultain was to become all too familiar, McDonnell agreed.
On 16 June he took part in the initial selection of men for the
Wellington corps, and left next day for Wanganui, armed with
Haultain's instructions 'to use your best endeavours to attack and
punish the tribes who have been concerned in the recent murders
of peaceful settlers'. Haultain, who had never been comfortable with
the events at Pokaikai in 1866, saw fit to add this rider:

> The Governmnent desire that the severest punishment should be inflicted
> on the actual murderers; but I need hardly remind you [sic] that it is your
> duty to exercise your influence to restrain men whose passions are naturally
> excited by horrible outrages, from unnecessary bloodshedding, to save women
> and children, and to spare life when resistance ceases.

McDonnell returned to Wanganui on 19 June, and set about raising
his Native Contingent. Despite help from Featherston, this proved
easier said than done. Hori Kingi decided to go to Wellington to
advise the government in person. His colleagues decided they had
better go too. 'Though I tried hard to persuade them that two would
be sufficient,' wrote a despairing McDonnell, 'six insisted on going
at the least.' The fact was that Whanganui interests were not yet
threatened by Titokowaru. They were willing to provide limited
help, but on their own terms and at their own pace. They demanded
the same pay as the constabulary (three shillings and sixpence a day,
plus rations) and more government rifles, though they had already
been issued with 500 for 450 warriors. Eventually, they got what
they wanted. But it was not until 24 August, ten weeks after
McDonnell's first urgent appeal, that Kawana Hunia, Kepa, and 131
warriors set out for Camp Waihi.

Compared to this, the mobilisation of the local militia ran smoothly,
and soon 200 settlers, mostly veterans, were in arms. 'I have to go
into the Militia "damn it",' wrote Harry Lomax. Half, obliged under
the Militia Act to serve only within twenty-five miles of their homes,
were used to garrison Patea and reoccupy the redoubts at Hawera,
Mokoia, Manutahi, Manawapou, and Kakaramea. The other half
entered local volunteer units, exempt from the Militia Act. One

already existed, O'Halloran's Light Horse, soon to become the Patea Yeomanry Cavalry. Two more were now formed: the Patea and Wairoa Rifle Volunteers. These units elected their own officers and made their own rules, but they took soldiering seriously, even to the extent of fining themselves a shilling for talking in the ranks. Recruited largely from old military settlers, fighting in defence of what they saw as their own homes, led by competent officers and even better sergeants, the Patea militia and volunteers were good troops, almost equal to the constabulary.

These local volunteer units were distinct from the government volunteers being raised in Wellington, known as the 'Wellington Rangers'. The Rangers were recruited by Captain A.M.A. Page, 'a very intelligent and excellent officer' and winner of the Kakaramea horse race. 'Any number of the genus homo were obtainable' at Osgood's Hotel, where Page set up his desk. He chose physically fit men, mostly with previous military experience, 'rejecting large numbers of drunken useless vagabonds'. He also found himself two subalterns, Lieutenant Harry Hunter, Major William's brother, and Lieutenant Harry Hastings, both 'genial, dashing' young gentlemen. Hastings was a journalist with the *Wellington Independent*, and continued to act as its correspondent. Despite the casual bigotry of his class and time, it is difficult not to like him. His reports from 'The Front' enlivened the *Independent*'s pages for the few remaining weeks of his life.

About 20 June, Hastings and his comrades embarked for Wanganui on the *Sturt*, the 157-ton paddle steamer which was the centrepiece of the military transport system. By the 24th they were at Patea, being trained to use their new revolvers and breech-loading Terry and Calisher carbines. The Terrys were modern weapons, capable of producing the high short-range firepower needed in bush fighting, but they had their drawbacks. They had a strong recoil, tended to jam when hot, and their skin cartridges burst easily and did not include a firing cap, so that the carbine had to be capped separately, like a muzzleloader. The Rangers struggled to master these difficult weapons, and Hastings at least was pleased with the result. The men 'have attained such proficiency in drill that they can load and fire their breach-loading carbines and revolvers with remarkable precision,' he commented. Hastings was less pleased with Patea itself, which he found 'decidedly dull and abominably dreary desolate and ugly'. But his natural cheerfulness soon reasserted itself. 'It contains however, some capital barracks, jolly officers quarters and a few respectable "publics".' On 26 June, camp life was enlivened by news of a bloodless skirmish near Waihi. Hastings passed on his own version to his Wellington readers: 'Our fellows, though within 15 yards of the niggers, escaped without loss, but the black man is supposed to have suffered.' On 1 July he reported further excitement – the arrival of one hundred well-trained and experienced constabulary reinforcements from Sentry Hill and Waikato and, above all, their commander: Major Gustavus Ferdinand Von Tempsky.

Von Tempsky was the one colonial soldier who matched McDonnell in contemporary renown, and far outshone him in retrospect. He had come to New Zealand in 1861 after a decade fighting Indians in Central America and gold mining in California and Australia. He commanded a company of the Forest Rangers from 1863 to 1866, and served with great success and greater applause in Waikato and South Taranaki. A Germanised Pole, son of a colonel in Prussian service, he had received the finest conventional military training available, in the Prussian army. He was a confirmed Anglophile with a writing style almost too English, and his and the British colonists' mutual admiration was greatly helped by a shared concept of 'the Anglo-Saxon races', which embraced both.

There were two Von Tempskys. One was described as 'the Lion of the Hour' by Premier Frederick Weld in 1865, and as 'the finest soldier in the colonial service' by Colonel Sir Harry Havelock. These were somewhat barbed accolades. Weld sought to make Von Tempsky a symbol of the self-proclaimed success of his 'Self-Reliant Policy', while Havelock, who inherited both his baronetcy and his reputation from his father, the Indian Mutiny Sir Harry, was widely believed to be medically insane. And the other Von Tempsky was described by one subordinate as 'quite, quite mad' and 'not fit to be in charge of men'. Both Von Tempskys existed, but it is too easy to caricature the man. His frailties were human enough. He had just won a personal struggle with the demon drink, 'although it is sometimes very hard to sit with a dry mouth with others who are all making themselves tolerably comfortable'. He was soon to receive news of his father's death, shattering a dream shared by many immigrants before and after him: 'I had always firmly believed that I should meet my beloved father again.' Despite his love for his wife, Emilia Bell, and his three children, there are signs that he had a Maori mistress at Patea. 'I believe he had a Maori wife [sic]', wrote Wanganui settler John Wright, 'This is something which may not be known.' She was probably Lucy Lord or Takiora, widow of Von Tempsky's 'most

Gustavus Von Tempsky
'Making of New Zealand
Collection', Alexander Turnbull
Library

Photograph alleged to be
of Lucy Takiora – the
identification is
uncertain *Danbury Album,
Auckland Institute and Museum*

trusted scout', Te Mahuki, and herself an excellent scout and spy.
A strong and able woman, she was half Ngati Ruanui, a female Katene
– though her doubts about her own role emerged much later.

Von Tempsky was protective towards Takiora and sought to prevent
her from accompanying colonist expeditions, although she was well
able to take care of herself. This was one cause of friction between
Von Tempsky and McDonnell, who needed her services, and there
were others. Von Tempsky was four years the elder, with a broader
education and experience, and more non-military talent. He was a
fair novelist and a fine painter. But the two had much in common:
courage, prickly pride, and charisma; frenetic energy, a real penchant
for irregular warfare, as well as a certain instability. They were
not only kindred spirits but old friends. They had served together
in the Waikato War, and then shared the frustrations of what both
saw as the government's weak-kneed Maori policy. 'I also have a

Von Tempsky's painting of a scene from Chute's campaign, 1866. Takiora is in the foreground   *Alexander Turnbull Library*

way of disposing of painful thought,' wrote 'Von' to 'My Dear Tom' in this context, 'by whirling a horizontal bar around in gymnastic furor.' But friendship was now soured by rivalry. Von Tempsky was outranked by his younger comrade for the first time, and he did not like it. McDonnell felt similarly piqued by Von Tempsky's reputation. Newspapers occasionally described the field force as 'Von Tempsky's men', and the Prussian's speed in bushfighting had earned him the Maori name of Manu Rau, 'Many Birds'; McDonnell had to be content with various transliterations of 'Colonel Mac'. Both were driven by a romanticised vision of themselves; legends in their own time living their own legend. Ultimately, there was not room for both. But at Patea in July, these tensions lay beneath the surface. What mattered was that McDonnell had gained a hundred more veterans and the most formidable deputy available.

The arrival of Manu Rau was bad news for Titokowaru, but at least he could hope that his plan to provoke an early offensive might now take effect. His measures had certainly had the desired impact on public opinion. As early as 18 June, the *Wanganui Chronicle* was 'chafing at the vexatious delays which are taking place in following

up the murderers'. Highly coloured accounts of Tom Smith's fate
were circulating: 'We have it from the best authority that the body
of the unfortunate trooper, Smith, was boiled down and made into
soup and partaken of by every member of the tribe, who afterwards
declared that they had never tasted such excellent fare.' And the
demand for vengeance was focusing on the desired point. Harry
Hastings wrote:

> They have fortified a devil of a place rejoicing in the name of Tengutatamana,
> near Pungarehu, and if they mean to fight anywhere it will be there. Strong
> as the pa with the unpronounceable name may be, led by McDonnell, who
> is a host in himself and a terror to the rebels, we will take it.

All this had its effect on McDonnell, who was in a state of high
excitement, reportedly leaping ashore at Wanganui shouting, 'A horse,
my Kingdom for a horse' to take him to the front. But, unfortunately
for Titokowaru, psychological pressure had not yet carried McDonnell
beyond military rationality. He received timely restraint in a letter
from James Richmond, who cautioned:

> One of the greatest difficulties the Govt. has to contend with is the common
> idea . . . that our leaders are bonebrained and hasty men who invite aggression
> and precipitate disloyalty . . . As much dash as you like after deliberation,
> but pray do not let there be even the appearance of haste in your undertakings.

McDonnell did intend to act with caution. He planned a 'move across
the Waingongoro River and [the] establishment of a post, to the
west commanding the road to the Kauae and to the north commanding
the entrance to the Pungarehu Bush'. He hoped this would force
Titokowaru to battle on the Waimate Plain, but, if not, he would
strike suddenly into the bush at soft targets. In such terrain, he wrote,
'only from a succession of unexpected blows can any good be expected'.
This was exactly what Titokowaru feared most: the bush-scouring
strategy. But before he could begin this systematic campaign,
McDonnell wanted yet more men.

Public and political pressure forced Stafford to accept McDonnell's
demands. He abandoned his retrenching budget and approached
Parliament for an extra £42,000. Despite the distraction of a debate
on Bellamy's, arising from 'the bad wines sampled and selected by
the committee', the people's ire aroused that of their representatives.
The money was voted, and Stafford found himself presiding over
its distribution at the rate of £3,000 a week. Haultain set about

recruiting four further government volunteer units, and called out the militia of Wanganui Town, theoretically several hundred strong.

The militia and volunteer system had worked well in the Patea district among military settlers whose own farms were threatened and who were only recently out of uniform. But the institution was roundly hated in most other parts of the colony. In Auckland, at the outbreak of the Waikato War in 1863, the calling-out of the 1st Class Militia (unmarried men aged between sixteen and forty) was said to have generated a rash of hasty marriages. Wanganui Town shared this basic dislike of service in the militia, all the more because its experience of district commanders had not been a happy one. Major Isaac Rhodes Cooper had lost his command in 1861 for the seduction of a twelve-year-old Maori girl – or rather, for allowing the seduction to become officially known. Colonel Charles Cecil Rookes had left in 1865 amidst veiled accusations of corruption. Rookes' replacement, Colonel Edward Gorton, the present commander, was relatively a model of probity, and he did his job as head of the field force's logistics extremely well. But he had his failings, and in the eyes of the townspeople these were even worse than those of his predecessors: 'Thanks to the commandants, the very name of the militia is the most hateful that can grate upon our ears.' An efficient but officious young man, Gorton was still intensely pleased with himself for becoming a lieutenant-colonel at the age of twenty-seven, and in Wanganui he was 'not at all liked'. On 15 July, at McDonnell's request, the government ordered Gorton to call out the town's 1st Class Militia. The Militia Act laid down that he notify each eligible man separately in writing, but with a tiny staff this was not practicable. Gorton therefore posted notices of an initial parade 'when upwards of 200 men ought to have been present'. But 'at the hour fixed there was hardly a 1st class militiaman there and half an hour later there were only about 16 and no appearance of more coming'. The Wanganui militia was on strike.

Their leader was the twenty-nine-year-old editor of the *Wanganui Evening Herald*, John Ballance, later premier of New Zealand. Ballance was to become a notable reforming statesman, but in 1868 he shared the feelings of his fellow-townsmen: that the only good Maori, 'friendly' or otherwise, was a dead one, and that a compulsory militia was the first step to dictatorship. Ballance seized upon the technical illegality of Gorton's notification, and in his newspaper advised militiamen not to attend the parade. Ballance was himself liable for service, and Gorton sent him at least a personal notification to attend

John Ballance
Alexander Turnbull Library

his own parade. Ballance again failed to turn up and subjected Gorton to the humiliation of parading by himself. The two young men exchanged angry letters and then argued in person. Gorton ended the debate by arresting Ballance and clapping him in a cell. So John Ballance began a peculiar New Zealand tradition whereby future prime ministers were imprisoned for opposing compulsory military service.

Wanganui was predictably enraged. 'Military Tyranny: Editor in Gaol', shrieked the *Evening Herald*, 'in the largest type'. There was wild talk of opening a second front. 'I know for a fact', wrote one settler, that if Ballance was not released it would be done by force, and a petition for Gorton's removal was 'got up'. Ballance was soon released, 171 1st Class Militia finally appeared on parade, and the storm subsided a little. But there was a continued friction between Ballance and the authorities. Gorton was so regularly portrayed in the press as 'a perfect fiend in human form' that Haultain felt obliged

Edward Gorton
Auckland Institute and Museum

to comfort him: 'I see you are well abused by the Press; that is a sure sign you are doing your duty.' The Wanganui militia continued to be sullenly unco-operative and for some months the district failed to match Patea by providing local volunteer units for the field force. Titokowaru's most effective ally in this period was the vehemently anti-Maori John Ballance.

Gorton was a desperately busy man. His Wanganui militia district acted as a supply and support command for Patea, and he functioned as McDonnell's quartermaster, wagon-master, inspector of stores, and recruiting officer, as well as struggling with his own militia. Newly recruited units arrived at Wanganui only partially equipped, and Gorton had to make up the deficit. Finding the myriad necessary items of equipment drove him almost mad: carbines and revolvers or rifles and bayonets; muzzle-stoppers, pouches, belts, and slings;

oil bottles, cap packets, cleaning rods, wire brushes; tin pannikins, plates, forks, knives, and shoe brushes; uniforms, greatcoats, caps, and boots; lanterns, bell tents, mallets, ball bags, and waterproof sheets.

Poor Gorton had also to arrange transport and supply. He bought 'Maori bullock carts' from Mr Street of New Plymouth, small, narrow drays designed to cope with Taranaki dirt tracks, attached to the bullock-yoke by poles which merely turned in a ring if the cart upset. He let the ration contract to David Peat of Wanganui, in partnership with George Lethbridge and James Alexander, at one shilling and fivepence ha'penny per daily ration of bread, meat, salt and pepper, and tea or coffee. The troops had one shilling and sixpence deducted from their pay to meet this cost. These merchants must have made a handsome profit, because the constabulary complained that they had been able to buy all this, plus candles and vegetables, for a shilling before the war. By early August, Gorton was disbursing £500 a week to Wanganui merchants, but even this did not improve his popularity in the town. Nor did his problems stop there. Gorton had to recruit one of the new government volunteer units himself at Wanganui: the 'European Contingent' (as against the long-awaited 'Native Contingent'). He hoped for 200 men, was initially able to find only seven, and eventually managed to scrape up fifty-six. They reached Patea on 29 July but, put together from reluctant dribs and drabs, they were never very reliable. Gorton also had to handle a substantial inflow of recruits from Wellington and the South Island town of Nelson.

The second government volunteer unit raised in Wellington was the 'Wellington Rifles'. Commanded by portly Imperial veteran Captain George Buck, and known to themselves at least as 'Buck's Bravos', they left the capital to some fanfare. On Saturday 25 July, the Rifles marched down Lambton Quay for the wharves, watched by a good part of Wellington. Some of these men were Page's rejects, and, as the *Wellington Independent* observed, their calibre was mixed:

A motley collection truly! Runaway sailors, unemployed clerks, unsuccessful miners, unfortunate mechanics – some well; some ill-looking; some with a gentlemanly bearing, and in whom traces of a good education and gentle training were visible – others suggested that Captain Buck had fallen among social outcasts.

The Rifles may not have been doing themselves justice, for many, like their spectators, were in the arms of 'the prevailing epidemic

Wellington goes to war   *From Punch, or the Wellington Charivari,* 1868

– beer or brandy'. Some 'betrayed a peculiar weakness of knees', and the bugler's 'Assembly' call was 'a weak and utterly farcical attempt'. On the wharf, as their ship set out, a local character, 'the irrepressible Linley, arrayed in a bell-topper hat, which was encircled by tri-coloured ribbons, was holding a kind of "corroboree" with two inebriated females of fearful aspect'. So Wellington went to war.

The forty-one-strong Nelson contingent arrived at Wanganui on 30 July. Haultain had intended that Captain Harvey Spiller should command them, but he had not yet arrived and they were led by their ensign, Walter Long Wrey, who had allegedly been 'refused employment at Nelson because he was a common drunkard'. At Wanganui, Wrey and his men found that the Wellington Rangers and Rifles and the European Contingent had almost exhausted the reserves of equipment: 'Unfortunately,' wrote Gorton, 'I have no tents, no clothing, and only about 15 stand of [Enfield] medium rifles complete with accoutrements, consequently I am unable to arm or clothe them.' There was spare gear at Patea, but the *Sturt* was unavailable and since Gorton had no boots either he could not send them overland. Nor could he put the men on rations, because he could not supply cooking equipment. So he had to give them their daily pay and 'billet the men in the different hotels'. Wrey and his men roistered happily for the best part of a week.

Gorton eventually managed to charter a vessel to take them to Patea: the *Woodpecker*, a tiny ketch-rigged paddle steamer of only 29 tons gross, under the command of Captain John Johnson. Since the Nelsonians would have to travel on deck and Gorton could issue them with only one blanket each, they were in for an extremely cold and uncomfortable ride. At 5.30 pm on 4 August, they reflected on this as they clambered over two large and comfortable steamers to get to the *Woodpecker*. It was not good enough. Wrey 'landed himself without leave and was followed by all his men', and 'adjourned to a public house close to the wharf'. Here Colonel Henry Reader, visiting from Wellington, found them and managed to persuade them to re-embark at 8 pm. The *Woodpecker* steamed off and the Nelson volunteers were now McDonnell's problem. Gorton must have breathed a sigh of relief. But at 11 pm, to his chagrin, he was roused out to view the *Woodpecker* steam back in to the Wanganui wharves. The ship had crossed the bar and stood out to sea, but the Nelsonians had 'mutinied and broached the cargo'. Since they had done so 'under the direction of their officer', the charge of mutiny was difficult to sustain, but there are no prizes for guessing the nature of the cargo: 'a quarter cask of brandy and two crates of bottled beer'. While the Nelsonians were consuming this, blithely assuming they were still en route for Patea, Johnson quietly put the ship about. Wrey was as surprised as Gorton to see the *Woodpecker* at the Wanganui wharves again. Neither Gorton nor Haultain saw anything amusing in this affair. Wrey and eight other 'ringleaders' were dishonourably discharged and the rest of the Nelson volunteers finally staggered in to Patea on 24 August.

Titokowaru's War was arguably the greatest organisational challenge yet to have faced the infant Pakeha state, the first war that New Zealand could really call its own. Given that Haultain and Gorton had an administrative staff of barely a dozen between them, they met this challenge quite impressively. Within ten weeks of the outbreak they had mobilised, armed, and equipped 1,000 men, of whom only 200 came from the permanent force. To be sure, there were difficulties with the kupapa, the Wanganui militia, and the Nelson volunteers, together with frequent lesser irritations. A sick cavalryman was charged for horse forage while still in hospital; Captain Buck, who must have assumed his men shared his own appetite, had to be reprimanded for drawing two days' extra rations for the Wellington Rifles, and there were poignant appeals from the likes of Mrs Atkins 'whose husband had deserted her to join the Patea force and requests that a portion of his pay be stopped for her support'. One of the three surgeons, Dr Brewster, 'had to be given the dirty kick-out for insobriety at the front'. Perhaps a quarter of the Patea Field Force were soldiers of questionable calibre. But a third (the constabulary and Patea volunteers) were first-class troops, and the balance were rapidly improving. McDonnell was soon to describe the Wellington Rangers as 'one of the most efficient and best conducted units in my command'. Overall, from Ngaruahine's point of view, Haultain and Gorton had done an unpleasantly good job. How was Titokowaru faring in the race for men?

As he had anticipated, Katene Tuwhakaruru was suspected for complicity in the 9 June killings, especially by Booth. On 25 June, while McDonnell was in Wanganui, Hane Wiremu of Hatepe informed Booth that Katene intended to turn his coat again. Booth promptly imprisoned the scout for the second time, 'greatly to his grief', according to Takiora. Then McDonnell returned, and in a series of long evening conversations Katene again managed to convince the colonel of his 'trustworthiness'. 'I . . . am more and more convinced,' wrote McDonnell on 6 July, 'that his counsels are both reliable and wise.' McDonnell arranged his release, together with that of his comrade Te Katu, and gave each a new revolver and a breech-loading carbine. But Hane Wiremu had been right. Katene had made his decision, finally triggered by the sight of a dead kinsman on 12 July. That night he and Te Katu went over to Titokowaru, and they did not go alone.

On 7 July, McDonnell had sent Von Tempsky to order the insider Ngaruahine of Paramena's Mawhitiwhiti in to Camp Waihi. In their own words, they were 'imprisoned . . . so that there would be none of them to go and tell Titokowaru [where] the troops were going to fight'. They too were suspected of involvement in the killings, and when Katene came secretly to their quarters outside the camp on the night of 12-13 July, he was able to persuade them to join him. One of them later stated that 'McDonnell began to think that these things were committed by the friendly Natives, who thereupon became afraid of McDonnell, and fled to Titokowaru in the night-time'. But sympathy with Titokowaru was probably also a factor – there were safer refuges than Te Ngutu o te Manu. In any case, virtually the whole population of Mawhitiwhiti, perhaps fifty people, went with Katene to join their embattled kin. When he arrived at Te Ngutu, Katene was welcomed with open arms, and he seems to have replaced old Haowhenua as battle leader of Titokowaru's forces. He was to perform this role with a skill and commitment that would make McDonnell regret his breech-loaders.

A few days later it seemed possible that equally unlooked-for help would come from another direction: Hone Pihama, Natanahira, and the insider Tangahoe. From the outbreak of war, these people had been subjected to the same kind of ill-concealed suspicion that had so affected the insider Ngaruahine of Hatepe and Mawhitiwhiti. In mid-July, matters came to a head when the people of Natanahira's Matangarara were accused of taking part in attacks on the colonial forces. Pihama, sometimes portrayed as a weak-kneed collaborator, immediately sent the government an ultimatum:

What I wish you to understand now is, that I am afraid those of my tribe who have surrendered to the Government will be liable to another Pokaikai attack, as accusations of this sort had commenced. That if it ever occurs I am determined to leave you and go to the bush, and you will see that every friendly Native in the district will follow me. I would rather die fighting with my race than subject any more of my people to such treatment as that was.

Parris and Richmond, who respected Pihama and realised his defection would double their problems, hastened to reassure him. Unfortunately for Titokowaru, they succeeded, but he was now beginning to hope for much more substantial support from further afield.

James Booth's first reaction to the Te Rauna killings had been to claim that the King Movement had instigated them from its capital at Tokangamutu (present-day Te Kuiti): 'I believe this murder has been committed in consequence of a message from Tokangamutu. brought by More.' This was not true, but Titokowaru must have wished it was. The King Movement was still a major force in New Zealand, more important in many areas than the colonial government. It had great influence with possible allies close at hand, such as the Taranaki and Upper Whanganui tribes. Titokowaru's negotiation with the King Movement was potentially the most important aspect of his struggle for support, a diplomatic war in itself, with Titokowaru's messengers and sympathisers on the one side and government officials, kupapa, and insider chiefs on the other.

As early as 27 June, a representative of the Waikato and Taranaki Kingites visited Te Ngutu o te Manu to investigate the cause of the conflict. Te Whiti of Parihaka, a Kingite supporter, was not impressed with the resulting report. He felt that Titokowaru had broken his own absolute commitment to peace, consecrated most recently at the March meeting at Te Ngutu. At a meeting in early July,

Te Witi, the most influential chief present . . . [said] that there was to be an end of bloodshed [and] after saying that the understanding come to in March had been broken by Titokowaru, gave those present to understand that if they went to assist Tito, they would not be allowed back.

The initial Upper Whanganui reaction was no better. The Turoa family and Topine Te Mamaku informed their anxious kupapa kin that they had no plans to support Titokowaru. Pehi Turoa said 'he disapproves of the murders at Ketemarae and did not intend to fight'. For Titokowaru, this was a bitter pill. Te Whiti, in particular, seemed a natural ally. Yet both Te Whiti and the Upper Whanganui chiefs were staunch Kingite adherents, and there was still hope that they would be influenced by the decision of King Matutaera and his chief

advisers, Rewi Maniapoto and Tamati Ngapora. All therefore turned
on that decision.

The colonists were aware of this. They themselves had no influence
with the Kingites, but they persuaded the Lower Whanganui chiefs
to act on their behalf. These sent an envoy, Epiha Patapu, to
Tokangamutu, carrying a letter from Mete Kingi. Epiha arrived about
17 July and approached Rewi Maniapoto, who called a meeting next
day. Titokowaru's rejection of the King Movement during the latter
stages of his peace campaign may have rankled, but this had been
primarily for Pakeha consumption. Ngaruahine had quietly retained
the Kingite flag. It was the policy of armed peace that was probably
foremost in the minds of the Kingite leaders as they met to decide
Titokowaru's fate. Rewi reiterated this policy. Land leasing, surveying,
and gold prospecting were to be stopped and the native land courts
obstructed, but 'goodwill was to effect all these': 'the sword was
to be sheathed'. He continued: 'Listen, Waikato: the island has erred
in the wrong doing of Titokowaru; but Titokowaru's evil doing is
with himself alone, even though through it he sink down into the
world of spirits; he sought out his wrong doing himself.' Tamati
Ngapora then said, 'Hearken, Rewi: there is nothing to say. Leave
Titokowaru to be pecked by the sea-gulls; he sought it himself.' The
King Movement had made its decision.

At the beginning of August, the Kingite ambassador, More, took
this fateful message to Te Ngutu o te Manu. He was accompanied
by Wiremu Kingi Te Rangitake of Waitara fame, who now espoused
the Kingite peace policy. In what must have been a tense and tragic
meeting, Kingi may have tried to persuade Titokowaru to give up
his resistance. If so, he failed. More then conveyed the King
Movement's resolution and demanded the return of its flag. The great
Maori organisation which had long been the backbone of resistance,
which had sent 1,500 warriors to support this very Wiremu Kingi
in 1860-1, would leave Ngaruahine to its fate. Titokowaru returned
the flag as requested, but in the bitterness of shattered hopes he formally
cursed the King: 'Let the birthday of Matutaera be eaten, because
his Kingdom was of man not of God.' His hopes of support now
rested solely on his Pakakohe and Ngarauru kin.

The first concern of both groups had been to allay Pakeha suspicion.
On 17 July McDonnell met the Pakakohe at Manutahi. Wharematangi
greeted him 'in peace and friendship', and the colonel reported that
'nothing could be more satisfactory' than the Pakakohe attitude. Next
day, officials from Wanganui met Ngarauru at Weraroa. After a

feast of 'pork pidgeons and potatoes supplied on the most liberal scale', the tribe 'expressed their loyalty to the Queen, and their anxiety to be faithful and protect the Pakeha'. A week later, on 24 July, Pakakohe and Ngarauru held a meeting together at Waitotara. The speakers 'highly disapproved of Titokowaru's proceedings . . . They wished to remain neutral, which was the general wish of all the natives at the meeting.'

The real attitude of these people was complicated. The need to allay Pakeha suspicion was real and urgent. McDonnell had wished to seize the Pakakohe on 6 July, and had been restrained only by Haultain and Richmond. Soon afterwards, Booth had compelled Taurua to visit Wellington, where he had the dubious privilege of meeting Governor Bowen, to explain the Pakakohe position. Wharematangi had managed to change McDonnell's attitude at the 17 July meeting, but a sudden reversion to the policy of striking first and questioning later was an ever-present threat. The shadow of Pokaikai and the other campaigns of 1865-6 loomed large. But there was also real sympathy for Titokowaru, which gradually began to take the form of tacit support. Tito Hanataua began to doubt the pro-government attitude of his Tangahoe colleagues, Pihama and Natanahira. He was superior chief of Rupe and Bent, who had actually joined Ngaruahine. Wharematangi secretly wrote to Titokowaru in late July with information and encouragement. The next month, he renewed the muru campaign, taking settlers' sheep from disputed land. When caught at it, he claimed he had done so 'because he thought the sheep were sick', but Booth believed that 'Wharematangi is making preparations to break out, and the thefts are part of the programme'. When asked by the colonists for information on Titokowaru's plans, Ngarauru denied they had access to them: 'Should [any] Ngarauru have evil intentions it will be known at once for are we not all one? Ngatiruanui is another tribe, how therefore can we know of their intentions?' In fact Ngarauru were in communication with Titokowaru, and he had his supporters among them.

This support went further than sympathy and encouragement. Two Ngarauru are known to have visited Te Ngutu with a gift of gunpowder, and this rare surviving evidence suggests other such acts occurred. Kimble Bent remembered that Ngaruahine 'managed to get plenty of gunpowder, I have often seen it brought in in casks and 25 lb weights. They got a good deal of it from neutral and so-called "friendly" tribes'. Apart from the South Taranaki people, Te Atiawa helped in this way. Ngaruahine occasionally had to use

scrap metal for bullets when they ran short of lead and often re-
used copper firing-caps by inserting match heads in expended ones
(which increased the chances of misfire), but their own small numbers
and the help of the neutrals reduced their supply problem to a
manageable size. Treasonable Pakeha traders may also have been a
source of supply. Two such men, Whitelock and Edgecombe, were
subsequently arrested. There was also an important symbolic gesture
from Upper Whanganui. The chief Te Kere sent Titokowaru a fine
white horse. It was said to have been stolen from Kepa and to be
invulnerable to bullets. It was named Niu Tireni – New Zealand
– and even the Pakeha troops were later to hold it in some awe.

   This still did not give Titokowaru the warriors he needed. Apart
from the arrival of Katene and company, his recruitment drive was
a failure, and the break with the King Movement had been an
unmitigated diplomatic disaster. But the ambivalence of his neighbours
did indirectly serve his other purpose by pressuring the colonists
towards prompt action against the desired target. James Booth
observed that:

*If a blow sudden and effective is struck at the root of the evil (Te Ngutu-
o-te-Manu), the Pakakohi will remain friendly; but if the murderers gain the
slightest perceptible advantage over us, I am afraid that other hapus, with the
hopes of getting back their land, will be induced to join.*

This was a telling argument, and through July it was coupled with
increasing public pressure in the same direction.

   A growing wave of nervousness among the country settlers gradually
moved south, well in advance of Titokowaru's warriors. The Ohawe
settlers had lost their crops, stock, and houses in mid-June, as had
those of Ketemarae. The settlers of Manutahi, Patea, Wairoa, and
even Waitotara began to fear that they would be next. On 11 July,
Harry Lomax scoffed at some of his 'very funky' neighbours who
had 'bolted' at the rumour of a Maori attack. By 25 July, his attitude
had changed: 'I sleep with a loaded revolver by my head and must
confess to a little nervousness when a dog barks in the evening.'
Four days later, he told Robert Pharazyn: 'Things really are in a
very very ticklish state and do not be surprised if you hear I have
bolted or been tomahawked by the buggers.' His personal arsenal
now consisted of two loaded revolvers, a shotgun, an Enfield rifle
and bayonet, and a sharp knife. The fears of the settlers were reflected
in the press: 'The public expect some effective work to take place
very soon.' At first, some were illogically inclined to blame Parris

[A Card.]
TITO-KAWARU & Co.,
BUTCHERS AND DRYSALTERS,
The Gorge-Patea-West Coast.

Families waited on in Town or Country at surprising short notice. A large supply of Cured Constable, Potted Pakeha, and Dried Militiamen always on hand.

N.B.-Sole agents for Stafford and Co.'s Aboriginal Irritant. Place of business in London, Exeter Hall, Strand, W.C.

PRELIMINARY ANNOUNCEMENT.

MESSRS. TETO KAWARU & CO., with a view to extending their already gigantic business, intend shortly to erect a Bone Mill, and will supply at very moderate rates any quantity of bone dust to the families residing at Tokangamutu and the neighbourhood.

Bitter jokes — the second refers to Titokowaru's supposed connection with the King Movement *From Punch, or the Auckland Charivari, Vol. 1*

for the delay in aggressive operations, but soon McDonnell's personal immunity to criticism began to wear thin. His friends at the *Wanganui Chronicle* stated that he was 'perfectly right not to move until he could move effectually but now time presses and something must be done'. Private comments on his apparent procrastination were much stronger: Lomax wrote that 'McDonnell's conduct is considered by the settlers as *insane.*' McDonnell's sensitivity to popular approval was great, and he could not help but be influenced by this mood. Nor could the government.

At the same time, events elsewhere were beginning to have a similar effect. On 4 July, a group of Maori prisoners of war, led by Te Kooti Rikirangi, escaped from the Chatham Islands and landed near Poverty Bay on the 15th. On 20 and 24 July they successfully skirmished with parties of troops sent to apprehend them, and by the end of the month they were still at large. From Wellington, this situation did not seem terribly serious in itself. Te Kooti had fewer armed

men than Titokowaru, and had even less apparent chance of support
from the neighbouring tribes. But why, the East Coast settlers and
their political representatives asked, should McDonnell sit doing
nothing at Patea with 800 European troops, while they scrabbled
to protect themselves with barely a hundred? So the government
came under increasing pressure in Parliament. On 24 July, in the
tortured double-talk that was to become another New Zealand
political tradition, Leader of the Opposition William Fox suggested
Haultain should go to Patea himself to stir things up. 'Without saying
whether his honourable friend was the right man in the right place,
he thought that if he were elsewhere at the present than where he
was, he would then be the right man in the right place.' Fox's final
comment had more bite. Haultain should be at the front generating
offensive action, not in Wellington 'assisting in the passing of Bills
with respect to the regulation of perambulators'. Haultain had in
fact already been to Patea. Gently at first, but with ever-increasing
firmness, he too was pressing McDonnell to act. 'Mutterings of inaction
are beginning to be heard,' he wrote privately, 'from those who
are ready to attack the Government on any weak point.'

By early August 1868, it was clear to both sides that McDonnell
had won the race for soldiers by a very long chalk indeed. Titokowaru
had a maximum of eighty warriors, and several of his own followers
and the Kingite emissary More put the number he could muster for
battle at any one time at sixty. On the other hand, McDonnell had
937 men effective on 25 August. Naturally, with posts to garrison,
supply lines to protect, the Pakakohe to 'overawe', not all of these
were available for an expedition. But the gross odds were twelve
to one. The result of the other competition, the struggle for
McDonnell's plans, may seem less clear cut. In fact the turning point
had already occurred, at the little redoubt of Turuturu Mokai near
Camp Waihi, on the morning of Sunday 12 July.

Chapter Five

THE DEATH OF KANE

The remains of Turuturu Mokai redoubt, ploughed up for pasture by war veteran John Flynn in 1888, stand today in a scenic reserve of the same name maintained by the Hawera Borough Council. It is a pleasant spot, with the great mountain as its backdrop and barbecues and wooden tables placed for picnickers by benign authority amid the ancient pa sites. Turuturu Mokai pa itself is one of these, standing close by the redoubt, taken from its builders by the Ngati Tupaea hapu of Ngati Ruanui in the sixteenth century. The words 'Turuturu Mokai' indicate the sharpened stakes on which the heads of slain enemies were mounted to warn prospective attackers of their likely fate.

Turuturu Mokai redoubt was built in 1866 near the old pa by a company of the 18th Royal Irish. It was very small: about fifteen yards square measured within the defences, and twenty yards square without. The ramparts, made Maori-style of earth and fern, were five feet high from the redoubt floor and eleven feet high from the floor of the ditch running right around the outside. Two circular protruding bastions, at diagonally opposite angles of the redoubt, allowed for crossfire against an attacker. The redoubt had been abandoned in 1867 and had fallen into disrepair. It was reoccupied by the Patea Field Force in June, and garrisoned by twenty-five constabulary. Renovation began, but on 12 July was not yet complete. The plank-walk inside the ramparts was unfinished and very slippery when wet; the ramparts had no loopholes, and the gate was just a gap in the west wall, reached by a makeshift two-plank bridge across the ditch. But it was screened by a solid earth parapet just inside the redoubt. From behind this the defenders could exact a heavy toll from enemies seeking to enter. The site was said to have been selected by Governor Grey, who had visited the area in October 1866. Grey, a brilliant strategist, grossly over-rated his own tactical military ability and induced many historians to do likewise. He demonstrated this again at Turuturu, choosing a site which was dominated by higher ground about 150 yards to the south. This left the garrison vulnerable to good marksmen.

Sketch of Turuturu Mokai *From T. W. Gudgeon, The Defenders of New Zealand*

Twelve miles away at Te Ngutu, on the evening of Saturday 11 July 1868, Titokowaru summoned his people to their great meeting house with a chant which began 'Here am I, at the Beak of the Bird'. Sitting cross-legged in front of them, he led prayers to Uenuku and then began pointing his finely carved taiaha, 'Te Porohanga', at individual warriors. Those picked out were the Tekau-ma-rua, The Twelve, an élite force or vanguard which actually varied in number. They would lead an attack on Turuturu Mokai that night. Each man indicated by Te Porohanga was questioned about his readiness for this particular fight, and chosen on the basis of his answers and divine guidance. With The Twelve as its core, the taua or war party totalled sixty men, virtually Titokowaru's whole force, but he himself did not accompany it. Instead, it was led by Haowhenua and another old veteran, Tautahi Ariki, or Tautai, who had fought at Otapawa and earlier lost all the flesh of one arm when pushing a shell away from his rifle pit. Haowhenua was close to seventy years old; among his younger subordinates was Te Kahupokoro, a lad of sixteen, who had fought his first battle at Sentry Hill four years before. Other members of the taua included Rapata Te Rangiora Nuku, Titokowaru's younger half-brother, and the priest Tihirua, as well as Taketake and Taruhae, all young men of proven courage, whose boldness Haowhenua and Tautahi's experience was intended to keep in check. Uruwhero, another reckless young soldier, was warned by Titokowaru not to join the expedition, but went anyway.

Another member of the taua was an Irishman, Charles Kane, a deserter from the British army. Kane also went by the names Tiaki, or Jack (the generic Maori slang for a Pakeha soldier), James, and the alternative surname of King. He cannot be traced in the records of his regiment, the 18th, and any or all of these names may be false, but the man himself definitely existed. Kimble Bent remembered that he was 'exceedingly bitter against his old officers'. Like Bent, he was protected and kindly treated by Titokowaru, who allowed him to marry his niece. They had at least one child, for their descendants still live in South Taranaki. Kane was a fierce and courageous man, who would not brook ill-treatment from anyone. He felt vengeful towards the British and did not share Bent's inhibitions about shooting those of his countrymen in Victoria's service. Turuturu Mokai was his chance, and it was to be neither the first nor the last time that Irish blood was to be shed on both sides of a battlefield.

Though Haowhenua and Tautahi led the taua it was Titokowaru who planned the attack, and his spies and scouts made him well informed of the redoubt's strengths and weaknesses. His prime consideration was to minimise his losses. He had no warriors to spare, and he wore the brand of Sentry Hill on his face. He therefore forbade an attack on the gate: 'Do not charge at the gate way of the fort; there stands the lion! Should you disregard this command, the lion will devour you.' Instead, he decided to exploit two less obvious weaknesses. The lack of loopholes meant that the ditch itself was the safest place for an attacker. Once there, Ngaruahine's guns and long-handled tomahawks would make it very dangerous for the garrison to lean out over the parapet and fire down on them. Titokowaru therefore planned for most of his men to creep as close as possible to the redoubt undetected, then sprint for the dead ground in the ditch. Naturally, the garrison's attention would then be focused entirely on them. Meanwhile the best Ngaruahine marksmen would take up position on the high ground to the south, armed with Enfields. It would be these men, 150 yards away, who shot down the garrison.

This plan did not necessarily demand the actual taking of the redoubt. Two dozen constabulary carbines would be a welcome addition to the Ngaruahine armoury, but they were not worth the lives a frontal assault would cost, and the main aim was to damage the garrison without losing warriors. Doing this, under the very noses of Hunter and Von Tempsky and their tough constabulary divisions at Camp Waihi only three miles away, would surely crack McDonnell's restraint. But the very proximity of Waihi, which made Turuturu

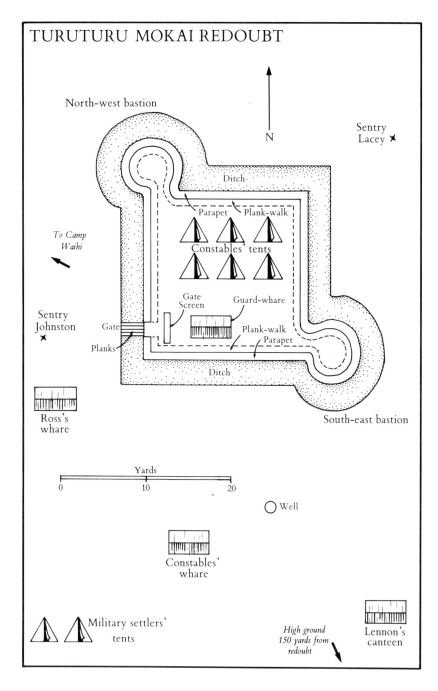

TURUTURU MOKAI REDOUBT

North-west bastion

Sentry
Lacey ✗

N

Ditch

Parapet   Plank-walk

Constables' tents

To Camp
Waihi

Gate
Screen   Guard-whare

Sentry
Johnston
✗

Gate

Plank-walk
Parapet

Planks

Ditch

Ross's
whare

South-east bastion

Yards

0   10   20

○ Well

Constables'
whare

Military settlers'
tents

High ground
150 yards from
redoubt

Lennon's
canteen

so suitable a target, was also a great danger. Hunter's mounted constabulary could cover three miles in twenty minutes. Titokowaru had chosen a night when a strong wind was likely to obscure the sound of gunfire at Turuturu for listeners at Camp Waihi – this use of the wind, 'the breath of Uenuku', gave rise to the saying that 'even the winds of heaven are Titoko's'. But gunshot flashes, fugitives, or even a sentry with particularly good hearing could still alert the camp, and a question mark remained.

The farewell poi dances over, the taua marched out of Te Ngutu into the night. As they did so, Titokowaru chanted, 'Kill them, eat them! Let them not escape! Hold them fast in your hand.' The taua marched south-east through dense rata forest to the Waingongoro River. Despite the cold and drizzling night, many were lightly clad in the usual mixture of European clothes, flax cloaks, and kilts; boots, bare feet, and flax sandals. Crossing the Waingongoro, they covered the fern and flax land north of Turuturu and crept into a gully a few hundred yards inland of the redoubt. There they sat silently, waiting. Before them, they could dimly make out their target, the dense black mass of Turuturu Mokai redoubt.

Meanwhile, the garrison went unsuspecting about their evening routine. Most were Irishmen, like the Beamish brothers of Cork, John and Alleyne, and many were veterans of the 57th Regiment – 'The Diehards' – which had served six years in Taranaki. Men like Ralph Ross, Michael Gill, William O'Brien, and Michael O'Connor had taken their discharges in New Zealand in favour of peaceful occupations but, bred in the close knit military tribe of the 57th, they soon found themselves drifting into the colonial forces. Apart from the constabulary, there were two local military settlers, Coslett Johnston and Lawrence ('Larry') Milmoe, also Irishmen, come in for protection. Johnston and Milmoe slept in tents close outside the redoubt, as there was no room inside. The redoubt commander was Captain Frederick Ross, son of a substantial Rangitikei settler, an officer well liked by his men. Ross was young but experienced; he had been badly wounded in the arm during the Pokaikai campaign, and was a friend of McDonnell's. On the evening of 11 July, Ross farewelled another friend, Captain Henry Morrison, now farming his land grant. Morrison had been sharing Ross's whare, which was also outside the redoubt, while gathering some scattered sheep. Morrison, luckily for him, had decided to leave that day for Patea.

Ross's men occupied themselves with the normal off-duty activities: talking, eating, smoking, and drinking. We do not know what they talked about, but they smoked Davidson's and Yachter Baltic pipes, and drank beer from black bottles lead-stoppered like champagne. Those in funds might drink V. Haytema and Co. Dutch square gin, or James Henart's Superior Malt Whisky, doctoring themselves with Davis's Vegetable Pain-killer in cases of over-indulgence. A less innocent pastime was hollowing the noses of bullets to make them expand on impact – home-made dum-dums. They ate ration biscuit, pork or beef, and locally bought or looted peaches, supplemented by tinned sardines from the little canteen outside the redoubt run by the fastidious storekeeper, Richard Lennon, whose mirrors Waru had taken. This evening, the bill of fare was also supplemented by onions bought from some insider Tangahoe, visiting the redoubt as they often did. The Maori had 'larked about' in friendly fashion, but sentry George Tuffin had noticed one man carefully examining the redoubt. Tuffin told Sergeant John McFadden, 'That fellow is up to something,' but McFadden replied, 'Oh, he's only looking for old clothes.'

Gradually, the pipes went out, the campfires died down, and the twenty-seven men at Turuturu Mokai made their way to bed. Most of the constabulary slept in six bell tents inside the redoubt, where there was also a whare used as guard hut and store. But two, Constables Hamilton and Cowper, slept in another whare outside the redoubt like Ross, the military settlers, and the storekeeper Lennon. Theoretically, all were close enough quickly to man the ramparts in the case of an alarm. Constable Garrett Lacey, another ex-57th Irishman, and military settler Coslett Johnston had drawn the pre-dawn shift of guard duty and, just before he turned in, Johnston asked Captain Ross if they could stand sentry outside, as the day's rain had made the plank-walk dangerously slippery for a sentry's pacing. Ross agreed, so when they were wakened around 5 am Johnston and Lacey armed themselves and took post outside, Johnston to the south, near the gateway, and Lacey to the north, near the north-east bastion. There they paced slowly up and down, as they had done a dozen times before, now and then blowing into their hands to warm them.

In the gully nearby, Ngaruahine huddled against the freezing night. Hours earlier, bitterly cold and with the tension mounting to an almost unbearable pitch, the younger warriors had urgently whispered their wish to get it over with. With difficulty, Haowhenu restrained them. He wanted more light, and although the mid-winter sunrise would not come until 7 am, the beginnings of dawn would soon lighten the blackness a little. When it did, a little after Lacey and Johnston began their beat, he murmured the order to commence a stealthy approach. Slowly, with infinite care, the taua began to creep foward through the long grass. Years later, Tautahi wriggled his hand snake-like to illustrate the manner of their movement.

Constable Garrett Lacey had sharp eyes, and, in the murk more than a hundred yards away, he thought he discerned several moving forms. At first he thought they were Henry Morrison's sheep, but as they got a little closer he made out that the figures were human. Fugitives? Friendly Maori? A patrol from Waihi?

'Halt! Who goes there?' he yelled, levelling his carbine.

No response. Lacey challenged again, without response. So he fired, and shouted, 'Stand to your arms boys!'

Surprise at last lost, Haowhenua leapt to his feet and roared, 'Kokiri! Charge!', and several men returned Lacey's fire. Lacey's bullet went wide, but Taketake, aiming carefully, hit the sentry in the shoulder. Lacey dropped, and the Maori raced forward parallel with the east face of the redoubt towards the little group of exterior buildings. Cut off from his friends, Lacey lurched to his feet and staggered off into the fern clutching his wound.

Captain Ross was up and out of his whare in an instant, dressed only in his shirt but carrying a revolver. He yelled to his men to stand to, and the constables inside the redoubt grabbed for their carbines and ammunition belts hanging on the tent poles within easy reach. Johnston, the other sentry, on duty near the gate, 'bolted in' with time to spare. His fellow settler-volunteer, Larry Milmoe, dragged suddenly from sleep in his flimsy tent outside the redoubt, was badly frightened but also made it inside. Constables Hamilton and Cowper, sleeping in the whare near the well, closer than Ross and Milmoe to the source of shots and shouts, panicked or decided they were cut off, and fled into the dark bush. Richard Lennon was less lucky or less prudent. Closest of all to the charging Maori, he stopped to dress himself and was cut down by Tihirua and Charles Kane as he stepped out of his canteen: 'Storekeeper Lennon, when the alarm was given, coolly dressed himself, laced his boots, and saw to it that every last button on his tunic was correct. As he walked out of his whare door he was cleft in two, and his heart torn out!' When Lennon fell dead, Tihirua, the war party's priest, stooped, neatly cut open his chest, and removed the heart: 'He certainly made a clean job of it.' With bullets now flying thick around him, he held the heart up, lit a match, scorched it slightly, and as the smoke rose cried, 'Tu, The God of War, is with us.' This was the ancient Whangai Hau ceremony previously applied to Tom Smith.

Lennon's corpse was used for the Whangai Hau because he was the Mata Ika, or 'First Fish', the first enemy slain in the battle. His killer gained considerable mana for the deed. Both Tihirua and Charles Kane believed the honour to be theirs, and this was later to cause another tragedy. At the time, Tihirua put his incongruously modern wax matches to a different use by firing Lennon's canteen and the other outbuildings, on Haowhenua's orders. About half the taua, under Tautahi, had meanwhile made straight for the redoubt's ditch. It took only a minute from Lacey's first challenge for them to attain this objective and they suffered no casualties in doing so. As the official report put it: the Maori 'seem to have got into the ditch of the redoubt at once'. Haowhenua then sent his marksmen to the rise in the south. Thus far, everything had gone according to Titokowaru's plan.

Tautahi and his men spread out along the ditch, mainly on the south side of the redoubt, pressed close to the wall so that the garrison could not depress their guns sufficiently to fire at them without leaning out over the parapet and fatally exposing themselves. Here, though the garrison fired as fast as they could load, the Maori were relatively safe, as Titokowaru had expected. But some of the men's blood was up; the long cold wait in the gully, the sudden flaring release of tension, and Tihirua's ringing cry of 'Tu is with us' was too much for their usually tight battle discipline. Springing up, ignoring Tautahi and Haowhenua's shouted commands, Taketake, Nuku, Taruhae, Uruwhero, and a few others charged straight at the gateway. Among the young hotheads was an old warrior, Paipai, as deaf to orders as any.

Constable George Tuffin, the alert sentry of the previous day, stood on the plank-walk at the southern parapet and fired his revolver, then his carbine, at the dark mass of Maori close up against the wall. As he rose to fire his carbine a second time, a Maori caught sight of his head and snapped off a shot which 'ploughed a deep furrow right across the top of my head, making a bad skull-wound'. Tuffin fell, and momentarily blacked out. Coming to, he saw Captain Ross near him, asking, 'Where are you hit, old man?' Tuffin tried to answer, but could not, though when Ross asked where his carbine was he managed to point to it. Ross, his five-shot revolver empty and with no time to reload, picked it up just as Taketake and the others massed on the other side of the ditch to rush the open gateway.

'Come on, lads!' yelled Ross, 'the devils are coming in at the gate!'
He called for volunteers to man the earth screen which guarded
it.

'I'll make one sir,' said Michael Gill.

'All right, Gill,' replied Ross, recognising his voice in the dark.

Gill was followed by Constables Peter Swords, Henry McLean,
and William Gaynor. From behind the screen, Ross and these men
faced Taketake and the others; the two groups blazed away at each
other in the flickering light of the burning whare. It seemed impossible
that any shot could miss but, as is always the case in battle, most
did. The constabulary worked their carbines with frozen fingers, and
some of their Terrys may have jammed. Nuku was able to charge
right into the redoubt and kill William Gaynor – not with the
tomahawk as the legend has it, but by shooting him through the
heart and spine. Gaynor fell dead in a sitting position, his back against
the earth screen, his carbine in the crook of his arm. Peter Swords
fell mortally wounded beside him, shot through the lungs. Ross picked
up their revolvers and fired them off – in all he fired some twenty
rounds in the battle, one of which hit Taketake in the arm. Taketake
was helped away, and Nuku withdrew unscathed, but it was Taruhae
who killed Ross with a 'gunshot wound of the left temple entering
the brain sufficient to cause instant death'. Running, like Nuku, right
into the redoubt, Taruhae bent amidst the bullets and cut out Ross's
heart, perhaps unaware that Tihirua had already performed the
Whangai Hau. As he turned to follow Nuku and Taketake, he was
shot dead by Gill or McLean. Ross's heart rolled into the ditch, where
it was picked up after the battle by Larry Milmoe.

This Maori attack was made with almost incredible courage; but
it was rash even if aimed at taking the redoubt, and Taketake, Nuku,
and Taruhae seemed more interested in glory. Three Pakeha were
down, but the Maori had lost four or five killed and wounded. They
had charged the mouth of the lion and it had devoured them.
Titokowaru's prophesying was also correct in another particular: in
the ditch, beside the plank bridge, lay Uruwhero, his feet touching
those of the corpse of old Paipai. From the garrison's viewpoint,
Ross was dead, but the gate had been held. There were still twenty
men, each with carbine and revolver, holding the redoubt wall, and
it was, surely, only a matter of minutes before Hunter's cavalry came
up from Waihi.

At Camp Waihi, about 6 am, the corporal of the guard noticed
some flashes in the dawn sky in the direction of Turuturu Mokai.

Captain Frederick Ross
Taranaki Museum

He gazed intently for a few minutes and, satisfied that the flashes indicated heavy gunfire, woke Senior Sergeant William Anderson. Anderson got up; he too thought the flashes were gunfire, and sent the corporal to rouse the officer commanding, Von Tempsky. Von Tempsky came out and asked Anderson where the firing was. The sergeant pointed out more flashes, but Von Tempsky, an old hand, was dubious: 'I listened but could hear no sound, as the wind blew against Turu Turu.' He decided to investigate without urgency, using his own men, the infantry of No. 5 division instead of the cavalry of No. 3. He sent Anderson to tell William Hunter to take command of the post in his absence. But it was a cold morning, and these alarms were two a penny. Major Hunt told Anderson 'that he was not going to turn out of bed, and to tell Major Von Tempsky that it was all right.' Anderson asked for, and received, permission to saddle the horses of the mounted part of No. 3 division – about thirty men. But Von Tempsky did not take them 'for the following reason: no firing being heard on account of the wind, and but a few flashes seen by myself, I deemed the affair of little importance, not requiring special speed.' The breath of Uenuku was serving Titokowaru well.

At Turuturu, the garrison's situation was worsening by the minute. Earlier, men had kept up a heavy fire into the ditch, leaning over to fire their carbines and holding their revolvers at arm's length over the parapet and emptying them. The fire was random; it caused no more than one Maori casualty, but it did keep Tautahi's men pinned down. But when Constable William Holden leaned over to fire he had his head smashed by a long-handled tomahawk and was shot in the chest for good measure. He lay now atop the parapet in the growing dawn light, blood and brains visible to everyone, and his comrades were not anxious to repeat his experiment. Moreover, in the improving light, Haowhenua's marksmen on the rise to the south were beginning to make themselves felt. Corporal John Blake was their first victim, shot dead through the head at a range of 170 yards. Soon after, Sergeant McFadden fell, calling out that he was hit in the leg – in fact he had been mortally wounded in the chest.

With their leaders, Ross, Blake, and McFadden gone, some of the men began to panic. Someone maintained that, as he fell, Captain Ross had called out, 'Take care of yourselves, boys. I am done for' in 'a queer manner, as when wounded', and that this meant they should flee the redoubt, every man for himself. The fact was that Ross had been killed instantly, and Michael Gill said, 'No, there's wounded, and we must protect them.' But the last surviving non-commissioned officer, Lance-Corporal H.P. Cobbe, was among the waverers and this encouraged four other men – Ralph Ross, Philip Kershaw, Wilkie, and Burrows – to join with Cobbe in obeying their captain's spurious last command. Larry Milmoe wanted to go with them but was prevented by his mate Johnston. Cobbe and the rest fled, jumping down from the walls into the ditch and away cross-country. Though Tautahi's men had not yet completely encircled the redoubt, this desperate expedient might be thought to require as much courage as staying in the redoubt, and in fact Ross (no relation to the captain) was killed in the ditch and Kershaw badly wounded – he lay hidden in a clump of scrub close to the redoubt and so survived the battle. The other three, like the rest of the garrison barefooted and wearing only the shirts they had slept in, ran hard for Waihi, shadows jumping at them from behind every bush.

Nearly an hour had passed since the first alarm, and both sides could scarcely believe that Hunter's cavalry had not yet arrived.

Haowhenua checked that his sentries were posted to give him good warning, and Tautahi spread his men right around the ditch. Some began digging away at the redoubt wall with their tomahawks, using the unlooked-for time to good effect. The garrison was now concentrated in the two bastions: Johnston and Milmoe, Stuart, Flanagan, and William O'Brien in the south-east; Gill, the Beamish brothers, Patrick ('Paddy') Shields, Michael O'Connor, Henry McLean, and George Tuffin in the north-west.

The south-east bastion was partly protected by its parapet from the sharpshooters on the rise, and Johnston, a veteran of the Royal Irish Constabulary and an ex-sergeant of military settlers, kept his nerve. He and Milmoe were the only members of the garrison with Enfield rifles and bayonets, and they later credited their two bayonets with mighty feats. Johnston claimed that 'it must of been the glint of our fixed bayonets as much as anything else which kept the Maoris from rushing us'. Larry Milmoe went even further: 'those who tried to scale the parapet were met by a charge of bayonets.' There was a cruel but persistent rumour that Milmoe never fired a shot, much less used a bayonet, during the whole battle. These tall tales helped give Turuturu Mokai its utterly false reputation as 'the Rorke's Drift of the New Zealand Wars' when hundreds of maniacal Maori were 'beaten off again and again by the little garrison'. Even so, it was a trying time in the south-east bastion. The thinly clad men began to suffer from exposure in the cold morning – the effects stayed with one survivor for the next fifty years. Flanagan was wounded twice in the arm, and the tension of waiting for the long-delayed relief while the Maori chopped away coolly at their protective wall was almost unbearable. But it was in the north-west bastion that the worst nightmare occurred.

Though the other bastion was closer to them, the Ngaruahine snipers on the rise had a clearer line of fire into the north-west. They were shooting into its exposed inner side, where there was no parapet, and they moved position until they found a good line of sight between two of the tents. As the sun began to glow redly just below the horizon, they picked off man after man with deadly accuracy. Apart from Blake and McFadden, who were killed there earlier, Paddy Shields was shot dead, John Beamish was hit in the shoulder, O'Connor in the leg, and the unfortunate George Tuffin was hit four more times after his first wound suffered at the gate. Young Alleyne Beamish did not fall victim to the snipers on the rise. He rose to fire, saw a white man level his gun from close by the redoubt, and fell mortally

wounded in the stomach. Charles Kane had got his strange revenge.
Kane himself was slightly wounded in the cheek soon after, and retired
from the fight.

The rising sun found the garrison of the north-west bastion literally
more dead than alive: three dead, one dying, two wounded, and two
unhurt. Gill was one of the unhurt, firing two or three weapons
in succession as John Beamish passed him cartridges with his uninjured
arm. Beamish, his young brother in agony beside him, was 'hoarse
with shouting' as the two sides exchanged words as well as bullets.

'Come out, come out,' yelled the Maori, along with 'all the English
"swearwords" in their vocabulary'.

'Come on, come on,' responded the garrison, or 'Look out! The
cavalry are coming!'

'Gammon, Pakeha, gammon,' replied the Maori, or else they just
'laughed fiendishly'. They continued to chip away at the ramparts.

Meanwhile, Cobbe had outpaced his fellow fugitives, Wilkie and
Burrows, in the race for Waihi. Disregarding severe cuts to his feet
from broken bottles in the redoubt ditch, and suffering further
'lacerations of the feet caused by running through fern', he staggered
into Waihi soon after Von Tempsky's infantry had left, missing the
major because he had cut across country. Lucy Takiora saw him
come in, dressed only in his shirt. In Sergeant Anderson's words,
Cobbe 'ran into the stables, and told me that the garrison at Turu
Turu Mokai was surrounded, and the greatest portion killed, and
that some of the wounded men were on their way into Camp Waihi'.
Anderson immediately ordered his men to mount and went to Hunter's
whare to ask if he could go to succour the wounded. Hunter refused:
Von Tempsky would do all that could be done. Anderson and his
men were furious; they could still see flashes of gunfire, and Anderson
had difficulty preventing his men from riding to the rescue against
orders. Hunter, still in his whare, sent a further order: dismount
and feed the horses. Letting Anderson go would dangerously deplete
the Waihi garrison, and by now Von Tempsky would beat the cavalry
to Turuturu anyway.

About half-way along the frozen track, Von Tempsky came upon
'two men in their shirts' – Wilkie and Burrows. They told them
that 'the redoubt was carried by surprise and most of the garrison
killed'. At last realising that he faced a genuine emergency, Von
Tempsky picked up his speed but, thinking he could no longer do
any good at Turuturu itself, made for a point north of the redoubt,
hoping to intercept the retreating enemy. Thus Wilkie and Burrows'

self-justifying misinformation allowed time for another couple of men to die at Turuturu Mokai. Back at Waihi, Hunter had at last decided to send his surgeon, Dr Samuel Walker, with a dozen mounted constabulary under Anderson as escort, to help any wounded, and to send out a stretcher-party on foot as well. After impatiently waiting fifteen minutes for Walker to get ready, Anderson galloped off. Because of Von Tempsky's misinformed diversion, it was Anderson who got to Turuturu first after all, a few minutes before the major. But there were no Maori there.

Haowhenua's well-posted sentries gave him ample warning of Von Tempsky's approach. The Maori had time to evacuate the ditch carefully and without casualties, take up their weapons and wounded, and make off. Von Tempsky pursued hard for a short distance, but Haowhenua had too good a start and he soon gave up. As they retreated, young Te Kahupokoro remembered looking over his shoulder and seeing two of the survivors jump up. They 'shook their rifles at us and danced a *haka*, and shouted at us in derision "Te bloody Maori – *hau, hau*".' Perhaps it was Milmoe and Johnston.

The survivors of Turuturu Mokai were entitled to celebrate, and they had certainly displayed great bravery. Historians have construed this to mean that the engagement was a noble British victory. They were wrong. British and Maori casualties were sixteen and six respectively, and most contemporaries saw Turuturu Mokai for what it was – a sharp and embarrassing little Pakeha defeat. The Ngaruahine achievement in crippling the garrison of a fortified post with small loss to themselves was a minor triumph of tactical planning. As for the strategic effect, that depended on Thomas McDonnell.

Some hours after the attack, McDonnell rode up from Patea and reviewed the carnage: Lennon, his corpse dreadfully hacked, lay beside the ashes of his canteen; Beamish, McFadden, Swords, Gaynor, Blake, Ross, Holden, Shields – all dead; McDonnell's companion of many expeditions, Frederick Ross, dead, a gaping hole where his heart had been. Above all, there was the insult. The defeat had occurred a mere twenty minutes' ride from the main constabulary camp at Waihi, under the Patea Field Force's very nose. That evening, in a state of barely suppressed rage, Fighting Mac asked Turuturu's new commander, young John Roberts, to stroll outside the redoubt. After a moment, McDonnell asked Roberts to sit. 'Drawing his sword he extended the blade, gleaming brightly in the winter moonlight, and brought it back up to his lips, kissed it, and said dramatically, "Roberts, I shall have revenge for this." ' From that day forward, McDonnell

Some of the defenders of Turuturumokai
Kershaw Flanagan, Beamish, O'Connor

Taranaki Museum

Larry Milmoe, on the site of Turuturu Mokai in 1898, pointing to the spot where
Ross was killed   *Taranaki Museum*

thought of little else but attacking his enemy at Te Ngutu as soon
as he possibly could.

Turuturu Mokai had served its purpose and there remained only
the attribution of praise and blame. There was plenty of blame, and
William Magee Hunter got most of it. He was pilloried mercilessly
in the press for not sending his cavalry, for remaining in bed while
Turuturu Mokai burned. He could not enter a public place without
an exchange of malicious whispers. He went up before a board of
inquiry in August, and though he was formally exonerated Haultain
publicly reprimanded him – and it was the sleeping-in that rankled:

*Inspector Hunter's conduct in not turning out of bed when a post, within
sight of his own camp, was reported to be attacked, showed so much apathy
and want of alacrity that, had he not on former occasions proved his general
zeal and courageous conduct, he could no longer be trusted in any position
of responsibility. His character as an officer has suffered.*

Hunter took it hard: 'I have been made the scapegoat of an unfortunate
and untoward affair . . . My case may be any one's to-morrow.'

As for praise, on the Pakeha side John Beamish, Coslett Johnston,
and Michael Gill – who in fact had the best claim – all came in
for a share, each appearing in newspaper articles as 'the hero of
Turuturu Mokai' in later years. Even Larry Milmoe made a bid for
the position, regaling his mates with his heroism at the pub in Hawera
decades later. When doing so for the umpteenth time, his mates,
as they had often done before, said, 'Now Larry Johnston is in town.

We'll bring him along and soon find out who the hero of Turu Turu is.' Larry 'got so annoyed' that 'he pulled out his rosery and shied it at his tormentors'.

The plaudits were not undisputed on the Maori side either. Both Kane and Tihirua claimed the Mata Ika, First Fish. The latter had the greater influence, and it was he who was believed. Enraged, Kane spoke of returning to the Pakeha and, with Bent, was interviewed by Titokowaru and made to promise that he would remain. Some time later, Ngaruahine found a letter, allegedly from Kane and ostensibly left for colonial troops to find. It stated that Bent and Kane planned to kill Titokowaru and bring in his head to Camp Waihi, on the assumption that this would temper their own reception. Hearing of this, Kane tried to escape but was caught and taken back to Te Paka village. That night, in some secrecy because it was still not clear that Titokowaru would approve, several Maori crept into Kane's whare while he was sleeping. One man, Patumutu, struck his sleeping form a terrible blow with a bill-hook but, because Kane had his blanket drawn up partly over his face, it missed its aim and only gashed his nose. Kane leapt up and grappled with his attackers. In the end, it was an old warrior, Uruanini, who brought him down by grabbing his legs. He was then tomahawked to death and thrown into a potato pit. There, at Te Paka, lies Charles Kane, Irish soldier, victim of two worlds.

Chapter Six

McDONNELL'S REVENGE

McDonnell reacted to Turuturu Mokai 'like one demented', but his melodramatic rage soon cooled into something more dangerous. By 24 July at the latest, he had firm plans to attack Te Ngutu, abandoning the bush-scouring strategy. To this extent, Titokowaru had succeeded in bending the colonel to his will. But McDonnell was resolved to accept the challenge in his own way. Titokowaru had determined the place and month of the attack, but it was McDonnell who would decide the day and direction. He would use this leeway to the full, aiming above all to gain tactical surprise. Titokowaru knew this, and sought surprise in his turn. Throughout August 1868, the two resourceful minds duelled for the unexpected.

Today, the scene of their duel, the forty square miles between the Kapuni and Waingongoro Rivers, inland of the Waimate Plain, seems small and accessible. The country is mainly fenced farmland, pocked with natural-gas wells, and it is easy to miss the old locations from a speeding car, then miss them again as you backtrack. But 120 years ago, the area was twenty times the size in terms of travelling time. To the uninitiated, the forest seemed almost impenetrable: a mass of great rata, totara, matai, and mahoe trees, with a dense undergrowth of fern and supplejack creeper. In fact it was a complex web of routes and clearings, in three dimensions. First, there was the major track, leading from Camp Waihi across the upper ford of the Waingongoro to Mawhitiwhiti, with branches to the other fringe villages. From Mawhitiwhiti, this became the Pungarehu Track, leading to Te Ngutu o te Manu. The second dimension was numerous lesser tracks, leading to lesser clearings in which grew maize, potatoes, and grass for Ngaruahine's stock. These clearings were not well known to the colonists, but good scouts could find them and they would have been the targets of bush scouring. Finally, there were infinite trackless routes, sometimes with steps cut or paths indicated, but most merely the memory of the best way to get from one place to another. This was the true secret of Maori bushcraft, which the British sometimes attributed to inborn monkey-like or rat-like skills. But if you had learned these routes, you could move where others could not, or at least do so much more quickly.

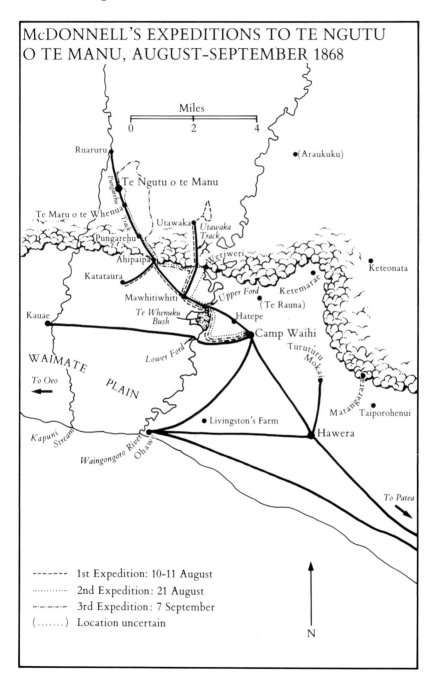

McDONNELL'S EXPEDITIONS TO TE NGUTU
O TE MANU, AUGUST–SEPTEMBER 1868

Miles

0   2   4

Ruaruru

Te Ngutu o te Manu

Te Maru o te Whenua

Utawaka

Utawaka
Track

Pungarehu

Ahipaipa

Weriweri

Keteonata

Katataura

Upper Ford

Ketemarae

(Te Rauna)

Mawhitiwhiti

Te Whenuku
Bush

Hatepe

Camp Waihi

Kauae

Turuturu
Mokai

Lower Ford

WAIMATE

PLAIN

To Oeo

Matangarara

Livingston's Farm

Taiporohenui

Kapuni Stream

Waingongoro River

Ohawe

Hawera

To Patea

(Araukuku)

N

- - - - - - -   1st Expedition: 10–11 August

. . . .   2nd Expedition: 21 August

— ·— ·— ·—   3rd Expedition: 7 September

(. . . . . . .)   Location uncertain

Against this background, Titokowaru laid his plans. Because of its mana as the centre of his power, Te Ngutu was the right choice as a target to provoke attack. But it was not a fighting pa. An Atiawa woman, Maata Ahuroa, who visited at the end of June 'stated that they had not done the slightest thing in the way of fortifying the place up to the time of her leaving'. Apart from one outwork, this remained the situation in August, for Titokowaru intended Te Ngutu as the symbol of a decisive battlefield, not the thing itself. Instead, he concentrated his remarkable engineering talents on Te Maru o te Whenua, a clearing one mile south-east of Te Ngutu on the Pungarehu Track, the route which any attacking force was likely to take. Te Maru pa

> *was constructed in a most ingenious manner; the palisades were erected right across the track, and for some chains on either side, and supported by rifle-pits in the rear. Yet it was intended only as a blind, to distract the attention of the attacking party from the more dangerous (because unseen) rifle-pits that flanked the whole line of advance, and ended in a gully, by which the enemy could escape without being exposed to fire. Any enemy attempting to storm the palisades would be enfiladed from these hidden pits.*

Te Maru was a deadly trap, an ambush within an ambush, and McDonnell did not have the faintest idea of its existence. But the essence of Titokowaru's generalship was his balance of innovation and precaution. There remained a chance that the colonists would find their way to Te Ngutu. If they did, Ngaruahine were doomed, because Te Ngutu was their economic base. Titokowaru therefore set about reducing its economic importance. It was not planted that season, and other cultivations were expanded. The main new base was a little-known pair of clearings two and a quarter miles north of Te Ngutu on the bank of the Kapuni, known as Ruaruru, the 'Owl's Nest'. Ngaruahine shifted their reserve supplies, equipment, and livestock to Ruaruru, and built storage pits and dwellings for their non-combatants, signs of which were still apparent many years later: 'They were cleverly constructed . . . it looked as if families could live in them, while anyone coming onto the clearings would look across and not see any signs of life or man-made constructions.' Ngaruahine still spent much of their time at Te Ngutu, and it retained its moral significance for both Maori and Pakeha, but it was now economically expendable. Its material heart beat at secret Ruaruru.

The secret of Ruaruru, however, was not quite so well kept as Titokowaru supposed. McDonnell had lost his special source of inside information – Katene – but Von Tempsky still had his – Takiora. She had heard of Ruaruru as 'a clearing they keep their horses in', and she knew where it was – roughly. She believed it to be 'quite a mile from Te Ngutu', not two and a quarter, an important difference in dense forest. She believed that an old track, inland of the Pungarehu Track, led to it through Utawaka, but 'she unfortunately knew only a portion of the track'. Still, McDonnell and Von Tempsky seized upon this chance. They would take the Utawaka Track to Ruaruru, not because they were interested in Ruaruru itself – they were unaware of its new importance – but because they could then attack Te Ngutu, by surprise, from the rear. Meanwhile, a diversionary force would demonstrate at the fringe villages near the entry to the Pungarehu Track, the expected route of advance. It would not go far into the forest, but it would focus Ngaruahine attention on itself. This too was a very clever plan.

Given the need for bushcraft, it would have been wise to wait for the Whanganui kupapa, whose departure was reported to be imminent at last. But here Titokowaru took a hand with a couple more goading raids. One took all James Livingston's sheep, but the more important occurred on 29 July, when The Twelve, under Katene, attacked a supply convoy. The attack was made a mile south of Camp Waihi, whose routines Katene knew so well. Naturally, the colonists assumed full drays were the attractive targets, so Katene attacked a convoy of empty ones. His purpose was to provoke, not destroy, and after wounding two of the escort, he slowly retired to the edge of the bush and danced a defiant haka in full sight of Camp Waihi. Von Tempsky and his men came out at the double, and Katene withdrew into the bush, where he had probably prepared hidden rifle-pits, hoping to tempt them in. Von Tempsky was bold, not rash, and he wisely declined the invitation. Katene's only loss was the young warrior Ngana, one of the killers of 9 June. He was shot dead as he danced by Richard Blake, one of three tough half-Maori brothers in the Patea militia, all crack shots. Like Cahill, Ngana had had a short war. But Katene returned to Te Ngutu well satisfied. He had made his point.

For McDonnell, it was yet another well-placed Picador's dart. He believed that Captain James Hirst, an officer he had dismissed from the Patea militia, was 'constituting himself a spy' for the government, reporting ' "want of energy", "inaction" and "unnecessary loss of time" on my part'. Even his admirer Harry Hastings was getting sick of apologising to the Wellington public for 'the apparent delay

in commencing operations'. McDonnell waited until the Wellington
Rifles arrived on 9 August, but decided he could wait no longer
for the kupapa. He picked out 300 of his best troops, issued two
days' rations, and marched out of Waihi at 11 pm on 10 August
to implement his plan of attack. Titokowaru's scouts might have seen
them leave Waihi, but in the darkness they did not see the force
split at Mawhitiwhiti. Captain Page and 135 men, the diversionary
force, marched off to the mouth of the Pungarehu Track and camped
there to await daylight. McDonnell, Von Tempsky, Takiora, and
166 troops – the striking force – pushed cautiously up the Utawaka
Track, 'maintaining the strictest silence'. Four miles up, at the limit
of Takiora's precise knowledge, they too halted to await the dawn.
Takiora slept in an old whare with the surgeon Samuel Walker, 'an
Irishman and a wag' on one side of her, Harry Hastings on the other,
and 'Von at my head'. McDonnell slept outside with his men.

Page's task was to 'entice the rebels from their stronghold', or
at least to hold their attention. When dawn broke, he burned the
little village of Katataura to advertise his presence. Takiora alone
recorded that he 'took some loot and burned some whares and killed
an old Maori'. (Old people often remained alone in an abandoned
village.) Seeing the flames, Ngaruahine rushed to man their trap at
Te Maru, but Page did not come on. Mystified, Titokowaru sought
to encourage him. 'The natives in the bush . . . yelled and called
for them to come on.' A few warriors showed themselves and 'many
others were heard inviting them to go to Te Ngutu'. Still Page did
not move. His diversion was functioning perfectly. But, on the
Utawaka Track, the main expedition had begun its descent into farce.

First of all, at 5 am, it began to rain heavily. The troops, bivouacked
on the ground without tents or old whares, soon became 'very
uncomfortable'. McDonnell and his men shook off sleep nevertheless,
and moved on, but Takiora found the track increasingly difficult
to follow. A party under Hastings had already got lost, before camping
for the night, and she had had to go back for them. She found them,
she wrote, 'in a creek pottering about', and brought them up, but
now, only half a mile from Utawaka, Captain Michie Brown of No.
5 armed constabulary 'seriously sprained his ankle by a fall over a
log'. The heavy rain continued, some ammunition was spoiled, and
the force was 'thoroughly wet through'. Eventually, even Takiora
got a little lost and the force began 'going away from Te Ngutu'.
McDonnell reluctantly decided to abort the expedition.

So a frustrated McDonnell returned the way he had come. He sent Von Tempsky to bring off Page, who was still at Katataura turning the other cheek to Ngaruahine's taunts. He was going to send Takiora 'but Von would not let me come back by myself'. To vent his ire, McDonnell burned Mawhitiwhiti on his way. His men shared his frustration, and tempers frayed on the tedious march back to Waihi. Sergeant C.D. Bennett of No. 3 found Constable Patrick Ready reluctant to fall in for the return march. Ready 'was standing in front of the Division. When I ordered him to fall in he said he would when he was ready and not till he pleased. I ordered him to be confined.' Being 'confined' on the march meant one was disarmed and deprived of one's trouser belt and braces so that the need to hold them up hampered escape. Constable Ready was 'greatly irritated'. 'Just as we arrived at Waingongoro River,' continued Bennett, Ready 'rushed up to me and knocked me down'.

Though Brown's ankle and Bennett's chin were the only colonist casualties, this first expedition against Te Ngutu o te Manu was an embarrassing fiasco. McDonnell would no doubt have been relieved to find that it has disappeared from history – even from the compendious tomes of the Gudgeons and James Cowan. Ironically, Titokowaru must have been almost as frustrated, because he too wanted a full-blooded colonist attack on Te Ngutu – up the Pungarehu Track. McDonnell drew some comfort from the performance of his raw recruits on a difficult night march, and this made him all the more determined to try again as soon as possible. 'I trust I am not premature in saying that I think they will give a good account of the enemy when we succeed in meeting the Hauhaus which I trust will be *very* shortly.' The emphasis is McDonnell's.

McDonnell's attempt to gain surprise by using an unexpected route had failed. He now decided to try an unexpected day – one when the weather was so bad and the Waingongoro so high that a colonist attack would be the last thing Ngaruahine expected. But for a week the weather continued frustratingly fine. On 18 August, he went to Patea to deal with administrative matters. As so often happens when one gives up, his luck turned. On 20 August it began to rain, and by noon it was 'very wet'. He sped back to Waihi and, after consulting with Von Tempsky, gave orders for an early start next morning, which 'broke with torrents of rain'. At 5.30 am on Friday 21 August, his troops paraded for their second attempt on Te Ngutu, wet but ready. This time, Takiora was left behind, probably on Von

Armed constabulary group. Colonel McDonnell on the right and possibly James
Livingston, standing, second from left. Note the shawls, worn as kilts by colonial
veterans in the bush for ease of movement   *Taranaki Museum*

Tempsky's insistence, along with Page, who was left in command
at Waihi. 'Von came and said goodbye to Page and I,' wrote Takiora,
'I could not sleep that night.'

The striking force now totalled 350 men, including the pick of
the raw Wellington Rifles, stiffened by some officers and sergeants
from the Patea militia. There was also the newly arrived Taranaki
volunteers, recruited from New Plymouth from the best militia in
the country – the fifth and last of the government volunteer units.
The force was divided into two equal wings under Von Tempsky
and Hunter, the latter determined to clear his name after Turuturu
Mokai. Other men had private axes to grind. Constable Burrows
also wished to regain a reputation lost at Turuturu. His trouserless
flight with Wilkie and Cobbe had been the butt, as it were, of unkind
remarks. He now volunteered to take charge of the unreliable but
fearsome hand grenades McDonnell had ordered from Wellington.
Hunter's orderly, Constable James Dwyer, created more undercur-

Another 'shawl party', at Camp Waihi   *Taranaki Museum*

rents. Compared to the popular McDonnell and Von Tempsky, Hunter
was something of a martinet, and his orderly was probably expected
to inform on his comrades. They therefore hated Dwyer, and one
or two eyed his back thoughtfully as they marched out.

The force reached the upper ford of the Waingongoro about 7
am and managed to cross the raging river with the aid of a rope,
in torrential rain. The river was chest high, but the men were
encouraged by the promise of a gill of rum at the other side. 'When
all cross a tot of rum was served out to each man,' wrote James
Livingston, 'which I was looking long for as I was suffering pains
in my bowels.' The force then marched on to the Pungarehu Track,
where Livingston's state was not improved by signs of his stolen
sheep – 'tracks of wool all along the road'. McDonnell was capable
of caution, and he left O'Halloran and his dismounted troopers at
the mouth of the track to secure his retreat before advancing up
it.

Titokowaru knew full well that McDonnell would try again. For
nine days after the first expedition his people remained on the alert,
with Te Maru permanently garrisoned. The outwork was now built
at Te Ngutu, a curved line of trenches and palisades covering the
egress from the Pungarehu Track. This was probably a precaution
against enemy scouts or minor raids, for the village itself remained
unfortified. But economic activity could not be suspended for ever.
On the night of 20 August, as the rain set in, he withdrew the garrison
from Te Maru. McDonnell would surely stay at home in such a
downpour. Next day most of the warriors, under Katene, went off

to shoot wild cattle, Kimble Bent and a party set off for the Tangahoe village of Turangarere to get ammunition, and the younger women went out to the various clearings to collect maize in the rain. The old women and children were mostly at Ruaruru, and only Titokowaru and twenty men remained at Te Ngutu, 'never dreaming that the Pakeha would come out in such weather'.

The colonists continued to pick their way carefully up the Pungarehu Track, leaving another detachment, the Taranaki volunteers, at Pungarehu itself. About 10 am, the rain began to let up a little, giving way to sporadic showers and a 'thick mist [which] shrouded the whole country; this was even better for our purpose than darkness'. Suddenly, the scouts came upon 'breastworks and entrenchments . . . flanking the road' – the secret fortifications on which Titokowaru was pinning his hopes. McDonnell cautiously explored them. 'I now found that rifle pits and defensive posts had been made on each side of the track, right up to Te Maru te Whenua, and they had evidently been used the preceding night, as the embers [of the campfires] were still smouldering.' 'But fortunately for the attacking party,' observed another relieved colonial officer, 'this strong work had no defenders.' Titokowaru's deadly surprise had been spoiled.

'Using great caution and enforcing the strictest silence', McDonnell and his men went on their way, closing on the Te Ngutu clearing about 11 am. Some 500 yards from the pa, the scouts glimpsed the palisading of the new outwork 'supposed to be the advanced post of the enemy; the column was then halted, and the Colonel with Sergeant R. Blake advanced cautiously from the bush to reconnoitre'. After inspecting the position, McDonnell decided that the outwork, which he could see had 'small manholes . . . cut in it, here and there', should be attacked frontally from the north-east, with Hunter on the right (with No. 3 constabulary and the Rifles) and Von Tempsky on the left (with Nos. 2 and 5 and the Wellington Rangers). Without pause, both wings would then assault the village itself, Von Tempsky's in the lead. With surprise on his side, it was a good, straightforward plan, and McDonnell crawled back to the waiting column to give his orders.

There were a few sentries in the outwork while Titokowaru and the rest of the twenty were in their houses. They included Whakataka, Toi's old father, and were probably mainly older or injured men, not up to chasing cattle through a rain storm. They sat talking, making cartridges, and singing. 'The natives were heard singing and had not the least suspicion of our approach.' Now it was Ngaruahine's turn to sit unsuspecting, like the garrison of Turuturu Mokai, while their doom crept up on them.

The peaceful sounds of slow singing and falling rain filled Te Ngutu clearing for a long moment. Then they were shattered by 'a terrific yell, the bugle sounding at the same time' – a roar described as 'a cheer that those who heard can never forget', but really a sound much more primitive, the Pokaikai yell. McDonnell and his men, after crawling on their bellies for fifty yards, leapt to their feet and charged straight at the outwork, perhaps a hundred yards away. The few Ngaruahine sentries got off one volley despite their shock, hitting Constable Timothy Collopy of No. 2 and Private Henry Sedgewick of the Rangers. Both men received glancing head wounds, which suggests that the sentries were huddled in the rifle trench against the wet, giving them a poor outlook into the bush, and that they were startled into firing high. They then sprinted for the village and the colonists scrambled in and through the outwork palisade behind them. William Wallace remembered 'crawling in through one of the manholes in the stockade and thinking what an easy target I would make for any Hauhau'. The colonists paused for an instant in the shelter of the rifle trench, then ran across the clearing towards the village at its southern end, Von Tempsky in the lead.

McDonnell maintained that he 'now found' that the village 'was strongly stockaded' in contrast to his visit before the war. This was not true. 'This Village was not fortified,' wrote William Newland, 'beyond upright fencing not intended for defence purposes but for a quiet place to live.' There were 'many *whares* scattered about the clearing' outside even this. Titokowaru and his men had no defences and only a minute's warning, but these were not the sleeping victims of Pokaikai. They seized their guns and threw themselves down behind the village fence. A few, perhaps from the houses outside the fence, took up positions in the bush on the western edge of the clearing. All opened fire on the colonists. Von Tempsky's No. 5 lost Samuel Whiteside, shot through the stomach, and Edward Hope, shot in the mouth. Thomas Lloyd, of Hastings' Rangers, was badly hit in the left leg, and William Wallace lost his young brother, Richard: 'I ran back and bent over him, but he was gone in a few moments. He was hit in the jugular vein and bled to death.' Hunter's wing was well to the rear, but it did have one casualty – James Dwyer, mortally wounded from behind.

The charge lost its impetus a little. 'Orders had been given to reserve fire until within pistol shot of the enemy', but it is very

difficult to sustain gunfire without returning it, and many men paused
to do so. 'Volley after volley was poured into the village.' But, urged
on by Von Tempsky, No. 5 and the Rangers quickly resumed their
charge, closely followed by No. 2. The Ngaruahine veterans now
knew that the game was up. Twenty guns could not stand against
300 and the village had to be abandoned very fast. They made their
decision without their leader. 'Titokowaru retired to his praying-
house when the firing began, and sat there muttering incantations,'
they later told Kimble Bent, 'and it was only with the greatest difficulty
that he was persuaded by his people to leave the *whare* and retire.'

The colonists entered the eastern end of the village just as the
last Maori were leaving at the west. Now was the time to pause
and fire, but the whooping troops ran in pursuit instead, weaving
among the whare that straggled the 200-yard length of the village,
and they missed the few warriors they could see. The exception was
Richard Blake, the crack shot. He stopped, aimed, and fired, hitting
old Whakataka, who later died; he reloaded his Enfield and fired
again, wounding a second man, so causing as many casualties as the
rest of the force put together. Some Ngaruahine stopped to fire in
return. '[Ranger W.A.] Kerr was shot through the lungs inside the
palisading, and expired after twenty minutes dreadful agony – poor
man, he suffered dreadfully.' The troops ran on into the little west
clearing, but the bush beyond this was too dense and McDonnell
called off the pursuit. He now held Te Ngutu o te Manu.

McDonnell must have guessed that he had ejected only a fraction
of Titokowaru's force and that the rest might soon appear. He posted
most of his men around the perimeter facing the bush, and hurried
the rest into searching the houses as quickly as possible. The search
turned up Kimble Bent's diary, an incriminating letter from
Wharematangi to Titokowaru, some coils of homegrown tobacco,
and a tame kaka parrot. Livingston 'saw plenty of sheepskins but
no live sheep'. There were also possessions of Katene's, including
his tupara, and eleven other guns, together with fifteen or twenty
pound-cannisters of powder 'wrapped in the paper as sold', a large
box of government ammunition, and a number of Ngaruahine's home-
made cartridges. John McLay of No. 5 made another discovery. He
poked his head into a whare and received a bullet in it, from a Maori
who had remained behind, possibly wounded in the legs. The
unfortunate McLay fell dead. Constable Burrows came up, and tossed
a grenade into the wounded warrior's whare 'to prevent him from
doing further mischief'.

Richard Blake
Taranaki Museum

The plunder was disappointing. Katene's tupara was his reserve gun – he carried McDonnell's new carbine – and the other guns were probably muskets and single-barrelled shotguns, all second-class weapons. McDonnell would certainly have specified other tupara, rifles, or carbines – he listed Katene's trousers amongst the spoils. Like Katene, the owners of these guns had left them behind because they had better weapons. There was not much food, though the loss of the ammunition would no doubt be a blow to Ngaruahine. All was destroyed, except the pet kaka, which Von Tempsky took back as a present for Takiora. McDonnell 'ordered the houses to be set on fire, and commenced with Titokowaru's house', taking care also to destroy the great house of peace, Wharekura: 'I caused the larger house to be fired in several places', waited until 'it was so far gone as to be impossible to be extinguished', and began his retreat, leaving Hunter with a strong rearguard to complete the destruction. Burrows went from house to house, tossing one of his grenades into each burning building. It was not yet noon.

McDonnell and the main body were only a few hundred yards down the track, and Burrows' work was still far from complete when shots rang out from the bush adjoining the village. Katene and the majority of Ngaruahine's warriors had left their cattle-hunting at the first sound of distant gunfire at 11 am, and had covered several miles of dense bush in under an hour. Hunter could not risk being cut off from the main body, and he promptly made off after it. Ngaruahine moved in as he moved out. We may guess that a tense discussion took place in the burning village. The enraged warriors wanted to press home an immediate counter-attack against the retreating enemy. Titokowaru forbade it. Even at this dire moment he would not break his inflexible rule of avoiding unnecessary losses to his tiny force. There would be pursuit, yes; but it would be carefully controlled. His men would keep strictly to cover and fire only when the colonists were exposed and they were not. Some warriors remained to fight the fires, the others went out to fight the colonists.

The main body slowly negotiating the muddy track, with forty men carrying the dead and wounded on stretchers, soon came under long-range fire and picked up their pace. McDonnell realised this was not quite appropriate for a victorious force and felt obliged to apologise in his report: 'I was anxious to follow them but could not find any track, and, as they seemed to be hid in bush which I could not possibly penetrate, without great labour and loss, I thought it better to move steadily on.' The main Ngaruahine pressure fell on Hunter and the rearguard. They were sniped at as they passed through each clearing and were occasionally subjected to quite heavy volleys – always from cover too dense for an effective return of fire, and from too far away to allow a counter-charge. The Wellington Rifles soon suffered their first casualties. Joseph Geary was shot dead through the head, and his brother Hamilton was severely wounded. On reaching Pungarehu, McDonnell ordered the Taranaki volunteers to remain and join Hunter. These fresh troops were apparently sorely needed, for 'in crossing one of the numerous clearings the rearguard was heavily pressed and they had all their work to do to keep the enemy back until reinforcements came up'. Joseph Thompson of the Rangers was badly hit in the shoulder, and lay under fire, in danger of being left behind. Dr Walker was unable to reach him and got a bullet through his coat in the attempt. But Major Hunter 'gallantly dashed out into the clearing under a perfect storm of bullets' and brought Thompson in. French Catholic missionary Jean Rolland, who accompanied the expedition as chaplain, also distinguished himself in attending the wounded. The heavy rain set in again, and the rearguard were pinned down in the ravine near Te Maru. McDonnell had to bring back part of the main body to assist them.

Ngaruahine ceased their pursuit only at the edge of the bush, six miles after it had commenced. Even then, a small party cut in front of the colonists and opened fire from an old pa site as they reached Weriweri. They retired when Albert Fookes led some of the Wellington Rifles towards them, 'but our troubles were not quite over, for on reaching the Waingongoro, it was found that there was a heavy freshet in the river'. There was mute consternation amongst the weary men at the thought of getting thirteen stretchers across this torrent. Edward McDonnell, 'one of our strongest men', stripped and crossed with a rope, making it fast to the other bank. With Livingston, the Blake brothers, and a few other strong men, he then managed to get the heavy stretchers across 'after a severe struggle'. The bone-weary troops, wet through, hauled themselves on to the far bank and safety. All in all, wrote one, 'the retreat was far worse than the attack'.

The exhausted force reached Camp Waihi about 6 pm, but Thomas McDonnell's day was not yet done. At 8 pm, he mounted his horse and rode off for Patea to announce his great victory. Early next day, he sent Sergeant-Major David Scannell to Wanganui with the news. Scannell reached Wanganui at 4.30 pm with the despatch and McDonnell's request to Gorton to forward it to Wellington with all speed. John Walker of Aramoho, a noted rider, left immediately overland, changing his horse six times along the way. At 4 pm, forty-six hours after the Te Ngutu expedition had returned to Camp Waihi, the weary Walker handed McDonnell's despatch to Haultain. One of the fastest pieces of paper in the history of New Zealand overland communications up to that time, it was also one of the briefest:

Ngutu attacked – taken – and burnt this day. Enemy well thrashed . . . behaviour of all ranks splendid – could not be surpassed. Great success. Very tired, can say no more.

McDonnell had not been so 'very tired' that he could not ride the extra thirty miles to Patea himself, and he did not go to the lengths of special orderlies and seven changes of mount for bad news – or unambiguously good news. He was concerned to outstrip less rosy rumours, and for a while he succeeded. Haultain was delighted, particularly with the financial and political implications. The victory should enable McDonnell to strike a couple of units off pay, he wrote, and would allow Stafford and him 'completely to rebut some of the abominable lies which have been circulating'. To this end, McDonnell's message was read in Parliament with unusual promptitude, the dramatic effect of its telegraphic brevity somewhat spoiled by the fact that there was no Wanganui telegraph.

For a few days after the receipt of McDonnell's first despatch, the government and the public celebrated his 'great success', but very soon cracks began to appear in the official version. As early as 23 August, Wiremu Hukanui came into Waihi with information that there had been 'only one killed on the Maori side' (Whakataka died later). He was sent away again and obligingly returned next day with a more acceptable report of eight killed. But other accurate reports filtered in through the insiders, and there was the inconvenient fact that honest men such as James Livingston had seen only three Maori, dead or alive, 'the whole time'. The damage was done. By 25 August the *Wanganui Chronicle* was saying it was 'absurd' to enthuse 'over a victory which looks like a drawn battle, and of which the enemy will probably claim the advantage, seeing that they followed our retiring men for some distance'. A similar change of tone occurred in other newspapers, and in Parliament Stafford's relief was shortlived. The Opposition was soon claiming that McDonnell's report, now supplemented by a fuller despatch, was 'anything but correct'. 'McDonnell fell back, the natives rallied and so hotly pursued the colonial forces that it was with difficulty that they saved their wounded,' stated Colonel H.C. Russell, MHR. 'Thus an operation commenced so gallantly ended with disaster.'

Russell was too harsh, and the first Battle of Te Ngutu o te Manu is probably best seen as a draw. After all, McDonnell had succeeded in surprising Titokowaru, despite the fact that the whole Ngaruahine strategy was designed to provoke attack, and Maori losses were not restricted to Katene's trousers and a pet parrot. They had lost Wharekura, the great house of peace, other houses, and valuable ammunition. It was true that the destruction of Te Ngutu was only partial, that only two Ngaruahine had been killed, and that Kimble Bent was able to replace some of the lost ammunition with gunpowder from Burrows' grenades, many of which failed to explode. But McDonnell and Von Tempsky, whatever their other faults, had again shown themselves to be leaders of great skill and resource, and their men had proven themselves. Even the new recruits, wrote McDonnell, had displayed 'all the fine qualities of tried veterans'. McDonnell's own subordinate, Walter Gudgeon, made the fairest assessment:

The skirmish was not very favourable to us, for we had lost four killed, and had eight wounded [actually nine], whereas as far as we could tell the enemy lost only two men; but on the other hand, most of our men were new to bush fighting: and no one expected great things from them, so the old hands were agreeably surprised to see them retreat so steadily and quietly in the face of an active, daring, foe, and predicted great things in the future.

Newspaper pressure for another attack on Te Ngutu mounted again, and on 7 September Haultain wrote to McDonnell that 'immediate advantage must be taken of your present large force and of the limited numbers of the enemy to attack them wherever they may be found'. In fact this letter was unnecessary, and it arrived too late to have any effect. The very day Haultain wrote it, McDonnell was marching on Te Ngutu yet again. In theory, he continued to trumpet the 'great success' of 21 August. In practice, he agreed with his critics. The attack had failed in its aim, and another was necessary. He hoped the third time would prove the lucky one.

Chapter Seven

THE BEAK

For two weeks after the battle of 21 August, McDonnell alternated between Patea and Waihi, making complaints to Haultain – of ten dozen port and brandy ordered to 'comfort' the one dozen wounded, only half had arrived – waiting for the kupapa, and harassing the Pakakohe. On 2 September, the kupapa arrived at long last, some 130 strong. Officially, they were led by William McDonnell; in practice, the colonists accepted that they were led by Kepa. In fact there was a third level of leadership, for if they had to choose, most of these men would follow Kawana Hunia. Despite these complexities of control, the kupapa were good troops, veterans of the campaigns of 1865-6, and well armed at the government's expense. McDonnell immediately added 110 to his striking force and dropped a similar number of his least experienced Europeans. As a result of repeated selection processes his striking force of 369 men was now of high quality and it outnumbered Ngaruahine by a factor of six. As for Pakakohe, both McDonnell and Booth believed that 'Wharematangi is making preparations to break out,' and Booth wrote, 'I . . . will certainly take him prisoner as soon as I can do so with safety.' Meanwhile, they had to be content with threats, sending the 'European Contingent' to Patea 'to overawe the Pakakohe'. In fact Wharematangi was not yet ready to risk his people in so unpromising a war, and the majority of Pakakohe remained peaceful. One small group, probably led by the priestess Tangamoko, and including her fifteen-year-old nephew, Tutange Waionui, did join Titokowaru, his first reinforcement since the coming of Katene.

At Te Ngutu, Tangamoko and Tutange found themselves in the midst of frenzied activity. Titokowaru had no doubt that McDonnell would come again to complete his work, and men, women, and children alike laboured desperately to prepare for his reception. There was one symbolic act, the rebuilding of Wharekura, but Te Ngutu village itself at last received some military engineering attention. The young son of Toi Whakataka, Pou Whareumu, then a small boy grieving for his grandfather, helped with the work, and remembered it clearly:

The pa had a stockade, ditch, and low parapet. The ditch was outside the tall stockade of totara timber [10 or 12 feet high] and the parapet, just inside the fence, was formed with the earth thrown up by the diggers. The trench surrounded the greater part of the pa; it was not dug on the west side, where the Mangotahi Stream, with its abrupt bank, closely approached the stockade.

These defences did at last turn the village into a pa proper, but they were still 'not formidable, and could have been taken by a determined assault'. The stout totara logs occurred only every few feet, there was much weaker split timber between them, and gaps even in this. There were rifle pits within the pa (no anti-artillery bunkers because the colonists could not bring cannon into the bush) but there was no proper rifle trench around the perimeter, and only a single line of fire, from behind the low parapet, was possible. But, visually, this fairly weak pa seemed to dominate the clearing, and this was the function designed for it. The real defences were elsewhere. Te Maru had failed, but Titokowaru had not given up his search for surprise.

Neither had McDonnell. He and Von Tempsky decided they would again try to attack Te Ngutu from the rear, through Ruaruru. With fitter troops and the experience of 10–11 August, it should, they thought, be possible to leave the Utawaka Track where it had misled them before, and strike out towards Ruaruru by lesser trails or no trail at all. McDonnell wanted Takiora as guide, and this occasioned a bitter argument with Von Tempsky, by no means the first in recent weeks. 'There was an altercation,' wrote Takiora, 'as Von did not want me to go as my information was quite sufficient.' Von got his way. Instead, McDonnell procured the services of Horopapera of Waitara, son of Hapurona, Te Atiawa's general in the Taranaki War but now an insider. Horopapera had lived at Te Ngutu for some time before the war. The expedition was set for 7 September.

McDonnell and Von Tempsky were wary of enemy spies, and their preparations were made in great secrecy. On 6 September, the men of the striking force went to bed knowing that something was up but not what. 'All this time if I except perhaps two or three of the principal officers,' wrote George O'Halloran, 'none of us had any idea of our destination.' There were really no prizes for guessing that, but the route and time of departure were carefully kept secret. At about midnight, after the men had been in bed barely an hour, Von Tempsky went from tent to tent rousing them, 'whispering in his foreign accent'. No lights were permitted. Like lovers leaving an adulterous bedroom, the men of the striking force stole out of Waihi in the dead of night. As they went, Lieutenant Albert Fookes discovered he had forgotten his revolver and returned to his tent to get it. Fumbling in the dark, he 'managed somehow to explode it', despite its being holstered and uncocked, wounding himself in the leg. 'This accident [sic] probably saved his life.'

After a long delay, carefully to check equipment and organise the line of march, the force set off about 3 am and crossed the Waingongoro, 'breast deep and freezing cold', an hour or so later. McDonnell forced the pace to pass ruined Mawhitiwhiti, a likely locale for spies, 'under cover of night'. He reached the entrance to the Pungarehu Track and advanced along it a short distance further to deceive any enemy or scouts. He then moved inland off the track, concealed his force, and waited for daylight. 'It was bitterly cold, in fact freezing, and the [kupapa] Maories, who were mostly without boots were crippled for weeks after the frost of that night.' As dawn broke, and the men could see their way, they started off again, going cross-country to the Utawaka Track and following it for a few miles. 'We struck inland,' wrote McDonnell, 'to Te Rua-ruru; after proceeding some distance on a very old trail it ceased altogether. We then headed in the supposed direction of the place named.' Silence was still 'insisted on', and the troops crept cautiously through the dense and trackless bush.

Despite all McDonnell's precautions, Titokowaru was waiting for them. Late the previous night, he had called his warriors into the rebuilt Wharekura and told them: 'O friends, be on your guard! This is an evil night – a night of danger, and the morrow will be a day of danger!' His followers believed this to be a divinely inspired premonition. But, for the sceptic, there is another level of explanation. Takiora later discovered a concealed lookout post in a rata tree 'where the natives got on and can see Waihi from it, and can see every movement of the Pakehas'. When McDonnell's preparations began on the evening of 6 September, a scout may have left this tree and run to Te Ngutu. Titokowaru guessed the colonists' objective while the great majority of them were still wondering. That night he sat praying in Wharekura while his people slept.

Early the next morning, the people breakfasted and Titokowaru addressed them on the marae: 'Friends! I salute you! You have eaten and are content; for the proverb says, "When the stomach is filled, then man is happy and satisfied." Now rise up and grasp your weapons, for I wish to see you dance the haka.' Among the songs that accompanied the war dance was that first chanted at the Manawapou landholding meeting of May 1854: 'Taranaki shall not be lost, shall not be abandoned to the stranger.' Then Titokowaru again prophesied that battle would occur that day, and his people set about their preparations.

Titokowaru sent most of the children and some of the women, under the old chief Te Waka Takereinui, to Ruaruru. Some women remained to support the warriors, as did a few young boys of ten or twelve and all those youths old enough to fight. The young Pakakohe warrior Tutange Waionui was called by Tangamoko, along with others about to experience their first battle.

She called us to her, and told us she was about to make us tamariki tapu, that is, sacred children, for the coming battle. She girded us each with a fine waist-garment, the korowai, made of soft dressed and closely woven white flax . . . These . . . she had made herself. These were the garments of war; she had karakaia'd [prayed] over them and charmed them so that the bullets of the enemy should not touch them, and so that we, their wearers, might conquer in the fight.

So these young boys made ready to face the likes of Kepa Te Rangihiwinui, Richard Blake, and the dreaded Gustavus Von Tempsky.

The colonists struggled through the trackless forest. 'We got into a very rough country, intersected with gullies and streams, and a perfect network of supple-jacks.' It was 'a most tedious march'. The force must have entered the forest about 7 am, and at 2 pm they were still marching, or rather struggling forward in a long straggling line, two abreast. The decision to avoid the major tracks, itself a gamble on the men's fitness and bushcraft, had paid off in that Titokowaru's scouts had lost them after their departure from Camp Waihi. But eventually it became apparent that they had also lost themselves. Again, the problem was the mistaken assumption that Ruaruru was one mile north-west of Te Ngutu, not two and a quarter as was in fact the case. In the dense bush, with visibility normally restricted to a few yards, even so small an error meant that the colonists saw no sign at all of Ruaruru, and they silently cursed Horopapera and the absent Takiora. But Horopapera kept his sense of direction, and succeeded in guiding the force to the supposed location of Ruaruru, a remarkable feat of bush navigation. The colonists were still cursing when they heard voices.

Ngaruahine knew the colonists were coming, but they expected them by the Pungarehu Track, or at least by some track. In accordance

with the custom which isolated the ill, two sick children had remained
in a small clearing between Ruaruru and Te Ngutu, a little over
half a mile from the latter. One was a young girl, the other was
the crippled nine-year-old son of Katene. They were tended in a
makeshift hospital of a few bark huts and a tent by a woman and
a man, probably the chief Paramena of Mawhitiwhiti. As luck would
have it, this clearing was close to where Takiora supposed Ruaruru
to be, and it was voices from there that the colonists heard.

On hearing the sound, McDonnell had Horopapera climb a tree
to pinpoint the direction. Frozen in silence, the force waited.
Horopapera 'could only see smoke' but this was enough. They had
found Te Ngutu. Kepa suggested that the attack be delayed till night,
but McDonnell felt this would increase the chances of detection and
give the advantage to an enemy more familiar with the ground. He
decided to attack immediately and whispered his orders. The kupapa,
who had been leading the march, would now move to the rear, except
for Horopapera, Kepa, and a few scouts. With these scouts and 140
Europeans (Nos. 2 and 5 constabulary, and the Wellington, Patea
and Taranaki Rifles), Von Tempsky would again lead the advance,
with McDonnell, Hunter, and 100 Europeans (No. 3, Wellington
Rangers, and O'Halloran's dismounted cavalry) in the centre.

The kupapa scouts soon came upon the hospital clearing, with the
woman standing unsuspecting outside the huts. 'For a moment she
stood petrified by our sudden appearance, then ran screaming down
the track pursued by the Maories.' She was never heard of again,
and Ngaruahine believed she was caught and killed. As Von Tempsky's
men passed the tent, Paramena sprang out. It seems he fired, one
against hundreds, for the colonists, though anxious to avoid warning
Te Ngutu, had to shoot him down. The troops found the sick children.
'The little girl was very ill' and they left her. Katene's son 'would
not keep quiet' and a kupapa seized the crippled boy and 'dashed
out his brains'. Von Tempsky did not do the deed, but he did not
stop it either. Another boy, Omahura, son of Te Karere, about ten
years old, had wandered away from Te Ngutu – tight Maori battle
discipline never applied to children. He too was found and brought
to the hospital clearing. There, remembered Omahura, 'I saw two
other children who were known to me. One was a cripple, and was
killed, but there was no suggestion that I and the other child should
be killed also.' Omahura was eventually taken back to Camp Waihi
where 'he gave a good deal of information'. He was later adopted
by William Fox, trained as a lawyer, and became a respected mediator

William Fox Omahura
Alexander Turnbull Library

between the two peoples. So his story ends more happily than that of Katene's son, though William Fox Omahura did not look very happy in his new life.

Katene's son had been killed for nothing. Ngaruahine, on the alert at Te Ngutu, heard the shots which marked brave Paremena's death. Titokowaru's first reaction was to call Kimble Bent to him. Though outwardly the picture of confidence, the chief gave Bent a small flax kit (kete) and quietly said: 'Friend, take this *kété* of mine in your charge. It contains some of my tapu treasures; take great care of it, for I may not see you again; I may fall with my tribe. Take it and leave the pa, and join Te Waka.' The renegade obeyed. At Ruaruru he, Te Waka, and the others anxiously awaited the day's result, knowing that, at last, Titokowaru and McDonnell were locked in decisive battle at Te Ngutu o te Manu.

As Kimble Bent slipped away, McDonnell pressed on past the hospital clearing, with Von Tempsky leading the way. The force advanced to the gully of the shallow Mangotahi Stream. Before them, 200 yards away, they could see the new stockade of Te Ngutu at the southern end of the clearing. Almost immediately, they came under fire – but not from the pa. This was Titokowaru's surprise.

Though the published accounts miss this, subsequent visitors to the Te Ngutu clearing found 'numerous underground passages', some literally tunnels, other camouflaged pathways. These led to dozens of firing positions in the bush around the clearing, all carefully sited, constructed, and concealed, covering every possible approach to the pa. Contrary to legend, these firing positions included few treetops. Stages set high in two rata trees to the north and east of the clearing were used as lookout posts, but these were vulnerable and easily pinpointed, and were probably abandoned as the colonists approached. Another tree, a pukatea, had 'a square hole cut out three feet from the ground where the native got in, being covered up afterwards so that no opening could be seen: he then ascended inside until some twenty feet from the ground, firing through loopholes.' There was also at least one decayed rata hollowed out and loopholed at the base, not the top. But most of the secret firing positions were probably rifle pits. Forgotten Pakeha eyewitnesses spoke of 'the ground honeycombed with rifle pits', 'protected rifle pits and ambuscades planted in every part of the bush'. One needs to think of the camouflaged bunkers of more recent jungle warfare, with foliage laid over a covered entrenchment, its occupants firing from ground level. But, tree or pit, these positions provided secure cover and good lines of fire for Ngaruahine and a terrible shock for their enemy. The green, innocent forest around Te Ngutu clearing was a carefully designed death trap.

As McDonnell approached, Titokowaru sent most of his men out of his pa in small parties under Katene, Toi, and Haowhenua to occupy these positions. They probably moved up the west edge and around to the north of the clearing in a wide outflanking move, a surreptitious left hook, with Toi and Haowhenua's parties in the lead. They quietly moved from position to position to improve their lines of fire, and soon men began to fall. Constable Joseph Hogan of No. 3 constabularly had his thigh smashed by a bullet, lucky to be the first to fall. He was a large man, 'fully fourteen stone in weight', but Michael Piercy and three other devoted comrades carried him all the way back to Camp Waihi. This was to be a battle in which wise men booked their stretchers early.

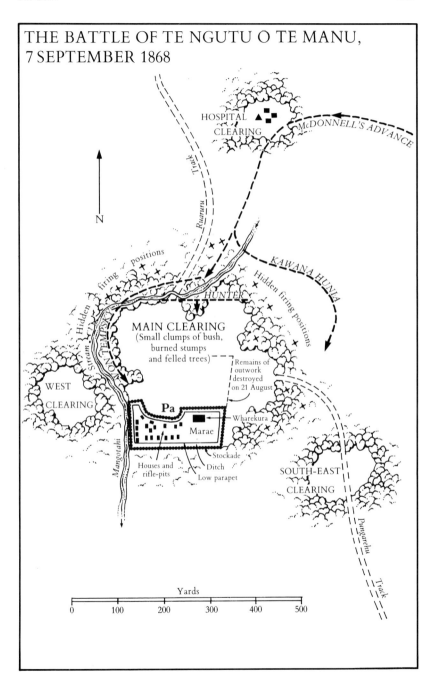

THE BATTLE OF TE NGUTU O TE MANU, 7 SEPTEMBER 1868

HOSPITAL CLEARING

McDONNELL'S ADVANCE

Track

Ruaruru

N

positions

firing

Hidden

KAWANA HUNIA

Hidden firing positions

HUNTER

Stream

NON-TEMPSKY

MAIN CLEARING
(Small clumps of bush,
burned stumps
and felled trees)

Remains of
outwork
destroyed
on 21 August

WEST
CLEARING

Pa

Wharekura

Marae

Mangotahi

Houses and
rifle-pits

Stockade
Ditch
Low parapet

SOUTH-EAST
CLEARING

Pungarehu Track

Yards

0   100   200   300   400   500

The Maori fire increased in volume and accuracy, coming from
the colonist right and rear as well as the pa itself. Soon Hogan was
joined by other casualties, but the troops had yet to see a Maori.
'In a very few minutes,' wrote McDonnell, 'we were fired upon
from front, right and rear, but except within the palisading to our
front we could see no enemy.' McDonnell, Von Tempsky, and Hunter
held a hasty council of war, 'talking in an animated manner'. The
enemy firing positions could not be pinpointed, and the pa seemed
the obvious target. Von Tempsky and Hunter were keen to attack,
and indeed the pa's own defences were not especially strong.
McDonnell initially agreed. The kupapa would move east and south
through the bush in their own wide outflanking move. Von Tempsky
would move up the western fringe of the clearing along the Mangotahi
to an outcrop of bush close to the pa and assault from there. Hunter
would assault frontally across the clearing. The colonist leaders then
went their separate ways.

Standing in a rifle pit inside Te Ngutu, Titokowaru watched the
enemy begin to deploy for an assault. In his hoarse, powerful voice,
he shouted orders to the warriors outside: 'Whakawhiria!' 'Encircle
them!', repeated again and again. The colonial troops could actually
hear him 'yelling "Surround them, surround them!" in Maori'. Toi
and Haowhenua worked around the north-east of the clearing and
engaged the bulk of the kupapa under Kawana Hunia, a cautious
fight between skilled bushmen. Both sides exchanged heavy fire but
kept closely to cover. Ngaruahine probably lost the Araukuku chief
Kaake at this stage, but no one else. The story that the kupapa had
no casualties at all was probably false, but their losses too were light.
With about seventy men – Kepa and the rest were with McDonnell
– Hunia had greatly superior numbers, but Toi and Haowhenua had
the advantage of prepared positions and pathways. Hunia held his
own, but the price of low casualties was being pinned down. He
was in no position to assault anyone.

Von Tempsky's force picked their way along the opposite edge
of the clearing. Harry Hunter and some Wellington Rangers got
to within thirty yards of the pa. Hunter, with Hastings, 'the life
of the camp at Waihi', told his men 'that the ball was about to
commence and he would advise them to choose their partners'. His
men were cut off from the pa by a bush outcrop, but there was
a ten-yard gap in it and Hunter was one of the few who could actually
see the enemy. He ordered his men to fire massed volleys into the
pa: 'Give it to them boys, give it to them! I can see the whites

of his eyes!'. 'I was passing the opening in the scrub,' wrote Sergeant-Major David Scannell,

and saw Lieutenant Hunter walking up and down quite unconcernedly. He called me to him, and on my going he showed me the natives in the pa, quite visible through the opening, shouting and yelling in the most frantic manner. I remonstrated with him on the unnecessary manner in which he was exposing himself; but he merely laughed and said it was capital fun to watch them.

Major William Hunter's force had the most difficult task of all, assembling in sparse cover preparatory to an attack across the clearing. His officers, William Newland and young Forster Goring, gathered the men together. But this exposed them to Katene's marksmen and the Maori fire redoubled. 'The firing was something awful just then,' remembered Newland, 'men were being knocked over like ninepins.' To McDonnell, who was with Hunter's division, it was clear that this was a cleft stick. If his men stayed under cover, they were picked off slowly; if they assembled in the open to assault the pa, they were picked off fast. And assaulting the pa seemed the only possible decisive action. The firing positions outside it were wrongly believed to be in treetops. 'Volley after volley was poured into these trees, but so well were the natives protected that their fire was never for a moment checked. Men now began to drop fast.' The Ngaruahine warriors, adept at quick loading and with some carrying two guns, kept up a remarkable fusillade: 'dreadful', 'deadly', 'withering'. 'The firing from the rebels was fearful, coming from almost every point', and aimed 'with a precision the proportion of killed and wounded speaks for all too surely'. The Taranaki volunteers fell foul of a particularly well-sited firing position and quickly lost nine men out of twenty-six. Hunter's own No. 3 division had four killed and several wounded as it broke cover and began to deploy for the assault, and it was clear that losses elsewhere were also heavy. McDonnell saw that the game was up. He ordered Hunter to give up his assault and began preparations to retreat.

McDonnell decided 'to push to my left, the only point that appeared open', and so 'into the main broad track' leading from the clearing – the Pungarehu Track. The problem would be extricating the wounded. There were only a dozen stretchers, each of which required four bearers. Any further wounded would have to be taken out on rifles, three rifles and six men to a casualty. McDonnell ordered Captain Brown of No. 5 division to gather up what wounded he could from Von Tempsky's command. Newland was to do likewise

An artist's inaccurate impression of the Battle of Te Ngutu o te Manu   *From the Illustrated New Zealand Herald, 1 December 1868, Alexander Turnbull Library*

for Hunter's while Hunter himself formed a vanguard to protect them. The stretcher parties were to move around the clearing to the Pungarehu Track as soon as they collected their bloody loads. 'It took a long time to get away,' wrote Newland, 'in consequence of having so many to pick up.' McDonnell asked Kepa 'to collect as many of his men as he could and send them to join Captain Newland'. The colonel then went to see Von Tempsky and 'desired' him to await the departure of the main body, then gather his men and follow, forming the rearguard. He told Buck to support Von Tempsky with the Wellington Rifles: 'Of this order I myself informed Major Von Tempsky and Captain Buck.'

An artist's more accurate impression   *From a painting by J. McDonald, Taranaki Museum*

Von Tempsky was angry. His force had advanced inside Titokowaru's left hook. Though closest to Te Ngutu, it had so far suffered least. He was not aware of the heavy casualties behind him, or of the fact that Ngaruahine had almost completed a straggling circle around the outside of the colonist positions, numerically thin but hard to break because well concealed. McDonnell had no time to explain himself. Von Tempsky believed that he could still take the pa by assault and that McDonnell was yielding too soon. He must have regretted the accidents that had cost him his seniority over McDonnell. Captain John Roberts remembered him at the time as being 'curiously listless. He was cutting away with his sword at a hanging bush vine . . . cutting shavings from it'. Von Tempsky told another subordinate, James Shanaghan, to take cover, but did not do so himself, pacing up and down beside the Mangotahi. He told Shanaghan: 'I am disgusted. If I get out of this scrape I will wash my hands clean of the business.' It was strange that he should confide his last thoughts to a nineteen-year-old private.

Titokowaru must have realised that the colonist right – Von Tempsky's command – had escaped his outflanking move and found shelter from the prepared firing positions. The warriors in the pa could no doubt glimpse Harry Hunter through the gap in the bush outcrop, just as he could them. Titokowaru therefore sent out another party, of ten men, perhaps led by the Mawhitiwhiti tohunga, Wairau, and also including Tihirua, young Tutange, the noted warrior Te Rangihinakau, and his eighteen-year-old son, Whakawhiria, subsequently so named for his part in carrying out Titokowaru's battle plan. Wairau and his men crept up the west bank of the Mangotahi, opposite Von Tempsky's men, who were also under cover. They killed one strayed colonist, the first body to fall into Ngaruahine hands, and performed the Whangai Hau on him, with Tihirua again using his Vesta matches:

> *Wairau held up the bleeding heart, and Tihirua applied fire to it . . . Wairau watched [the smoke] intently to see the direction of its drift . . . The smoke rose and drifted out through the trees in the direction of the pakeha force . . . Wairau knew then that the white soldiers would be the vanquished ones that day.*

He then led his men into an unprepared but naturally concealed position at the foot of a karaka tree. Tutange remembered that an officer with a curved sword 'came out into clear view of us, within a very short distance of where we were crouching – I should say less than half a chain. I fired with the others. One of our bullets struck him – I have always believed it was mine.' Whakawhiria and other Maori disagreed. According to them it was the veteran Te Rangihinakau who, 'taking careful aim', shot Von Tempsky through the centre of the forehead, killing him instantly.

The Pakeha had their own 'superstitions' and the body of such a leader was a symbol some men were prepared to die for. Young Shanaghan and a Frenchman named P.F. Jancey 'went to the major and lifted him up and laid him on his back'. Then Wairau and his party fired, wounding Jancey badly in the side and hitting a cartridge box on his back as well. Shanaghan dragged Jancey to cover and, unable to carry Von Tempsky by himself, ran to get fresh help. He soon found Harry Hunter, who had at last withdrawn from his advanced position at the bush outcrop, and together they broke cover and ran across the clearing towards Von Tempsky: 'When we were about ten paces from Von Tempsky's body,' wrote Shanaghan, 'Hunter was shot dead', the bullet knocking him flat on his back. John Roberts saw him later 'lying on the broad of his back, dead, staring at the tree-tops'. It was no longer 'capital fun'. Shanaghan remained almost hysterically determined to save his commander's corpse, but he was running out of assistants. He wandered back through the western fringe of the clearing from clump to clump of crouching men, saying, 'Come along for Major Von Tempsky's body.'

Shanaghan approached several men but, understandably enough, his appeal was refused. Then he reached the north-western corner of the clearing and found George Buck. 'Captain Buck was the only one who responded, saying, "I will go with you, young fellow. Do you know the spot where the Major fell?" ' Just as they reached it, Wairau's party began firing in sections of three – textbook 'platoon fire'. One bullet from their first volley hit Shanaghan's left thumb, 'which was shot nearly off'. He had changed his carbine to his right hand when a bullet from a second volley pierced that and knocked him down. Buck asked where he was hit, and Shanaghan held up his bloody hands as the third section fired, knocking off Shanaghan's cap and killing Buck outright. There he lay, with Hunter and Von Tempsky, while Shanaghan managed to stagger off. Both the officers aware of McDonnell's order to retreat were now dead.

McDonnell had not yet begun his retreat. We know this because it was his party which carried James Shanaghan off the field. But Shanaghan, badly injured and perhaps unconscious, did not tell the colonel of Von Tempsky's fate. The colonial forces were now in some confusion. The enemy fire could not have been quite the storm of lead many remembered – sixty men could only do so much – but it was constant and well directed. The troops lay flat on their bellies in the undergrowth along the Mangotahi Stream, blazing away into the bush. The officers had to shout above the din or go from group to group to give their orders. 'There were a few men with me,' recalled one, 'an officer cannot see more than ten or fifteen when he is skirmishing under such conditions.' Moreover, four units had lost their commanders, and McDonnell had contact with only parts of Von Tempsky's command, which he incorporated into his own force. The battle had collapsed into a shifting mosaic of isolated human pockets, increasingly out of touch with one another. McDonnell, having gathered up what wounded he could find, moved off south-eastwards towards the Pungarehu Track, assuming Von Tempsky would cover his rear. But he sent his brother William to find him and make sure. The time was perhaps 2.30 pm.

As the colonist retreat began, Titokowaru called in his scattered warriors and took stock. Paramena and Kaake were dead. At least one of Wairau's party, Motu or Hotu, was wounded, and there may have been a few more. But Pakeha corpses dotted the clearing. The main colonist force was now withdrawing towards the Pungarehu

Track, with the kupapa moving parallel inland of them. The rump of Von Tempsky's command had withdrawn to the bush off the north-west corner of the clearing, and Ngaruahine had possession of his body. Young Tutange Waionui gave the corpse a cut on the temple with his tomawhawk to make sure of it. 'You *pakehas* will not regard my action . . . as . . . a murder?' he inquired, when telling the story around 1910. 'I was but a very young man then, just a boy, and it was my first battle.' Te Ngutu rang with cries of 'Ka horo', 'They are beaten', but Ngaruahine's work was far from done. The warriors performed a brief haka, to the chant 'See the government soldiers flee away/And turn and fearfully gaze at me', and flung themselves into a vigorous pursuit. Again Titokowaru restrained his men, instructing that the pursuit be tightly controlled – harassment from cover without unnecessary risk. Katene led the pursuit and he accepted and implemented these orders. But still he intended to take full revenge for his son.

McDonnell's force was the first to feel the impact. As the heavy Maori fire continued, despite their disengagement, some of his men began to panic. They had marched and fought well the whole day, but now it seemed as though the battle would never end. 'Great difficulty was experienced in getting men to carry the stretchers the new men especially thinking they had enough to look after themselves.' As the retreat left Te Ngutu clearing, Captain Alfred Palmer of the Patea Volunteer Rifles was mortally wounded in the lungs. He was left where he lay. Now some men began to run. McDonnell sent George O'Halloran and his dozen dismounted troopers ahead to secure the line of retreat. O'Halloran saw one man 'who had neither a cap on his head nor any arms in his hands but was striding along at a great rate'. O'Halloran called out to him from behind a tree. 'He jumped as if he had been shot.' O'Halloran, a man capable of cracking jokes at his father's funeral, found this 'a very amusing incident', but his runaway was not the only one. Others began to seep past the wounded and McDonnell's vanguard. McDonnell later claimed that some 'did not stop till they got to Rangitikei and Manawatu', and the tale grew in the telling until the whole defeat was blamed on these few fugitives. In fact only about forty men actually 'fled'. Most were Wellington Rifles, the least experienced unit. They did not run until the battle was well and truly lost, and most joined Kawana Hunia and made their retreat in fairly organised fashion. Indeed, Hunia, who of all the government commanders received least credit, made by far the best withdrawal.

Kawana Hunia
Taranaki Museum

Moving inland to evade pursuit and sending out a screen of skirmishes to discourage it, he kept his bearings and brought both his Maori and his Europeans in safe to Camp Waihi at 8 pm, leaving a few men to hold the Waingongoro ford for McDonnell.

As his brother's retreat began, William McDonnell made his way through the bush at the north-west of the clearing, trying to find Von Tempsky. Small groups of increasingly demoralised men lay scattered about under cover. McDonnell was told that Von Tempsky had been killed. At last, he came upon a live officer, Harry Hastings, and told him 'that the only chance was to carry out the orders given to Major Von Tempsky at once'. Hastings, probably feeling that immediate retreat would leave several isolated groups in the lurch, replied, 'Captain Buck is senior and he would consult him.' McDonnell pressed him, but Hastings refused. McDonnell gave up, and set off to join his brother, collecting ten officerless Europeans and eight kupapa as he went.

Meanwhile John Roberts and a few men, another isolated fragment of Von Tempsky's command, waited for orders in the bush not far from Hastings. For Roberts, the battle had so far been relatively quiet. Positioned well behind Harry Hunter and Von Tempsky, he could see the pa way across the clearing, but he had yet to see a Maori. 'I had fired a few shots at the palisade, more for the sake of making a noise than anything else, for I could not see a single Maori,' he later reported. Now he heard firing moving away to his left and he began to suspect that Colonel McDonnell was 'fighting his way out'. Roberts had a bugler with him, and he ordered him to sound the Officers' Call. Ensign Charles Hirtzell, the Manawapou publican, James Livingston, a mere volunteer sergeant in theory but an important leader in practice, and Hastings heard the call and made their way to Roberts. They established that Von Tempsky and Buck were dead, and they withdrew a little further into the bush north-west of Te Ngutu before halting to decide what to do. They 'could distinctly hear the firing and shouting of the rebels following up McDonnell's party'. On these four young men, all in their early twenties, rested the responsibility of saving the remaining troops.

Titokowaru now switched most of his warriors to attack on this group, the only enemy left on the original battlefield. Led by the eager Katene, Ngaruahine closed in, still keeping carefully to cover and perhaps using the 'underground passages' again. The four colonist leaders had decided to retreat but, the unfortunate concern for officers' corpses surfacing again, Roberts went to see if he could bring out Buck's body first. When he returned unsuccessful ten minutes later, he found that Katene had struck. Again, the tension between the need to separate for cover and safety and to concentrate for some concerted move had given him his opportunity. Of Hastings' group, three or four men were dead, Corporal William Russell had had his thigh smashed, and Harry Hastings himself was very badly wounded.

The loss of yet another leader, the renewal of heavy fire, and the dawning knowledge that they had been abandoned was very nearly too much for veteran and raw recruit alike. A disgusted James Livingston confided to his diary: 'a panic seized the whole and they fled through the bush leaving dead and three wounded on the field'. A few ran south-east, outpacing William McDonnell's group and joining the main body ahead of him. One or two got separated, lost their sense of direction, and ran due north, where they were later killed by Ngaruahine or wandered in circles until they starved to death. The skeleton of one was found fourteen years later, three miles north of Te Ngutu. But most fled north-east as a body, away from the enemy fire. They were pursued by their own leaders, but not by Katene. For Titokowaru had again switched his attention to the main body, like a sheepdog shepherding two flocks.

McDonnell was making very slow progress. He had to detour around the clearing to avoid exposing his men on open ground, and in doing so he lost the Pungarehu Track. 'Our way had to be cut through supple-jacks and undergrowth which with the eight stretchers we now had was a work of toil and difficulty.' He was still less than a mile from Te Ngutu clearing when a little group of Roberts' and Hastings' fleeing men caught up with him. They told him that Von Tempsky, Buck, Major Hunter's brother Harry and his own brother William had all been killed. Just then, to the colonel's relief, William turned up with his eighteen men, followed closely but stealthily by Katene and the pursuing Ngaruahine. Thomas McDonnell later claimed that his brother's report reassured him about Von Tempsky's division. 'Knowing that a large proportion of the force was in the rear with several good officers, I moved on, feeling sure they were covering our retreat.' In fact William confirmed the deaths of Von Tempsky and Buck, the only really experienced officers, and Thomas stated elsewhere that he tried to go back, 'but the enemy still attacked our rear'. The reality was that Titokowaru had split the colonist force. Colonel McDonnell now had to be his own rearguard.

This crisis brought out the best in him. As the pressure from Katene's marksmen grew and the route became still more difficult, the stretcher parties began to lag behind. They again began to wonder aloud if they could save the wounded as well as themselves. One stretcher would have been abandoned if McDonnell, at the rear of the straggling column, had not taken a turn carrying it himself. To some men, especially the grateful wounded, he seemed to be everywhere at once: 'Colonel McDonnell's must be a charmed life, his clothes are shot through in several places.' 'How he escaped death twenty times is more than his adjutant could tell.'

Hunter's rearguard at last came upon the Oura Stream, which ran through the Te Maru clearing and would lead them back to the Pungarehu Track. Hearing of this, and fearing that the enemy might get in front and head them off at the gully near Te Maru, McDonnell sent his brother William ahead with a dozen kupapa to hold the clearing. This idea had indeed occurred to Katene, and he too had sent off a party to Te Maru. Its two leading scouts, one of them probably a popular young chief named Reweti, arrived first and concealed themselves to await their comrades. The kupapa gave Walter Gudgeon their account of what transpired:

Captain McDonnell and his men arrived at Te Maru breathless; fortunately they had a dog with them who ran on in front, and they had just reached the bush, [when] a voice asked in Maori, 'Who are you?' They could see the dog was a Maori. Our Maories answered, 'It is us, come on'. Out stepped two athletic young Maories from under the trees, and were immediately shot down; they were the Hauhau advanced guard who had nearly been too quick for us.

Reweti was killed; the other managed to escape, presumably wounded. This incident was the nearest thing to a success the colonial forces had the whole day. Reweti was the third and last Ngaruahine warrior to die in the battle.

Foiled at Te Maru, Katene pressed McDonnell's rearguard even harder. He actually succeeded in cutting it off twice, but each time McDonnell managed to restore his link with Hunter, although not without cost. One man was shot dead and Dr William Best was severely wounded in going to ascertain his state. Other men fell, and soon McDonnell was burdened with thirteen or fourteen wounded, 'besides several slightly hit, but could walk'. Ironically, Dr Best had the worst time of it. There were no stretchers left and he was carried on rifles, an agonising mode of transport for a badly injured man. With at least fifty-four men needed to carry the wounded, besides van and rearguards, there were now no more spells for the stretcher-bearers, and in the rear exhaustion, panic, and utter rout were only a hair's breadth away. As they passed through another clearing, McDonnell resorted to a gesture as brave and flamboyant as he was himself. David Scannell wrote that

when the fatigued bearers, who could get no relief, and the hard-pressed rearguard were for a moment inclined to waver, [I] again saw the Colonel (he was then on a high stump in the most conspicuous part of the clearing) calmly announcing to his men that, happen what would, he would not stir from that spot until every wounded man had passed on.

The reserve supplies of ammunition had been lost and bullets were now running short. McDonnell and a few of the best marksmen, including Richard Blake, did most of the firing as the weary column passed Pungarehu. Despite their skill, the marksmen caused few if any casualties, but they did keep Katene's men at a distance. Now that they were on the track, progress was a little easier, and as night fell they emerged from the forest at Ahipaipa.

As they thankfully moved out into the open, they 'received a parting volley from the enemy'. Triumphant or not, vengeful or not, Katene had no intention of engaging on open ground. He and his men contented themselves with a victory haka and derisive yells from the edge of the bush. But, wrote McDonnell, a hint of honest relief creeping into the defensive bombast of his report, 'they did not molest us any more'. Using ropes and long sticks, the main body, including the wounded, managed to cross the Waingongoro, with McDonnell, like a sea captain leaving his sinking ship, the last man to cross over. The force dragged itself into Camp Waihi at 10 pm, after nearly twenty-four hours marching and fighting. Even O'Halloran was 'weary and rather depressed', and most men were utterly spent: 'the majority of them, as they arrived entering their tents in silence and lying down'. Kawana Hunia's division, with few if any wounded to carry, had arrived two hours before. But nearly half the expedition's Europeans were still missing.

While most of their men panicked, Roberts and Livingston kept their heads, supported by Pehira Turei, one of four kupapa with them, and a few other men. They dragged Hastings, Russell, and the other wounded to temporary safety, and sought to rally their men. Fortunately for them, Ngaruahine were again concentrating on the main body, and they succeeded, although the men remained very nervous. The party included fifteen wounded – four more than could be carried. Roberts now had to make the terrible choice of who to leave behind. How he did so in most cases we will never know – this is the kind of thing soldiers never talk about. But Harry Hastings made his own choice. When first hit, he asked Hirtzell 'to hide the circumstance from the men, dreading to create further panic'. Now, heroically or duped by a public-school code to which others paid lip service, 'he requested them to leave him, as they would have enough to do without being encumbered by him'. Hastings was 'desperately wounded', and saving him would entail dumping another man, so his comrades obeyed.

Corporal William Russell, his thigh smashed, was another man left behind. 'As there was no means of carrying him off, his fate was sealed; in fact he recognised this himself and asked his comrades to shoot him.' No one would. James Livingston smashed his carbine against a tree so that the Maori would not get it, but he would not do the same for Russell. They put his revolver in his hand, and left him, propped against a tree trunk. Legend has it that when the pursuing warriors came upon him he 'stood them off' with his revolver, hitting one or more before being shot at long range. 'So he died a soldier's death, and was not even tomahawked.'

Livingston and Roberts and their party then pushed on for a couple of miles, probably moving north-east in a wider half-circle than McDonnell. They still had eleven wounded, proportionately an even heavier burden than that of the main body. There was no track, they were more or less lost, and a small Ngaruahine party picked up their trail and followed at a cautious distance, firing when a target offered, keeping up the pressure. 'We went very slowly,' remembered Roberts, 'occasionally turning to fire. I don't think we travelled more than half a mile in the hour. All of us were now very exhausted.' But none was as exhausted as Private G.H. Dore. Dore was an ex-sailor who had joined the Rifles in Wellington in the heady days of July. His photograph suggests he may have suffered from Down's syndrome, victims of which are often short-lived and considered 'below average' in intelligence, but are endearing, stubborn, and tough. Early in the battle, Dore had his left shoulder smashed by a bullet, 'a most fearful wound'. When Roberts' party began its retreat, he was already 'weak from loss of blood and pain'. 'He asked for assistance to get away, but could get none.' Now, with another man who had been shot through the mouth, he struggled desperately to keep up with the retreating column, staggering along clutching his bloody shoulder. He could still persuade no one to help him, though Livingston 'stopped and gave him some brandy'. The man with the head wound fell out exhausted, pleading for help like the other wounded who had 'piteously implored that they might not be left behind'. Deadened with exhaustion, strained faces looking away, his comrades passed on. Soon Dore too fell out and collapsed. But Dore lived to tell his tale.

The pursuing Ngaruahine came up and began to strip him of his gear. 'He feigned death, and after his trousers, boots, revolver, and a haversack had been taken, he heard the natives ordered away to follow the pakeha.' He crawled further into the bush and 'hid himself in the flanges of a Pukatea tree'. He was still quite close to Te Ngutu and he could hear other wounded Pakeha calling for help. Later 'he heard the natives dragging two wounded men along, and heard one of them say, "why don't you kill me at once, you wretches?" ' The other was speaking in broken Maori, presumably pleading for his life. Once night fell, Dore could hear the Maori victory celebrations

Privates Campbell (left) and G. H. Dore, wounded at Te Ngutu *Taranaki Museum*

at Te Ngutu, and he imagined he could hear the terrible screams of the two men as they were 'roasted alive'. He was wrong, but this did not help him at the time. He lay where he was for the best part of forty-eight hours, miraculously not bleeding to death. 'As the dogs were barking he expected to be found at any moment', but he was not, and on 9 September 'he thought he would make an effort to save himself'. For three more days he wandered in the bush, with no food except some watercress 'which griped him, and caused great pain'. He kept going. 'He was delirious at times; and had very little recollection of the latter part of his journey, and none whatever of crossing the Waingongoro river', but somehow he did so. At 7 am on 12 September, he walked in to Camp Waihi 'in a frightful emaciated state', his wound 'alive with Maggots'. He was operated on, and recovered with remarkable speed. 'This,' Gudgeon observed rightly, 'is certainly one of the most wonderful instances of endurance on record.'

Back on 7 September, the Ngaruahine gave up their pursuit of Roberts and Livingston as dusk began to fall, soon after they had left Dore for dead. 'We pushed on about two miles after they lost

More Te Ngutu wounded   *Wanganui Museum*

us,' wrote Livingston, 'then we lay down until the moon should rise by which to steer a course out of the bush. All the time we heard shots fired from the Colonel's party.' The tired men slept, amidst the moaning of the wounded and other noises: 'We were still within cooee of the *pa*; in fact we could hear the Hauhaus' yells and war songs all night, we were that close.' The seemingly hostile bush was in fact neutral, and the men lay undiscovered but not undisturbed. Charles Hirtzell slept 'but was awakened by Livingstone clutching me by the throat and telling me to shut up. I had been dreaming and in my dream had yelled out.'

At 2 am, with the moon high, the force started off again, still without a track and guided only by Pehira Turei's sense of direction.

'We . . . scrambled cross gullies and through swamps as well as we could, but made slow progress as the wounded were very stiff, it having been extremely cold while we were lying.' Turei hoped they were moving south-east, inland of McDonnell's route. As dawn began to break, they came to a hill and, climbing it, saw the Pungarehu Track 'to our joy'. By 7 am they were at the Waingongoro, with no enemy in sight. Livingston laconically recorded the fording of the river 'over which I carried several of the wounded'. By 9 am they were 'home to Waihi, where we were met by the whole camp who had given us all up for lost'. 'There was cheering, and shaking of hands,' continued Livingston in his private diary, 'and crying in turn which was rather a queer sight among strong bearded men.' He and Roberts had brought out sixty-six men including ten wounded, but still there were many missing faces. One memory stuck in Charles Hirtzell's mind: 'Major Hunter, with tears in his eyes, coming out to look for his brother.'

Chapter Eight

THE LITTLE TYRANT

In England, on Friday 30 October 1868, a country gentleman, Edward Palmer, perused his two-day-old copy of *The Times* over breakfast. Amidst the usual news of court and country, and of worsening relations between France and Prussia, his attention was drawn to a report on hostilities in New Zealand. *The Times* had its 'Own Correspondent' in Wellington, and it reported Titokowaru's War more extensively than New Zealand's own history books. It had received prompt news of Te Ngutu via ship, telegraph, and overland mail, and Edward Palmer read with alarm of the death of a 'Captain Palmer' on 7 September. He wrote immediately to the Colonial Office in London. Was this, he asked, his brother, Alfred Palmer? It was, but typically the Colonial Office did not know it yet, and Edward had to wait weeks to have the bad news confirmed. In Ireland, Mr N.C.G. Hunter had the same painful experience. By the time he learned for certain that one brother, young Harry Hunter, had fallen, he had lost another. So the news of Titokowaru's victory rippled across 12,000 miles, diminishing with distance but still spoiling breakfasts as far away as Dublin.

The previous month, the news had hit harder still in New Zealand itself, and the bereaved had been no more fortunate in the receiving of it. 'From end to end of the colony the calamitous reverse of the Ngutu created a painful feeling.' It was 'the most disastrous affair that ever took place in New Zealand'. In Auckland, Amelia Von Tempsky had dire rumours of her husband's death confirmed by the arrival of his last letter, with 'killed in action' scrawled tactlessly across the envelope. Word of the battle steamed into Wellington with the *Sturt* on 9 September, and only the prophets of doom, proved right, could take any satisfaction from it. That day, the distinguished politician, James Fitzgerald, wrote: 'I look upon matters with extreme gloom and only this morning was in the very act of saying that I was daily anticipating some great disaster, when a friend walked in and said it had *come*. This catastrophe on the west coast is only the first.' The editor of the *Wellington Independent* announced 'the most serious and complete defeat ever experienced by the colonial forces'. Enraged by the death of his friend and colleague, Harry Hastings, he demanded vengeance. Titokowaru and his people 'must be shown no mercy. They should be treated as wild beasts – hunted down and slain . . . [they] are the curse of the colony *and we should exterminate them.*'

But Stafford and his beleaguered ministry knew revenge would have to wait. Their resources were already stretched, few reinforcements were available, and it was soon to become clear that the Patea Field Force had been damaged very badly indeed. No government likes 'catastrophe' when Parliament is in session, and the ministry had to weather a barrage of invective from Fox, Featherston, and a rising Jewish politician from Otago, Julius Vogel. It was Vogel who, on 15 September, managed so to incense Stafford that he stormed from the House. His supporters were reduced to pathetic quips in his defence: Why is Fox's face 'as long as Jew's harp'? Because 'he *has been* properly played up by Vogel.' The one immediate measure Haultain could take to reinforce McDonnell made the political situation still worse. Major James Fraser's No. 1 Constabulary, stationed at Napier, was promptly ordered to Patea. Led by Donald McLean, the Hawke's Bay settlers protested vehemently that they had been abandoned to Te Kooti. McLean, hitherto a lukewarm supporter of Stafford in Parliament, changed sides and took a couple of allies with him. Harry Atkinson, who disliked Fox but considered Haultain 'an evil so enormous' that even Fox was preferable, did likewise. The ministry survived a motion of no confidence only by the Speaker's vote. Right across the colony, the wolves bayed for scapegoats.

Nominations for this unwelcome distinction had already been made at Camp Waihi on 8 September, the day after the battle. The troops rested after their exertions in the bush. They rose from their exhausted sleep in dribs and drabs, and sat about the camp talking over their humiliating and bewildering defeat. Lucy Takiora, mourning Von Tempsky, was one of the first to blame 'McDonnell's mistake for taking the men away . . . if Von had had more men on his side he would have given them pepper'. 'The whole of the men are very incensed against Colonel McDonnell,' wrote a sergeant in one of the Wellington units, 'and they say they will never go out with him again.' McDonnell himself was trying to write the most difficult report of his life. Compared to his subsequent allegations against both his superiors and subordinates, it was relatively generous, but the seeds of an attempt to shift the blame were there. During the battle, he wrote, his raw troops could not be prevented from 'huddling together in small lots, affording a good target to the enemy'. This was true of a few units late in the battle, especially the Wellington Rifles, and McDonnell made no secret of it. As the day wore on the Rifles' invective against their commander became increasingly bitter and mutinous. Some even proposed to 'hang or drown Colonel McDonnell'. McDonnell struggled with draft after draft of his report, finally completing it next day. On 10 September, amidst the ashes of his treasured popularity, he left for Wanganui to visit his sick wife.

Across the Waingongoro, at Te Ngutu, the aftermath of battle was very different. Non-combatants from Ruaruru and tired pursuit parties trickled back, and 8 September built gradually into a celebration of victory. One by one the enemy corpses were brought in, stripped of clothing and equipment, and laid out on the marae. As the number grew, and Von Tempsky and other officers were identified, the significance of the victory was brought home. Speaker after speaker recounted the deeds that had created it, and all joined periodically in the appropriate chants and haka.

The spoils, including fifty modern carbines and much ammunition, were piled in front of Titokowaru, who then allocated something to each warrior. A warrior named Rameka got Constable F. Darlington's pocket watch and a gold chain belonging to Harry Hastings – items that were later to get him into trouble. To his great delight, young Tutange Waionui received Von Tempsky's revolver. Titokowaru himself had Von Tempsky's sword taken away and hidden. The corpses themselves were ceremonially allocated to the various hapu but, despite the wishes of the grieving relatives of Ngati Ruanui's own dead, ritual mutilation was not allowed, although Titokowaru did permit one corpse to be cooked, and a few partook of it. They included Katene Tuwhakaruru, taking the ultimate revenge for his dead son by reducing his killers to food. About noon, once this rite had been performed, Titokowaru rose and said: 'Oh friends, men and women – I salute you! Bury the sacred bodies of the slain lying before us here . . . It is not well that they should be left to offend. They must be consumed in fire!'

A large pyre was built – not on the sacred marae itself but in the south-west clearing. Von Tempsky's body was laid on first and the others were piled on top of it. Gustavus Von Tempsky, Manu Rau, feared by Maori across the whole North Island, had at last met his match. His death was a triumph in itself. A pioneer of a form of warfare of which man and woman, young and old, were alike the victims, his achievements were not the sort to elicit a chivalrous epitaph from his enemies. Yet, as Kimble Bent remembered it, Titokowaru gave him one:

In the days of the past you fought here and you fought there, and you boasted that you would always emerge safely from your battles to the bright world of life. But when you encountered me your eyes were closed in their last sleep. It could not be helped; you sought your death at my hands. And now you sleep for ever.

Titokowaru had no intention of resting on his laurels. After two days' recuperation, he decided to cross the Waingongoro and set up a new base in the Pakeha zone. On 11 September he sent a strong party to scout his route, harassing Camp Waihi along the way with haka and long-range volleys. Next day his emissaries visited the neutral Tangahoe at Matangarara and put the question that was in many minds. Would his fellow-tribesmen join him now? Natanahira and Maata said no; they were not compelled, and departed peacefully, but only a dozen of their people went with them. The sections of Tangahoe living elsewhere, at Oeo and Keteonata under Pihama and Ahitana, also remained neutral. But most of the Matangarara people, the main section of Tangahoe, led by Tukino and Tito Hanataua, now joined Titokowaru.

On 13 September, with all his people, Titokowaru himself crossed the Waingongoro and encamped at Taiporohenui, once headquarters of the whole Ngati Ruanui tribe – a politically significant choice. It was also just one mile from the colonist garrison at Turuturu Mokai, and in full sight and sound of it. For months the Patea Field Force had hunted Titokowaru's band, seeking urgently to force him to give battle. Now, at Taiporohenui, in fairly open country, he offered battle every hour of every day, but the Pakeha no longer wanted it.

Demoralisation among the colonial forces was growing. The Ngaruahine harassment on the night of 11 September succeeded in rousing the whole camp in heavy rain: 'We had a very miserable night of it,' wrote Livingston. Next day, Dore was found, and his story of the torture of prisoners did nothing to cheer the men up. That night, there were two further alarms. In this context of fear and loss of confidence, many men sought the traditional solace in drink. The Patea Field Force had never been notable for its sobriety and in the week after Te Ngutu it surpassed itself. At Camp Waihi the troops had just received their month's pay – 'everyone is in a great state of funds just now' – and the three canteens did a roaring trade. Run by private contractors, these canteens were supposed to supply a range of goods, but one had 'only two pairs of boots in stock, but plenty of liquor'. The orderly who took McDonnell's report of 9 September to Wanganui celebrated his safe arrival in style. When Gorton sent for him to take return despatches he was found in gaol 'in a beastly state of drunkenness'. Another drunken despatch rider fell off his horse six miles from Wanganui and was put to bed by a kindly farmer. 'Patea appears to have been abandoned to Bacchus', reported the *Wanganui Evening Herald*. 'Rum ad libitum, and as much license as the most thirsty could desire.'

Mistaking the results of disaster for its cause, and taking the broad hint in McDonnell's despatch, the colonial press began to blame the defeat at Te Ngutu on the drunkenness and ill-discipline of the troops, 'a rabble of drunken mutineers'. 'There is little doubt that our gallant friends fell through the cowardice of a class of men who were not even decent "loafers".' Parliament itself followed suit with a heated debate on drunkenness at the front, in which the piquantly named Mr Barff participated. Stafford defended the troops, drily noting that 'charges of occasional and even habitual drunkenness might be brought much nearer home'. But the men soon learned that they had been described as cowards, drunks, and 'the offscourings of the streets' in both press and Parliament, and this lowered their morale further. The public and, still worse, publicans were advised to shun them, and one deserter, Private William Anderson of the Wellington Rifles, committed suicide.

Initially, open disaffection had been limited to the government volunteer units; now it began to spread. Men who had served long with McDonnell (Nos. 2 and 3 constabulary and the Patea volunteers, largely recruited from his old military settler units) remained loyal, but Von Tempsky's No. 5 became increasingly resentful. They disliked Major William Hunter's rigid discipline, contrasting it with Von Tempsky's 'kind and gentlemanly' treatment of them; they believed a wounded comrade had 'died through neglect', and they 'were imbued with a very lamentable spirit of hostility to Lieutenant-Colonel McDonnell, most unjustifiably connecting him in some way with the death of the late Major Von Tempsky'. On 13 September, they mutinied.

As Major Hunter was inspecting the normal morning parade, he found a man smoking his pipe and told him to put it out. A neighbouring man, Constable John Keenan, interjected: 'Oh we might as well all be smoking as standing here', and Hunter retorted, 'What the devil is it what you think.' Keenan replied that '. . . if the Major [Von Tempsky] had been alive this would not be the case, and he would not be trampled on'. Hunter ordered two files of men to confine him to the guardroom. Keenan 'threw down his carbine violently on the ground and said but for a wish not to give them [his comrades] trouble six files would not put him in confinement'.

Keenan was imprisoned and Hunter dismissed the troops, but they paraded again later in the day, at their own request, and demanded Keenan's release. Hunter refused, and delivered a homily on discipline. Constable George Maunder, an intelligent but poorly educated (he spelled his name 'Gorge') veteran of the Waikato militia, yelled, 'We won't serve any longer. Let us take our swags and go to Patea.' Hunter claimed he also said, 'Boys, let's rush the guardroom' – to free Keenan. Realising matters were in a 'ticklish state', Hunter ordered the men to lay down their arms, but Maunder countermanded him: 'No, we shall need our arms to go to Patea.' The parade broke up without orders, and most of the men jeered Hunter. Now there was certainly talk of freeing Keenan by force, and Hunter was determined to resist: 'I was glad to find I could depend on No. 2 + 3 Divisions even if I had to fire upon the men in case the guard room was rushed.' New Zealand's first battle between Europeans was a hair's breadth away.

But Hunter was wise enough to allow No. 5 division's own leaders time to reassert some authority. Captains John Roberts and Michie Brown, popular young officers, moved among their men seeking to cool tempers. But it was the sergeants, William Fenton, John Toovey and, especially, Edward McMinn, who really had the men's confidence, and it was mainly their efforts which defused the crisis. Twenty men set off for Patea, but McMinn, an able Irish veteran of the Forest Rangers, told them 'not to make fools of themselves', and managed to persuade them to return. He was helped by an error so strange it may have been deliberate. Dr Samuel Walker rode into the middle of this tense situation with 'the sad news that Colonel McDonnell's wife is dead'. The report later proved false, but at the time the troops were less inclined to revile a man who had just lost his spouse. Hunter ordered yet another parade and succeeded in arresting Maunder and two other 'ringleaders'. Four men deserted the next night, but order was restored – for the moment.

A few days later, when Defence Minister Haultain visited the front, he found the situation dire indeed. Titokowaru's force was increasing while the colony's appeared to be crumbling. The Wellington Rangers' term of service had expired and, despite efforts to dissuade them, they had gone home to a man. No. 5 constabulary and the Wellington Rifles were mutinous, and the terminally ill Hori Kingi had ordered the kupapa chiefs to his deathbed. 'Fox would have had a nice job on his hands if we had resigned a fortnight ago,' wrote Haultain to Stafford. The Patea settlers were far from grateful for Haultain's presence among them, claiming that 'he exulted over the depopulation of the district' and that his strategy consisted of writing to Titokowaru 'to solicit his forbearance'. To cap it all, McDonnell was in a sorry state. Growing public abuse of his troops did not save him from the same treatment. He was accused of 'madness', 'bull-headed rashness' and 'want of proper courage' by turns, often by the same newspapers which had eulogised him before Te Ngutu. Combined with contempt from his own men, this cut him to the quick. Furthermore, although Walker's report had been false, it was true that Rose McDonnell was extremely sick – she died the following year. Harried and depressed, McDonnell virtually abdicated the command for days at a time. At the end of the month he wrote to Haultain: 'I am sorry I have not been able to send a report – but the combination of troubles domestic and public that have lately fallen upon me has been nigh sending me distracted and I am far from strong.'

Under the weight of these circumstances, Haultain too came close to despair. He would 'ignore popular clamour and vituperation', he told Stafford, 'but if you and other colleagues believe all is going wrong and that our whole system is bad, I should lose heart – if not break down altogether'. Haultain was saved by his own stereotypical stiff upper lip. He collected himself and, backed by Stafford, made a determined effort to rescue the situation. He took measures against indiscipline and drunkenness which met with some success. He managed to persuade Kepa and Kawana Hunia to remain at the front, despite the death of Hori Kingi on 18 September. And he saw to it that Fraser's excellent No. 1 constabulary came up promptly. He resisted pressure to sack McDonnell, and instead encouraged him and promised full support. McDonnell had always swung easily from self-pity to confidence, and he responded.

The revived McDonnell rode in to Camp Waihi on 17 September, accompanied by Haultain, and confronted his men on the parade ground next day. No. 5 was sent to Patea, and McDonnell addressed the remainder in an effort to boost morale. With his loyal military settler veterans, Fraser's fresh division, and the kupapa, he was still able to muster a formidable striking force of 300 men. He decided to use it to take the bull by the horns. At 4 am on Saturday 20 September, he marched out of Waihi to engage Titokowaru at Taiporohenui. The colonists waited for full daylight at Turuturu Mokai, then advanced on the enemy camp. Soon, they could hear the Maori 'singing out in surprise that here were white men . . . [and] see them standing on the housetops looking at us'. Apparently unfortified and on open ground, Taiporohenui was a tempting target, but recent experience made McDonnell wary. He approached to within a few hundred yards, fired a volley, then withdrew a short distance, hoping to draw out the confident Maori. But 'they were too "wide awake" '. McDonnell now advanced in earnest. William Newland of No. 3, advancing with him, was sure the position could be 'taken quite easily in a few minutes. There was no formidable obstruction to get through.' The colonists approached to within 300 yards, 'some of the Maori bullets coming pretty close to us'. There the men paused, 'waiting for the word "charge" '.

But, with a sinking heart, McDonnell now observed entrenchments, partly hidden in the bush flanking his approach route. It was another of Titokowaru's traps. Reluctantly, McDonnell called off the assault. Newland wrote: 'why the place was not rushed I do not know, as it was quite in the open'. He could not see the concealed trenches. As he withdrew, McDonnell tried one more ploy of his own. Once out of sight of Taiporohenui, Fraser's division quietly peeled off from the main column and hid in an overgrown ditch to ambush any pursuit. McDonnell and the rest of his men awaited the result at Turuturu, ready to rush back in support. But Ngati Ruanui were too shrewd. They approached the ditch, 'supposed that we had left men and fired a few shots from the bush which made our men jump up and return [fire]'. Foiled again, McDonnell marched back to Camp Waihi. Though it was not immediately apparent, he had played his last card.

The bitter disappointment at Taiporohenui recommenced the slide in field force morale. On 22 September, the kupapa left for home, claiming that they had to attend Hori Kingi's tangi and see to their crops. 'But, in truth, they were cowed like the rest, and glad to avoid further collision with a tribe which seemed likely to win in the struggle.' Two days later, Haultain made a last-ditch effort to solve the problem of No. 5 division, addressing them on parade at Patea. Ironically, Von Tempsky's men had been further disgruntled by being sent to Patea 'on the eve of an expected engagement', considering themselves 'under the imputation of cowardice'. There was now a strong solidarity between rank-and-file and sergeants – a decisive change. At the trial of the four men arrested on 13 September, Sergeant Fenton refused to name the ringleaders 'because though I endeavoured to prevent the men from being insubordinate, I share the reasons which were the real cause of it'. Sergeant Toovey went further, despite the advice of the presiding officer to hold his tongue: 'I am, and I believe I speak for all the men of the Division too, unwilling to go into action again under Colonel McDonnell.' McMinn acted as spokesman for the whole, and when Haultain ordered 'the well-disposed men to step forward and separate themselves from the others', only Sergeant William Anderson did so. Haultain denied that No. 5 was suspected of cowardice, but stated that 'insubordination was more inexcusable than cowardice' and that he would disband the division. By 1 October, Von Tempsky's proud unit, the heirs of the Forest Rangers, no longer existed. Despite his dishonourable discharge, McMinn later joined John Ballance as a military defaulter in Parliament.

With No. 5 and the kupapa gone, and most of the government volunteers still unreliable, Haultain and McDonnell now had to face the harsh reality: they no longer had enough effective troops to hold their position. In the last week of September, they abandoned Turuturu Mokai, Hawera, Manutahi, Mokoia, and Manawapou – all the redoubts north of the Patea River. Above all, on 24 September they abandoned Camp Waihi, their main frontier base. 'Some of us had been stationed there nearly three years,' wrote Newland, 'and quite felt leaving it.' With shocking suddenness 'the front' had moved south twenty-five miles. 'There is no doubt we are making a regular run for it,' wrote Livingston. Titokowaru had achieved the first substantial reconquest of Maori land since the Taranaki War.

So October opened with Pakeha troops and civilians streaming back to Patea, having abandoned six redoubts in as many days. Titokowaru followed them up. Still heavily outnumbered, his war parties did not engage the retreating colonists head on, but snapped at their heels, hastening their retreat all the more. The colonists tried to carry off or destroy supplies and equipment, but a great deal was left in the abandoned redoubts and it was Ngati Ruanui who profited. The farms south of the Tangahoe River, hitherto untouched, now burned in their turn. On 29 September R.B. Hamilton and other Manutahi settlers watched their own homes go up in smoke. 'We perceived our houses in flames, and worst of all, the Maoris were after us, thirsting for our blood and our heads. We ran ten or twelve miles till we nearly dropped.' The settlers of Mokoia also suffered from their own side. 'For them I felt really sorry,' wrote Livingston, 'as their chests were broke open by the men, and valuable books, pictures, and old relics which were prized highly by them and which money will not restore, were carried off.' The confusion was such that on 30 September two colonist detachments fired on each other near Manawapou, and a Scots constable, Robert Smith, was killed. Some ebullient young warriors were said to have found his body and put part of it in a barrel of salt pork for hungry Pakeha scouts to find. By courtesy of the motion picture *Utu*, this macabre little practical joke has become the best-known incident of Titokowaru's War.

On 1 October, Titokowaru's main force moved south again and set up a temporary camp near Manutahi. A party captured two of Pihama's 'mailmen' – he and Natanahira still maintained a despatch-carrying service for the government. Patohe visited the Ngati Ruanui camp and secured their release, but Titokowaru demanded that the mail-carrying cease: 'Do you hearken: let the mail on the roads be altogether stopped, take warning by this word.' That night his warriors fired on the Kakaramea redoubt, and there were two false alarms at Patea itself. On 3 October, Titokowaru advanced again, to Otoia, covering the move by planting rumours that he intended a still greater advance, to Waitotara or even Wanganui itself. Three weeks before, his base had been a comfortable forty miles from Patea Town. Now it was only a few miles upriver.

At Patea, there was great alarm. We 'expect an attack every night', wrote members of the garrison; 'Titokowaru is now in full possession of all the country beyond 200 yards from the orderly room.' Many settlers fled, reportedly paying up to fifty pounds for steamer passage to captains 'trafficking on the desperate fortunes of the Patea refugees'. They were made still more desperate by the disappearance of one of their number, Alexander ('Sandy') McCulloch. It was said that he had been captured by Ngati Ruanui and subsequently killed for refusing to carry potatoes, and that his posthumous fate was gruesomely similar to Robert Smith's. 'Months after, his bones were discovered in a water-hole at Kakaramea, from which the camp had been using water in happy ignorance.'

The rumours of Titokowaru's intention to advance on Wanganui, conveyed in good faith by Patohe, Pihama's mailmen, and others, caused alarm further south. At Waitotara, Harry Lomax wrote proudly that 'I am looked upon as a madman for staying out here', and at

Wanganui there was a 'great panic'. 'Not only have all the Patea settlers come in,' wrote Basil Taylor, 'but many of the Wanganui as well; and even in town so great was the panic at first that a few availed themselves of the steamer going to Auckland.' There was a flurry of urgent despatches to the government from Gorton, for once in full agreement with the Wanganui settlers, demanding more men and money. Booth went off to Wellington to pound the message home. Fearing a real threat to their tribal interests, Lower Whanganui commitment to the war increased several notches. Mete Kingi himself led 300 warriors to Perekama on the Waitotara to bar Titokowaru's path.

Titokowaru was unimpressed by this move. 'I have heard that a war party of Whanganui are at Perekama. What of it? What is that to anyone?' He was more immediately concerned with the attitude of the Pakakohe. Wharematangi, previously sympathetic, had taken umbrage over something, possibly their relative jurisdiction in Pakakohe territory, and had not yet joined Titokowaru. This problem might be resolved, but the influential Ngawaka Taurua still wished to remain neutral. McDonnell was also worried about the Pakakohe. Yet again he urged the government to allow him to arrest them – mistakenly describing them as 'the Pokaikai', a classic Freudian slip. But Haultain refused, and McDonnell resorted to intimidation instead.

He ordered Taurua to a meeting at Patea, and gave him a frightening dose of the McDonnell brand of 'Maori' symbolism. He pricked his finger with a pin and showed Taurua the blood and a rifle bullet. 'He said look at this,' remembered Taurua,

if this blood is shed among you, this [bullet] will go into you; we went to the wharf where McDonnell loaded a gun with that bullet, and fired it at a post; he hit it . . . and afterwards . . . fired into the waters of the Patea . . . when the firing was over we said this is very important . . . I became distressed about the bullet and the blood of McDonnell.

Pakakohe discussed this incident at length, and decided that McDonnell would hold them responsible for any hostilities in their area. They might as well be hung for a sheep as a lamb. On 15 October, settlers Jem Southby and T. Collins, a lance-corporal in O'Halloran's cavalry who was due to be married in a few weeks, were riding near the Whenuakura River, well south of the war zone. Suddenly a flurry of shots rang out, fired for the first time by Pakakohe warriors. One shaved Southby's brow; another killed Collins. 'They cut off his head and took his heart and right hand away [and] put his head on a post looking at his body.' Pakakohe had declared war. The last of Ngati Ruanui's three subtribes had thrown in their lot with Titokowaru.

Haultain was very displeased by McDonnell's 'mishandling of neutral chiefs', as he understatedly described it, and by his attendance at an anti-government meeting in Wanganui on 29 September. But he was still not ready to bow to pressure to be rid of him. 'He has not behaved well in several matters,' the defence minister told Stafford, 'but he is very angry and some ill-advised friends are backing him up.' The 'ill-advised friends' included Isaac Featherston, who encouraged McDonnell's growing conviction that the government had forced him into the attack on Te Ngutu, and that its failure to give him full discretion was at the root of all his troubles. The government's refusal to permit him to imprison the Pakakohe, and so prevent what he saw as their inevitable outbreak, was the last straw. On 3 October McDonnell wrote Haultain a contradictory but furious letter, disclaiming any intention to resign, but ending, 'under no circumstances will I again serve under the present government'. Both personally and in writing, Haultain offered to let him withdraw this statement, but he refused, unless given full control of the war effort with only Dr Featherston to 'assist me and even direct me in my movements'. On 14 October, his patience finally exhausted, Haultain wrote:

As you have not availed yourself of the opportunity which has been afforded you of withdrawing this very objectionable remark you leave me under the painful necessity of acquainting you that His Excellency will be advised to accept the resignation of your services and that you are relieved from the command of the Patea District.

Thomas McDonnell will reappear in this story, but always in a subordinate role, and another chance of glory would elude him during the summer of 1869-70 in operations against Te Kooti. One might assume that his rivalry with Von Tempsky had ended with the latter's death at Te Ngutu, and that McDonnell had had the better of it simply by surviving. But the Von Tempsky legend burgeoned after 7 September, rising like a ghost from his funeral pyre. Eulogies of the Prussian adventurer jostled for space in the newspapers with abuse of his commander. In the succeeding century, it was Von Tempsky who got the biographies. Reputation, wrote McDonnell, was 'more dear to me than life itself', and now he had irretrievably lost it.

For the remaining thirty-one years of his life, he walked in the shadow of Te Ngutu. Since his legend had been so vital a part of him, this was literally a living death. McDonnell paid for Pokaikai. Titokowaru had swept away both his great opponents: one dead, one destroyed. Unfortunately for him, an equally able replacement waited in the wings.

In 1861, when he came to New Zealand as General Cameron's military secretary, Major George Stoddart Whitmore had been one of the most promising young officers in the British army: academically gifted, well connected, and widely experienced in fighting Bantu, Boers, and Russians. But in New Zealand in 1862 his brilliant career was aborted by a quirk of fate. At this time, apparently balked of the war he had come out to lead, General Cameron had resigned his command, and Whitmore followed suit. But a major was easier to replace than a commanding general, and Cameron's resignation was refused while Whitmore's was accepted. Whitmore bought and stocked a large sheep and cattle station in Hawke's Bay. A small man, with a cultivated steely gaze and a staggering capacity for hard work and privation which he expected others to emulate, he made his station manager's life a misery. In 1863, at the age of thirty-two, he was appointed to the Legislative Council and reconciled himself to life as a prominent member of the colonial gentry. With his background, this was inseparable from part-time military service, and between 1863 and 1868 he held various senior positions in the Colonial Defence Force, the militia, and the armed constabulary. This second military career climaxed with the Battle of Omarunui on 12 October 1866, when Whitmore and the Napier militia crushed a Pai Marire 'invasion'. It was not Whitmore's fault that the invading army was only eighty strong, that it probably consisted of missionaries, not soldiers, or that most colonist casualties, according to Premier Stafford himself, 'resulted from the crossfire of our own people'. When Te Kooti escaped from the Chatham Islands, Whitmore took up arms again and gave the prisoners their hardest fight yet, at Ruakituri on 8 August 1868. He did not win, but tactically he did not lose either, and his stubborn pursuit of Te Kooti in the face of great difficulties was impressive. Whitmore had a thorough professional grasp of the military arts, yet he was not some hidebound, stereotypical British regular, imprisoned by the rulebook. His intelligence, energy, and determination gave him a genuine capacity

George Stoddart Whitmore
Alexander Turnbull Library

to improvise. In most respects, he was the perfect colonial commander. But he did have one great weakness: nobody liked him.

The nicest way to put it is that Whitmore was hypocritical, elitist, arrogant, and tactless. He praised Premier Stafford to his face and damned him behind his back, begged to be allowed to flog his troops and indignantly denied the thought had ever crossed his mind. He always stressed the importance of being 'a gentleman by birth and in manner', which did not endear him to men with no such claim. His colleague, James Richmond, wrote: 'Whitmore is a capital fellow full of energy. What a thousand pities he should be impaired in his usefulness by incurable and extreme egotism. I have never met his equal in that regard.' His handling of the Poverty Bay militia before Ruakituri, when he had some defaulters dig their own graves as though he were going to execute them, had turned Donald McLean, one of his few friends, into a secret enemy, and McLean's chief lieutenant,

John Ormond, was quite blatant in his hatred: 'He is a contemptible little brute . . . no epithet is too foul for him.' Others described Whitmore as 'the great tyrant', 'that chip of the Devil', 'a diminutive beast', an 'inflated imbecile', a 'miserable pretender', 'a little, conceited, egotistical, self-sufficient ass', 'a perfect donkey without brains'. Much of this stemmed from his manner but his tendency to demand as much from his men as he did from himself was also a factor. 'I have the pleasure of a slight acquaintance with him,' wrote one of his officers, 'and am not keen on intimacy – as he is a disgusting little pig, as hard as nails and can walk any two men off their legs.' The Little Tyrant would never be popular, but the universal dislike of him would soon be tinged with grudging respect.

When Haultain finally became fed up with McDonnell, it was to Whitmore that he naturally turned. In the same parliamentary office that had witnessed similar discussions with McDonnell only four months before, with James Booth present to detail the plight of the Patea district, Haultain appealed to Whitmore's strong sense of duty. He also offered him reinforcements, support, and promotion to full colonel, a rank shared only by Haultain himself. Whitmore professed reluctance. He returned home to Napier to ask the advice of his wife, Isabella, whom he had married on a visit to England three years before. 'Though it was hard upon her,' wrote Whitmore, 'my wife recognized that I must not evade my duty.' After last attentions to the cattle-breeding programme he had just commenced at his station, he steamed back to Wellington and on to Wanganui to deal with Titokowaru. 'Little Whitmore', wrote Ormond, 'left Wellington saying three days would settle the West Coast question and that then he would hop across to [fight Te Kooti] and settle that business.' Whitmore's arrival at Wanganui on 18 October was marked by 'a heavy earthquake'.

In Wellington, Haultain had briefed Whitmore on the situation at the front, which he believed to be now under control. Two companies of the 18th, the last Imperial regiment in the colony, had arrived in Wanganui on 7 October. They had strict orders not to leave the town, but their presence helped restore confidence. The Wanganui people themselves were at last showing signs of taking up arms, and Mete Kingi now had 457 men at Perekama – his tribe's whole force. The European field force was still more than 600 strong, and 400 of these, 'confident and cautious' under Major James Fraser at Patea, blocked Titokowaru's advance from Otoia. Whitmore had over 1,000 men, said Haultain, and it was time to resume the

A and C companies of the 18th Regiment, parading outside the Rutland Stockade, Wanganui. Their orders permitted them to do little more   *Wanganui Museum*

offensive. This was too rosy a picture, and Whitmore lost no time in saying so. He replied querulously that he could not make out 1,000 men anywhere. The Wellington Rifles were 'real brutes, thoroughly funked', the European contingent was 'beginning to mutiny', and the Patea Yeomanry Cavalry had asked for their discharge. There were no more than 200 Europeans effective, and 150 was nearer the mark. Far from confidence, 'all hope had been abandoned' at Patea: the mood 'resembled that of men in a shipwreck'.

With demoralisation went drink, and the problem started at the top. James Fraser had real qualities – he was courageous and very popular with his own men. But he was also an alcoholic; 'one of the old "two bottle" men – or, rather, he was contented with two bottles when he could not get three'. Others followed his lead. 'Major Fraser and the other officers are frequently intoxicated' – even Kepa was not immune. The Patea guard picket celebrated Whitmore's arrival with a drunken binge. A quarrel broke out, knives appeared, two men were 'seriously stabbed', and twenty-one were arrested. By 30 October Whitmore was writing to Haultain:

since I have been here (and they tell me it is play to what it was) I have seen more, and worse crime than I ever saw before . . . What staggers me is that everyone talks of the wonderful change in the behaviour of the troops . . . What a mistake it is not being able to flog! One flogging would stop it all perhaps. Can I do it?

Major James Fraser
From T. W. Gudgeon,
The Defenders of New Zealand

For their own reasons, Haultain and Whitmore painted very different pictures of the state of the Patea Field Force. The truth lay somewhere between the two. On 23 October, far from the 150 to 200 he claimed, Whitmore had 516 'effective' European troops. It was true that he also had 116 'ineffective' and that demoralisation, indiscipline, and exceptional drunkenness were again rife in some units. But Whitmore set about these problems with great energy, and he understated his success in overcoming them. First, he moved most of the troops at Patea out of the cramped township and into a new camp between the river and the sand hills, setting up his own headquarters at Booth's comfortable house well outside the town. This demonstrated confidence in his men's capacity to repel attack and created space for a greatly increased amount of drill. It also stopped 'all intercourse between the township and the camp' and so 'removed the men from the nightly orgies which of late had been too common'. To make sure, Whitmore used a new law to close the Patea pubs, leaving only a strictly regulated official canteen. The field force had several types of unit, each with different conditions of service, and to Whitmore it was clear that this contributed to disunity and indiscipline. He advised Haultain to enrol all future recruits in the armed constabulary and himself dismissed the Wellington Rifles, re-enlisting a few of the best men as constabulary. Apart from the rump of the European contingent and a few other remnants, the government volunteers, who had made up the bulk of McDonnell's force, now virtually ceased to exist.

From the outset, Whitmore made it clear that his was a different style of command: 'I go on a totally different principle to McDonnell. I keep my distance from . . . all the Force. I am never "hail fellow well met" with anybody. I live at my own establishment with Mr Forster [his aide and cousin] (who is a gentleman and suits me very well).' 'Distance', authority, and discipline were the watchwords. Whitmore arrested, court-martialled, and imprisoned offenders right and left. The flogging issue was more difficult. Brutal flogging, a punishment which the Maori looked upon as mere savagery, was still the mainstay of British army discipline. However, many considered it inappropriate for the colonial forces and the legal situation was ambiguous. At the risk of being charged with assault, Whitmore did eventually permit Fraser to flog one man who had refused the lesser punishment of pack-drill. The punishment stopped three short of the stipulated twenty-five lashes because the victim fainted – 'he would not have stood 3 more lashes'. But, with the 'worst', or least malleable, of the men imprisoned or dismissed, Whitmore's tongue was lash enough for the remainder. Within a week of his taking command, the newspapers were reporting that 'confusion, disorder and mutiny which had reached a frightful pitch under his predecessor had been reduced to order'. The ineffectives had been weeded out and 'the remaining force is in a state of perfect order and effective discipline'. Such measures did not make Whitmore popular. Fraser and other officers returned his low opinion of them with interest, and unflattering anecdotes about the new commander were gleefully told and retold. 'Whitmore saw a soldier lying drunk. Riding up to him, he abused him and said, "You are drunk, sir." The man said, 'Well I am drunk but I'll get over that; but you are a fool and you'll never get over that".' But Whitmore was no fool and, on the whole, his tough new measures worked. By the beginning of November the colony again had a force to be reckoned with.

Haultain and Whitmore were fully agreed on one problem: the kupapa. They had yet to grasp that Whanganui were allies, not

The Whanganui kupapa levée en masse, including many young boys *Wanganui Museum*

subordinates. Matters first came to a head on 12 October, when Mete Kingi objected to Haultain's attempt to give orders direct to subordinate chiefs. Haultain was enraged that 'that scoundrel Mete Kingi' thought he 'knew better than anyone else' how to run the war. Kingi told Haultain plainly that 'he was Chief of the tribe and not a man should move without his orders'. Haultain wrote,

I felt inclined to kick him out of the room but I smothered my wrath. [I] told him that I knew he was a great talker, but that he was the first man who had ever told me that he was a great warrior, [and] that his tactics were ridiculous . . . and I finished my Philippic by saying he was not the Chief of the Tribes. That Kemp was the Rangitira now that Hori [Kingi] was dead.

It was fortunate that Haultain had 'smothered his wrath'. Mete Kingi stormed out, although it was in fact he who controlled his temper and attempted to be conciliatory. 'Within five minutes Mete came back like a whipped cur . . . and begged that I would not think badly of him.'

Whitmore was initially unimpressed by Kepa – 'a chief who, I am sorry to perceive today, cannot be kept sober' – and hopeful about his relations with the established Whanganui leaders. He even made one or two attempts at tact. But he soon came around to Haultain's view of the situation. When Mete Kingi urged that the

allies should content themselves with protecting Wanganui until
reinforcements came up, 'I answered him very shortly that I looked
to Kemp, not to him.' Kepa, a man with qualities Pakeha could readily
appreciate, soon gained Whitmore's good opinion. He was promoted
to major and treated as chief of the kupapa. Kepa himself was by
no means averse to this boost to his mana, and he increased his personal
following, but he still felt some obligation to the tribal leadership.
It was true that Mete Kingi was more a politician than a soldier,
and that he consistently sought to assert his status as an ally – for
example, by reporting direct to Governor Bowen rather than to
Haultain and Whitmore. But Titokowaru's advance south had created
a real willingness to co-operate, and the danger was that the colonist
leaders' attitude would erode this.

Morally, Titokowaru still had the upper hand and he wished to exploit
it by forcing another battle as soon as possible. But his force, though
greatly increased to 150 or 200 warriors, was still outnumbered five
to one by the colonists. Again, he would have to induce them to
attack him in a prepared position. Only a week after taking up the
command, it seemed that Whitmore might do just that. On the morning
of Sunday 25 October, influenced by Haultain's confidence, pressure
from plundered settlers, and the fact that the kupapa could keep
the field only for a limited time, Whitmore and Mete Kingi advanced
against Otoia.
    They found that Titokowaru's camp was 'pitched in deep jungle',
no doubt replete with hidden positions, at the base of the hill 'Gentle
Annie', with a steep ravine to the south. Titokowaru paraded his
men on top of the hill to tempt the enemy in and exchange haka
with the kupapa. Whitmore fired a couple of volleys and a few shells
from his two six-pounder Armstrong guns 'to try and draw the
Hauhaus out'. Like McDonnell at Taiporohenui, Whitmore advanced
again but found the ravine blocking his way; he claimed that working
around it 'would have occupied more time than we could devote
to the movement'. 'We have made two attempts to attack
Titokowaru's pa,' reported Mete Kingi to Bowen, 'but could not
get at it from the badness of the road; and he refuses to come out.
If there had been a good road, we should have extinguished his pa.'
But Titokowaru too might have wished for a better road, and the
fact was that each set of leaders was too shrewd to oblige the other.
Titokowaru stayed at Otoia, and Whitmore and Mete Kingi withdrew
to Patea.

It was stalemate. But, within a few days, Titokowaru had hit upon another plan to force battle upon his cautious enemy. It was to be his most ambitious strategic manoeuvre. On 30 October, colonist scouts observed that the campfires no longer burned at Otoia. Titokowaru and all his people had left. This, theoretically, was what Whitmore and Mete Kingi had wanted. The enemy had left their strong position. The only questions was: where had they gone?

For three or four days, 'though the Wanganui natives have been very indefatigable in looking for him', it seemed as if Titokowaru had vanished into thin air. Whitmore himself was anxious and in Wanganui the most alarming rumours flew thick and fast. Far away, the *Auckland Punch* was safe enough to exercise its wit:

YE NURSERY RHYMES TO SUIT THE TIMES.
(For Children)

Colonel Whit--re (loq.)
> *Riddle me, riddle me,*
> *Where can those Maoris be?*
> *Where do you think we'll find them.*

Colonel H--lt--n (loq.)
> *Leave them alone,*
> *They are picking a bone*
> *Or two they've left behind them.*

Moral

Little Whit--re is fast asleep,
The Hauhaus know where to find him;
If he doesn't look out, and mind what he's about
Tito will get behind him.

Punch was wiser than it knew. Titokowaru did get behind Whitmore. In a wide outflanking movement, he and his people marched through the dense bush well inland of the colonist positions and patrols. They rested at Putahi, on the Whenuakura River, intending to go to Okotuku Hill, inland of Wairoa, and eighteen miles in Whitemore's rear. Despite the best efforts of the colonist scouts, they had not yet been discovered. But Titokowaru no longer wanted secrecy. While he and the rest of his people made for Okotuku, he sent The Twelve, the Tekau-ma-rua, still further south. Very early on the morning of 1 November, in the dead of night, they struck the unsuspecting Ngarauru and Pakeha settlements clustered around Perekama and the Weraroa redoubt on the Waitotara River.

There were still several dozen settlers on the Waitotara, keeping nervously to their farms on the assumption that Whitmore's force would block any Maori advance. Most, warned by their Ngarauru neighbours, now snatched up a few possessions, mounted up, and bolted through the night for Wanganui, Harry Lomax, courageous 'madman' or not, among them. Charles Durie allegedly ran out one door of his house as Ngati Ruanui entered at the other. But two were caught. Settlers Reece and Richards were asleep in a house at Karaka, sharing its one bed, when two Ngarauru, Etapu and Mihaka, awakened them with the news that the Tekau-ma-rua was upon them, surrounding the house. Reece said 'just two words, "My God". As my friend Mr Richards was sitting up close to me in bed, I distinctly felt his leg shake (for the second only) as if you had struck a tightened rope and felt the vibration.' Reece spoke Maori, and Richards said to him: 'For Gods sake, Reece, if they are going to kill us, tell them to do it quickly, and not to torture us with their tomahawks.' The two settlers were taken across the Waitotara to Papatupu, where The Twelve were assembling their plunder. There they waited for five anxious hours while the Maori debated their fate. Then, to their great relief and surprise, they were released.

This unusual act of mercy had two causes. Despite subsequent claims to the contrary, most Ngarauru were willing to join Titokowaru if he had some chance of protecting them from government retaliation. The Weraroa raid suggested he had, and Big Kereopa and some of the other warriors enlisted immediately. But that did not mean that they were willing to see 'their' own Pakeha killed, and it was their intervention which helped save Reece and Richards. 'Big Kereopa' spoke on their behalf, and it was Etapu who turned the scale. Etapu, though Ngarauru, was said to be another of Titokowaru's younger half-brothers, and his views carried some weight. Furthermore, his young daughter, Wairoa, burst into tears at the crucial moment, 'making the Hauhaus turn on her with "What are you crying for?" "Oh", she said, making more noise than ever, "You are going to take our Pakehas to Okotuku, and kill them." At which the Hauhaus relented.' The other cause of the two settlers' salvation was less laudable. The Weraroa raid was a propaganda exercise, designed to show Whitmore that Titokowaru's advance to Okotuku had laid open the soft Pakeha underbelly south of the Waitotara. In Wanganui, Reece and Richards would pound the message home. The Maori 'released the Pakehas telling them . . . Titokowaru was going to use the Waitotara as the centre of his future operations'.

This news naturally caused consternation in Wanganui. Before noon on Sunday, Gorton received a despatch from Acting Sub-Inspector Colin McDonnell (no relation to the colonel), who commanded the thirty-two constabulary garrisoning the Weraroa redoubt. McDonnell clearly thought his time had come, and planned to die heroically:

I have the honour to inform you that the Hauhaus are within a quarter of a mile of here, and I expect to be attacked every moment. I can only say that we are quite ready for them . . . We are sure to be attacked this day. I have no time to write you any further, as I must get the messenger off at once before the roads are closed. I can only say you can depend upon myself and my men to the last extremity.

Gorton sent off the newly constituted Wanganui Cavalry Volunteers, seventy strong, to Weraroa, called out his old enemies the 1st Class Militia ('P.S. I don't expect to get more than 50 Militiamen'), and prepared to march with them himself to relieve the prospective hero. He also sent an urgent despatch to Whitmore, including information from Reece and Richards. The Twelve did not attack Weraroa – much to Colin McDonnell's embarrassment, no doubt – and they soon withdrew to join Titokowaru at Okotuku. But they had made their point. It seemed, wrote Gorton, 'that Titokowaru's intentions are to harass the district on this side of the Waitotara River'.

Whitmore received Gorton's despatch early on 2 November. It seemed to him that he now had no option but to march south himself, find Titokowaru, and attack him before he ravaged the Wanganui hinterland and perhaps threatened the town itself. Within four hours of his hearing of the Weraroa raid, he was marching south with every man who could be spared from Patea. By 10 pm on 2 November he was at the Wairoa redoubt, 'from which place I shall be in a position to move in such direction as may be required'. Here he learned from the leader of the local volunteers, Captain Robert Hawes, that he would not have to move very far at all. At the foot of Okotuku Hill, only four miles from Wairoa, Titokowaru had just begun building a new pa. Hawes, wrote Whitmore, 'assured me there was no kind of fortification [there], only a day or two before. I saw that in that case the sooner we attacked the less probability there would be of a pah being erected, or at least completed, and therefore the more hopeful my chances.'

The new pa at Okotuku was called Moturoa. Soon it was to have another name: Papa Tihakehake, the Corpse-Strewn Battlefield.

Chapter Nine

THE BATTLE OF MOTUROA

Moturoa was a battle that everyone knew was going to happen. Since Whitmore's arrival at Wairoa on 2 November, the troops had known that something was up. By Friday 6 November, when two days' rations were served out, there was no doubt what it was: an attack on Titokowaru's new pa, Moturoa, next morning.

Veteran soldiers say that waiting for a battle to take place is worse than a surprise encounter, and that this is particularly so when you are on the attacking side. Why, you ask yourself, should I get out of this nice safe tent into a hail of bullets and be killed trying to take a piece of dirt from someone I don't know? This dilemma is old, and was as real to Lance-Corporal Philip Putnam, in his tent at Wairoa redoubt on the morning of 7 November 1868, as it was to the ANZAC at Gallipoli forty-seven years later. Putnam had come with his constabulary division, Fraser's No. 1, from the East Coast after the Te Ngutu disaster. Ordered to 'the front' on 17 September, he asked for his discharge but was refused. The auction of the Ngutu deads' property on 21 September, a macabre military tradition, was disconcerting – next time it might be his prized possessions selling at bargain prices. At Patea on 3 October – Putnam's birthday, when his mates shared two looted turkeys with him – he heard that Von Tempsky's division had been disbanded, and was himself involved in guarding shattered fragments of the first Patea Field Force – 'any amount of prisoners every day'. On 18 October, with a hint of envy, he observed a 'mutiny among the Wellington Rifles'. He marched to Wairoa with the rest on 2 November, spent 'Guy Fawkes day in a great funk of being attacked at night', and next day was told off to join Whitmore's assault force at Wairoa. That morning, when his mates rose to enter the bush and fight the ferocious victors of Te Ngutu, Putnam took his cowardice in both hands: 'I was too tired, and stopped behind.' He escaped official reprimand, but his own conscience did not let him off so lightly. He sought solace in Father Rolland's masses. Three weeks after 'stopping behind', in an age when this was still a remarkable thing for a Protestant Englishman to do, he was 'Baptised into the Holy Roman Catholic Church'.

George Cumming
Taranaki Museum

Philip Putnam was not the only man grappling with dreadful fear that morning. Captain Richard Kenrick 'got ill' as he had done before Te Ngutu. As an officer, he was less lucky than Putnam and was dismissed by Whitmore. Another officer, Major George Cumming, Whitmore's adjutant, was also haunted by Te Ngutu. He told James Booth, in confidence, 'that if he was asked to go into the bush [again] he would resign his commission'. In confidence or not, Booth lost no time in telling Whitmore. Cumming, the chief staff officer and sufficient of a gentleman for Whitmore's taste, lived with the colonel, and the two of them may have talked it out. For whatever reason, Cumming overcame his fears and marched out into the bush with the rest. The surprising thing is that Putnam and Kenrick were the exceptions, and George Cumming the norm.

For Kimble Bent, on the other side, the knowledge of imminent battle was just as disturbing and considerably more complicated. He had marched with Titokowaru's main force from Otoia to Okotuku on 2 November, and spent the night at a camp beside potato cultivations planted on the flat below Okotuku Hill. Here, Titokowaru decided to make his stand, explaining to his followers that he had had a 'foreboding . . that we would be attacked here by the soldiers . . .

he said he was sure the *pakeha* scouts would find us sooner or later'. Titokowaru sent the children and old people away, and for four days his men and women laboured mightily on their new pa, using traditional teamwork techniques, considerably more efficient than European methods. Bent worked with them. He knew that he himself would not be fighting – Titokowaru always respected his scruples about fighting his fellow-Europeans. But he would have to face gunfire like the fighters on either side, and a turncoat has few friends with whom to share his fears. At night, in his hut, he tossed and turned: 'Though I was dog-tired I could not sleep – thinking, thinking over the past, and dreading what the future might bring me.'

Bent did have some friends, and one, Te Waka Taparuru, was his hut-mate that night. An older man, with a big head and moko on both cheeks, 'wiry and wonderfully quick on his legs', he was an exceptionally skilled warrior. Tutange Waionui recalled that 'there was no-one so expert as he in loading a muzzle-loader'. In 1865, Waka had killed a government interpreter, Charles Broughton, reportedly shooting him as he stood lighting his pipe on the marae at Otoia. Remembered by the Pakeha solely for this, Waka was also a good friend to Kimble Bent, a trusted comrade of Titokowaru's, and a much-loved brother and father. On the night of 6 November, while Bent tossed restlessly across the hut from him, Waka dreamed he saw his own face reflected in a Pakeha mirror. Disturbed, he consulted Titokowaru, who 'interpreted the dream as an omen of death' and warned Te Waka 'not to leave the shelter of the stockade during the impending engagement or he would be killed'. Waka went away unconvinced. Such portents had a way of eventuating, whatever one did.

Another member of the Maori force was Tu-Patea Te Rongo, a powerfully built youth, one of the newly joined Pakakohe. At seventeen years, Tu-Patea was already a veteran, having fought his first battle at Nukumaru in 1865, against all Cameron's army. Half a century later, on 4 March 1921, he paced over the battlefield of Moturoa with James Cowan, describing the fortifications. They were personally laid out by Titokowaru, and included a wooden palisade with a firing trench behind it. Tu-Patea and Bent, who did the work, emphasised the palisade's heavy tree trunks but, as at Te Ngutu, these were only the main struts of the fence. The palisade was actually quite flimsy, a screen rather than a wall. The first line of fire would come from the firing trench. The earth from it was used to form a low bank behind, from which more warriors could produce a second line of fire through gaps in the palisade. Yet another line of fire could come from three taumaihi, squat towers or bastions, about fifteen feet across and twelve feet high, made of wood and earth packed in a web of fern for greater solidity. These must have blended in with the palisade because, though Maori evidence leaves no doubt of their existence, the colonist accounts do not mention them. These defences had immense disguised strength – the capacity for a triple 'sheet of fire' – but they covered only the southward face of the position, in a single crooked line about 110 yards long. Tu-Patea stated that:

We had been at work four days when we were attacked and did not have time to finish the fortifications. We only had one side done, besides three taumaihi, one in the elbow of the work and one at each corner . . . The pa was not closed in; it consisted then of only one line.

But, if Tu-Patea thought this a consequence of lack of time only, he underestimated his leader.

Looking south from outside the farmhouse which stands today on Okotuku Hill, you can still follow Titokowaru's logic. The hill top itself appears to dominate the surrounding countryside and would seem the obvious place to fortify. But it was here that the people of Okotuku village were defeated by Chute on 4 January 1866, and it did not suit Titokowaru's purposes. Instead, he put his single line on the flat land below, resting its right on the steep gully to the west and its left on an area of broken ground and thick bush to the east. Here, he supplemented nature with concealed rifle pits and hidden breastworks of wood and supplejack, linked with the pa proper by secret pathways. From in front of the pa, looking towards Okotuku, this left flank looked fairly open. Like Te Ngutu, Moturoa was partly an illusion, designed to look weak in front and vulnerable on the left. In reality, it was neither.

At Wairoa, very early on the morning of 7 November, the colonial forces began marching out for the attack. They left the redoubt in three columns between 1 am and 3 am, making for a rendezvous at the edge of Moturoa bush. The first column consisted mainly of the men Whitmore had brought from Patea, detachments of Nos. 1, 2 and 3 constabulary, the Patea Volunteer Rifles, and Yeomanry Cavalry. They were the pick of the old Patea Field Force, 155 men selected from a total of 245 in their units. They were accompanied by thirty-two of the local Wairoa Volunteer Rifles under Captain Robert Hawes and Lieutenant Andrew Middlemas.

A newly recruited constabulary division, No. 6, formed the second column, 106 strong. Raised in Auckland and led by John Roberts, they had only arrived at Wanganui on 5 November, and had had a lively march to the front. Hustled onward from Wanganui by Gorton, they had marched from the Kai Iwi to Wairoa on 6 November, under fire from Titokowaru's patrols for the last couple of miles. Despite youth and recent recruitment, they were good troops. Many had seen service before, twenty of the least fit were weeded out and left at Wairoa, and even Whitmore approved of them: 'I have never seen a finer body of men.'

The third column consisted of the Wanganui kupapa, some 420 in all. The previous day they had enthusiastically driven off the Ngati Ruanui patrols that beset Roberts, inflicting the only casualty of the action. By 6 am, most had joined the other two columns at the rendezvous, and the rest were on their way. But Whitmore now ordered the young chief Aperahama and twenty men to join Middlemas and the Wairoa volunteers as a reserve force at the edge of the bush, building an earthwork as a field base for the main advance. Aperahama, a veteran of Chute's campaign who may have aspired to a status similar to Kepa's, obeyed. This was enough to break the fragile reconciliation between the military authorities and Mete Kingi. Repeatedly insulted by Haultain and Whitmore, angered by their persistent attempts to replace him with Kepa as leading chief, Mete saw the direct order to Aperahama as an attempt to wean yet another section of his tribe away from him. Supported by other senior chiefs, including Kawana Hunia and three-quarters of the tribe, he refused to continue the advance. Kepa, Wirihana, Aperahama, and a hundred men of a like mind from a mixture of hapu, joined the Pakeha.

Deprived of nearly half his force, Whitmore now had to decide whether to proceed with the attack. Even without Mete Kingi and the bulk of Whanganui, he had 400 men. Whitmore knew they outnumbered Titokowaru, though he could not know by how much, and, for all the carping of the previous weeks, he also knew that his troops were good. The Pakeha units had all been sifted to eliminate the least fit, and Kepa's men had selected themselves: 'The force is in excellent spirits and there is no doubt that if they get anything like an opportunity they will give a good account of Titokowaru.' This, combined with Whitmore's own characteristic tenacity and the strategic and moral pressure so carefully created by his opponent, was enough. Whitmore decided to give his men something like an opportunity, and renewed his advance.

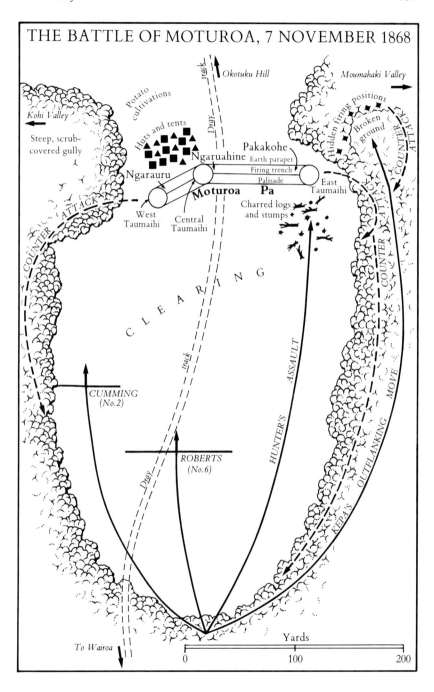

THE BATTLE OF MOTUROA, 7 NOVEMBER 1868

Okotuku Hill

Moumahaki Valley

Kohi Valley

Steep, scrub-covered gully

Potato cultivations

Huts and tents

Hidden firing positions

Broken ground

Ngaruahine

Pakakohe

Earth parapet

Firing trench

Palisade

Ngarauru

Moturoa **Pa**

West Taumaihi

Central Taumaihi

East Taumaihi

Charred logs and stumps

C L E A R I N G

COUNTER ATTACK

COUNTER ATTACK

COUNTER ATTACK

HUNTER'S ASSAULT

CUMMING (No.2)

ROBERTS (No.6)

KEPA'S OUTFLANKING MOVE

track

track

Drag

Drag

To Wairoa

Yards

0   100   200

Leaving Middlemas and Aperahama holding the earthwork, the colonists entered the bush, dumped their personal swags and other gear not needed for battle, and proceeded quietly and cautiously along the broad dray track that led to Okotuku. Almost immediately there was another mishap. One man, probably of the Patea Rifles since he carried an Enfield, had his gun at full cock. He stumbled, and the gun went off, wounding Sergeant Edwin Kirwan of No. 6 in the back of the neck. There was, however, little chance that the sound had carried to the enemy through the thick bush and drizzling mist, and the advance continued. Kirwan was left on a stretcher to be picked up later, along with his comrades' swags.

Less than a mile from Moturoa pa, the colonists were rejoined by their scouts who had gone forward to reconnoitre. These included Kepa and some of his men, together with Hawes and a few other Wairoa volunteers brought along for their local knowledge. Whitmore halted the force and moved forward through some high fern to look at the pa for himself. Listening to the reports of his scouts, particularly Kepa, and inspecting the Maori position in the grey dawn light, he made the three assumptions that were to determine the course of the coming battle. First, all was quiet. The advance had not been perceived by the enemy and there was still a good chance of surprise. Second, the Maori defences seemed to consist of simple palisading with no special firing positions of any kind. 'The palisades were new and neatly put up,' wrote Whitmore, 'but in no way different, I think, to ordinary kainga palings.' They were 'miserable affairs[.] I could easily have cut the lot with my clasp-knife.' The internal defences were not visible. Hawes had seen no defences at all a few days earlier, and the simplicity of these hastily erected fortifications therefore came as no surprise. Finally, although the steep gully west of the pa, at the edge of the Kohi Valley, protected the Maori right flank, their left seemed vulnerable. Taking all this into account, Whitmore accepted a plan suggested by Kepa: that one force creep through the bush east of Moturoa and suddenly fire into its open left rear while another launched a strong surprise assault across the clearing against the left front. At some time between 7 am and 8 am the first force moved out, led by Kepa.

Kepa's outflanking force included his eighty Whanganui warriors with Walter Gudgeon tagging along. There were also twenty-five veterans of No. 1 constabulary, Philip Putnam's braver comrades, including several 'de-tribalised' Maori such as Constable Henare Kepa Te Ahururu. With Fraser commanding the Patea garrison, No. 1

Forster Goring
From T. W. Gudgeon,
The Defenders of New Zealand

was led by Forster Goring, a twenty-three-year-old veteran of Te Ngutu. A cool young man with a quizzical expression, his gentlemanly Anglo-Irish lineage did not prevent his being 'always ready for a scrap, as befitted a lad from County Galway'. Kepa, Goring, and their men worked their way slowly and cautiously around the eastern edge of the clearing, eventually taking up a concealed position southeast of the pa's front and about forty yards from it. At this distance, even in the mist, the detail of the pa was clearly visible, and all still seemed quiet.

In fact, within Moturoa, the sentries were alert. The previous night Titokowaru, fully aware of Whitmore's preparations at Wairoa, had gone around the camp warning his warriors: 'This is an evil night. Be vigilant, and keep a keen lookout for the enemy.' He put Katene in command of the sentries. As the colonist forces began their deployment, it was their erstwhile colleague who peered at them through the mist from his position in the central taumaihi. Katene's first inkling of the colonists' presence is said to have come with the

faint sound of steel striking steel as a trooper's accoutrements jangled
despite his caution. Soon he glimpsed dark, moving figures, and he
silently climbed down and made the rounds of the camp, waking
the men and women of each tent and hut.

'The soldiers are on us!' young Tutange Waionui, shaking himself
from sleep, heard Katene whisper urgently. 'They are by now entering
the clearing. Get your arms quickly! Man the trenches! But don't
make a sound.'

The warriors quietly took up their arms. Many Ngaruahine had
breech-loading carbines taken at Te Ngutu. Kimble Bent and others
were 'very clever at making cartridges for our breech-loaders', using
such things as eel bladders for covering, in place of the normal gold-
beater's skin. Some, like Tutange, still preferred tupara to carbines
'because something was always going wrong with them'. Tutange
also had Von Tempsky's revolver. Apart from a few of the new
recruits, who still had muskets or single-barrelled shotguns, this was
an unusually well-armed Maori force. All now went to their allotted
positions: the new Ngarauru recruits on the right, perhaps led by
Big Kereopa and a fierce, lean warrior named Timoti; Ngaruahine
in the centre under Katene and Kokiri, and Pakakohe on the left.
Taurua was present, but tactical command of the Pakakohe seems
to have been held by the old veteran Paraone Tutere of Manutahi,
Tutange's grandfather. Wharematangi, Haowhenua, and others,
including most Tangahoe, may have been absent, perhaps guarding
the children, and Maori accounts state there were only a hundred
warriors in Moturoa. They were few, but they were awake and fully
prepared. Whitmore's first assumption had proved false.

To Kepa's men, who had now remained hidden close by the pa
for twenty minutes, it seemed almost too quiet, hardly the morning
bustle of an unsuspecting camp. Realising this, one man of the garrison
began to cut firewood, but the homely sound came too late. 'Do
they think us fools?', whispered one of Kepa's warriors, 'now I know
they expect us.' But this knowledge, in its turn, came too late. Just
then Whitmore unleashed his assault party: the Patea volunteer units,
under Captains P. Gilling and O'Halloran, and No. 3 constabulary
– together about a hundred men. At his own repeated insistence,
William Hunter was in command, for Turuturu Mokai still rankled.
The night before, at Wairoa, he had asked Whitmore to let him
lead the attack, and told a friend that 'he would show the world
that he was no coward, and avenge his brother Harry's death'. Now
he repeated his 'earnest wish' and Whitmore agreed. The rest of

William Hunter
From T. W. Gudgeon,
The Defenders of New Zealand

the force, Roberts' large No. 6 division in the centre and No. 2 on the left, was to enter the clearing behind Hunter and keep up a heavy fire on the front of the pa, adding their crossfire to Kepa's in support of Hunter's assault.

The assault party left the cover of the belt of bush in skirmishing order. As he moved out, Hunter told Roberts: 'Follow me up like the Devil.' The assault party ran diagonally across the 300 yards of open ground towards the left of the pa. They made it unharmed to within about thirty yards of the silent stockade. Hunter's deputy, William Newland, remembered that 'up to that moment not a sound could be heard – some thought the Rebels had cleared out. But when we had got to within a chain or so of the Position one shot was fired . . . killing one of our men. In an instant the whole face of the Pah was one line of smoke and bullets flying like hail.' Hunter's point of attack was the eastern taumaihi, held by Pakakohe, and it was their leader, Paraone, who fired the first shot. At this signal, the Pakakohe all opened fire in the single volley that Newland likened to hail. Some warriors fired at ground level from the firing trench, some from the earth parapet behind, and some from the top of the taumaihi. One colonist veteran said, 'I never saw the like of that sheet of fire.'

Their momentum carried Hunter's assault group to within ten or twenty yards of the stockade. Kepa's men fired from their hiding places, a few charged to support Hunter, and the rest began trying to work around behind the left flank of the pa. To Whitmore, 300 yards away, it seemed as if the assault was succeeding. Constable Henare Kepa actually scrambled to the top of the stockade and peered down into it. But he was soon shot through the lungs, and as the smoke and fog cleared a little it became obvious that Hunter's assault had been shot flat. More than a dozen men lay dead and dying, and the survivors were pinned to their sparse cover of stumps and logs by the terrible Maori fire.

William Keneally was among the first to fall. A strapping twenty-one-year-old private in the Patea Rifle Volunteers, he was shot within a few yards of the east wing of the pa. Deciding that Keneally was the Mata Ika, Tihirua sprang from the stockade, ignoring bullets, and dragged his body inside, removed the heart, and performed the Whangai Hau. The smoke from the scorched heart drifted in the direction of the enemy – a good omen. William Hunter was another Pakeha whose luck had run out, but his demise was in the best Victorian tradition. Determined to prove his courage after the Turuturu Mokai smear, he is said to have walked upright among the prostrate men despite the terrible fire. 'Lie down, sir, for God's sake lie down,' they shouted. 'But he refused to do so, saying, "No, no, boys; I must show the world today I am no coward." ' Soon a bullet struck him high on the thigh, cutting the femoral artery, and he bled to death in Newland's arms, but not before he had managed a few last words: 'I am done for. Take command of No. 3. Don't leave me for God's sake. Remember my poor brother Harry.'

Whitmore still hoped to renew the assault. No. 6 under Roberts and No. 2 under Cumming were now deployed along the southern edge of the clearing, firing massed volleys into the pa with great rapidity. Kepa and the assault party were still blasting away with a will from close range. 'The palisades,' wrote Whitmore, 'appeared to me to give no protection to its defenders except concealment, and . . . I am sure there must have been many casualties.' He noted that 'we all heard the women crying inside', presumably lamenting dozens of dead. Convinced that the garrison was severely weakened,

Whitmore went forward to see if he could galvanise the assault force into another effort. 'To give the wee devil his due he never lacked for pluck or enterprise'. But Whitmore's second assumption was also false. The palisades were flimsy, but the other defences protected the garrison very well indeed. The women's cries were encouragement, not lamentation. A group of women, some armed, crouched in an inner rifle pit, ready to tend the wounded, bring ammunition, or fight themselves if the enemy broke through. Indeed, it was they who had suffered the only Maori casualty thus far in the battle. Kimble Bent saw one woman 'shot dead through the head as she rose to wave her shawl and yell a fighting cry to the men at the palisades'.

Coming up to the assault party, Whitmore found Newland, Gilling, O'Halloran, and their men hugging the ground close to the pa and firing away blindly but hotly from behind logs and stumps. Hunter's body was picked up and carried some way to the rear by Newland and three or four others. But this itself cost two more casualties, and men were still being hit. Without help, the assault could not be renewed. Still worse, bullets were now beginning to come not only from the pa but from the bush on the colonists' flank. Where was Kepa?

Kepa and Goring were finding that to work a way through the bush to the left rear of Moturoa was much less easy than it looked. For one thing, the ground east of Moturoa was not as accessible as it seemed from the south. Though not the precipitous ravine of the western flank, it was rough and broken, the fringe of the Moumahaki Valley. It was made still more difficult by design. 'Branches interwoven with undergrowth and ground vines' had been made into 'an impenetrable abatis'. The tangled bush was 'penetrable only by steps which had been formed by the natives with supplejacks'. Still more important, in the first hint of Titokowaru's willingness to fight outside his pa, a party of the garrison engaged the outflanking force in the bush. They fired from hidden positions and, in contrast to Te Ngutu, they caused the kupapa heavy casualties – five or six men killed or mortally wounded, plus lesser wounds. Whitmore's third assumption, that Moturoa's left was vulnerable, had proved as false as the others, and Kepa's outflanking effort was stopped dead.

The two prongs of the colonist attack, Hunter's assault and Kepa's outflanking move, had both failed with loss. The Pakeha tide had reached its full and could go no further. At this point in many earlier New Zealand battles, the Europeans had simply cut their losses and withdrawn unhampered to try again another day, the Maori victors too few, too exhausted, or too diffident to launch any kind of counter-attack. Not so with Titokowaru. At this moment, inside Moturoa pa, came the order 'Kokiritia', and most of the garrison left their defences and went over to the attack. Whitmore had hitherto been striving to take Moturoa and crush Titokowaru. From now on he struggled to preserve his force and prevent Titokowaru crushing him.

The battered assault party, still clinging to its sparse cover close by the pa, was the first to feel the effects. William Newland, having returned from carrying off Hunter's body, noted that:

some of the Rebels had come out of the Pah into the bush on our flank. We were very much exposed to their fire which was very close. One poor fellow was coming to where I was with about a dozen men when he was shot through the chest and fell with blood running from his nose and mouth. I asked two men that were nearest to fetch him but no one seemed inclined to venture [out from cover] so I said 'who will volunteer to come with me' and one man named Brewer said 'I will go with you'. We rushed out and got hold of the wounded man. I had his left arm over my shoulder and my mate the right. We dragged him a few paces when Brewer was shot dead and fell across the man we were helping, so I had to leave them as it was impossible to do anything further. The Rebels were pressing us very closely in great numbers on our flank and trying to cut off our retreat.

Newland felt that his command was in danger of being 'cut to pieces (wiped out)'. It was no use expecting help from Kepa, who had his own problems. Now reinforced from the pa, the party in front of him was no longer content to hold up his outflanking move. Extending to its left further into the bush, it 'threatened to outflank No. 1 A.C. and the Kupapas under Kemp' in their turn. In this crisis, Whitmore kept his nerve. He ordered Kepa to pivot back, so countering the threat of his being outflanked. In Whitmore's military parlance, 'to prevent the enemy turning our flank, we refused our right'. He also ordered up No. 6 division, hoping to extricate the battered assault party with its help.

This order reached John Roberts and his men as they stood in their central position at the south end of the Moturoa clearing, still emptying their breech-loaders into the pa as fast as they could load. To obey it, Roberts had to lead his young recruits out from cover at the edge of the bush and across 300 yards of open ground to support the right wing. Seeing that Cumming was under increasing pressure on the left, Roberts first detached one section to support him. He told the rest of his men to await his order to enter the clearing

John Roberts
From T. W. Gudgeon,
The Defenders of New Zealand

then to 'follow me, and every man for himself until you get across to the other side – don't look behind you!' They made it across with little loss, and formed line, firing steadily. Under this cover of eighty fresh rifles, Whitmore was at last able to extricate the assault party. If Roberts had not come up when he did, wrote O'Halloran, 'the natives would . . . have annihilated us'. Goring's No. 1 division was also withdrawn to the south of the clearing, and Kepa's men soon after began making their way back through the bush to the dray track. Roberts covered the gradual withdrawal of all these units, calling out to his men occasionally: 'Be steady, my men, stick together', and each time a cheery reply "We will, sir." '

But the fate of some of the brave No. 6 constables was anything but cheery. In one of two exceptions to Titokowaru's rule of pressing the retreating enemy as hard as possible while keeping carefully to cover, a small party of warriors charged home against No. 6. They were probably Ngarauru, under Kereopa and Timoti, not yet fully conversant with Titokowaru's methods. They dashed in on Constable Charles Eastwood with tomahawks, cut at him, and tried to carry him off. Instead of firing, Eastwood's comrades tried to wrestle him free in a bizarre tug of war. In doing so, they allowed Ngarauru to escape unpunished for their rashness. Eastwood, without a gunshot wound on him, was picked up by his comrades 'frightfully tomahawked – his head is cut in slices and the expression on his face is something awful his eyes are almost turned in their sockets'. Whitmore tastelessly likened his appearance to that of a 'crimped fish'. A dozen others of No. 6 fell to Ngati Ruanui gunfire.

The second exception to the rule of Maori caution involved Bent's friend, Te Waka. As his comrades rushed out into the bush and the enemy began their retreat, Te Waka is said to have gone into a fit of whakamomori, a berserk disregard of death. According to Bent, he leapt straight over the palisade under the horrified gaze of his sister, Te Haukarewa, and his young son, Ratoia. Whatever the truth of this, the subsequent event is confirmed by the other side. Alone, Te Waka charged straight across the clearing at the colonial forces, getting to within tomahawk-reach of the foe before he was shot dead through the head. His premonition had been self-fulfilling.

On the colonist left, where the brave coward George Cumming and No. 2 constabulary were stationed, more Maori moved from the pa into the bush. As they had done at Te Ngutu, they moved in tiny parties along trackless routes explored and memorised before the battle, always careful not to expose themselves to the Pakeha fire. With no good targets, the best the constabulary could do was fire at the Maori gunsmoke: 'Whenever we saw a puff of smoke we fired at the spot.' In this way, the colonist left struggled 'to keep the Hauhaus from working round through the gully on that side and outflanking us', just as Kepa and Goring did on the right. 'The whole of the force was actively engaged. The enemy now in great force [sic] was enabled to extend his front and threatened to outflank us on the right and left'. The confident colonist attack had become desperate defence, and Whitmore knew the time had come to retreat.

With a few exceptions, there was no fragmentation into small, isolated parties as had happened on the retreat from Te Ngutu two months before. Whitmore kept control of most of his men and organised a textbook retreat. No. 1, No. 6, and Kepa's kupapa alternated as rearguard, one retreating through the other then forming line 150 yards further down the dray track and being retreated through in its turn. Whitmore, used to muzzle-loading weapons, noted 'the terrible rapidity with which the breech-loaders enabled our men to fire'. Most volleys blasted the bush at random but, combined with Titokowaru's orders, they did keep the pursuing Maori to cover. Kepa impressed Whitmore enormously, going back twice to look for wounded, and Roberts and Goring might have come straight from a *Boy's Own Annual*. After a spell commanding the rearguard, Roberts said to Goring: ' "You try this billet for a change". "All right, mate," replied Goring, in his drawling way.'

But the retreat was no promenade. Kepa told Whitmore that no wounded had been left, but he spoke only of his sector of the battlefield. At the front of the retreating column, Newland and the remains of Hunter's assault party knew differently and eventually told Whitmore that many had been left behind – the worst possible blot on a commander's reputation. 'This seemed to astonish him,' wrote Newland. 'He repeated "left behind?" half a dozen times.' For those wounded who were lucky enough to be carried off, there was still agony and danger. Most stretchers had been lost, or left with the swags, and badly injured men again bumped along in terrible pain on rifles. Some became victims of the leading pursuers, who now began to cut through the bush to get behind the main retreat. One party found the first casualty, Edwin Kirwan, and finished the job his own comrade had begun. They also killed three of his bearers – the fourth, David Meldowie, wandered for days lost in the bush, mentally unhinged, living on grass and fleeing from colonists as well as Maori. Another party, led by Kokiri, posed as kupapa and came on to the dray track amidst the retreat. They might have done great damage if Richard Blake had not recognised Kokiri. The Maori van came too close to another stretcher party, carrying a slightly wounded man. 'He jumped out of the stretcher and ran for his life out to the Wairoa Redoubt. The stretcher bearers were too slow for him. He afterwards exchanged into a mounted force.'

At last, the beaten colonists reached the edge of the bush a mile from Wairoa and made for the redoubt. James Livingston, who was acting as quartermaster at Wairoa, came out to help them with a few others. After handing out makeshift stretchers to the wounded, Livingston took post near the earthwork 'to assist the tired men in keeping the devils back'. Kawana Hunia could not bear to remain inactive and he too brought up some men to the earthwork. About 1 pm, the rearguard reached the edge of the bush and ran for a few hundred yards 'so as to get out of range of the bush before it was lined with the enemy'. But the pursuers soon shot three Europeans with a volley at 500 yards' range. Hunia's relative, the

Ngati Apa chief Anita, was shot through the lungs while yelling defiance at the enemy from the earthwork. The retreat, hitherto steady, picked up its pace. The earthwork and the men's swags were abandoned. The pursuers came to within a few hundred yards of the redoubt, burned a house outside it, and withdrew a little only when Whitmore began firing shells from his Armstrong guns.

The last colonists to emerge from the bush were a dozen of No. 2, the one organised group which had become isolated from the rest. Without officers, but ably led by Corporal Hugh Talty and including veterans, Michael Gill, Henry McLean, and William Wallace, this detachment managed to extricate itself from the closing jaws of the Maori pursuit just in time. 'If we had remained a little while longer in the bush', remembered Wallace, 'our small detachment would have been done for as the Maoris were nearly all around us.' They brought out two wounded, but another two men were missing: Constables Anderson and Joseph Savage. It was probably one of these two who was the last to die at the Battle of Moturoa. Cut off from his comrades, he was wandering lost through the bush when he heard Maori coming upon him – Big Kereopa's Ngarauru party, who later told the story to Kimble Bent. The constable feigned dead, but one English-speaking warrior, possibly Kereopa himself (who had had a mission-school education), stopped and looked at him closely. He shook him and said, 'Wake up!' The constable begged for his life and was told, 'Go on your knees and pray to your God to save your life.' He did so, and was asked, 'Well, are you saved now?' Evidently not, for with a cry of 'Say farewell to your God!' the Ngarauru smashed his head with a rifle butt. Mercy, on either side, was a rare commodity in Titokowaru's War.

The colonists, together with the recalcitrant kupapa, still outnumbered Titokowaru several times over, and there was no question of his assaulting Wairoa. About 1.30 pm, he drew off his warriors to Moturoa to mourn Waka and celebrate victory, leaving his enemies to stew in their own juice. Stew they did. With some 800 men crammed into a redoubt built for a hundred, Wairoa was extremely crowded. Whitmore later claimed that his men pressed him to renew the attack, but in reality the mood was grim. There was no collapse of morale comparable to that after Te Ngutu, but losses were equally heavy – between fifty and sixty – and the defeat nearly as comprehensive. Titokowaru now seemed invincible. A few men lost their nerve completely. Many were upset at having lost their personal gear in the swags left at the edge of the bush – bedding, diaries, miniatures of loved ones, as well as reserve ammunition. Livingston and Putnam, for their different reasons, had retained their diaries. 'Every person in bad spirits,' wrote the former, while the latter listed his dead friends and reflected that the morning's decision had been wise if not glorious.

After a night in which the Maori spared time from their celebrations to rouse Wairoa three times with volleys, Whitmore and his sleepless troops marched off to Patea at 6 am, leaving the Wairoa Rifles again to garrison the redoubt alone. Whitmore maintained that he left because he had to get the wounded to hospital quickly, but they had actually been sent separately at 4 pm the previous day. Perhaps the truth was that the walls of Wairoa could not contain his whole force for long and he now felt that walls were needed.

Whitmore reached Patea at noon on 8 November, found the *Sturt* about to depart, and had hastily to write a report for it to take. Throughout the afternoon he struggled with the task, just as McDonnell had done at Camp Waihi two months before. He was twice interrupted by Newland, who wished to take Hunter's body to Wanganui for burial aboard the *Sturt* – a very ill-timed request. Whitmore sent Newland packing in no uncertain terms. The despatch, and the private letter to Haultain which accompanied it, was Whitmore's own curious mixture of fairness and fortitude, hypocrisy and venom. He offered Haultain his resignation, he refused to blame his Pakeha troops, and he gave Kepa the most generous praise. But he understated his casualties by half, and ten days later was still expressing the hope that some of the killed were merely lost and would turn up. Privately, he complained about Cumming, Fraser, and even Roberts, and he was later to describe the importunate Sub-Inspector Newland as 'a big girl [who] should not be ever made an inspector'. He reserved most of his venom for the kupapa, and the original despatch fairly sizzles with accusations, somewhat toned down in the published version: 'Bullying and insolent and braggart as Hunia has always been where he dared, on this occasion he had no voice to speak.' The kupapa were to blame for the defeat, he insisted. Their motive was not his own clumsy interference with tribal politics but either treachery or cowardice. He inclined to the latter, 'rather than treachery or anything experience might detect'. That evening, this schizoid despatch went south in the *Sturt*, along with the dead Hunter and the living Newland, who managed to get his way in the end.

Whitmore had no illusions about the military situation, though he had some about its causes. He concluded that, until greatly reinforced, he could do no more than protect Wanganui's immediate hinterland south of the Waitotara. 'I shall cover the settled districts,' he told Haultain, 'and protect Weraroa, and hope that recruits may arrive.' On 9 November, he left Patea and marched south to Nukumaru, eighteen miles from Wanganui. His force was only 250 strong, for he had left Fraser to garrison Patea with 200, and the kupapa, including Kepa, now left for home. A fortnight before, Whitmore had criticised Fraser for keeping his troops behind trenches at Patea. Now he too began to entrench.

Titokowaru and his people remained at Moturoa for four days, recuperating and giving thanks as they had after Te Ngutu. Again one Pakeha corpse was cooked, but this time only Kereopa and ten newly joined Ngarauru ate of it, possibly as a kind of initiation. They did so at their own insistence: 'Titokowaru did not like this man-eating,' remembered Tu-Patea. There was no longer any need for it. Bent, who did not like Kereopa, remembered that the latter seemed to enjoy the human flesh, and one can imagine the huge warrior choosing to give the nervous renegade that impression. On 11 November, in the familiar strategy of taking up the slack left by his retreating enemies, Titokowaru advanced to Papatupu on the Waitotara. Here he commenced negotiation with the remaining Ngarauru, beginning a process which was to double his force within a month.

The senior Ngarauru chiefs were still reluctant to join. Pehimana and Hare Tipene went off to their upriver refuge of Piraunui. Aperahama Tamaiparea stayed in Titokowaru's camp for some days, but 'although Titokowaru sent for him three or four times, he refused to go to him'. Aperahama then went to his Whanganui relatives, at Putiki, where he reported all this to James Booth. But the senior chiefs were followed by very few of their people. Apart from these, said Aperahama, 'all the Ngarauru have joined'. Some joined Kereopa in Titokowaru's ranks immediately; others, under Uru Te Angina, the senior remaining chief, promised to follow shortly, and they kept their word.

This may have added seventy or eighty warriors to Titokowaru's following, and Moturoa brought in as many recruits again from other sources. 'Very wonderful reports of Titokowaru's successes are sent through the country,' bemoaned Robert Parris. The major contributors were Atiawa, Taranaki, and Ngati Maru. The chiefs of Te Atiawa, including Wiremu Kingi Te Rangitake and Hapurona, confirmed their

wish for peace in their territory at a meeting later in November
– Te Rangitake threw a proffered taiaha over a cliff into the Waitara
River to symbolise his feelings. But they could not stop small groups
leaving for the south and perhaps they did not wish to. Among
Taranaki, Te Whiti was still firmly for peace, but his partner, Tohu
Kakahi, may have been less adamant, because at least one family
which acknowledged him as chief joined Titokowaru's ranks. Peace
at home and war at a distance was an old game in Anglo-Maori
conflict. The small Ngati Maru tribe, linked to Ngaruahine by inter-
marriage, sent most of their warriors. Titokowaru's following soon
grew to nearly 1,000 people, including 400 warriors – perhaps half
Ngati Ruanui, a quarter Ngarauru, and a quarter Ngati Maru,
Taranaki, Atiawa, and individuals from other tribes, including several
Ngati Maniapoto and Waikato. In South Taranaki terms, this was
now an army. Since many warriors were accompanied by their
families, it might even be called a people in arms.

Meanwhile, the *Sturt* made its way south, discharging one grim
cargo, Hunter's corpse, at Wanganui and reaching Wellington with
the other, Whitmore's report, on 10 November. Its impact can be
imagined. Haultain ordered the Defence Department to redouble its
recruiting efforts. District militia commanders were stung into
renewed activity with telegrams like 'I am not satisfied with your
want of energy in this matter', and Captain Stack was sent to
Melbourne to buy modern Snider carbines and recruit 200 men. He
and the Victorian police were to get one pound each for every man
who proved effective after six months. Leaving James Richmond to
handle these efforts, Haultain turned the *Sturt* around and set off
for the front himself, arriving at Nukumaru on 12 November.

Whitmore was no friend to subordinacy, but he confessed that
in this crisis the defence minister's stolid presence was a comfort,
particularly when hard decisions had to be made. Haultain did bring
some good news. A fresh division of armed constabulary, No. 7,
under Michie Brown, had arrived in Wanganui 120 strong and would
be up that night; forty-one more constabulary recruits were on the
way from Hokitika and Greymouth, and others were due soon. These
troops were good but raw, and the hard decisions remained.
Titokowaru was on the move, Wanganui itself was in real danger,
and the three outposts – Patea, Wairoa, and Weraroa – could not
all be maintained. The two leaders seriously considered abandoning
Patea, so recently the base of operations. They sent Cumming up
in the *Woodpecker*, hired to supplement the *Sturt*, to evacuate

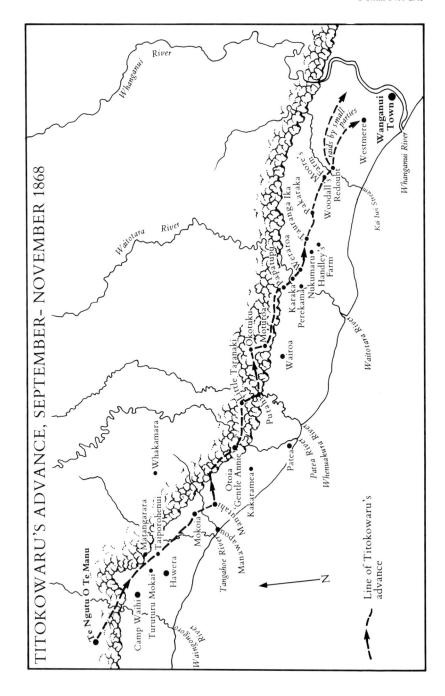

TITOKOWARU'S ADVANCE, SEPTEMBER– NOVEMBER 1868

Whanganui River

Waitotara River

Waitotara River

raids by small parties

Wanganui Town

Westmere

Woodall's Redoubt

Moore's Farm

Kai Iwi Stream

Whanganui River

Paakakaraka

Taumaranga Ika

Weraroa

Karaka

Nukumaru

Handley's Farm

Perekama

Papatupu

Okotuku

Moturoa

Wairoa

Little Taranaki

Putahi

Patea River

Whenuakura

Patea

Waitotara River

Otoia

Gentle Annie

Kakaramea

Manutahi

Manawapou

Tangahoe River

Mokoia

Matangarara

Taiporohenui

Whakamara

Hawera

Turuturu Mokai

Camp Waihi

Te Ngutu O Te Manu

Waingongoro River

N

Line of Titokowaru's advance

government property, including the two Armstrong guns, together with the remaining women and children. 'So Patea is doomed,' concluded Livingston. And they decided to evacuate Weraroa.

Titokowaru was indeed on the move. After only a couple of days at Papatupu setting the process of recruitment in train, he sent out The Twelve in his usual tactic of masking the movement of his main force with raids elsewhere. On the night of 12-13 November, The Twelve burned a half-finished blockhouse outside the Weraroa redoubt, slaughtered some stock, and exchanged shots with the garrison. Captain Wilmot Powell and his fifty Wanganui militia blasted the black bush with heavy volleys for five hours, long after the Maori had gone. On 14 November, Titokowaru's whole army arrived at Nukumaru, burned the local farmhouses while the colonists huddled in their entrenchments, and began building a new pa, Tauranga Ika, barely a mile from Whitmore's position.

Before this, Friday 13 November had proved black indeed for Haultain and Whitmore. In the midst of their struggles to contain one disaster, they received news of another. Three days before, on the East Coast, Te Kooti had raided Poverty Bay in the dead of night, slaughtering young and old, men and women, Maori and Pakeha. Terrible tales of the attack, some of them true, were sweeping the colony, and McLean and the Hawke's Bay settlers were blaming the government and demanding immediate help. Haultain and Whitmore decided to hasten and extend their planned withdrawal. Newland was sent to Weraroa and given ten minutes to clear out the garrison. He found Powell and his men about to dine and eager to describe their feats of the previous night. 'There is no time for eating, get your men and their swags outside,' ordered Newland, 'I am going to burn the tents!' Burn them he did, along with ammunition, rations, and supplies of all kinds. Peyman, the canteen keeper, tearing his hair at the loss of £1,000 worth of goods, locked himself into his store. Newland, prompted by word that 'Col. Whitmore was in a devil of a way as I had been longer than I should have been', smashed down the door and had him forcibly removed.

On Sunday 15 November, Whitmore abandoned Nukumaru as well and fell back behind the Kai Iwi to Woodall's redoubt, an old Imperial post only nine miles from Wanganui. As the troops held the first church parade at their new base, Titokowaru's pursuing vanguard fired a long-range volley at them and the presiding parson, the Reverend Elmslie, fell to the ground. All thought him hit, but he had only fainted from the shock – a reaction which symbolised that

of the colony. Three days later, Maori raiders struck south of the
Kai Iwi to the fringes of Wanganui itself, burning six farmhouses
within five miles of the town. John Cameron of Marangai and other
settlers south of Wanganui, 'after living in what is considered the
safest part of the district', began digging escape tunnels, fortifying
their woolsheds, and building private blockhouses, 'loop-holed, musket
bullet proof and fireproof'. The less wealthy or well positioned fled
into town. 'Whitmore doesn't seem to be doing any better than
McDonnell did,' wrote Cameron to his old crony, Charles Rookes.
'Tito Kowaru's headquarters is now at the Pakaraka, and if he goes
on at this rate he will soon be in Wanganui . . . in short Rookes
the whole place is going to the devil.'

As fuller information came in from the East Coast during succeeding
days, both Whitmore and Haultain concluded that the situation there,
terrible though it might be, was less serious than that in the west.
Outside Hawke's Bay, the press and public tended to agree: 'The
stoppages of success on the East may be vexatious and galling, but
the continuance of failure . . . on the West Coast is simply humiliating.'
Poverty Bay was a raid, which did not endanger Napier. Moturoa
was a lost battle, which did threaten Wanganui. Titokowaru's men
had come within five miles of the town, and if they attacked it they
might. multiply the horrors of Poverty Bay a hundredfold. But
Whitmore no longer had confidence in his ability to defeat Titokowaru
with his present force: 'I feel strongly that the district from Wanganui
to Patea is far from being one in which a rapid success is probable.
The force required needs more discipline, and more training, and
perhaps more numbers than anywhere else.' Whitmore felt it would
be easier to defeat Te Kooti. He therefore came up with a secret
plan: at the beginning of December, the best of the field force would
suddenly be shifted to the East Coast. There, they would crush Te
Kooti while the growing flow of constabulary recruits assembled,
trained, and stood on the defensive at Wanganui. Then Whitmore
would rejoin them with his crack troops and the expanded force
would overwhelm Titokowaru. Haultain accepted the plan, with
considerable hesitation. He was concerned about the defence of
Wanganui and insisted Whitmore leave ample troops to hold the
newly contracted defensive line and that he return from Napier
promptly. If not, he warned, 'I shall say you have failed in your
promises, and have no right to expect me to believe you again.'

As yet, the Wanganui settlers knew nothing of this. But they did
know of disaster at Moturoa, massacre at Poverty Bay, retreat to

THREE MINISTERIAL WITCHES.

" Hail ! Tito, King of the Cannibal Islands ; hail ! all hail !"

·Tɪᴛᴏ : " Ye should be women ; and yet your beards forbid me to interpret that you are so."

Titokowaru as Macbeth. The witches, from left, caricature Haultain, Stafford, and James Richmond *From Punch, or the Auckland Charivari, Vol. 1.*

Nukumaru, and now this fresh flight to the Kai Iwi itself, and they were frightened and enraged. Like McDonnell before him, Whitmore was blamed and his unpopularity reached new heights. Making 'No Whitmore' placards became a minor industry in Wanganui, as it was soon to do in Napier, and one of his own soldiers wrote: 'There is a wonderful unanimity of opinion here about Colonel Whitmore; not only the men but the officers agree that he is a perfect donkey without brains to plan or execute and utterly incompetent for an important command.' Beneath this torrent of blame ran a sub-stratum of shock and fear. It was difficult to understand how a distant frontier war had arrived at their very doorstep.

James Booth, who in his days of confidence had done much to bring the war about, now wrote to his brother in England:

We have had a succession of disasters, we have given up one post after another, almost every house in the district is burnt and all our best officers, some of

The 'Heroes of Weraroa' in later life   *Wanganui Museum*

*them my particular friends, have been killed in several engagements we have
had with the enemy who is now threatening the town of Wanganui . . . It
is a dreadful thing to see young fellows knocked over as I have seen them
. . . I shall write more fully next mail if spared.*

And on 17 November, the *Wanganui Times* waxed still more lyrical
in despair:

*From Waihi and the line of the Waingongoro . . . where little more than
three months ago a flame was lighted which has burst into such a dreadful
conflagration . . . down to the Kaiiwi as our boundary, is a transformation
sufficient to make men of British name and lineage almost question their identity.
The very idea of such a thing would have been scouted as simply preposterous.
The greatest alarmist, the most faint-hearted of croakers, could not have dreamed
of a retrogression so great. Where is it to end?*

The sole gleam of light had been Powell's defence of Weraroa
on 13 November. It was a false dawn – there remains no real evidence
of any Maori casualties. But the Wanganui press was determined
that Powell and his townsmen-in-arms should not miss out on the
heroic status that had eluded Colin McDonnell two weeks before.
Large headlines announced the repulse of a fully fledged assault. 'Traces
of bodies dragged through the fern', 'pools of blood', and 'great clots

of gore' proved that four Maori had been killed and precisely eighteen wounded. Weraroa, Wanganui's main bastion, had been held against the odds. It was the much-maligned Wanganui militia, brayed the newspapers, which had been 'the first to give the Hauhau a check in this miserable war!' Then, the very day after their triumph, Haultain had abruptly withdrawn Powell and his heroes and abandoned Weraroa to the enemy.

Whitmore might have been pleased to see Haultain, but he was the only one. When the Defence Minister returned to Wanganui from the new front along the Kai Iwi, he was received as warmly as a murderer at his victim's funeral. He and his colleagues, wrote John Ballance, 'have shut their eyes to the danger of the situation. The force is too weak to hold the country and there is at the present time nothing to prevent Titoko Waru from coming to Wanganui. He can pack his bags and make the journey in a single day.' Wanganui thought he had done so on the night of 15 November, when the alarm was raised and panicking men and women rushed through the dark streets with their children to the York and Rutland stockades. The alarm was false, but it made the settlers feel no more kindly towards Haultain. When Ballance proposed a motion of no confidence in him to a large public meeting, it was passed unanimously. Superintendent Featherston wrote that the abandonment of Weraroa had left the town at Titokowaru's mercy: 'How long will the colony submit to such imbecility,' he asked. One wit put the whole matter in verse, borrowing his metre if not his sentiments from 'The Young Lochinvar'.

H--LT--N, M.H.R.

Oh, the great Col. H--lt--n's come down to the west
In all our grand army his place is the best,
He has payment in plenty, and fighting has none,
And can live in the quarters he loves – Wellington.
One thing is quite certain, no people in war
E'er had chief in command like H--lt--n, M.H.R.

He's a stickler for form, and a lover of place;
Thinks retreating is strategy, never disgrace:
And though officers fret, and though soldiers may fume,
Unless Mr. Tito Kowaru will come
To a fair fighting ground free of bank, bush, and scour,
He'll never be seen by H--lt--n, M.H.R.

So boldly he landed, he came in the 'Sturt',
'Mong settlers and soldiers, Kupapas and dirt;
And directly he got here, although it was late,
He ordered old Wh--tm--e at once to vacate
An outpost – the troops there were rather too far
From the town to protect great H--lt--n, M.H.R.

And this morning they got sharp orders to 'clear',
To set fire to the tents, and to scuttle the beer;
To burn up the blankets, flour, sugar, and gear.
And leave two drays behind as a slight souvenir
So they did it, and left the old Warera pa:
Won't they run fast that catch old H--lt--n, M.H.R.

There was mounting 'mong chiefs of the Kupapa clan,
And the Yeomanry cavalry rode and they ran:
There was racing and chasing to Wanganui,
But the ghost of a Hauhau did nobody see.
So quick in retreating, so careful in war –
Was there EVER a chief like H--lt--n, M.H.R.?

Chapter Ten

HANDLEY'S WOOLSHED

Wilmot Powell came close to becoming the Hero of Weraroa, but he did not come close enough, and nearly twenty years later he too was to try his hand at heroic poetry, with even less success. He recalled 'jocund hours' with old comrades once 'full of bounding life':

> No thought of danger checked their fiery zeal
> With flashing eye, and agile bounding step,
> O'er many a gory stricken field they trod.
> Along the gloomy path, they tracked the foe.
> The deadly, echoing volley, and the ringing cheer,
> Resounded through the woods and told of victory.

Powell listed 'the fearless Ross', 'Von Tempsky, the bravest of the brave', 'Hunter, Hastings, Buck and Palmer too', none of whom had heard much victory resounding through the woods in this war. But the most prominent, and the only non-officer in Powell's pantheon of heroes, was a young Manutahi farmer named George Maxwell:

> Again and last of all, on fair Kaiiwi's heights
> Young Maxwell sped, fit type of border chivalry.

George Maxwell was born in 1842 in the Scots border county of Clackmannanshire. His forebears had no doubt raided deep into England with the Black Douglas, much as Ngati Ruanui now ravaged the Wanganui hinterland – hence Powell's reference to 'border chivalry'. He had emigrated to New Zealand at the age of nine and settled in the Kai Iwi district with his parents and two sisters. In 1867 he bought his own farm at Manutahi – confiscated Pakakohe land – and there he worked hard, saw a great deal of his friends, including Diston Ginger, and occasionally 'got jolly well drunk'. Popular, convivial, and endearing, he does not seem the type who would split a child's head with a cavalry sabre.

Maxwell had so far served out the war on garrison duty with the Patea militia. He had had little opportunity to distinguish himself, and this was something he was very eager to do. It is said that he and his mates, Arthur and Henry Wright, were enamoured of the same girl and wished to outdo each other in impressing her. But Maxwell had also watched a year's hard work go up in smoke when The Twelve burned his house at Manutahi on 29 September. And he had lost friends: David Cahill, brained with his own mallet in the first killing of the war; Frederick Ross, Powell's 'fearless Ross', whose heart had been cut out for the Whangai Hau by fearless Taruhae at Turuturu Mokai, and seventeen-year-old Richard Wallace, who had bled to death in his brother William's arms at Te Ngutu o te Manu.

Maxwell had lived through the aftermath of the crushing defeat at Te Ngutu and had returned south to his parents' home when Titokowaru conquered his own district. After Moturoa, he became part of the new Wanganui war effort, for Wanganui Town was finally standing to arms. Haultain had decided to remove the main obstacle to Wanganui Pakeha co-operation: Edward Gorton. He was promoted inspector of stores and continued to act as quartermaster general. But to the delight of the Wanganui settlers he was replaced as commander of the militia district by his adjutant, Major Maillard Noake, an ex-officer (actually a riding master, though he preferred not to stress this) of the 1st Dragoon Guards who had charged at both Balaclava and Chartist demonstrations. Haultain went further. The New Zealand settlers had long believed, with a splendid disregard for both fact and probability, that left to themselves they were superior Maori-fighters to regulars, Imperial or colonial. The Wanganui settlers were no exception, and now Haultain called their bluff. On 23 November he authorised the enrolment of the 'Bushranging Volunteers' at a shilling a day more than militia pay, with a five-pound-a-head bounty for live enemies brought in, 'whether such prisoners be wounded or not'. 'A special reward of £1,000 is promised to the corps for the person of Titokowaru.' This was to get the colony into trouble with the Imperial government, which disapproved of bounty-hunting, but at the time it had precisely no effect. Haultain later explained he did it only 'to silence some Wanganui Braggadacio's, who declared they were ready to form themselves into a corps, to scout in front of the Troops, if only sufficient encouragement was offered them. I need hardly say the offer was not accepted.' And indeed the Wanganui Bushranging Volunteers were stillborn. Haultain had somewhat better luck with the militia, detachments of which now began to build and man the blockhouses that were part of Whitmore's plan to protect the Kai Iwi line in his absence. Service in volunteer units was preferred, and the Wanganui Veteran

The Wanganui militia, in uniform at last   *Wanganui Museum*

Volunteers under Captain Thomas Kells, eventually 200 strong, was the most notable among the infantry. But the major success, the most important Wanganui contribution to Titokowaru's War, was two corps of cavalry.

The first was Captain William Finnimore's Wanganui Cavalry Volunteers, about seventy strong, of which John Ballance became cornet for a time. The other was the Kai Iwi Cavalry, commanded by Lieutenant John Bryce, a tactless but determined man of thirty-five who had already done quite well at farming and politics and was to do even better. He had served previously in volunteer cavalry, and his old commander described him as 'the dirtiest and most negligent trooper we ever had'. George Maxwell was 'unanimously elected' sergeant. The Wanganui unit had been formed in July, and the Kai Iwi in October, but it was not until the aftermath of Moturoa that they saw action.

The volunteer cavalry elected their own officers and, in the main, they equipped themselves. It cost up to thirty pounds for a good horse, five pounds fifteen shillings for a carbine, six pounds eighteen shillings for a revolver, and eighteen shillings four and three-quarter pence for a curved, heavy cavalry sabre. The cavalry was therefore an upper- and middle-class affair and, for these young bloods, the war was quite fun. Off duty, they played cricket, rounders, and cards

John Bryce
Harding Denton Collection,
Alexander Turnbull Library

– sometimes the whole night long – and they drank. 'Several of the
Troop have been going about half drunk with swollen eyes and flaming
faces.' But they also drilled enthusiastically and had a real *esprit de
corps*. Even Whitmore was rather pleased with them, and after Moturoa
they were a godsend to him. He now desperately needed cavalry
to keep open communication with Patea and Wairoa, to give
information on Titokowaru's movements, and to patrol the newly
contracted Wanganui defences against raiders. The mounted
constabulary had 'dwindled to almost nothing' and Whitmore thought
little of their commander, William Newland. Finnimore, on the other
hand, was 'an officer of great smartness and high promise', and
although Bryce might lack his colleague's smartness he too was 'a
most intelligent officer (who always seems to be right in his reading
of Maori designs)'. Their men, 'splendidly mounted and gaily dressed',
were 'raw but good', and 'seem quite willing to do their share, but

I'd be glad if they'd drink and boast less'. They were, wrote Whitmore, 'almost too eager'.

The Kai Iwi cavalry were called out for full-time service on 18 November, but it was not until the afternoon of Wednesday 25 November that they had notice of their first major mission: 'the troop received orders to be saddled up at midnight for a night expedition, the object of which was kept secret'. They were to accompany the remaining mounted constabulary under Newland, who learned the purpose of the expedition in an uncomfortable interview with Whitmore at Woodall's redoubt. Whitmore needed to know the condition of the garrison of Wairoa so that he could decide whether to resupply it or evacuate it before leaving for the East Coast. There had been no communication with Wairoa for more than two weeks, and Newland was to go 'to see whether the people there were dead or alive'. Newland was vaguely aware of Whitmore's low opinion of him, and he wished to prove himself. He nervously asked permission to return by way of Nukumaru to see if Titokowaru was still there. Whitmore agreed.

The twenty-fifth of November happened to be Maxwell's twenty-sixth birthday, and preparations for the expedition put paid to any planned festivities. But he was no doubt pleased at the prospect of action and correspondingly disappointed when heavy rain postponed the expedition. Next day, however, the weather was better and the sixty-six-strong cavalry column set off from Woodall's redoubt at midnight. There were two dozen mounted constables, tough veterans such as Frank Shortt and Tom Lister, then a corporal but subsequently to be demoted to constable, third class, for unknown misdemeanours. There was also an Italian who went by the name of Blyth – perhaps the 'Italian of rank who, with a desire to hide his identity, passed under a very common English name'. Newland's second-in-command was Captain George O'Halloran who, with his few remaining Patea yeomanry, had been incorporated into the armed constabulary as part of Whitmore's reorganisation. O'Halloran had recently been the victim of one of Dr Samuel Walker's practical jokes. Untimely sun on 10 November had peeled the skin off his nose and Walker had given him an ointment which turned the tip 'quite black, nor would soap and water have any effect'. His superiors and subordinates had been exercising their wit about this, and O'Halloran for one was grateful for the darkness.

The remainder of Newland's force were Kai Iwi cavalry, including Arthur Wicksteed, a Wanganui militia lieutenant serving as a private

'Newland's Cavalry' *Taranaki Museum*

trooper; Cornet Roland Garrett, a surveyor and engineer; twenty-
three-year-old William Lingard, slightly deaf and very brave, and
fifteen-year-old trumpeter, John Wallace. The rest was rather a family
affair: Bryce's brothers-in-law, George and Allan Campbell; the three
Peake brothers, George, H.L., and John; the rather pompous young
diarist Moore Hunter and his brother Andrew, and his 'two very
intelligent mates Mr Kirk and Mr Hammond'. Maxwell's particular
friends were two more sets of brothers: Robert, James, and Tom
Morgan, and Liber and Arthur Wright. Robert Morgan wa a deft
hand with scissors – he regularly cut Maxwell's hair – and Maxwell
was a frequent visitor to the Morgan family home at Brunswick,
drawn by a female sibling, 'Miss Morgan', as well as by his three
male friends. The Wrights were sons of George Wright, a Brunswick
settler with extravagant whims. Poor Liber was living monument
to the moment when his father 'stepped ashore on the Wanganui
river bank [and] threw his hands in the air with the exclamation
"Liberty" . . . when his son was born he had him named "Liber".'
According to Moore Hunter, Liber managed to become 'a quiet good
natured cool and collected young lad'. Two more Wright brothers,
George and Henry, were in the Wanganui Cavalry Volunteers. They
were much older than Arthur and Liber, who at seventeen and sixteen

weie, with John Wallace, the youngest troopers in the unit by several years – mere boys.

The expedition reached Wairoa about 8 am without seeing any Maori. They found Robert Hawes and his garrison in fair spirits, considering the recent disaster at nearby Moturoa. Apart from the occasional false alarm and exchange of shots with Maori scouts, their worst problem was that some salt pork had gone bad, leaving them with only nine days' meat. At noon the two forces had 'a good dinner' together, reducing the Wairoa meat supplies still further. About 1 pm, the cavalry set off on their return journey. Not wishing to give the impression that he was too concerned for his comfort, Newland falsified their time of departure as 11 am in his report to Whitmore. The column retraced its route to the Waitotara River, passing the burned-out shell of Sherwood's Hotel at its mouth. Newland then turned inland into the sand hills toward Nukumaru, according to his arrangement with Whitmore. This was harder going and it was late afternoon before the column approached Titokowaru's position.

They reined in near 'The Soldiers' Graves', the spot where Cameron's men killed in the battle of January 1865 had been buried. A final ridge of sand hills blocked their view inland. They were now on Handley land – the model farm created by John Handley senior in 1866–7 after a successful career as a Wanganui builder. On these fertile Nukumaru acres Handley grew oats, wheat and potatoes, pastured sheep and horses, and kept pigs and geese. He also built to last: a comfortable homestead, substantial fencing, and a corrugated-iron woolshed. For all this, however, his farm had not recently been a happy place. Handley himself was killed in 1867 when one of his horses fell on him, and his wife died the day before Titokowaru's War broke out. His elder son, William, had the farm and his younger son, John junior, now rode as sergeant with the colonist cavalry. While the column waited behind the toetoe-covered sand ridge, Newland sent John Handley up to the top with Frank Shortt to reconnoitre. They clambered over the post-and-rail fence enclosing the Soldiers' Graves and gazed out over the farm. Below them and to their right were the ruins of the farmhouse, burned by the Maori two weeks before. To the right of that was the iron woolshed, still standing, with a sheep pen between it and a little lake fringed with bush and toetoe-covered swamp. North of all this stretched well-fenced fields and paddocks, and beyond them the ground rose to Titokowaru's new base, Tauranga Ika.

Tauranga Ika was a place of celebration on 27 November. A contingent of Ngarauru, led by Uru Te Angina, had arrived that morning from Perekama to join their kin in Titokowaru's ranks. The formal welcome had occurred that morning, and Titokowaru had quickly made Uru's people tangata whenua – no longer manuhiri, or guests, but part of the new community at war. The able-bodied men and women were all working together preparing food for a great feast. Except for a few scouts, the patrols and foraging parties had been called in for the festivities. There had been no sign of the demoralised Pakeha outside their fortifications for two weeks, but Titokowaru had not forgotten military precautions. That morning he had sent a double agent, a Ngarauru named Rimitiriu, to Woodall's redoubt to offer his services to Whitmore as a spy. Two mounted scouts were riding along the Kai Iwi–Weraroa road below the Soldiers' Graves at this moment, and the warrior Tawa Te Amo remembered that 'General Titokowaru had given orders to the elders not to scatter, but to keep together'. But, as ever, this discipline did not extend to children. 'The children did not know anything about these orders,' said Tawa, 'they did not apply to them.'

For the children it was an exciting day: the moving rituals of welcome, the prospect of a feast, and scores of new faces to befriend or patronise. After a while, several Ngati Ruanui, Taranaki, and Atiawa boys, blasé veterans of the war trial, made friends with some Ngarauru newcomers, and offered to show them the delights of the neighbourhood. Two of the Ngarauru boys, Whakarua Te Karihi, 'a good-sized lad', and Poharama Takarangi did not go. At all of thirteen or fourteen, they had reached puberty and been issued with weapons, and it was beneath their dignity to accompany the youngsters. 'They were children,' said Whakarua proudly, 'we were their elders and fit to fight.' But Poharama's brother Ihaka, about nine years old, and two or three other young Ngarauru, set off from Tauranga Ika with their new friends.

To Handley and Shortt, all this was no more than a vague hive of activity in the distance, but like good scouts they took note of what they could. Tauranga Ika stood on higher ground, in a horseshoe-shaped recess in dense bush, with a good view of the surrounding country. Since arriving to confront Whitmore at Nukumaru on 14 November, the Maori had worked hard on the place, and it was already a viable fighting pa, although not yet the engineering masterpiece it was to become. Most of the defences were concealed, and Handley and Shortt could not see them. They described Tauranga

Ika as a camp – to them its most prominent features were six large bell tents, probably Gorton's government issue. But they did see the two mounted scouts 'riding very slowly' along the track below them with more government plunder in the form of breech-loading carbines over their shoulders. Handley and Shortt slid and scrambled back down the slope to tell Newland.

With O'Halloran, Bryce, and Garrett, Newland now climbed up to the graveyard to have a look for himself. Encumbered by spurs and riding boots, the officers 'crept up the rise among the Fern and rushes keeping out of sight from the front'. Newland reluctantly concluded that there was no chance of catching the enemy scouts. Newland inspected Tauranga Ika for some minutes, and then he and the other officers returned to the column and recommenced the homeward journey. With luck's consent, that would have been that. The column slowly picked its way across the sand and scrub on the seaward side of the ridge, passing the points parallel to the woolshed, the pa, and the lake in succession. Then, about one mile from the graveyard, they 'heard Pigs squealing not far away'.

Meanwhile, Ihaka Takarangi and his companions ran down the slope from Tauranga Ika, a dozen strong. The tallest and eldest was Kingi Takatua, 'a stout boy' of about ten, possibly connected to both Ngaruahine and Taranaki – Titokowaru and Tohu Kakahi are listed as his chiefs. Kingi alone was close to puberty. 'It was only Kingi who showed signs of a few hairs about his person.' Akuhata Herewini was a much smaller, younger boy, a Pakakohe related to Ngawaka Taurua. His father, Herewini, had fallen at the Battle of Te Ngaio in 1865, whereas both Kingi's parents were in Tauranga Ika. Other Ngati Ruanui boys in the party were Hoani Tamou, Tonu, and Wi Taria, and there was one unnamed Atiawa, almost as tall as Kingi – between four foot and four foot-six inches. Apart from Ihaka, there were at least two other Ngarauru: Pehira Toheriri, a very small boy aged between six and eight, and Poharama Ngarutahi. Poharama wore a shirt and a blue coat, which he remembered proudly. The others wore shirts, some made from sacks in the manner of European peasants, and serge garments made from blankets which could be worn as either shawls or kilts. These had replaced dressed flax as what was commonly described as 'Maori mats'. That was it. 'No trousers, no boots, and no hats,' said Ihaka emphatically. The practice was to wear trousers only after puberty, and not one of the boys had reached that stage. Accordingly, none had weapons, though a few had pocket knives. There may have been one exception in the form of a tomahawk carried by Kingi Takatua. But ten Maori eyewitness accounts deny that there were any weapons, and Kingi's tomahawk, if it existed, may have been a toy.

After descending the slope, the boys ran across Handley's grass at the northern end of the flat ground, and then slowed right down as they clambered over the fence which Handley had built to keep his horses from the ripening wheat and the swampy ground on the southern and western sides. It was a solid affair, a ditch, bank, and gorse hedge which few horses could jump. They were veering left towards the lake, intending to swim, when someone noticed a few pigs and geese by the woolshed. These animals must have evaded the foragers who burned Handley's house and dug up his potatoes by hiding in the swamp and bush by the lake. Now they had come out for food. The excited boys sped towards them, but both geese and pigs were now wary, and all escaped bar one fat sow. This the boys managed to corner. While some struggled to open its belly, Ihaka Takarangi and Pehira Toheriri climbed on to the roof of the woolshed, 'simply for child's sport', in little Pehira's words: 'I clambered up with the assistance of a piece of timber.' With pocket knives, inexpert butchers, and a 150-pound sow, the pig-killing was a gruesome business, and the dying animal squealed lustily.

It was this sound that was heard by the colonists. Newland halted the column, dismounted, and clambered up the sand ridge for the second time with Bryce. When they reached the top and took in the scene at the woolshed below them, now over half a mile to their left, they saw 'some figures in the potato paddock' next to the woolshed. At this distance they could make out little detail, but they were obviously Maori from Tauranga Ika, and their party seemed small. Newland said to Bryce, 'This is good enough. We will have a go in here.' After scrambling back down he ordered the column to return the way it had come, to a point about 500 yards distant where he had noticed a gap in the ridge. 'Captain Newland . . . ordered the return of the troopers as quietly as possible,' remembered Frank Shortt, 'telling the men not to allow their sword scabbards to hit their stirrup irons, or otherwise make a noise.' With excitement mounting, the cavalry retraced their steps.

They reached the gap in the ridge and could now see the woolshed almost directly below them and only 420 yards away. Bryce wished to charge immediately, but Newland decided to fire a volley first – a mistake. The range was still too great for really effective shooting and it would give premature warning. While the remainder held the horses, he ordered most of his men to dismount and proceed down to a fence at the bottom of the woolshed side of the sand ridge 'for the purpose of shooting them'. As they did so, some of the boys saw them at last. One said, 'Look, those are Maoris coming down.' Another corrected him: 'No, they are Europeans.' All the boys peered intently at the figures in the scrub and some said, 'Yes, perhaps.' At that instant, a single shot rang out, followed by a crashing volley. After a split second of stunned silence – 'none of [us] were fit to fight, and we were very much frightened when we heard the [dis]charge of guns' – the boys fled for the distant pa. Ihaka and Pehira were delayed by the need to clamber from the roof of the woolshed, but only slightly: 'We tumbled down as fast as we could,' remembered Pehira, 'whether we hurt ourselves or not.'

As they deployed to fire their volley, the cavalry had a fair view of their targets. They could see Ihaka or Pehira (some did not see both) on the roof of the woolshed, and several later admitted that one was a 'young fellow, apparently about 15'. After they fired, and the boys began running for their lives, their youth and lack of weapons was quite evident. James Carroll saw 'four Maoris on the sea-ward side of the wood-shed . . . One was rather a small one. He was 11, 12, or 13 years of age. He could not be more.' Asked whether the figures he fired at were 'Fighting Maories', John Handley replied, 'No, it struck me that they were children – big and small boys.' Here was an easy target, and the troopers did not wait for orders. Handley recalled, 'I said they do not seem to have any guns. I jumped on my pony, threw down my carbine and sword belt. I galloped off in pursuit', closely followed by George Maxwell. Jostling each other in their excitement, the Kai Iwi cavalry ran for their horses, mounted, and charged in for the kill, not despite the fact that their quarry were unarmed children, but because of it.

From a drill-sergeant's viewpoint, the charge was a sorry affair. Newland may not have intended to charge at all, and there were certainly no officers in the leading groups. There were no ordered ranks: 'whoever got his horse came away.' Several did not get their horses for some time. Frank Shortt was holding the reins of six but, he said, 'I became so excited that I let the horses escape.' One constable, spurring his mount through a gap in the fence, 'got jammed' with James Carroll and hurt his leg. Carroll lost his horse and Bryce had to spend some minutes catching it for him. So the cavalry rode out in whooping dribs and drabs, pursuing the little Maori figures 500 yards away, and pursued in turn by their own officers.

In Tauranga Ika, Titokowaru's people were still busy cooking food when they heard the distant volley. The boys' parents instantly realised their children were absent, and put two and two together: 'We knew it when we first heard the attack. We missed our children, and then we knew it was the children who were being attacked.' To a man, the warriors dropped what they were doing, ran for their guns, and poured out of the pa in their hundreds, sprinting for the woolshed two miles away. Their children ran just as hard towards them. They quickly scrambled over the rail fence of the sheep pen. Kingi vaulted it in a single motion, using only one hand. Alex Cunnabel, one of the leading riders, claimed that he saw the tomahawk in the other 'raised over his head' as he leapt. They 'ran as fast as possible' through the wheatfield, perhaps a hundred yards broad, and the gap between the boys and their elders closed at several hundred yards a minute.

The cavalry crossed the 400 yards between the foot of the sand ridge and the woolshed even more quickly. Those who had started first, and who 'happened to be good riders and well mounted', gained the front – mostly Kai Iwi troopers, but including one or two constabulary such as Frank Shortt. With all three advantages, John Handley held the lead through a slight dip near the sand ridge, across the 'potato paddock', and in and out of the sheep pen. he pulled up at the big ditch and bank fence, which 'was next to impossible to get the horses through', and rode left along it, making for a gateway he remembered. To his frustration he found it 'banked up', and he leapt from his horse and began pulling at it with his hands. Most of his comrades were also blocked by the big fence. Some dismounted to help Handley; some rode along it looking for another gap; others milled around the woolshed, where they were soon joined by the slower riders. But two groups of about half a dozen each, made up of the best jumpers, put their horses at the fence and cleared it. One group, including Alex Cunnabel, Frank Shortt, and Tom Morgan, crossed well to the right, rode straight into the swamp, and got stuck in it. But the other group – Maxwell, Arthur Wicksteed, George Peake, Arthur Wright, and George Campbell – crossed to the left, avoided the swamp, and found itself amongst the rearmost children.

The ditch and bank fence had also been a problem for the Maori boys. Most managed to scramble over it fifty or a hundred yards before the troopers and ran on, lungs bursting, through the grass and scattered fern and flax on the other side. But Ihaka and Pehira, delayed by their descent from the woolshed, had just crossed, as had short-legged little Akuhata Herewini. Kingi Takatua brought up the rear, perhaps because he felt the responsibility of leadership or harboured silly dreams of emulating Katene and Tihirua with his tomahawk, but most likely because he helped Akuhata over the fence. He was just scrambling out the ditch himself when Maxwell and Wicksteed soared over.

The two riders first saw Ihaka and Akuhata ten or twenty yards away – Pehira 'got tired and hid myself in the fern.' The colonists reined in their horses, levelled their revolvers, and fired. One, probably Maxwell, hit Akuhata in the back, and the little boy fell, pumping blood. Wicksteed hit Ihaka in the thigh but, in his shock, the running boy did not notice the wound immediately and stumbled forward into a flax bush. Maxwell spurred forward, changed his reins to his revolver hand, and brought his sabre down on the crouched figure. Ihaka 'clasped his hands above and on his head to save himself', but the blow was angled and not at full power. The sword severed one finger of the right hand, slashed the others, and cut deeply but not fatally into Ihaka's head. He fell forward into the flax bush and out of sight. 'The person who struck me thought I had been killed,' said Ihaka, 'but he made a mistake.' All this took only a few seconds, and Wicksteed now noticed Kingi at the edge of the ditch. He fired at least two shots, hitting him in the back and the side of the stomach, and the boy fell back into the ditch, but somehow kept or regained his feet. Maxwell hauled his horse about, cantered the few paces back to the ditch, leaned down, and swung his bloody sabre. Though wounded, Kingi must have jerked his head away in reflex, for the blow glanced off the side, leaving a wound like Ihaka's. But this time Maxwell made no mistake. Peake saw him strike twice, and Wicksteed remembered him 'prodding at a native in the ditch'. In fact his second blow was one of great force and precision. Kingi's head was 'split in two halves, one half falling down over his shoulder'.

The officers knew that hundreds of furious warriors from Tauranga Ika were only minutes away from them, and they strove desperately to regain control of their men. Most of the constabulary were at the woolshed – Tom Lister remembered seeing the fat sow 'stuck and partly opened'. Newland and O'Halloran, who never crossed the ditch and bank fence or came close to any Maori, managed to get them formed up and gave orders that no man should dismount. The Kai Iwi troopers were much more scattered, and Bryce and Garrett had the harder task. Bryce had gone after James Carroll's runaway horse, and was still chasing it when Maxwell killed Kingi.

Like a jockeyless race horse, the runaway had followed its fellows all the way to the big fence and here Bryce finally caught it. He handed the reins to one trooper and rode after other men who were trying to get through the fence, ordering them back to the sand ridge. 'Lieutenant Bryce passed me,' said Robert Morgan, 'and ordered me at once to retire to the main body, and also to induce any other trooper I saw to do the same.' Bryce then jumped the ditch and bank fence himself, close to the swamp. He found that Garrett had preceded him, and ordered him 'to bring back the men to the foot of the sand hill as quickly as possible', which meant some furious work getting the bogged horses out. Bryce then rode off after Maxwell and his companions.

After Kingi, Maxwell and his comrades put spurs to their horses again and rode hard after the remaining boys. They passed Ihaka and Pehira, both hidden, and they passed Akuhata, who lay bleeding profusely from his bullet wound. As they did so, the little boy must have made some movement, perhaps getting up on to his hands and knees. Realising he still lived, one of the troopers leaned right down from his saddle and swung his sabre. The single blow slashed both Akuhata's head and shoulder, and flung him over on his back. Humans, even small ones, can be hard to kill and even this second terrible wound did not kill Akuhata immediately. He lay dying, face to the sky, only ten yards or so from the big fence.

Within a couple of hundred yards, Maxwell's group had overtaken the rest of the boys. One or two successfully hid themselves in the toetoe fringing the swamp; 'another boy hid in the water, like a little crawfish'. But most were flushed from cover and were ridden down by the troopers 'who at once began to slash and cut away at them as they ducked under the horses to avoid the sword-thrusts and the revolver-shots fired at them. The lads ran hither and thither.' With the rescuing warriors now only minutes away, the colonists had less leisure to make sure of their victims, and may even have shown a glimmer of mercy. Bryce, catching up with the milling men and boys at a fast canter, passed one lad 'who threw himself in terror before him, but Mr Bryce rode on'. George Campbell saw two boys thirty yards away and forbore to fire at the smaller one: 'I did not make any attempt to harm him.' But Campbell did fire at the 'larger' of the two figures he saw, probably Poharama Ngarutahi, all of nine years old. Poharama emerged from a flax bush and stood stock still, frozen with fear, as Campbell fired. The bullet ripped across his chest from nipple to nipple, making a slash-like wound.

Poharama fainted, events blurred in his mind, and to the end of his days he believed it was a sabre wound, although his elders knew better. Either Arthur Wright or George Peake cut Hoani Tamou on the back of the head. Wi Taria was also wounded, and Tonu was hit by a bullet in the sole of the foot as he bounded over the grass. Then Bryce at last caught up with his leading men.

He found them in a state of high excitement, ready to take on Titokowaru's whole army, which was now almost within gunshot. The five were clustered together, comparing scores and bursting to renew their charge. Bryce 'got in front of Sergeant Maxwell,' according to Campbell, 'and at once ordered him and all of us to retire'. Maxwell refused. Peake remembered: 'He called on me and some of the others to follow him and he would take the pah.' Bryce now drew his sword for the first time; 'I did it,' he said, 'for the purpose of threatening the men.' Peake recalled him saying, 'The first man who passes me I will cut him down.' Maxwell was not afraid of Titokowaru's army, let alone John Bryce, and he still hesitated. It was not until Bryce 'told us that our own men were in the swamp bogged, and that we had better see about getting them out' that he consented to retreat.

Obedient to orders at last, Maxwell and the others went and helped Garrett get the bogged horses out. After a glance at the oncoming warriors, Bryce cantered quickly back to the big fence. Handley had finally crossed, and he and a few others were gathered around Akuhata. Bryce joined them. Years later, questioned about what he saw, Handley replied frankly:

> Q. *Was he a small boy or a large boy?*
> A. *He was about four feet six inches in height.*
> Q. *Was he nude?*
> A. *He had only a shirt on.*
> Q. *Could you see his private parts?*
> A. *His penis was sticking up and not skinned as a boy of 14 or 15 would be.*
> Q. *You judge from what you saw of his private parts as to his age?*
> A. *Yes.*
> Q. *Did you notice whether there was any hair on his private parts?*
> A. *I noticed there was no hair there.*

With the true nature of their deed dawning on them, Bryce and his men watched Akuhata die, just before his oncoming elders, at extreme range, fired the first Maori shots of the day. 'We all stood round for a moment looking at the body until the bullets came whistling round through the fern, when we left.'

Bryce got his men away in the nick of time. They rejoined the constabulary, crossed back over the sand ridge, and resumed their homeward march more hastily than before. Try as they might, the warriors from Tauranga Ika could not come up in time – the whole affair had taken only ten minutes. Some Maori slanted south of the lake to cut the cavalry off, without success. In their fury, all wasted ammunition freely, for the range was too great. By sunset, the cavalry were back in the safety of Woodall's redoubt reporting their triumph to Whitmore. Apart from falsifying the time of his departure from Wairoa, and concealing his error in ordering the initial volley, Newland noted the 'gallant example' set, from the rear, by O'Halloran and Bryce, multiplied the two killed into eight, and failed to mention that the victims were children, although rumours soon got out. But he did justice to Maxwell's prominence: 'I wish particularly to mention the extreme gallantry of Sergeant G. Maxwell of the Kai Iwi Cavalry, who himself sabred two and shot one of the enemy, and was conspicuous throughout the affair', which was all perfectly true. Whitmore, noted the nervous Newland, 'seemed pleased with what had been done'.

A postscript to these events took place in London in 1886. George Rusden, an Australian civil servant and historian, had two years previously published a *History of New Zealand*, in which was included an account of Handley's Woolshed: 'Some women and young children emerged from a pah to hunt pigs. Lieut. Bryce and Sergt. Maxwell dashed upon them and cut them down gleefully and with ease.' Bryce sued Rusden for defamation; the case went to the Privy Council in London, the colony's ultimate Court of Appeal. Bryce won, and Rusden was forced to pay £2,531 in costs and damages – an immense sum. In fact there had been no women at the woolshed, and Bryce did not cut anyone down himself. But he was fully aware that his men had done so, and that very young boys were their victims, and he took no disciplinary proceedings against them. Poor Rusden had got the right tragedy and the wrong details. As London's *Daily Chronicle* observed when reporting the case: 'writing history is a somewhat dangerous undertaking'.

In 1868, Handley's Woolshed made headlines in Wanganui as 'a dashing affair', and it made Maxwell's reputation. But public attention was soon focused elsewhere. Early on Sunday 29 November, Whitmore received final confirmation of the East Coast move from Haultain, who had returned to Wellington. Whitmore decided to march out next day with his whole field force to resupply and reorganise the Patea and Wairoa garrisons before leaving. He also hoped that, during the expedition, Titokowaru might be tempted into battle at a disadvantage on open ground. Whitmore now had 500 constabulary and 120 volunteer cavalry, and he hoped to exploit Handley's Woolshed. 'We well know,' he wrote, 'they burn to avenge the surprise carried out by Captain Newland and Lieutenant Bryce.' Titokowaru did burn for vengeance. He too wanted battle, and was prepared to take unusual risks to get it. But he still had fewer men, his few mounted scouts were no match for the colonist cavalry, and he would fight on his own terms, not Whitmore's. For the next forty-eight hours, the two engaged in a deadly game of manoeuvre, like swordsmen probing for an opening.

It was Titokowaru who took the initiative. While Whitmore finalised his plans for the morrow, Titokowaru advanced with most of his warriors and suddenly appeared before Woodall's redoubt, where they 'threw up some rifle-pits and some slight palisading'. He then sent a detachment south of the Kai Iwi, where it looted and burned a couple of farmhouses in broad daylight. This was Titokowaru's classic strategy: stabbing at the enemy's settled districts to lever his fighting force into an attack on a fortified position. But it was an economy version – his fortifications were slight, the work of a few hours only – and Whitmore was presented with a unique opportunity. Whitmore, however, 'took no notice of this impudent demonstration'. Such hesitation was a far cry from McDonnell's eager hunting of August, and perhaps McDonnell himself, who had returned from leave to take up a subordinate post, reminded Whitmore of this that evening: 'McDonnell . . . kept me up all night on the 29th – talking over his wrongs and "Willie's" (William McDonnell). He is a dangerous fellow.'

At 5 am on 20 November, a weary Whitmore marched out of Woodall's to find Titokowaru now positioned at Pakaraka, flanking the road to Tauranga Ika and Wairoa. 'His mounted men hovered in front of my advanced guard,' wrote Whitmore, who this time rose to the bait. He sent in the cavalry under Newland and Finnimore 'to cut these off by a rapid movement'. Pursuing the mounted Maori, the colonists were very nearly led into ambush. Several horses were hit, including Newland's, but the cavalry managed to withdraw just in time: 'The enemy had evidently prepared a trap into which the cavalry were almost led, having taken up a position behind a bank, and rifle-pitted the edge of the bush.' Foiled in his vengeance on the cavalry, Titokowaru now paralleled Whitmore's march to Nukumaru and took position at Tauranga Ika while the colonists faced him from Handley's farm. Whitmore deployed his troops in 'semblance of intention to assault', while sending a convoy of supplies to Wairoa and seventy-two constabulary recruits to Patea to replace Fraser's division which was to join him on the East Coast. Titokowaru 'put up signals of recall to all his outlying parties', and, when the assault failed to eventuate, brought his men out of the Tauranga Ika defences. With an Enfield rifle one of his warriors mortally wounded a colonist at 1,400 yards distance. The two armies faced each other across Handley's paddocks, but neither would attack. Whitmore eventually broke the stand-off by marching to the Waitotara River, where he camped for the night. Next day he picked up Fraser and the returning convoy from Wairoa, and set off for home. He made one more attempt to draw the Maori into a trap, using the calvary 'like a red rag to irritate a bull', but Titokowaru would not oblige. The two generals had proved well matched in the bout of manoeuvring. 'They would not give me a good chance', complained Whitmore, and Titokowaru would no doubt have echoed the sentiment. On 2 December, with 250 of his best constabulary, Whitmore at last left Wanganui for the East Coast.

As he had promised Haultain, Whitmore did not leave Wanganui undefended. Redoubts and blockhouses sprang up like mushrooms in and around the town, and there were now over 400 Wanganui volunteers and militia who were genuinely useful for defensive purposes. The two companies of the 18th – 180 Imperial troops – were available for the defence of the town. Apart from the 260 men garrisoning Patea and Wairoa, there were also 230 constabulary, and the trickle of recruits had become a stream, adding 500 more men by the end of the month. In Whitmore's absence, the command was held not by Gorton or Mc Donnell but initially by Lieutenant-Colonel Jasper Herrick, and then by Lieutenant-Colonel William Lyon, a forty-three-year-old, one-armed Imperial veteran of the Crimean and Waikato Wars. Lyon could load and fire a breech-loading carbine with his single arm. Though 'brusque and blunt' in manner, he was much more popular than Whitmore.

With a garrison of 800, rapidly increasing to 1,300 effective troops, it might be expected that the Wanganui settlers would feel reasonably secure. They did not. 'I regret to say,' wrote Whitmore on his departure, 'that the feeling of the population seems to me to be one

of panic.' In the succeeding week, fears that Titokowaru might renew
his advance led Lyon to pull back the base of operations again, this
time to Camp Westmere, a mere three miles from Wanganui Town,
leaving Woodall's as yet another outpost. Maori raiders fired on a
settler five miles out; one nervous sentry shot another by mistake,
and work began on a ditch and bank wall around the town. Worst
of all, at noon on 4 December, two Maori walked into Woodall's
redoubt with a letter from Titokowaru.

MATTERS FOR YOUR CONSIDERATION

To Whitmore,–

Salutations to you. This is a question to you. To whom does England
belong? To whom does this upon which you stand belong? This is my
word to you. The heavens and the earth were made in one day, and man
and all things bearing fruit therein were made in one day. If you know
that God made these, it is well. A covenant was entered into with those
people. You were made a Pakeha, and the name of England was given
to you for your tribe. I was made a Maori, and New Zealand was the
name given to me. You forgot that there was a space fixed between us
of great extent – the sea. You, forgetting that, jumped over from that place
to this. I did not jump over from this place to that.

This is my word to you. Move off from my places to your own places
in the midst of the sea. Move away from the town to those other places.

Arise, that you may be baptised, that your sins may be washed away,
and call upon the name of the Lord. Sufficient.

From TITOKOWARU

We can only speculate about Titokowaru's motives in sending this
ultimatum but he, like other Maori leaders before him, certainly
overestimated Pakeha respect for a flag of truce. His two emissaries
– Rimitiriu, the Ngarauru agent, and the Ngaruahine warrior Rameka,
on whom Darlington's watch and Hastings' gold chain were found
– were instantly seized and imprisoned. The colonists tried to dismiss
the letter as barbarous insolence or to ridicule it with weak satire.
But this was all too unconvincing, and an Auckland newspaper
observed that the letter concluded 'somewhat after the manner of
an English judge in passing sentence of death on a criminal in the
dock'.

At this time, 'in our hour of extremity', as the Wanganui Times
put it, Thomas McDonnell travelled to Pipiriki to appeal to the
Whanganui tribe for help. 'Fighting Mac' still believed he held great
sway over Whanganui and neighbouring tribes, and he assured

TELEGRAPHIC INTELLIGENCE
FROM THE WEST COAST.

December 14.

TITO KOWARU has sent in a message to Wanganui, demanding
the heads of Sir George Bowen and a couple of Bishops
for his Christmas dinner. "The bone of Mr Stafford's
proboscis he also requires for a toothpick. If his request
is complied with, he will spare the inhabitants for a few
days longer.

A gallant *sortie* has been made, and a double-barrelled
gun taken from the enemy.

December 15

The rumour of the double-barrelled gun was unfounded.
It was either a double-breasted coat or a barrel of Dublin
stout. They are all to be sent home to the British Museum.

December 16

It has been ascertained beyond a doubt by a party of
scouts that no gun was taken on the 14th, consequently
Woodall's Redoubt was immediately abandoned.

More bitter humour   *From Punch, or the Auckland Charivari, Vol. 1.*

Whitmore he would soon assemble 800 kupapa. But Whanganui were
still smarting from the government attempt to interfere in tribal
politics and from various slanders which had recently appeared in
the local press. John Ballance in particular had been playing variations
on the theme that the only good Maori was a dead one, accusing
Natanahira of being 'a spy and a traitor', advocating mass reprisal
killings for Poverty Bay, and 'threatening the lives of friendly natives
in the service of the Government'. At a meeting with Lyon,
McDonnell, and Booth, Kawana Paipai became so enraged by this
that his 'feelings overcame his versality and he gave the assemblage
a pantomimic illustration of the manner in which he would serve
the promulgator of such calumny if he had his way with him'. In
the crisis, the government tried to be conciliatory. They must, wrote

Haultain of the despised Mete Kingi, 'yield a little to him to induce him to co-operate with Kemp, who feels he cannot work successfully in defiance of him'. Ballance lost his cornet's commission for his statements, but McDonnell's efforts to recruit kupapa came to very little. The sole fruit of his efforts was a small corps of sixty 'Native Cavalry'. Some young warriors had observed the fine equipment and growing mana of the volunteer cavalry and decided they wanted the same at government expense.

To Ballance, Maxwell, and their comrades in the Pakeha cavalry, the formation of this unit seemed the height of kupapa arrogance. The Native Cavalry was 'a motley band of Maoris in the regulation forage cap, some with boots, some with shoes, and others in their more natural costume of nudity. If this ridiculous exhibition were not both expensive and mischievous it would be amusing enough, but being both the one and the other it is simply preposterous.' Matters came to a head when Lyon tried to take all the cavalry on a reconnaissance patrol. He placed the kupapa in the lead, the Pakeha cavalry gave 'ironic cheers' as they passed, and Finnimore and Bryce claimed the advanced position was theirs by right. 'Lyon said that his orders were that the natives should lead, and his orders must be obeyed. The men, considering this an insult, refused to proceed.' Finnimore and Bryce were arrested but subsequently reprimanded and released.

There were two other cavalry patrols during December. The first was a 'looting expedition' mounted by Finnimore's Wanganui Cavalry Volunteers, probably including Trooper John Ballance. Finnimore rode out on 13 December, moving by night to keep his presence secret from the Maori. Finnimore intended to give them a dose of their own medicine by ravaging the unoccupied and undefended villages in their rear. He reached Patea by 5 am on 14 December and remained there during the day. After playing cards and drinking all evening, his men rode out at 1 am the next morning to burn villages, accompanied by a few of the Patea garrison including Livingston, John Gibson, and one of the Ginger brothers. They reached Manutahi at 4 am, found it empty, burned it, and proceeded to a nearby small hamlet where an old Pakakohe couple were keeping the home fires burning for their people. According to Livingston, a reliable source, 'they murdered two old Maoris, a man and a woman, burnt their bodies, and did other atrocities which if done by the Maoris on us would create a great sensation'. The 'atrocities' included some form of sexual mutilation – the grim likelihood is that the man's genitals

were severed and placed in his mouth. Acting on information from
Livingston and Ginger, Booth complained bitterly about the 'brutality
and mutilation of a Hauhau man and woman'. The incident was
investigated, the volunteers were exonerated, and Booth's complaints
were described in the press as 'totally unfit for publication. The moral
filth they contain, from mere hearsay, is enough to make one's very
blood run cold.' But no one denied that an old woman had been
killed. 'It is impossible sometimes, as it was the other day,' wrote
Ballance of the affair, 'to distinguish between the men and the women.'
Finnimore and his men went on to burn Mokoia and two other villages.
They took thirty horses and a copy of 'the "Works of Martin Luther"
in German with a Maori war song written on the flyleaves' and
returned to Wanganui well content. Titokowaru sent all his mounted
men after them, but too late. Again he had failed to avenge himself
on the Pakeha cavalry, and now the utu debt was even greater.

The second patrol, the last of the year, took place on the night
of 27 December, when the Wanganui Volunteers and Kai Iwi Cavalry
rode out to see if the Maori were still at Tauranga Ika. As dawn
broke the next day, they reached Handley's farm and inspected the
pa. It was totally silent, seemingly abandoned. With or without
permission from Finnimore and Bryce, a party of ten troopers went
to investigate more closely. They included Arthur and Henry Wright,
Allan Campbell, George Small, Tom Cummins, and William Lingard,
led, of course, by George Maxwell. All were fine horsemen and
they again jumped the ditch and bank fence, scene of former exploits,
and rode up the slope to the pa, which was newly palisaded but
completely quiet.

They approached to within one hundred yards. They still could
not see a soul, but Maxwell and Lingard fired into the pa to make
sure. Suddenly the palisades blazed with 'a storm of lead'. It was
a trap, sprung a little prematurely. Several horses were hit. Henry
Wright's was killed and fell, pinning him by the leg, though its body
was between him and the bullets from the pa. No help came from
the main body of cavalry, and the Wright family was bitter against
Bryce thereafter. Seizing his chance of utu for his relative Ihaka,
Big Kereopa leapt from the pa and ran towards Wright, carrying
a long-handled tomahawk. The troopers had begun to flee, but Arthur
Wright yelled, 'Call yourselves men!' and some turned to help his
brother. Tom Cummins fired his carbine, hitting Kereopa, according
to the unfriendly Kimble Bent, in the buttocks. 'The big fellow
clapping a hand to his wound – which was in his posterior parts

– bolted back into the *pa* nearly as quickly as he had come, yelling "I'm shot! I'm shot!" ' Lingard then caught a Maori horse, on which Henry Wright made his escape. Lingard was later decorated for this, and for freeing Wright from his dead horse, although Wright maintained he freed himself at his third attempt.

The troopers galloped from the scene, shaken but apparently none the worse for wear. Then, without a word, George Maxwell slid from his horse to the ground. Superb rider to the end, he had ridden 150 yards mortally wounded. Now he breathed his last, not far from the spot where Kingi Takatua had done likewise one month before.

Chapter Eleven

THE BRINK

On 1 January 1869, the people of Wanganui opened John Ballance's *Evening Herald* to find two sentences that spoke for most of them: 'The New Year brings no joy or gladness to Wanganui. Suspense is everywhere and hopes are ebbing fast.' The *Wanganui Times* reported 'general stagnation and distress' and the emigration of no fewer than 200 townspeople during December. A cruel fate had seen Christmas celebrated with a major fire at the Ridgeway Bowling Saloon. Some irrepressible young boys had managed to save much of the stock from a nearby sweet shop, but theirs was the only faintly festive Christmas. Land prices in the town had fallen by 75 per cent – if any buyers at all could be found. One settler wrote to Australian friends that 'distress is general owing to the destruction of property and the stoppage of business . . . the town is full of poor people who have been warned in, and whose whole chance of support is at present gone . . . bread for the most destitute is all this letter asks for.'

The sense of crisis was not restricted to Wanganui. Titokowaru's War was now a national and even international affair. In the aftermath of Moturoa, a stream of dignitaries had visited the front in accordance with the familiar Wellington policy of sending VIPs to a disaster area in preference to more practical help. From the government came Stafford, who broke his firm principle of colonial 'Self-Reliance' by appealing to the Imperial naval and military commanders in Australia for immediate assistance. James Richmond's visit led him to urge Whitmore to hasten his return from the East Coast, 'as the people here are in great alarm'. Haultain took radical military measures, as we have seen, and he was also rumoured to have mentioned the unmentionable: the possibility of returning all confiscated land.

From the Opposition came William Fox, its leader, and Superintendent Featherston. Fox was soon 'in a great state of alarm about the peace of his district', but managed to boost morale no more than the government ministers: 'Mr Fox may visit Whanganui and other places, but he will require to be born again before he inspires the Legislature or the country with confidence.' After Te Ngutu, Featherston had written: 'I am awfully disgusted with the panic of the Wanganui people.' Now he sang to a difference tune. 'If things are bad on your Coast,' he wrote to McLean, 'they are still worse with us on the West', and to McDonnell: 'Certainly things never before looked so bad at Wanganui and I dread losing. Now I fear that a great part of the town has been burnt.' The most eminent visitor, Governor Bowen, was shocked by what he found: 'It is a piteous sight which the streets of this town now present almost hourly, destitute men and women flocking in for food and shelter.' 'The hinterland,' he said, 'has already been laid desolate by the ravages of the present rebellion, which has swept away the civilization of 20 years.' He received a petition from 605 'Wives, Mothers and Daughters' of Wanganui, begging Queen Victoria 'to avert the extinction of ourselves, and those dearest to us, under circumstances equal to if not exceeding the barbarities perpetrated in the Poverty Bay district'.

It was not necessary to visit Wanganui to experience the crisis at first hand. Throughout November and December, rumours flew thick and fast that Titokowaru had crossed the Whanganui River with his main force, or sent a raiding party, or that the Manawatu tribes had decided to support him. The second and third of these rumours were all too credible. Titokowaru's propensity to raid well in advance of his main force had been clearly demonstrated, and many of the mixed tribes of Manawatu and Horowhenua were professed Kingites and Pai Marire adherents who were now beginning to sympathise with him. A Waikanae hui told James Richmond that, while they disapproved of Te Kooti, 'Titokowaru is fighting for his land which you took by theft.' Richmond said, 'Do not dirty your tongues with talk of Titokowaru . . . his throat thirsted to drink the blood of Europeans.' But they replied, 'That was wrong, you provoked him.'

As early as 16 November, Haultain wrote that 'the panic is I am sorry to say extending towards Rangitiki', and four days later he reported 'considerable alarm at Turakina'. On 25 November, Stafford wrote that 'arrangements have been made and are making for the defence of Turakina, Rangitikei, and Manuwatu districts in case they are attacked'. The same week a report was received, via Kepa, that some of Titokowaru's men had crossed the Whanganui River, and a small scouting party may actually have done so. A settler was killed by unknown Maori near the mouth of the Manawatu River, and throughout this district and the Rangitikei people fled their homes for places of safety. There was 'great alarm' in Wellington itself.

'Apparently something like a panic exists in Wellington.' From the Manawatu, John A'Deane wrote the 'reports are rife' of imminent attack: 'Mrs A'Deane is in a great state of alarm, and goes to bed every night with the expectation of a visit from those fanatics to murder her children.' Parliament feared that Titokowaru intended to link up with Te Kooti: 'Some combined movement may be made between the two cannibal leaders.' A year later, Takiora was to discover that this fear had not been groundless.

Among Titokowaru's indirect victims was a one-time Danish prime minister, Bishop Ditlev Monrad. Monrad had led Denmark into the disastrous Slesvig-Holstein War of 1864, the first coup of a certain Otto Von Bismarck, against Prussia and Austria-Hungary. After the war, with his family and a few retainers, Monrad fled Denmark and emigrated to New Zealand, as far from his old world as possible, eventually settling at Karere on the Manawatu River, close to the embryonic settlement of Palmerston North. His sons, Viggo and Johannes, served in the Patea Field Force, and the latter was present at Moturoa. In late November, dire rumours of a Maori advance south of Wanganui seemed to be confirmed by a message from the government that settlers and 'loyal' Maori must look to themselves. Like other local Pakeha, Monrad buried his valuables in his garden and fled down the Manawatu to Foxton. While there, one of Monrad's entourage, Frederik Kornerup, was attacked and mortally wounded by a Maori. Whether the killer's motives were personal, whether this was a local Maori gesture of support for Titokowaru or whether it was the act of his own scouts, is not clear. Naturally enough, Monrad and his fellow refugees drew the more pessimistic conclusions – as did Colonel Whitmore. Foxton too was evacuated, and in January 1869 Monrad left the colony to return to Europe. The only thing Titokowaru and Bismarck had in common was that each had chased the same Danish prime minister 12,000 miles.

In retrospect, it is easy to mock Monrad and the other settlers south of Wanganui who fled to Wellington or to local redoubts, or who armed and drilled to face the onset of Titokowaru. But the threat seemed real, and the government certainly took it seriously. Lyon had withdrawn to Camp Westmere the better to oppose a crossing of the Whanganui, and a redoubt was built at Turakina and strongly garrisoned with armed constabulary. The militias of Rangitikei, Manawatu, Wellington, and the Hutt Valley were all called out, armed, and drilled. Whitmore wrote, of Manawatu, that 'people must go into central defensible posts', and blockhouses and rcdoubts began to spring up as they had done around Wanganui. Richmond told the Wairarapa militia commander that 'letters from Upper Wanganui call for redoubled vigilance. Every man in the country should know his post in the case of alarm.' Not all the emergency advice was as helpful. 'In the case of being beleaguered,' Charles Haughton of the Defence Office told one garrison commander, 'cook several days food at once so as to economise on fuel.' Captain Henry Young, commanding C Company of the 18th Royal Irish at Wanganui, published a booklet of *Hints on House Defence.* It recommended that, 'works for local protection – to be garrisoned by settlers, and to which terror-stricken women and children may easily find their way – should be constructed near to the main road (and to an inn if possible).'

For the first time since the 1840s, war came home to the people of the southern part of the North Island. As they received their rifles and went off to their drills, 1,000 Wellington militia must have recalled the departure, with high hopes and drunken fanfare, of the Rangers and Rifles only four months before. Indeed, the sense of catastrophe, and the readiness for desperate measures, was New Zealand-wide, with mass additions to Titokowaru's ranks the foremost fear, and Imperial help the foremost hope. In the far south, at Dunedin, the *Otago Witness* stated: 'The conviction is universal throughout the colony that at no time in its history has greater danger been imminent. The Colonists are left to themselves and they have suddenly discovered that they are not able to protect themselves.' In Nelson David Munro, the Speaker of the House of Representatives, wrote:

If there be a general rising of hostile Maoris throughout the North Island, as appears to be threatened at the present moment, I do not think that the colony is capable of grappling successful with the difficulty . . . The North Island of New Zealand was never in so critical a state as at the present time.

Munro suggested suspending the constitution, returning to direct Imperial rule in return for troops, and his was by no means a lone voice.

From Wellington, *The Times* correspondent informed his London readers that:

the settled country has been overrun, and almost every vestige of civilization has been destroyed to within 8 or 9 miles of the Wanganui township. The loss of life and property had been great, and the prestige which a mere handful of savages had acquired had acted and is still acting as a leaven, leavening the whole native population south of Auckland.

At New Plymouth, on 27 November, some out-settlers abandoned their farms and came into town for fear of attack by Titokowaru's sympathisers. On the East Coast, Bishop William Williams of Waiapu wrote: 'The number of reverses we have received during the last six months is truly astonishing. There have been a great number of them, and not a single success to put on the other side. What does this seem to indicate, but that God's hand has been turned against us.'

In December, a 'monster meeting' in Auckland unanimously moved to petition for the suspension of the constitution and a return to direct Imperial rule. The *Weekly News* explained why:

From first to last the military history of the year 1868 has been one long melancholy record of misfortune . . . Our position 12 months ago was one of comparative security . . . we were in full possession of a lofty prestige. Our former wars had been successful . . . We felt strong, and confident in our strength to put down any rebellion likely to arise . . . We are now in a position of having lost our prestige, while we have vastly increased our forces. We have been surprised and out-generalled in every way: we have been defeated, massacred, driven back, almost cowed, by the successes of a handful of savages; and this is in short the change in our position during the year.

In his eleven months of office thus far, Governor Bowen had been something of a figurehead, in marked contrast to his predecessor George Grey. But in this climate, with appeals for Imperial help on many lips, he became more prominent. George Ferguson Bowen was a man of great education and some intellect, but Charterhouse and Trinity, the Presidencies of the Oxford Union and the University of Corfu, and a book proving that Ithaca was in fact the birthplace of Odysseus, were not the best training for inspiring resistance to Titokowaru. Bowen's wife, the Italian countess Diamantina Roma, was popular amongst a colonial aristocracy starved of titles, but he himself was considered pompous and too fond of his ease. According to James Richmond, he belonged 'to a fraternity too dignified to make haste' and was 'not a man of nerve or patriotism'. Insider circles in Wellington nicknamed him 'Pickle Polly', claiming: ' "Pickle Polly" is a humbug and he is Governor of New Zealand.'

Humbug or not, Bowen came up with a sound diagnosis of the New Zealand crisis in a confidential report to the Imperial government. He poured scorn on 'the present un-English panic' of the colonists, but in fact echoed their sentiments. Earlier he had written that 'the Maoris generally are watching the progress of the war with gloomy

George Bowen, caricature by
Tom Durkin
Alexander Turnbull Library

MASKS & FACES.   No. 2.—VICE-ROYALTY.

A Quoter of Poetry.

irresolution, and . . . will ultimately join that which may prove to
be the strongest party.' After Te Ngutu and Moturoa, this seemed
to be Titokowaru, and Bowen feared that the withdrawal of the
last remaining Imperial regiment, the 18th, would spark a general
rising. Stringent orders restricted the 18th to defensive duties in major
towns, a position which 'horribly disgusted' its officers, but even
so it remained a symbol of the Imperial link. 'All those best acquainted
with the Maoris,' wrote Bowen,

believe that if they once realise the fact that the Colonists are entirely abandoned by the Mother Country there will be a general rising, when we shall be able to hold, in the North Island, only Auckland and Wellington, and there will be massacres like those of Poverty Bay and Cawnpore all over the East and West Coasts . . . There is a general panic: and people here are like 'drowning men clutching at straws'. The fact is that the so-called 'self-reliance policy' has been an imposture from the beginning.

One of Bowen's answers to the problem would have delighted Titokowaru. As 'one of the few men in the North Island whose head is cool', he spoke of taking command of the field force himself, perhaps with the martial martyr King Leonidas as his model. But the rest of his solution was more sensible. He quoted a 'naval officer of high rank' on the difficulties of defeating the Maori in their 'd----d enchanted hole, impassable by land and impracticable by water; in which no man can get anything but disgrace and discredit'. He suggested major concessions in the form of 'a modified recognition within certain districts' of the 'so-called "Maori King" ', together with the prohibition of outlying settlements – in effect, the abandonment of confiscation. And finally he requested a couple of regiments of Imperial troops.

This last request was only one of many, and Bowen had first made it in the wake of the disaster at Te Ngutu in September. But between 1860 and 1865 the Imperial government had spent millions of pounds on the New Zealand Wars, and after years of bitter bickering had been unable to persuade the colony to meet much of the cost. It had then handed over entire control of 'Native Policy' to the colonial government, on the explicit understanding that it would make no further commitment of men or money. On 27 January 1869, Bowen received the reply to his first request for help from the Duke of Buckingham, then Secretary of State:

However lamentable this disaster [Te Ngutu] may have been, it affords no reason for doubting that the European population of the Colony, now amounting probably to near 220,000 souls, aided by the loyal natives, are fully able to defend themselves, if they make proper arrangements, against a few thousand disaffected Maoris, of whom only a few hundred appear to be at present in arms.

Even the 18th, insisted Buckingham, must go as planned: 'having regard to the numerical disproportion of the two races I find it difficult to imagine any such change in the state of affairs as can render it

AN UNNATURAL MOTHER.

Britannia to New Zealand: "THERE, THAT'S THE SWAMP YOU HAVE TO WADE THROUGH; SO START AT ONCE, AND DON'T EXPECT **ANY** HELP FROM ME."

Mother England abandons New Zealand   *From Punch, or the Auckland Charivari, Vol. 1.*

necessary for you to adopt the responsibility of detaining the troops after the receipt of these instructions.'

George Grey had taught the colonial politicians that Imperial officers on the spot could be induced to turn a blind eye to orders from distant London. Despite Buckingham's letter, appeals flew across the Tasman to the commanders in Australia. In January and early February, Major-General Trevor Chute, the Sherman of South Taranaki in 1866, and his quartermaster-general, Colonel Hyde Page, together with Commodore Rowley Lambert, made secret visits to Wellington and Wanganui. Military action against Titokowaru was the sole alternative to the boredom of garrison duty in Australia, and these officers were looking for ways to co-operate. Chute was persuaded to delay the departure of the 18th, and Lambert promised to help from his ships if he could. But their instructions were too watertight. Chute could not rescind the 18th's defensive instructions, still less reinforce them. Lambert's predecessors had lost so many men in the Waikato War that the efficiency of their ships was endangered. The Admiralty had issued standing orders against action on land, and with the best will in the world Lambert could not contravene them. He kept his powerful warships, *Blanche, Rosario, Challenger*, and *Charybdis* in New Zealand waters as much as possible, but the South Taranaki Maori took care not to expose themselves near the coast. Two days after Moturoa, on 9 November 1868, John Ballance had written: 'the self-reliant policy has failed, and the only hope left is to sue for protection to the Mother Country'. By the beginning of February 1869, it was clear this 'only hope' did not exist.

What Bowen and the colonists feared above all was the intervention of the King Movement. For a long time the movement as a whole had adhered to its July decision to leave Titokowaru to his fate, and some of its leaders still held to it. Ambassador More reassured Parris of its peaceable intentions at New Plymouth on 27 December, and another Kingite envoy, Rapihana Otaota, did the same two days later in Wellington to Bowen himself. But there were signs of a gradual and partial shift in opinion. In October, King Tawhiao had issued a proclamation to all Kingite tribes. It reiterated that Titokowaru was to be left alone, but the emphasis had changed from that of Rewi and Tamati Ngapora in July: 'Friends, do not allow your thoughts to dwell on the works of Titokowaru. Leave him alone to carry on his work. It is a work that has been appointed to him by God. Although he may eat men leave him alone. Those are his own thoughts.' The line between Kingites and kupapa was not always clear, and this proclamation seems to have advised waverers against joining Titokowaru's enemies.

As the impact of Titokowaru's victories resounded through the North Island, sympathy for him increased amongst the Kingites. Two Ngati Maniapoto leaders in particular began to advocate active help: Reihana, whose influence as a tribal chief was beginning to rival Rewi's, and Tawhana Tikaokao, who had helped fight Cameron at Nukumaru in 1865 and was still, with Rewi, the King Movement's leading general. Whatever the movement's previous relations with Titokowaru, the opportunity created by his victories seemed too good to miss. The Pakeha were on their knees. Would there ever be a better prospect of reversing the result of the Waikato War? Despite the opposition of Tamati Ngapora and those who still held to Te Ua's peace policy, despite the ambivalent attitudes of Rewi and King

Tawhiao himself, Tikaokao, Reihana, and other leaders began to prepare for war.

An Auckland land speculator, Josiah Firth, had major interests in Waikato near the confiscation boundary and had even been allowed to lease some Ngati Haua land inside it. Apart from a few virtual renegades such as Louis Hetet and 'the Fenian O'Connor', he was the best informed of all Pakeha about Kingite intentions. Firth noted Tikaokao and Reihana's activities, and wrote: 'Waikato, the heart of the island, though full of excitement and preparation, is still at peace. Until a blow has been struck there, the war will not have become general; and there is yet hope, though I confess a small one, that the final and terrible catastrophe may by God's blessing be averted.' Then, on 13 February 1869, the blow came.

As early as November, Tikaokao and Reihana had proposed a sudden attack on Pakeha North Taranaki. Even a small-scale raid, like the killing of Cahill and company on 9 June 1868, would constitute an effective Kingite declaration of war, divert colonial troops from those facing Titokowaru, a hundred miles to the south, and allow Ngati Maniapoto physically to link with him via Chute's Track around Mount Taranaki. It would also be an unscrupulous but clear-cut way of breaking the stalemate between pro- and anti-war factions within the King Movement. Rumours of the plan reached William Searancke, resident magistrate in the confiscated Lower Waikato in early December, and he sent a warning to his opposite number at New Plymouth, Robert Parris. Reihana is said actually to have set out to mount the raid, probably in January, with thirty warriors. But he was intercepted by Rewi Maniapoto and forced to return. The secret debate – war or peace – must have swayed back and forth among the Kingite leadership. In February, Tikaokao renewed the attempt, entrusting it to a subordinate chief, Hone Wetere Te Rerenga of Mokau. On 12 February, Wetere set out with fifteen warriors of his own hapu on his deadly errand.

Wetere was a mission-educated chief in his thirties, the son of the late Takerei of Te Awakino, near Mokau. He had a reputation for being helpful to Pakeha travellers (years later he was to save the surveyor, C.W. Hursthouse, from drowning) and his followers included a deserter from the colonial forces, David Cockburn, whom he treated kindly. Wetere was said to have been 'a very intelligent fellow', and to have owned a Kawhia-based trading vessel. He had fought in the Taranaki War of 1860 and joined the Pai Marire religion, which as usual strengthened rather than weakened his staunch adherence to the King Movement. He firmly believed that the proposed expedition was ordered by Tawhiao – it 'is not mine', he said, 'it is Tawhiao's' – and he may well have been right. There were other Maori reports to this effect, and Reihana recalled a conversation in early February in which Tawhiao had complained of the activities of some Pakeha. Reihana offered to kill them, and the King said, 'Suppose you do, there are plenty more to be caught.' Reihana replied, 'Yes, there are more at Pukearuhe.'

The Pukearuhe redoubt had been built in 1865 in a 'position commanding the pass by the White Cliffs, and cutting off communication from the north'. It was eleven miles north-east of the Urenui Redoubt, thirty-one miles north-east of New Plymouth, and twenty-five miles south of Mokau, a major Ngati Maniapoto coastal settlement. Though the area had been at peace since 1866, the garrison of Pukearuhe had not been disbanded until 28 February 1868 and, like Urenui, it was still a centre of military settlement. But it was now a fortification-in-waiting, rarely containing more than half a dozen military settler custodians. The commander was Lieutenant Bamber Gascoigne, a thirty-eight-year-old veteran and scion of a military family – his cousin, the eccentric Frederick, also a colonial officer and sworn enemy of Whitmore, told proudly of attacking an Indian servant with a toy sword at the age of eight. Bamber Gascoigne's current circumstances were hardly those of a frontier garrison commander. He lived peacefully in a small but pretty house, tending fields of corn and potatoes with his wife, Annie, aged twenty-seven, and three small children, together with two cats and a dog. A few single men of his old military settler company were also normally in residence, and others such as Fred Trent, Edward Gregory, John Skinner, and Ebenezer Naylor had farms nearby.

Robert Parris had not ignored Searancke's warning. But he had recently arranged for the resettlement of a large body of pro-government Atiawa in the area, and he expected that these would act as a buffer against any Kingite aggression. As additional precautions, Parris hired two of them, Epiha and Tamati Makariti, to scout the area around Pukearuhe. And on 5 December, he and Henry Richmond, superintendent of Taranaki, decided to pass on Searancke's warning to the local settlers and leave the question of evacuation to them.

The local Pakeha leaders were fully aware of the crisis created by Titokowaru, and of the general tension. Their missionary, sixty-two-year-old John Whitely, wrote on 2 December that 'during the

35 years I have been in New Zealand I have never felt so desponding as at the present time'. Whitely was a longstanding leader of the Wesleyan mission in New Zealand, and his hard work and knowledge of their language had earned him respect among the Maori. He was also involved in the underside of missionary activity – land buying and sending military information to the government in time of war – and he made no secret of his antagonism to Pai Marire and the King Movement. But he still had high standing and good channels of communication among his Maori neighours, and was sure he would receive warning of any attack. Bamber Gascoigne was equally confident. 'He would never have it that it was unsafe. He always said that ample notice would be given and that their lives at any rate would be spared.' So the settlers of Pukearuhe remained on their farms. Only Annie Gascoigne expressed some unease. When Fred Trent went to catch some stray horses after seeing a few Maori travellers on the beach below the redoubt just before Christmas, she half-jokingly told him that if he left he 'should hear of her and the children being tomahawked'.

Around midday on Saturday 13 February, two parties of Ngati Maniapoto met by chance near the Whitecliffs. One consisted of four men, including Henry Phillips, son of a Kingite Pakeha, Frank Phillips, and his Maori wife. Phillips and his companions, Titokarangia, Johnny Pihama, and one other were returning to Mokau from a trading trip to Urenui and Pukearuhe begun on 7 February. They had crossed the Mimi River at 10.30 am. The second party was Wetere and fifteen armed warriors, including Te Oro, Pene (Ben), Manuera, Tukirau, Tatana, Tanui, Herewini, Haupoe, and half a dozen others. Titokarangia asked Wetere where he was going, and he bluntly replied: 'on to kill the whole of the Europeans at Pukearuhe'. To ensure surprise, he persuaded or compelled the four traders to accompany him. He intended to use Henry Phillips as his interpreter, and it was Phillips who left the only full eyewitness account of the day's events.

The party stopped at a creek at the foot of Pukearuhe. Here, Wetere left his guns and most of his men and walked openly up to the redoubt with Phillips and five of his own men: Te Oro, who was second in command, Manuera, Pene, Tukirau, and Tatana. At that moment the redoubt contained only two men, military settlers John Milne and Edward Richards, who were sitting in the cookhouse on stools at either side of the fireplace. Another man, named Snell, who normally lived there was away that day, and the neighbouring military settler

The Pukearuhe Redoubt, 1868   *Taranaki Museum*

farms were all a mile or two distant. The two scouts, Epiha and
Tamati, were patrolling elsewhere, and the Gascoigne family had
gone for a walk. Wetere had Phillips call out something like, 'Anyone
home?', and Milne and Richards went out to greet their visitors.
One was reading a book which he put down, open at his place, beside
his stool. They knew Phillips, Maori traders and travellers came
frequently to the Redoubt, and they felt no need to take any of
at least five rifles and two revolvers available to them. Outside, they
shook hands with the Maori and asked them what they wanted. Wetere
replied through Phillips that he had pigs for sale down at the beach,
and that they should come and inspect them. Milne and Richards
were pleased at the prospect of fresh pork and asked Wetere whether
he had any peaches as well. He said he had, and the two settlers
walked off down the track to the beach, accompanied by Tukirau,
Pene, and Manuera. Tukirau carried a taiaha, a spear-like staff whose
function could be ritual, ornamental or practical. At a bend in the
track, out of sight of the Gascoignes' house but in view of Phillips
and Wetere, Tukirau suddenly struck Richards on the back of the
head with the taiaha, killing him with five rapid blows. Milne turned
at the sound and, according to Phillips, saw 'his mate fall'. Manuera
swung at his forehead with a long-handled tomahawk, with Milne
'holding up his arms for protection'. The tomahawk broke – the
handle was later found under his body – but Pene took Tukirau's
taiaha and finished Milne off with it.

Military settlers playing cricket at Pukearuhe before the attack   *Taranaki Museum*

As Milne and Richards strolled off to their deaths, Wetere sent his two remaining warriors, Te Oro and Tatana, to the Gascoignes' house. They found the whole family out. Wetere then ordered up from the creek the rest of his party, with the guns, and sent them to remove Gascoigne's rifle and revolver from his house. At this stage, they took nothing else – 'Wetere told them to leave the rest until their work was done.' Ngati Maniapoto then settled down to wait.

Within a few minutes, the Gascoignes appeared, walking towards them after enjoying the midday sun *en famille* in their fields. Annie Gascoigne may not have been feeling well and had risen late. She was still wearing her nightdress under another garment. Her husband was carrying baby Louisa, while five-year-old Laura and three-year-old Cecil walked behind with their mother. Gascoigne walked up to the group standing around his house, and recognised Henry Phillips.

'Hallo, are you back again?' he asked.

'Yes,' said Phillips.

Something in this curt reply, or the fact that the Maori were armed, aroused Gascoigne's suspicions: 'He went straight on for his house, walking fast', perhaps hoping to get his weapons. 'Ben (Pene) followed him close up, with his taiaha.' As Gascoigne reached for his door handle, Pene struck him twice in the back of the head. 'He fell forward on his face and never moved again.' But, to make sure, Te Oro sprang forward, seized a large wood-chopping axe lying nearby, and

hit him again, 'cutting the head in two halves'. Manuera leaned down
to where little Louisa had fallen and hit her with a short tomahawk,
'nearly severing the upper part of the head', as the coroner put it.

Annie Gascoigne watched this appalling scene but somehow retained
some presence of mind. Grabbing her two remaining children, she
ran and hid behind one of the redoubt's parapets. Te Oro and Manuera
went in pursuit. In a moment, they returned to find Wetere and
Phillips sitting at their ease outside the Gascoignes' house. Wetere
asked them if they had killed Annie Gascoigne, 'and they replied
"Yes, and the children too"'. Cecil had three tomahawk-wounds
on the back of the head; Laura had been killed with two blows while
lying in terror on the ground, and Annie also had two fatal head
wounds, together with bruises on her face as from a fist, perhaps
indicating some desperate attempt to protect her children. Wetere
said, 'Kapai' – 'Good'. The flying fish which had crossed the prow
of his war canoe had all met their fate. His men tomahawked the
Gascoignes' dog and the children's pet cats to finish the job.

But the killing had not yet ended. Throughout the afternoon, the
Ngati Maniapoto taua rested, ate ham, bacon, and potatoes taken
from the cookhouse, and divided other loot. Phillips got six boxes
of matches, a new pack of playing cards, and 'a clean white shirt'.
Wetere took Bamber Gascoigne's revolver, watch, and opera glasses
for himself – not many Ngati Maniapoto chiefs could boast a pair
of opera glasses. About 7 pm a sentry 'saw someone coming on
horseback in the distance. Wetere then said, "Whether it is a white
man or a native, we must kill him . . ." Te Oro sang out, "It is
a white man." Te Wetere answered saying to let him come.'

The missionary John Whitely rode north that Saturday evening,
heading to Pukearuhe to preach Sunday service the next day. Between
4 pm and 5 pm he called at Captain William Messenger's house on
the Mimi River, and at 6.15 pm, three miles short of Pukearuhe,
he took tea at Ebenezer Naylor's. Now, as he approached the redoubt,
he presented Wetere with a quandary. For it was Whitely who had
educated the Maori leader and baptised him 'Hone Wetere' – John
Wesley. He was not part of the plan; the last Pakeha Wetere wished
to kill. The legend has it that Wetere called out, 'Go back, Whitely;
your place is not here', and that Whitely replied, 'My place is here,
and here I remain, for my children are doing evil.' Another Maori
then said, 'Dead cocks do not crow.' But Henry Phillips remembered
none of this, and Wetere's doubts were probably silent and quickly
stifled. On his orders, Tanui fired at about thirty yards, killing

Hone Wetere Te Rerenga,
with his wife and son
Taranaki Museum

Whitely's horse. As the old missionary disengaged himself from the
animal, six shots rang out from the Maori's newly acquired Enfield
rifles. One merely grazed his clothes, the other five struck home,
creating wounds, wrote the coroner, 'each of which I should consider
mortal'. The taua took Whitely's watch, jacket, and saddle, and
finished looting Pukearuhe. They cut off Annie Gascoigne's wedding-
ring finger to get the ring, and put her and the rest of her family
in a whare and covered them lightly with earth. Whitely, Milne,
and Richards were left where they lay. After setting fire to the redoubt
and its outbuildings, they set off for Mokau.

Hone Wetere was luckier than George Maxwell. He survived the
war, came under a general amnesty in 1883, and died in his bed
in 1889. He even became something of a celebrity, a tourist's Te
Kooti, and his photograph, with his wife and young son, was used
as a picture postcard. Wetere's son looks younger than Cecil Gascoigne
would have been, and one wonders about the provenance of the fine
watch at his father's fob.

It seems possible that although King Tawhiao might have consented to the Whitecliffs raid he disapproved of the killing of women and children. When he received word of the raid and saw some of the plunder, including Annie Gascoigne's wedding ring, he said: 'This is not my work; Ngatimaniapoto have brought it to me.' But the King realised that, in Reihana's words, 'the sword was now drawn', and he gave orders for the immediate deployment of 1,300 warriors in various parts of his territories. Between 400 and 600 Ngati Maniapoto warriors, under Tikaokao, Reihana, and Wetere, assembled at Mokau to meet the expected Pakeha reaction. The chiefs warned neutral and kupapa tribes not to interfere in a letter dated 19 February 1869: 'To the Kupapas commencing at Te Pihanga, thence throughout all your boundaries. Come up to the interior. If you do not like the interior remain quiet. Leave me and the Governor to carry on our work. Lie quietly where you are; look not to the right or left.'

The Pakeha settlers of North Taranaki had no doubt about the meaning of the Whitecliffs. 'No-one supposes,' wrote the editor of the *Taranaki Herald* on 20 February, 'that this will prove to be an isolated incident.' Captain Thomas Good of Urenui 'thinks it is sure to be a general war'. His fellow settlers agreed, and abandoned their farms *en masse*; the New Plymouth militia and volunteers stood to arms. In Waikato, there were strong rumours of imminent attack and there too the settlers went into the towns and redoubts. The government also agreed that the massacre was 'to be regarded not as an act of individual vengeance but as a declaration of war on the part of a considerable body of hostile Maories' and scrabbled desperately to find troops for yet another front. All across Pakeha New Zealand there was despair at the thought of combined operations between Tikaokao and Titokowaru. The nightmare had come to pass. All now turned on the news from the south.

Chapter Twelve

TAURANGA IKA

We left Colonel Whitmore on 2 December 1868, steaming off for the East Coast with the cream of his troops. He reached Poverty Bay on 4 December, and found that Te Kooti had gone to ground at Ngatapa, a position of great natural strength deep in the interior, but one which could be surrounded. After a month of trials and tribulations, during which everything which could go wrong did so, Whitmore succeeded in besieging the place with his constabulary, now reinforced to 340, and 370 Ngati Porou kupapa under Ropata Wahawaha, a kindred spirit of Kepa's. On the morning of 5 January, as Whitmore's patiently woven noose tightened inexorably around his foe's throat, Te Kooti, escaped down an almost sheer precipice with his best warriors. But the colonial forces captured many of his other followers and, with Whitmore and James Richmond's consent, the kupapa slaughtered 120 of them 'after a few questions'. By 18 January, Whitmore and his constabulary were back at Wanganui.

At last Whitmore's energy and determination had gained him a substantial victory. But it was over the lesser of his two enemies, Te Kooti himself had escaped; and the Opposition did their best to deprecate the success. The victory was 'grossly exaggerated', wrote Featherston: 'as usual I suspect Te Kooti skedaddled through the back door without much loss'. The thick blanket of gloom lying over the colony did not lift appreciably and Whitmore remained as unpopular as ever. In Wanganui, 400 settlers petitioned against his return – 'Why should we have a man who was twice cast off as worse than useless in Hawke's Bay?' – and his eventual homecoming was far from triumphal. 'No Whitmore' placards made another appearance and among the troops 'many openly declare they will not go into action under Colonel Whitmore'. He was described in the newspapers as 'the bête noir of New Zealand', edging out both Te Kooti and Titokowaru for the title.

Whitmore shrugged all this off, and did likewise with gentler advice from his political masters. Both Richmond and Stafford tactfully suggested that he should be less hard on his men and less blunt in his public criticism of subordinate officers. Whitmore responded: 'I cannot succeed in keeping silly papers from saying ill things about me – and I can't prevent officers who have got all they can and don't care for fighting from now and then getting the rough end of my tongue.' He also confessed that 'my mode of dealing with my subordinates is natural to me and cannot be taught. To promise to act under advice in this respect would be to mislead you.' 'In this respect' was a subsequent insertion, and perhaps the original version was closer to the truth. As far as possible Haultain tended increasingly to give Whitmore his head, and Whitmore could easily overwhelm Richmond and even Stafford with superior military knowledge. Ngatapa did little to alleviate the grave military crisis, but it did place the colonial war effort firmly in the hands of the Little Tyrant. 'Colonel Whitmore is supreme with the Government,' complained the *Nelson Colonist*, 'he does as he likes, and they obey his orders.'

The army assembled by Whitmore at Wanganui in January 1869 was by far the largest solely colonial force ever raised – some 2,000 men in all. Apart from the 180 Imperial regulars of the 18th, still tied to their two stockades, there were more than 400 local Wanganui troops: some 200 'Veteran Volunteers', increasingly used to garrison the lesser redoubts and blockhouses of the Kai Iwi district; an average of perhaps 100 other volunteers and militia called out periodically for some kind of useful service, and the Kai Iwi and Wanganui Volunteer Cavalry, 120 strong. Despite Maxwell's death, the cavalry's morale was still high. They had seized sixty Maori cattle in a raid on 5 January, and on 13 January had accompanied Lyon on a four-day patrol to Patea, during which Moore Hunter had acquired an acute case of dysentry which confined him to hospital for a couple of days 'passing blood'. Whitmore's public praise in November had endeared him to the cavalry, and they at least were pleased to have him back. Finnimore's men actually gave three cheers at the news – a novel experience for Whitmore. When they rejoined his field force on 23 January, he found them still rather overimpressed with themselves and gave Bryce a 'pulling up' – 'but he is much the better for it now'. 'He came and dined with me with Finnimore,' wrote Whitmore, 'and sat up half the night very amicably telling me their feats and arranging their plans.'

The kupapa component of the colonial army presented the usual difficulties. Whanganui power grew with Pakeha desperation, and Whanganui knew it: 'This is a New Year and we want new arrangements.' In addition to the controversial Native Cavalry, Mete Kingi wanted four shillings a day, plus rations, per man – sixpence a day more than Pakeha troops. As Pakeha recruits streamed in, Whitmore toyed with the long-cherished idea of doing without kupapa altogether, but decided against it. Eventually, 405 kupapa, including the cavalry, took the field, although no more than 200 – Kepa's immediate following and that of the like-minded chief, Aperaniko – were useful from Whitmore's point of view.

Even Kepa was far from completely malleable. He, Wirihana, and the Native Cavalry accompanied Thomas McDonnell on a sentimental journey to Te Ngutu o te Manu on 17 January, an offshoot of Lyon's Patea expedition. The village had long been deserted, and McDonnell, of course, discovered that it had been 'utterly impregnable' on 7 September 1868. He also recovered Von Tempsky's bones, having been told exactly where to find them by the envoy Rameka, still languishing in prison at Wanganui. McDonnell believed he commanded the patrol; Kepa did in fact, and the two quarrelled bitterly. Kepa asserted that 'it had been a distinct understanding that he was to receive no orders and be under no command except that of the Commanding Officer' – Whitmore. A few days later, Kepa quarrelled with another officer. In the heat of the moment, he made wounding reference to Handley's Woolshed: 'If I knew you were going to kill children, I would have nothing more to do with the fighting.'

Kepa also consolidated his position within the Whanganui federation. His daughter, Wikitoria, married the son of Kawana Hunia. Starved of its own high society, Ballance's *Evening Herald* went so far as to report the wedding – the bride's dress was white silk trimmed with blue and red, 'which looked exceedingly picturesque'. Kepa's mana was on the rise, but not directly at the expense of Mete Kingi. Both were still manoeuvring to fill the vacuum left by Hori Kingi, and though Mete increasingly gave way to Kepa in the military sphere, he more than held his own in politics. On 9 January, he was one of only three Maori chiefs to accompany Bowen aboard HMS *Challenger* on a viceregal tour of the South Island, and was photographed in Christchurch eating grapes in state. Despite the government's best efforts, he and Kepa maintained a working relationship. The government paid and otherwise rewarded its kupapa, but still it did not command them.

The backbone of Whitmore's army was the armed constabulary, now greatly increased in strength to more than 1,000 men. All seven established divisions had arrived at Wanganui for the big push against Titokowaru. The old Patea Field Force divisions, Nos. 1, 2, and 3, had accompanied Whitmore to the East Coast and back, as had the

Wikitoria Kepa, leader of
Wanganui fashion
*Danbury Album, Auckland
Institute and Museum*

newer Nos. 6 and 7 – the last without its commander, Michie Brown,
shot dead through the head at Ngatapa. Two divisions were now
facing Titokowaru for the first time: No. 4, a well-trained unit from
Waikato under Major Dean Pitt and his subalterns, J.R. Watts and
Stuart Newall, and No. 8. No. 8 was actually Maori, recruited from
the Arawa confederation, but 'detribalised' – separated from its chiefs.
By this means, Whitmore fondly hoped he could avoid the kupapa
problem. No. 8 was indeed a good unit, and it replaced the two
Wanganui cavalry corps as his favourite. This aroused great resentment

in other units: 'Arawas were allowed to keep their loot – as usual favoured in everything'; 'Whitmore has sent 10 gallons of beer to the Arawas . . . It is disgraceful . . . these Arawas are treated like pets.' The Arawa were commanded by Captain William Gundry, half Arawa himself, with the nephew of an English earl, the physically powerful young Thomas Porter, as his deputy.

These divisions comprised about 500 veterans, and at Wanganui they found the same number of new recruits, with more coming. Many of the new men were failed gold miners from Westland, Otago, and Thames, and Captain Stack had sent 166 Australians from Victoria between 17 and 30 December alone. The average age of twenty-nine men recruited at Hokitika in late November was twenty-seven; the average height was five feet seven and a half inches – about the general average of the day. One was South African, three American, five Irish, nine Scots, and eleven English, but many must have passed through Australia. Such men were physically tough and potentially good soldiers, but did not always take kindly to military discipline.

Whitmore, of course, complained bitterly about the indiscipline of his veterans and the 'glaring inefficiency' of his recruits. He told Stafford he had had to discharge up to 150 unsuitable men during January, and that at least eighty had deserted – he had actually to 'attack' a camp containing sixty deserters, he said. Whitmore was also far from happy about his officers, including newcomers like Sydney Davis, known as 'the Yankee' because he had served in the American Civil War. 'Davis drinks. O'Halloran . . . does that and worse . . . Spiller is a goose . . . Pitt thinks too much of his whiskey.' Fraser 'will not yet face his Division and keeps to the sick list . . . there is a screw loose I am sure.' As for the McDonnell brothers, apart from Thomas, the 'perfect curse', William was someone 'who I do not care to serve with', and George 'may go or stay without making any difference except as regards his pay'. Poor Newland 'is quite absurd to promote. He is quite unfit for it, being neither wise nor sober'. Whitmore summed up: 'All the desire of the regular officers is not to fight and not to move – of the Volunteer officers to charge at windmills, gallop about, and boast. Between these extremes one is torn to pieces.'

There was some truth in all this. The Ngatapa divisions arrived back at Wanganui on 14 January, four days before Whitmore, and celebrated their return with 'great fighting amongst the divisions' and great roistering in the town. 'Full privates with their forage

Some of Whitmore's officers. Standing, from left: W. A. Richardson, Sydney Davis, John Handley, Walter Gudgeon, Harvey Spiller, Jasper Herrick. Henry Northcroft is in the centre of those seated   *Alexander Turnbull Library*

caps sat rakishly on their close-cropped heads ogled the girls and looked as killing as they could', drank everything they could lay hands on, and enlivened the night with 'bachanalian song' from the guardroom. Philip Putnam had managed to sit out the siege of Ngatapa protecting stores on the line of communication, and he was in good form. He received his backpay on 19 January, went into town with ten pounds and 'the chaps', but without leave, and got a dose of Moore Hunter's dysentery. A repetition of this behaviour later earned him 'an awful talking to' from Whitmore himself, 'the worst I ever heard of'. Among the new recruits, one demonstrated his mastery of hand-to-hand fighting by stabbing three comrades in a drunken bar-brawl. Another 'cut his [own] throat in a fit of delirium tremens'. Several men from Greymouth were over fifty years of age, 'old worn out men', and there were scores of desertions around 19 January. Constable Patrick Cullen got two years' hard labour and fifty lashes (flogging had been legalised) for striking a sergeant, and there were several lesser court martial sentences for 'insolent language' and 'disgraceful conduct'. As for the officers, poor Fraser had added epilepsy to his alcoholism, and the two between them had drowned his real merits. 'Yankee' Davis was 'a devil-may-care character', given to creeping out of camp and firing off his revolver to test his men's alertness, and to firing it into the roof at dinner parties for no reason at all. Apart from those Whitmore mentioned, two senior subordinates, Kepa and Lieutenant Colonel John St John, another Imperial veteran, renowned for his hardiness, were also very fond of their bottles.

But Whitmore was up to his old trick of exaggerating his difficulties. Drink and war had long been inseparable, and Pitt and Davis, like Kepa and St John, remained very effective officers despite it. And even Whitmore was impressed by some of the other officers, including Lyon, Roberts, Swindely, Morrison, and Northcroft. Of the men, the medically unfit discharged during January actually numbered only fifty-seven, and the mass desertion of 19 January was caused by the desire to follow Putnam's example and enjoy backpay in Wanganui rather than Camp Westmere. Most men returned to the colours with their hangovers.

In combat, the veterans were now normally good troops – indeed, the 'rakish' angle of their forage caps might suggest a new confidence born of Ngatapa. Among the recruits, many had seen service previously. Of one sample of twenty, three had served in the navy, one in the Royal Marines, one in the Cape Mounted Rifles, and six in the New Zealand colonial forces. Men such as Sergeant Samuel Austin and Constable Tom Adamson were returning to army life after substantial military experience. Austin had served with the Whanganui kupapa in 1865 and 1866 and now rejoined them, acting as Kepa's quartermaster. At twenty-one, the large and formidable Adamson was already a veteran of four years' campaigning on the East Coast, and had demonstrated courage and ruthlessness. Solomon Black, a thirty-four-year-old Scots veteran of the Waikato militia, and Benjamin Biddle, a twenty-year-old ex-sailor, also had experience and 'natural' courage, unlike their fellow member of No. 1 division, Philip Putnam. Thomas McKenzie, an older Indian veteran with Ghurka blood, had emigrated to Canterbury with the nabob, John Cracroft Wilson, and took this opportunity to return to warfare which, for men like him, was an addictive drug. Adamson and McKenzie joined a new 'Corps of Guides', formed by Whitmore for scouting duties, along with a Frenchman, Pierre De Fougeraud, a hard drinker and good cook who had been wounded at Te Ngutu. The guides, a dozen strong, were at first commanded by Maxwell's comrade,

Paddy Doyle's Lament

It was down in Otago they collared me
A Government soldier for to be
To go up and fight the wild Maoris
In the forests of Taranaki
For two-and-sixpence a day and the [ration,]
And fifty broad acres of swamp
Not to mention the two tots a day sir-
Which the same it was seldom I got

> *Chorus*
> So list to Pat's tale for a minute
> And by it you'll plainly see
> That I'm hemmed in around with misfortunes
> They've all got a down upon me!

That [comedian?] of an orderly-sergeant
Does be dogging me round the whole day
He's yelling "Doyle, come here when I call you!
Why the devil don't you heed what I say?
Sure, you're the dirtiest man in my room, sir
And the clumsiest one in the squad,
Faith, it's up to the Captain I'll bring you
And this time 'twill be 'Seven Days [Without] Grog!'

But whist! A substitute I'll get, sir,
And go back to my damper and tea,
Bid good-bye to the orderly-sergeant
And my estate beyant there in Patay [Patea],
By my soul, 'tis a sorrowful story
I'm treated far worse than a dog,
Do my damnedest, I never can please them –
They do always be stopping my grog!

Recruit's ballad, sung by J. P. Ward to James Cowan   *Fildes Collection, 631, Victoria University of Wellington Library*

William Lingard, and later by Christopher Maling, whose adventures were plagiarised in the publications of the English soldier-charlatan George Hamilton Browne.

Whitmore's new army was formidable: so large that there was no question of his not attacking Titokowaru very soon. Whitmore's information about enemy numbers was less exaggerated than usual, and he knew Titokowaru had no more than 500 warriors. But Titokowaru need have had no fear, for his new pa more than made up the deficit. The New Zealand Wars had thrown up several men of great military engineering talent – Kawiti, Te Wharepu, and Pene Taka among others. Titokowaru ranked with the best of them, and Tauranga Ika was his masterpiece. Even as a stark plan, a simplified shadow of itself, Tauranga Ika's symmetrical design has a certain fatal beauty, and the impression is well founded. The numerous sunken anti-artillery bunkers, roofed with timber beams and galvanised iron from Handley's woolshed and similar buildings, were topped with a thick, all-absorbing cushion of earth. There were many small bunkers, rather than one large one, so that if a shell did manage to find its way in, casualties would be minimised. Ordinary houses and tents, including Titokowaru's own in the north angle of the pa, were merely for day-to-day living. The bunkers were proof against much heavier artillery than Whitmore's few small Cohorn mortars and two six-pounder Armstrong guns. Similar bunkers had protected Ngai-te-rangi from 110-pound Armstrong shells at the Gate Pa in 1864.

Once a bombardment had harmlessly spent itself, the garrison could move from their bunkers through well-protected tunnels and covered passages to the edges of the pa, to find firing positions of three types. The most basic and important was the firing trench running right around the pa, 'traversed' or partially blocked with sections left undug to protect its occupants from stray shots passing right along its length, and roofed over as well. Riflemen in this trench fired at ground level, which helped counteract the tendency to fire too high for the curved trajectory of their bullets. There were two palisades outside the trench, formed of large tree trunks sunk deep in the ground as struts, with much thinner split timber in between. The split timber, held on to the struts by cross rails, did not reach the ground, leaving a gap of eighteen inches through which the riflemen in the trench could fire. The second type of firing position was on the roof of the firing trench, from where riflemen could shoot through loopholes in the palisade. The third was the four salients at the angles of the pa, two of which contained squat taumaihi, bastions like those at Moturoa, built of timber, bullet-proof flax matting, and compacted earth. The salients ensured that an assault on any face of the pa would be enfiladed from left, right, and front.

This was not all. On three sides Tauranga Ika was within easy gunshot of thick bush. There are strong signs that this bush contained

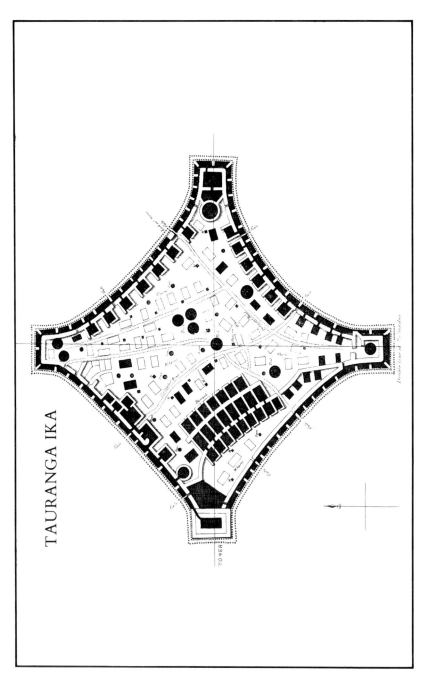

TAURANGA IKA

further defences: concealed rifle pits and other hidden firing positions. Not only would these enable the Maori to ambush any outflanking move, but they would also provide cover for firing unexpectedly into the rear of an assault. And the bush prevented any close reconnaissance. Tauranga Ika combined the deceptive strengths of both Moturoa and Te Ngutu. Whitmore suspected it was strong, but he could not know how strong. His attack would be careful and cautious, but it would come.

On Wednesday 20 January 1869, the colonial army began its summer offensive. Whitmore advanced slowly and methodically, perfecting his supply system and training his best recruits as he went. He began by throwing a strong bridgehead across the Kai Iwi to Moore's farm, and put the rest of his striking force – eventually 1,077 men – to work repairing the inland road. On 22 January, Lyon took command of the vanguard at Moore's farm, which was heavily reinforced with cavalry. Next day, under their noses, Titokowaru's thirty mounted men, supported by a hundred unmounted warriors, seized sixty of Moore's cattle and 'closed upon Lieutenant Bryce's troop' when it rode out to oppose them. On Whitmore's orders, Bryce tried to tempt the Maori in on his own infantry supports. His horse got stuck in a bog near the Okehu Stream, and he very nearly joined Maxwell as utu for Handley's Woolshed. But he escaped, and the Maori in their turn declined to enter the colonist trap.

During the next two days Whitmore continued with his training and roadwork, building a bridge over the Kai Iwi and completing the shift of his field base from Camp Westmere to Woodall's redoubt. Lyon, just north of the Kai Iwi near the Okehu Stream with the vanguard, fortified his camp, which became known as Fort Lyon. The inland road crossed the Okehu just beyond his position by an old bridge, and continued through a steep, bush-covered gorge. To the astute Whitmore, this seemed a likely place for an ambush, and on the night of 25–26 January he sent in two small patrols to scout it. One consisted of Kepa and some kupapa; the other of William Lingard and the new Corps of Guides. The guides spent the night near the top of the gorge, intending to pre-empt an ambush, but themselves fell into one at dawn on 26 January. Constable Thomas Cummings was killed, as was Thomas McKenzie, the old Ghurka, who was said to have died of a heart attack just before being tomahawked. Lingard, Chris Maling, and the remaining guides fled back to Fort Lyon. Another man, Kelly, was wounded and saved by Samuel Walker, the surgeon-humourist, who rushed out of the

Fanciful reconstruction of the ambush at Okehu *From a painting by J. E. Moultray,
Taranaki Museum*

fort and carried him in. The successful Maori ambushers came out
of the bush and made off on horseback. Some of Kepa's men saw
them but considered themselves too few to intervene.

The ambush took place within a few hundred yards of Fort Lyon,
and Lyon, soon supported by Whitmore, moved out in force. They
exchanged fire with more Maori skirmishers for half an hour, losing
another man wounded, but managed to save the Okehu bridge, which
Titokowaru's men had set on fire. During the course of the day
Whitmore pushed on to Handley's farm, opposite Tauranga Ika, with
the cavalry, kupapa, and four divisions of constabulary. The guides,
he felt, had saved his main force from falling into the ambush, but
Titokowaru had clearly had the better of the war of scouts, and
this reduced Whitmore's capacity to reconnoitre Tauranga Ika still
further. Whitmore spent the remaining days of January consolidating
his position. Improvements to the road were completed, and Gorton's
carts traversed it three times daily with rum, food, and ammunition.
More troops were brought up to a series of entrenched positions
stretching from Handley's farm to Fort Lyon. A further ninety
constabulary arrived from Poverty Bay under St John and Captain
Frederick Gascoyne, Bamber's cousin – though he insisted on spelling
his name differently. On 1 February, the last of the reinforcements
and several small Cohorn mortars, which fired an eight and a half-
pound shell, came up.

Whitmore was now 'ready to assail Titokowaru's camp', as he
put it. He conceded that his 'information was not perfect as to his

fortifications'; 'I am puzzled to make out if the place where Maxwell was killed is his true position.' The southern and eastern faces were 'the only place where the "Pah" was visible' through the bush. It seemed strong, but not impregnable, and Whitmore planned to advance methodically, entrenching as he went, bringing his right wing as close as possible to the east angle of the pa. He also intended to send a force into the bush still further to his right so it could fire on the east angle from the rear. 'Tomorrow', wrote a reporter attached to his staff, 'he intends advancing on the right flank by the rifle pits and a sap if necessary; and he will also take up a position on the reverse flank of the pah.' Despite Whitmore's subsequent denials, it seems he then intended to assault after a bombardment. Nos. 3, 6, and 8 divisions, under the fiery Colonel Lyon, were told off as 'the storming party'. For all his cunning and all his caution, Whitmore intended to plunge head first into the Tauranga Ika death trap with both an assault and a move into the bush. 'As far as I can judge,' he wrote cheerfully to Stafford that night, 'the claptrap expression "the force is in good spirits" has every reasonable foundation.' And, he told Haultain, 'the troops all seemed very anxious to close with the enemy'.

At 7.30 am on Tuesday 2 February, the volunteer cavalry under Finnimore rode over the two miles separating the colonist positions from Tauranga Ika. They advanced to within 500 yards of the pa, driving in Titokowaru's pickets. With the mounted constabulary and Kepa's kupapa, they then took position on the flanks of the main force as it advanced to Handley's long ditch and bank fence. The colonist centre under Whitmore himself then continued its advance to within 200 yards of the pa, where they entrenched securely despite a steady fire. On the right, Lyon pushed on in the afternoon to within 100 yards, and also entrenched. Apart from the storming party, he seems initially to have had No. 1 division with him. 'Saw the hau haus all day awful cheeky,' wrote Putnam. The colonists advanced from trench to trench, hard work which took the whole day but prevented casualties. It was not until about 5 pm that the Cohorns and Armstrongs opened fire. One Armstrong shell hit the palisade and threw off a splinter which wounded an incautiously exposed warrior in the head. The same shell ripped a hole in Titokowaru's own tent, but of course he was not in it. He and all but one of the garrison kept to their bunkers and survived the bombardment unharmed.

Throughout the day, the Maori fire had been desultory, but in the evening it increased. As Whitmore himself admitted, it was 'very well directed', but 'owing to the cover of the trenches' only one man was hit. A war of nerves had more impact. The men in Lyon's position were close enough to converse with the Maori garrison, and they did. 'We were able to have a chat with the hau haus,' wrote Putnam, although other participants described it as 'rather strong repartee between occasional volleys'. To keep their spirits up, the constabulary sang camp songs, including 'Marching through Georgia' from the recently ended American Civil War.

'Go on, pakeha, go on,' the Maori replied, 'give us some more.'

Less politely, one warrior shouted, 'Come on Pakeha and be food for the Maori; send all the fat ones in front.'

It was enough to make Philip Putnam nervous. 'This has been very harassing work up every other night sleeping in Belts turning up an hour before daylight. Marching. Entrenching in the day time. I wonder the men don't mutiny, hau haus came out and yelled at us awfully in the evening.'

His division was replaced in the night by the Arawa of No. 8, which made No. 1 'so mad', though one suspects Putnam did not share their anger. No. 1 moved back to the ditch and bank fence, no longer part of the storming party. Throughout the night, the Maori fire increased, reaching a crescendo at 3 am and slackening away to nothing thereafter. Dawn broke in silence, and at 7 am the *Wanganui Times* correspondent reported: 'an advance from the trenches will shortly be made'.

As they awaited the order to assault, the men in the front lines began to notice 'an unusual and even ominous stillness'. Solomon Black 'declared it was his opinion that the natives had bolted'. Others with more experience of Titokowaru's ploys demurred, perhaps remembering the fate of George Maxwell, who had died here for the same assumption. But, 'in spite of all opposition', Black, his mate Ben Biddle, and one other constable 'jumped over the ditch and bank fence, walked through the piece of bush, and straight up to the pa'. As the colonial army held its collective breath, they clambered over the palisades and in to Tauranga Ika. They found the great pa completely empty, except for one male puppy, 'the sole trophy that fell into our hands'.

What happened at Tauranga Ika? Why did the great Titokowaru, at the peak of his powers, abandon his strongest pa and the prospect of almost certain victory? Some Ngarauru and Ngati Ruanui elders, now living, may know, but they are not telling, and their reticence is in itself instructive. We are left with the conventional historian's tools of probability, shreds of evidence, and speculation.

Some possibilities can be eliminated. It was not a strategic withdrawal. The Maori army began to dissolve after 3 February and it would not have done so if it was merely exchanging a strong position for a still stronger one – which, as the event was to prove, did not exist. Whitmore maintained that it was fear of his attack which caused the evacuation. But, once they had inspected it, the colonists were all stunned by Tauranga Ika's strength. It was 'beautifully built', 'a fearful place to rush', 'without doubt the strongest Pah I have ever seen'. 'It is more than doubtful if we should have taken it by storm.' 'In all my experience during the last war I have never seen a more formidable rebel position.' Whitmore himself inconsistently confessed that 'no troops in the world' could have stormed the defences. It was 'a really strong pah,' he wrote privately, which 'could not have been rushed. *Quite impossible.*' So much for Whitmore frightening Titokowaru from Tauranga Ika.

The notion that the Maori had run out of food is scarcely more credible. Titokowaru had all the farms and stockpiles of South Taranaki to draw on, Maori and Pakeha, and the volunteer cavalry raids had burned mainly empty villages. The colonial forces found vast caches of potatoes in nearby settlements in the days after the evacuation.

A more serious possibility is that the Maori had exhausted their ammunition. According to a government spy, Titokowaru asserted in September 1869 that this had been the case. But the filter of neutral tribes that had previously kept him supplied was still operating. He had captured over 300 swags containing reserve ammunition at Moturoa, together with ammunition from settlers' houses throughout the whole Waitotara district, and the Weraroa supplies Newland had not had time to destroy in ten minutes on 13 November. The Maori army fired freely on the night of 2-3 February and, as we shall see, its rearguard was to continue doing so during the subsequent days. Weeks later, Titokowaru did lose most of his ammunition, and it may have been this he referred to in September.

The least unlikely explanation is that of Kimble Bent. Titokowaru, Bent told James Cowan,

was detected in a liaison with another man's wife. This misdemeanour was, in Maori eyes, fatal to his prestige as an ariki [high chief] and a war-leader. He had trampled on his tapu, and his Hauhau angel, who had so long successfully

guided his fortunes, now deserted him. His run of luck had turned. A council
of the people was held to discuss the cause célèbre, and many an angry speech
was made. Some of the chiefs went so far as to threaten Titokowaru with
death. At length a chieftainess of considerable influence rose and quelled the
storm of violent words. She appealed to the aggrieved husband's people not
to attempt Titoko's life; but urged that the garrison should leave the pa –
it would be disastrous to make a stand there after their tohunga, their spiritual
head and their war-leader, had lost his mana-tapu. This met with the general
approval, and on the night of the attack the people packed their few belongings
on their backs and struck quietly into the forest.

Another tradition has it that Titokowaru's partner's name was
Puarauranga, but nothing else is recorded about her.

Bent implied that the discovery of the affair, the meeting about
it, and the evacuation of Tauranga Ika all occurred on the same
night: 2-3 February. The swiftness and completeness of the evacuation
do not necessarily undercut this. Tauranga Ika had no doubt been
stripped down to a fighting pa – children, old people, and surplus
supplies had been sent elsewhere. Time after time in the New Zealand
Wars, Maori forces had shown themselves fully capable of organising
and implementing an efficient evacuation in a few hours. Another
consideration supports the notion of a sudden decision on the night
of 2-3 February. A Maori story indicates that Titokowaru's mana-
tapu was considered to be still at its height during the bombardment
that evening: 'Titokowaru's god and his great priestly mana prevented
the shells from entering the *pa*. He stayed them just outside the palisade
wall, just as if he had put out his hand and so they fell short, all
outside the stockade.' The story deals specifically with Cohorn mortar
shells, which did indeed all fall short. Furthermore, the repartee
between garrison and besiegers on the evening of 2 February suggests
that morale in the pa was high up to that time. Soldiers who have
just lost their invincible leader through a 'fatal misdemeanour' do
not normally exchange witticisms with the enemy before battle.

Kimble Bent had no reason to lie. His memoirs are generally
accurate, except about his own early career. He kept a journal, and
received a tohunga's training in the arts of memory. He was an
eyewitness, and as one of Titokowaru's immediate entourage was
in a position to be well informed. He greatly esteemed his leader,
who always treated him kindly, and would have been the last person
to blacken his name gratuitously. But there is reason to believe that
Bent's account, while true, was only part of the truth.

There is a Maori tradition that warriors should remain chaste before battle and this might have applied with still more stringency to a tohunga-warleader whose personal tapu was so important. Here, at first sight, may lie the clue to the puzzle of Tauranga Ika. But, while we know all too little about Titokowaru's religion and philosophy, we do know that chastity was not part of it. Te Ua Haumene had rejected missionary teachings about sexual relations, preferring the traditional practice of polygamy and perhaps going even further by discarding marriage ceremonies. Te Kooti Rikirangi did likewise, and is said also to have openly practised adultery with his followers' wives as an assertion of his mana. There is some evidence to suggest that Titokowaru went at least as far as his predecessor, Te Ua, and perhaps as far as his contemporary, Te Kooti. A month after Tauranga Ika, Robert Parris was told by Ahitana's Ngati Tupaea that 'Titokowaru's followers are leaving him in consequence of his intriguing with their women'. Tangahoe are also said to have objected to his plurality of wives, and a similar report made reference to a Ngarauru village on the Waitotara: 'It was at this village that Titokowaru introduced the Mormon custom of polygamy taking no less than five wives from the Waitotara tribe.'

Some of the senior chiefs of the hapu allied to Titokowaru seem never to have liked aspects of Titokowaru's code which appeared to undermine conventional behaviour. Perhaps these included his personal predominance which exceeded that of traditional leadership, his ceremonial cannibalism, and conceivably also his sexual practices. The established chiefs of Tangahoe – Hone Pihama, Natanahira, and Patohe – refused to join him, as did the equivalent chiefs of Ngarauru – Pehimana, Aperahama, and Hare Tipene. Taurua and Wharematangi of Pakakohe had also hesitated, despite their sympathy with his cause. There is a reliable Maori tradition that, at a Ngarauru village on the Waitotara, since wrongly known as Taratu, Titokowaru was rejected by the local chief, who was also an eminent relative. Titokowaru 'was ordered to return to his home and cease causing further trouble amongst the local natives. Because of his refusal, and of his barbarous rites, Titokowaru was banned from entering the pa of his tuakana (superior, his first cousin) the chief of the old pa site.' This may be the same Waitotara village in which Titokowaru is said to have taken five Ngarauru wives. But the crucial point is that the practice which these actions reflect, if not the actions themselves, must have predated Tauranga Ika.

All this suggests that Titokowaru practised polygamy, and perhaps even ritual adultery like Te Kooti, and that this was public knowledge amongst his followers before Tauranga Ika. The established chiefs strongly objected to this and other radical aspects of his creed, but the people as a whole accepted it, without detriment to Titokowaru's mana among them. Yet, according to Bent, the people were so horrified by the discovery of one particular relationship on the night of 3 February that some 'went so far as to threaten Titokowaru with death'. On the other hand, another traditional account states that on the night of 3 February, just before the evacuation, Titokowaru himself conducted a religious ceremony to establish the best route of escape. And it is certain that the evacuation was carried out in organised fashion, with nothing left in the pa but a puppy, and that Titokowaru was in full and masterly control of the rearguard.

It was not the mere fact of a sexual liaison, or even of adultery, which caused the people to reject Titokowaru. It may well have been the identity of Puarauranga. The most likely explanation, perhaps, is that she was the wife of some important chief. Yet who, given that Titokowaru's practice was known and accepted, was so influential that his cuckolding should arouse so strong and strange a reaction? For the rejection of Titokowaru seems to have been instant and almost universal, yet curiously regretful and incomplete, as though the prophet's offence, though fatal, was beyond his control. He was still allowed to conduct the retreat and the religious ceremony which preceded it. The mystery remains, and here we must leave it, except for one last guess. We know that Titokowaru had close relatives among the Ngarauru, possibly more than even he knew. Etapu, said to have been his half-brother, was one. Could Puarauranga have been another?

Chapter Thirteen

THE LION AT BAY

Whatever its causes, the abandonment of Tauranga Ika on 3 February 1869 began the collapse of Titokowaru's resistance. For several weeks the colonists remained unaware of this. Of course, Whitmore and the government tried to portray the occupation of the empty pa as a great victory. Yet they did so automatically, without real conviction, and nobody except some historians believed them. The official claims were 'a gross delusion', 'a great mistake': 'Colonel Whitmore makes a great mistake when he puts down the retreat of the enemy to fear'; 'It was a great mistake to proclaim his [Titokowaru's] masterly retreat . . . as a victory gained by us.' Far from the troops being 'delighted with their success', as Whitmore claimed, 'disappointment was terrible' among them. 'So, upon the whole,' wrote the London *Times* correspondent 'the "grand decisive blow" may be considered to have missed.'

Ten days later came Whitecliffs. The news created as much consternation among the Pakeha facing Titokowaru as it had at New Plymouth. Haultain wrote that 'the very suspicion of a general rising is most alarming' and went to New Plymouth himself. Whitmore did not receive the news until 20 February. He had hoped to do without Mete Kingi and the recalcitrant bulk of the Whanganui kupapa, but now he changed his tune: 'The late news from Taranaki is so serious as to modify a good deal my feelings regarding the employment of the Ngatihau [Whanganui]. I now think we should get them by a means short of asking for their services.' Numerous reports confirmed that Tikaokao and Reihana had 600 warriers assembled at Mokau. Neutral Maori opinion was that they were awaiting the counter-attack that they naturally assumed the Whitecliffs would engender. If it did not come, they might advance on New Plymouth. This possibility in itself helped Titokowaru by diverting colonial troops. The hundred constabulary sent initially to New Plymouth came from Whitmore's army, and more were to follow. But a still more horrendous possibility was widely feared. On 25 February the *Wanganui Times* expressed the common view: 'It is more than probable that Titokowaru may, within the present week, be joined by five or six hundred Ngatimaniapoto.'

These fears were misplaced, though the colonists could not yet know it. The events at Tauranga Ika on 2-3 February meant that Titokowaru had lost his value as an ally for the King Movement. His army was disintegrating, with 'whole hapus breaking away'. The North Taranaki Maori and the Kingites learned of this more quickly than the colonists. Within a few days of Whitecliffs, the Taranaki Maori were 'inclined to think that Titoko's game is nearly played out, and that any further chance of success is gone'. Titokowaru himself knew it, and is said to have admitted as much to the King Movement, perhaps to save them from joining a sinking ship: 'Titoko has written to the King, stating he judged it better to give up fighting and retire'. Tikaokao, Reihana, and their army remained ready for action at Mokau, but in the light of these developments they did not move. For the moment, the Kingite intervention in Titokowaru's War was suspended.

Titokowaru's ship was sinking. There were major desertions from his army immediately after 3 February, and his control over the remainder greatly diminished. Big Kereopa and at least some Ngaurau remained with him until about 20 February, but by the end of the month all but two or three had gone. Tito Te Hanataua and some Tangahoe also deserted, as did at least ten of the Ngati Maru. Pakakohe were still with Titokowaru in mid-March, but 'they are very dissatisfied with him and intend to leave him' and soon did so. His force ultimately shrank back to the level of the Te Ngutu o te Manu, and his struggle was now solely to block Pakeha vengeance. But the wounded lion still had claws.

On the morning of 3 February, after discovering that Tauranga Ika was empty, Whitmore, balked of his prey, set off in determined pursuit. His fastest-moving troops, the volunteer cavalry, the Arawa of No. 8, and Kepa and thirty of his best bushmen, Sam Austin among them, moved in advance, supported by Nos. 3 and 6 under Lyon. The enemy had a start of several hours, but Kepa's party found signs of their retreat, including a camp where the rearguard had stopped to rest and eat, 'the fires being still alive'. The trail led to the cluster of villages around Weraroa. Around midday the cavalry (under Bryce, because Finnimore had been sent to Wellington with Whitmore's Tauranga Ika report as a reward for his services) entered Weraroa, scene of Wilmot Powell's fictional triumph of 13 November. Bryce was fired on by Titokowaru and the rearguard, who were in high fern on the Karaka plateau, across a gully from the derelict redoubt. Kepa came up, and charged immediately across the gully to come to grips. Lyon's column also entered the fern, soon followed by Whitmore, who sent in No. 7 to support Lyon, and also brought up No. 1 and the Arawa. It is likely that Titokowaru retreated to the Weraroa villages because he wished to pick up his children and old people, sent there when battle at Taurangi Ika had seemed imminent. Now all that stood between them and the 700 eagerly advancing colonial troops was their disgraced general and his forty-man rearguard.

Kepa was as eager as anyone to get Titokowaru, perhaps because he saw Moturoa as a personal humiliation. With twelve of his party, he pushed on hard through the fern, and suddenly found himself in an ambush. His impetuous advance must have taken him in from an unexpected direction, for Titokowaru's men 'could not fire for fear of shooting each other'. Kepa managed to escape back to the rest of his party, losing only one man killed – a chief of high mana named Hori Rongo Raukawa. Kepa's band lay down and exchanged fire with Titokowaru through the thick fern, waiting for Lyon to come up so that they could renew the advance. 'But,' wrote Sam Austin, 'I am sorry to say we were left there until all our ammunition was spent, and had to retire through the bush as best we could.'

Lyon had tried to advance. But his force came under heavy fire almost as soon as it entered the high fern. Titokowaru had left a few men to hold Kepa and moved across with the rest to prevent Lyon from joining him. Lyon had 160 men of No. 3 and No. 6, including many veterans and excellent officers such as Goring and Roberts. But the Maori fire was accurate despite the foliage – perhaps hidden positions with good lines of fire had been prepared in advance. Three constables of No. 3 soon fell severely wounded; two more disappeared completely, and were presumed killed. The rest found 'it was impossible to get a view of the enemy', and dire memories of Te Ngutu sprang to mind among the veterans while the new recruits began to panic. Despite his best efforts, Lyon and his officers could persuade only twenty or thirty men to follow them and had to give up. 'Roberts, who is as good a man as could be,' wrote Whitmore, 'could not get his men on – and the enemy was not certainly above 50 strong if that, merely their rearguard.' The troops began to sidle back out of the fern, though they did not bolt. Lyon himself 'scorned to retire, and remained with his wounded, walking erect from one to the other'. Eventually he too withdrew, bringing the wounded, and joined Kepa, Whitmore, and the rest of the troops in the gully below Te Karaka.

Whitmore now sought to organise another attack, but unease had spread quickly to the uninvolved units, even to Arawa and Kepa's picked party. 'Whitmore wanted us to return back again,' wrote Austin, 'although he had 6 or 700 men who had done nothing. We had not broken out fast although they had had both breakfast and dinner. After some talk between Whitmore and Kemp we were allowed to fall out and get our breakfast.' Reluctantly, Whitmore withdrew the whole force to Weraroa for the night. Next day the two men missing from No. 3 walked into camp unharmed. They had got lost and, according to their own account, had almost stumbled into the midst of Titokowaru's force – though it seems most likely that they 'got lost' in the other direction. Hori Raukawa was also found, 'cut up in a frightful manner', 'the head in one place, the body in another' – probably in revenge for the volunteer cavalry's deed near Manutahi the previous December. The mutilation may have been of a similar kind, for it produced 'an extraordinary effect upon his comrades', ranging from rage to terror and sometimes both.

The tiny, forgotten skirmish of Te Karaka was one of Titokowaru's major victories. Kepa claimed to have killed five of his men, and Lyon several more, and Titokowaru certainly lost at least one killed – a Ngaruahine warrior named Te Ritemona. But, against enormous odds even for him, and in the most depressing circumstances conceivable, he had saved his people. On 4 February, all left the Weraroa villages and withdrew further inland. For the next fortnight, Whitmore had difficulty persuading his men to enter dense bush. On 9 February he wrote to Stafford: 'I am trying to raise a light column of Volunteers and to get natives but the Wanganuis don't come and since the mutilation of Hori are *cowed* I think.' His patrols searched all the open areas and margins of the bush as far north as Moturoa and burned the deserted Weraroa villages, but they did not enter the great inland forest, and so found no sign of Titokowaru.

Titokowaru's new encampment was actually not far from either Wairoa or Weraroa, forming the apex of a triangle drawn inland from the two. According to Kimble Bent, its name was Oteka – the colonists knew the locality as 'Seven Hummocks'. It was only seven miles from the Weraroa villages, but over extremely difficult country. Here, Titokowaru was safe for the moment, but his resources were melting away like ice in the sun. Ngarauru now began to leave him, at first moving up the Waitotara to their ancient refuges such as Piraunui. Though the colonist patrols did not find Titokowaru, they did loot or destroy horses, cattle, and potatoes in the villages around Weraroa which had recently been his main supply area. He had some reserve supplies, but they could not last for ever, and by 16 February the colonists had learned his approximate location and regained their confidence.

During this period, Whitmore shook himself free of the sense of anti-climax and disappointment, and did some more of the clear strategic thinking that had produced the East Coast plan and victory at Ngatapa. He was beginning to suspect that 'the enemy is to some extent scattered'. The nature of the war would change: the formal confrontation between two armies was over, and the hunt was on. 'To bring this campaign now to a close, the enemy must be hunted out of the bush.' Whitmore's raw recruits could eventually be trained for such a task, but there was no time. And his large army was too cumbersome. 'For such operations much of the force under my command is utterly useless,' he wrote. What was needed was the old bush-scouring method: flying columns of picked troops, accustomed to the bush and to travelling light. Whitmore therefore redeployed his troops. He discharged Finnimore's cavalry and 200 constabulary recruits. He still feared Titokowaru 'could endanger the settled districts behind', and left the Wanganui Veteran Volunteers, Bryce's cavalry, and most of the kupapa to hold the line of the Kai Iwi. He reinforced St John at Patea and Hawes at Wairoa, so that they could mount aggressive patrols to cut off Titokowaru if he retreated northwards. He left the main headquarters, guns, most of his wagons, and some constabulary at Nukumaru, and formed a slimmed-down striking force of 'Major Kemp's selected corps' of about a hundred kupapa and the best of the constabulary – in all around 600 men. But Te Karaka had shown that even these men were not immune to Titokowaru's aura of invincibility in the bush, and Whitmore set about encouraging them, characteristically using both the stick and the carrot.

The sticks were dismissal and sentences of fifty lashes and two years' hard labour for cowardice and desertion. Several men received such treatment for their behaviour at Te Karaka, though Constables James Quinlan and F. Lambe managed to escape on 15 February, before their sentences were carried out. Whitmore also revived his Poverty Bay tactic of threatening summary execution, telling 'the divisions that had misbehaved at Te Karaka' that 'I would fire into them if they hesitated again'. The carrots were more original, though based on the ancient incentives of glory, sex, and cash.

The glory, Whitmore suggested to the government, should derive

from a new colonial decoration: the New Zealand Cross. Bowen
authorised it, forgetting that his mistress Queen Victoria was supposed
to be the fount of all honour. He was reprimanded, but the Cross
was instituted, and competition for it was immediately intense. It
could be awarded retrospectively, and Thomas McDonnell spent most
of the rest of his life lobbying for it, eventually succeeding in 1886.
Sam Austin had a much easier road to the coveted decoration, receiving
it for saving William McDonnell from a tight spot during the Pokaikai
Campaign in 1866. McDonnell later wrote: 'I was taken out by Sergt.
White and not by Sergt. Austin who in mistake received the Cross
for doing so.' Despite such errors, the decoration served Whitmore's
purpose.

His other incentives were less innocent. The government had given
the Arawa of No. 8 division custody of some of Te Kooti's female
followers captured at Ngatapa, including one of Te Kooti's own wives.
They had brought these women with them to Wanganui in January,
causing a local paper to remark: 'What they propose doing with
Mrs Te Kooti we know not, but trust they may shortly have Mrs
Titokowaru to keep her company.' Whitmore did indeed promise
that if any of Titokowaru's women were captured, 'I will give them
to the Arawa'. Some were, and it may be these women who appear
in photographs of colonist and kupapa troops stationed at Patea a
few months later. It seems probable that the women became
involuntary sexual partners. This practice occurred elsewhere during
the wars, at Te Porere for example. It amounted to government-
authorised slavery.

Whitmore's cash incentive was an adaptation of Haultain's aborted
bounty for enemies brought in. This time it applied dead or alive,
at five pounds a warrior, ten pounds a chief, and 1,000 pounds for
Titokowaru. One man is said to have fraudulently claimed this last
prize by gouging out the eye of a dead enemy and claiming the
corpse was the one-eyed Titokowaru. The plan failed because he
chose the wrong eye. There is another story, probably equally
apocryphal, that Titokowaru responded by offering two shillings and
sixpence reward for Governor Bowen. But it is quite certain that
Whitmore's offer of five pounds a head was taken up, and taken
literally, in at least four cases. On one occasion Tom Adamson and
a kupapa dumped severed heads in front of Whitmore and claimed
the bounty. The colonel was shocked at this barbarism. According
to Thomas Porter, he had intended that they bring only the ears.

Thus motivated, the colonial striking force renewed the hunt on

Two views of Whitmore's pursuit force, with women   *Taranaki Museum*

16 February. Two columns scouted towards the Seven Hummocks area. One, 186 men under Kepa, was based at Wairoa and patrolled inland on 17 and 18 February. Kepa found signs of a foraging party, but none of the main body. The other column, Thomas McDonnell and his No. 2 division, was based at a new camp at Te Karaka and patrolled the north bank of the Waitotara. On 17 February McDonnell returned, convinced that the enemy position was around Seven Hummocks, and Whitmore ordered him to cut a packhorse track from Te Karaka in preparation for an expedition.

Even Whitmore had to admit that McDonnell searched vigorously for the enemy. Few hatreds can have been more intense than McDonnell's for Titokowaru: 'I . . . believe Titokowaru capable of anything horrible. I trust his future punishments will fall into my hands. I should hardly like to hear that he was dead, unless I had been by.' Now the prospect seemed near and on 18 February McDonnell urged on his men as they worked on the track in the heat of the day. Fraser, Herrick, and Cumming happened to visit Camp Te Karaka that afternoon, and the sociable McDonnell walked down from the working parties to talk to them. Someone had just told the officers that there was a grove of peach trees, laden with ripe fruit, just across the Waitotara. After a week of rations and no more, Herrick and Cumming wanted to go and collect some but, perhaps suffering from a hangover, 'Colonel Fraser demurred, objecting to walk up the steep hill'. Sergeant George Menzies, a big and rather stout veteran of the 57th Imperials, was nearby. With a veteran's instinct for avoiding hard work on the track, he offered to take a party to pick fruit for the visiting officers. McDonnell consented, and Menzies chose nine men. At 3 pm the party climbed the hill, crossed the river in a small canoe, and made towards the peach grove, leaving two men to guard the canoe.

The peach grove happened to contain a party of Titokowaru's men, perhaps as many of twenty. They were probably a reconnaissance unit, keeping an eye on McDonnell's camp, commanded by Big Kereopa and including Tutange Waionui. Kereopa ordered his party to lie quiet. As the constabulary began to pluck peaches, they opened fire at a hundred yards. Taken completely by surprise, Menzies and company fled towards their canoe. The leading men might have escaped, according to Tutange, but the others held up the canoe while attempting to clamber aboard. Kereopa, less careful a leader than most of Titokowaru's lieutenants, charged in to close quarters with his warriors, but the colonists were too intent on escape to punish them with a volley. Five men were shot or tomahawked to death near the canoe and their bodies thrown into the river. They included two Australians, George Horspool and James Banks, who had been recruited in Melbourne two months before. Sergeant Menzies was killed with a canoe paddle. 'I snatched up a paddle from the canoe,' recalled Tutange, 'and struck him a slanting blow on the side of the temple with it, the fatal blow called *tipi*, as delivered in a sideways fashion with the edge of a stone *mere*' – a short, sharp-edged club. Two men, Robert Henderson and Alfred Wakeford, got clean away by sprinting up the river bank. Two more, John McEvoy and Connell Boyle, managed to swim the river. As they staggered up the opposite bank of the river they received an accurate volley from Kereopa's men. McEvoy fell wounded and Boyle was killed with a shot through the head.

The Peach Grove Ambush, bloody and one-sided as it was, did not have the malign impact of Te Karaka on colonist morale. Whitmore claimed that, on the contrary, his troops were eager for revenge. But it did have some intimidating effect – 'this unfortunate affair cast a gloom over the whole camp'. This, combined with unseasonable rain which flooded the Waitotara and with news of the Whitecliffs, suspended the hunt for Titokowaru for another fortnight.

The ambush also marked the final disappearance of Thomas McDonnell from this story. He prided himself above all on his bushcraft and ability to predict Maori actions, and the loss of seven of his men in so amateurish a fashion was humiliating, as Whitmore subtly implied in his report. McDonnell could not bear it, and resigned again. Whitmore wrote vindictively: 'it's a ton weight off my mind to get rid of him, as I believe he has been my sole difficulty here beginning at Moturoa or before it'. Someone might yet take revenge on Titokowaru, but it would not be Fighting Mac.

Titokowaru remained at Oteka until early March, protected by the terrain, the rains, and the memory of Te Karaka and the Peach Grove. But by 4 March the floods had subsided. Whitmore had made a flying visit to Wellington from 1 to 4 March and persuaded the government to recruit some East Coast Maori, especially Ngati Porou, whom he believed to be the good bushmen he needed. But now he was back and, without waiting for Ngati Porou, he recommenced the campaign. He completed the dray roads and packhorse tracks around Wairoa and Te Karaka, established ferries across the Waitotara, and sent strong columns into the bush towards Oteka. It was time to leave, and Titokowaru did so, marching north with

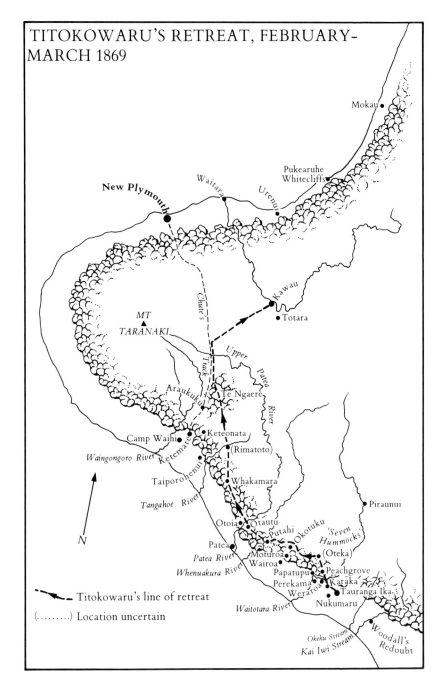

TITOKOWARU'S RETREAT, FEBRUARY–
MARCH 1869

Mokau

Pukearuhe
Whitecliffs

New Plymouth   Waitara   Urenui

Kawau

MT
▲
TARANAKI   Upper   Totara

Chute's

Track

Upper
Patea
River

Araukuku   Te Ngaere

Camp Waihi   Keteonata

Waingongoro River   Ketemarae   (Rimatoto)

Taiporohenui   Whakamara

Tangahoe River   Piraunui

Otoia Otautu
                    Putahi Okotuku 'Seven
Patea   Hummocks'
Patea River   Moturoa   (Oteka)
Whenuakura River   Wairoa
                    Papatupu Peachgrove
N   Perekama   Karaka
                    Weraroa Tauranga Ika
                    Nukumaru
            Waitotara River

■ ■ ■ ◀─ Titokowaru's line of retreat

(.........) Location uncertain

Okehu Stream   Woodall's
Kai Iwi Stream   Redoubt

his people to the Whenuakura River.

It was probably now that he suffered further desertions: Taranaki, some Atiawa, and most of Tangahoe, including Tito Hanataua. This left Titokowaru with Ngaruahine, some Atiawa, and the extremely discontented Pakakohe under Taurua and Wharematangi. Tiny loyal residues of his other allies also remained, such as Rupe and his few Tangahoe, and a Ngarauru named Tapa. There may still have been as many as 400 people, of whom no more than 150 would have been warriors. Perhaps about 8 March they moved down the Whenuakura, past Putahi, and across to the Patea River. They encamped at Otautu, a small Pakakohe village in dense bush at the edge of a great ravine on the south bank of the Patea opposite Otoia. Marching through steep, thickly forested country they had to abandon most of their remaining horses, including Titokowaru's own cherished steed, Niu Tirene. Only Katene and Tutange Waionui kept horses for scouting.

The colonial columns scouting towards Oteka therefore found nothing except Niu Tirene and six other horses. The capture of the 'great "Gray Horse" ' was itself something of a triumph, for the colonists were by no means immune to 'superstition'. And Whitmore was quite pleased that Titokowaru had left Oteka: 'I confess it is most satisfactory to get the enemy out of a place in which he could only have been attacked under every possible disadvantage.' On 9 March, Whitmore received word from St John at Patea that Titokowaru's force had been seen at Putahi. In a flurry of violent activity, he realigned his forces, shifting his baggage train from Nukumaru and his columns based on Wairoa and Weraroa to Patea. By 12 March, Whitmore had concentrated his striking force at the battered old district capital and was ready to attack.

Titokowaru was aware of the colonial redeployment and, despite the weakened condition of his force, made an effort to obstruct it. The colonists were using the coastal route to convoy supplies to Patea, and on 10 March a Maori raiding party prepared an ambush on it at the mouth of the Whenuakura River. The Maori allowed several individuals and small parties to pass through unmolested – a sophistication which Whitmore could scarcely believe. Then at 1.30 pm a supply convoy passed by – seven drays, a flock of sheep, and a forty-man escort under Lieutenant James Hunter of the Patea volunteers. The Maori opened fire, but their volley was mistimed, and they retreated prematurely after mistaking the dustcloud of two travellers for Pakeha reinforcements. Two horses were hit, and 'a tin of coffee put out of shape', but there were no human casualties on either side. Sergeant Taplin of the escort did not wait to establish this, but fled the scene all the way to Wanganui and reported a bloody defeat. He defended his conduct by saying that 'if a bullet had hit me on the back when retiring, I should have considered that I received it in the execution of my duty'. One can imagine Whitmore's reaction to this, and he had Taplin court-martialled. Indeed, he wanted him sentenced to death, but the court would agree only to fifty lashes and two years' hard labour. Paradoxically, Whitmore then remitted all but one of the lashes, 'as no flogging could make a man brave', whereas, presumably, a firing squad would. But Taplin's disgrace did not affect the fact that Titokowaru's attempt to cut Whitmore's supply line had failed. At 8 pm on 12 March 1869, Whitmore's striking force marched secretly out of Patea to attack Otautu. Sensing a bloody engagement, Philip Putnam, shrewder than Taplin, took sick and remained behind.

The colonists moved in two columns. One, 200 men under St John, marched up the north bank of the Patea to Otoia and the nearby fords to cut off the Maori retreat. The other, under Whitmore, marched up the south bank to assault Otautu. It consisted of the fittest men of Nos. 1, 2, 3, and 6 divisions, plus the Arawa of No. 8 and eighty Whanganui under Kepa – in all 400 men. The night march was a trying one – 'the most dismal march I remember', according to Frederick Gascoyne – and the men were all 'more or less uncomfortable from not being able to smoke'. But these were picked troops, and their bushcraft had improved greatly in the six weeks since Te Karaka, as Whitmore himself admitted: 'The troops have shown a marked improvement in moving through the bush . . . I am much more satisfied than I have ever been with the spirit of the men and their bearing when placed in the bush.'

Whitmore's column completed its difficult march undiscovered by about 5 am on 13 March. Dawn brought a thick fog, reducing visibility to twenty yards in some places, but the scouts established that Otautu was indeed the Maori position. A track led up the hill from the south, intersecting with a lesser track near some peach trees. The village was on a small plateau on the reverse side of the hill overlooking the Patea River. The plateau also contained cultivations and scattered clumps of bush. Behind it the ground dropped steeply into a wooded ravine, extending down to the river 200 feet below. There was a light village fence, but no fortifications. Quietly and carefully the colonists began climbing the track and reached the top at 6 am, still undiscovered. The Arawa and a few European constabulary scouts were in the van, led by Whitmore himself. Whitmore planned to keep Nos. 3 and 6 in reserve under Lyon and to deploy two assault forces: Whanganui and No. 1 on the right, Arawa and No. 2 on the left. With McDonnell gone and Fraser on the sick list in Patea, their divisions were commanded by junior officers – Fraser's No. 1 by Fred Gascoyne and McDonnell's No. 2 by David Scannell. Whitmore was therefore able quietly to promote two Maori, Kepa and William Gundry, to the command of his assault forces. Both were ruthless masters of bush warfare, and they and their men crept carefully but eagerly up Otautu Hill.

But the Maori were not completely unprepared. The previous night in Otautu, Kimble Bent had had a strange dream about a village with the houses cut in half, and this Titokowaru had interpreted as a warning. As he had done before Te Ngutu and Moturoa, the chief called his people together the following evening and said: 'Be on your guard! This is a night of evil and danger, and the morrow also will be a day of evil!' Again repeating his conduct at Te Ngutu, he especially cautioned his Pakeha, Kimble Bent, telling him to pack his most cherished possessions and be ready to fly at a moment's notice. Titokowaru received his foreknowledge of the enemy attack from a combination of the supernatural and sound military analysis. Their relative importance is for the reader to decide.

Titokowaru made his plans. He did not hope to repulse an attack on Otautu and win a victory of the Ngutu type. His people were in no state for that. He built no significant artificial defences, no trench systems or palisades. As his orders to Bent indicate, his plan was to evacuate the village itself quickly. But he would then seek to block the colonist pursuit while the non-combatants escaped by holding the lip of the ravine behind the village, a kind of natural firing trench. He added only a few concealed rifle pits. These radical tactics – aimed at keeping the enemy *in* Otautu not out of it – could be expected to have a surprise effect. The plan still required a few minutes' warning to enable the non-combatants and those Pakakohe warriors who did not choose to fight to move off with their gear in organised fashion. A sentry was thus posted on the top of the hill, which normally commanded a wide view. Behind him was an advanced picket of perhaps a dozen more sentries. On the morning of 12 March the sentry was Te Wareo, a Puketapu Atiawa, and the picket was possibly commanded by the wily old Mawhitiwhiti veteran, Hakopa Te Matauawa. But Titokowaru had not counted on the fog.

Whitmore and other colonists described the fog as 'unfortunate', but without it they would not have surprised Otautu. They are also said to have been helped by Te Wareo's drowsiness. In the fog, the colonist van got so close to him that several thought of silently tomahawking him. Ben Biddle was said to be about to do so when an officer said he was an Arawa. Whitmore claimed that if he had not happened to turn back to check on the rear at that moment he would have done it himself. 'I always carried in my girdle a tomahawk, a trophy from Ngatapa, and if I had been where I was a moment or two before the sentry would have been noiselessly killed.' But whatever the contents of Whitmore's girdle Te Wareo was probably neither so close nor so drowsy as that. He suddenly leapt up and dodged back through the bush, firing his revolver – carried by Maori sentries for signalling purposes – to raise the alarm. The colonists van then fired at him, but missed. They in turn were 'almost immediately fired upon with great precision by the enemy's guard or picquet, which turned out with great alacrity'. Tom Fleurs of the guides was mortally wounded, and two or three Arawa were also hit. But now Whitmore rapidly deployed his force as planned, Kepa and Gundry pushed on cautiously through the bush, and the picket fell back, though Hakopa himself did not.

At this first exchange the colonists were only yards from the plateau on which the village stood, separated from it by a narrow belt of bush and the insubstantial blanket of fog. The plan had failed: Te Wareo had provided too little warning, and the people in Otautu immediately understood they were in terrible danger. Kimble Bent's original account of their reaction – not the published version gentrified by Cowan – was as follows:

What a scurry there was! The people poured out of their whares just as they were from their sleeping mats – some with only a shawl or a bit of mat on, some stark naked. The women were worst of all – some of them hadn't a stitch of clothing on, and there they were yelling like the deuce, and running for their lives.

Bent grabbed his own flax kit, ready-packed with his diary, 'a little money', and other valuables, and scrambled down the ravine to the river with many others. 'Those who were with me were non-combatants, like myself, mostly women.' Some women remained, as usual, to support the fighting men. The women with Bent, encumbered by old people and children, had no chance at all of crossing the Patea before Kepa, Grundy, and their warriors caught up with them – unless something intervened.

The fighting men too flung themselves from their whare and out of the village, but at Titokowaru's command most did not flee. Some disenchanted Pakakohe may have done so, though young Tu-Patea Te Rongo stayed to fight, but Titokowaru may still have had as many as a hundred warriors. Taking only their guns and bandoliers, they left all their personal belongings, right down to their pipes, in their huts and tents. Despite the short notice they rushed to their assigned firing positions, most just under the lip of the ravine. The colonists did not yet know that the ravine existed.

Gundry and his men followed up the retreating picket. They emerged on to the plateau on the left of the village and may actually have entered it. They approached the ravine, still hidden in the mist, when, according to Constable J.H. Wilkes of No. 2, 'we received another sharp volley, from only a few yards distance, which killed one man and wounded several others'. The wounded included the noted Arawa warriors, Haihana Whakatau and 'Bonaparte', as well as William Gundry's young brother, Frederick, who had a terrible groin wound which proved to be mortal. Gundry's force recoiled a short distance and took cover.

On the right, the colonists also pressed forward towards the empty village. The Whanganui were on the extreme right, beyond the line of Titokowaru's hidden riflemen, with Gascoyne and No. 1 inside them. Gascoyne noted the retreat of the left, but pushed on towards the ravine. 'Immediately several of our men were knocked over by bullets from the foe hidden by the fog,' he wrote. Gascoyne too took cover, lying flat with his men only a few yards from the muzzles of the enemy guns. 'Just then Colonel Whitmore . . . rushed forward, shouting to me "Why don't you go on, sir? Charge instantly." ' In his own recollection Gascoyne replied, 'Down with you, Colonel, or you will be shot.' Whitmore was furious, until the death of his own orderly convinced him of Gascoyne's wisdom. In fact, mere captains did not give orders to George Whitmore, and with his own brand of cold courage the little colonel crawled forward with Kepa to try to make out the enemy position. He was mystified. His whole line, right and left, was pinned down and suffering casualties from close-range Maori fire. Yet their own far heavier volleys seemed to have no effect. For, in the fog, the colonists still could not see the ravine, and their fire passed harmlessly over the Maori's heads.

Down at the river, the non-combatants struggled to cross, ferrying themselves in a small canoe which could take only four at a time. With the river running broad and fast, it was a slow process. As the minutes stretched into an hour, groups of colonists on the plateau above began to edge forward, helped as well as hindered by the fog.

On the colonist left, Constable Charles Watt of No. 2 division 'in his eagerness to find out the position of the enemy, crawled to within a few yards of them'. Suddenly he was hit in the leg, the bullet breaking the bone, and called to his comrades for help. One of them wrote:

although we were within a few yards of the Hauhaus, and could hear every word they said, we could not discover whether they were entrenched or under cover of their pa, the fog still continuing so dense. It appeared almost certain death to advance to where poor Watt lay wounded.

Scannell's deputy, Captain Henry Northcroft, ordered three men to rescue him, led by William Wallace, now a sergeant. 'Wallace hesitated and then said "It is death to go there." ' Northcroft was a man of almost inhuman courage and rectitude. In later years he asked a boy of ten years, nine months his age. When told 'eleven', Northcroft said, 'That boy will never make good. He cannot tell the truth.' Now Northcroft stuck his sword in the ground and rescued Watt himself, under heavy fire. Unfortunately one of the shots which missed Northcroft mortally wounded Watt as he was being carried in, but that was not the point.

On the other flank, another party of seven men of No. 1 under Sergeant Richard Shepherd had also gone forward, possibly to cover Whitmore's reconnaissance. Elsewhere, the troops had taken to apparent cover only to find that the Maori had sighted lines of fire on it in advance. The same must have happened to Shepherd's party, because five of the seven men were quickly killed or wounded. Corporal William Guthries was hit in the mouth by a spent bullet but, despite losing two teeth, 'he coolly put his fingers into his mouth and pulled out the bullet'. Robert Barth, Thomas Kelly, Solomon Black, and Shepherd himself were not so lucky. Shepherd had his face shattered, but survived, and when he died in Wellington in 1913 in the midst of a general strike, his newspaper obituary must have turned him in his grave: 'These scraps with the Maoris in the old days must have been quite as warm as the street engagements that the police have been experiencing this week with the rabble up Taranaki-street way.'

'I regret to say,' wrote Whitmore, 'that during this interval we had to sustain many losses, hit from points which we could not see, but which afterwards proved to have been prepared for the purpose. At first the men thought these to have been shot from the rear.' According to the Maori, some were. Hakopa Te Matauawa had not withdrawn to the ravine with the rest of the picket. He was wearing a constabulary cap, tunic, and trousers, and carrying a Terry carbine – all taken in battle. He was therefore able to pass himself off as a kupapa and slunk about in the murk on the fringes of the colonial force, shouting impossible orders and shooting an isolated man when the opportunity arose. After wounding one of Kepa's warriors with his last carbine bullet, he managed to rejoin his comrades at the lip of the ravine. In 1911, according to James Cowan, the story of Hakopa's deed at Otautu was 'still told and retold with loving admiration by the old Taranaki Hauhaus'. Perhaps it was not quite so heroic as Henry Northcroft's, but it was rather more effective.

'This interval' proved to be longer than Whitmore subsequently cared to admit – two hours and five minutes, to be precise. The non-combatants all crossed the river. Titokowaru may have gradually thinned out his rearguard as well, and remained with about forty men and a few women, possibly the best swimmers. Eventually the morning fog lifted. The enemy position could now be seen, and Whitmore outflanked it on the right and prepared to renew his advance. Some Maori women were observed carrying away a wounded man 'in the midst of the heaviest fire'. Then Titokowaru and the last of his rearguard scrambled down the ravine and escaped by swimming the Patea.

The colonist troops now rushed the undefended village of Otautu, and Whitmore tried to push them on in pursuit. But, after their night march and the tension of the last two hours, the men were more interested in rest and plunder. 'If we could have stopped our men "looting",' wrote Whitmore privately, 'we might have killed a lot. But both Kemp and I did our best yet the golden moment past before it could be done.' To Whitmore's 'great disappointment', St John's column had not got past Otoia. It now fired off premature volleys, either at distant Maori fugitives or at nothing at all, from 'too far to be of the smallest use, but showing the enemy that his retreat was cut off in that direction'. Whitmore had lost eighteen men, while Titokowaru lost only one killed in the battle itself, a

Waikato warrior named Muhumuhu. Kepa eventually managed to mount a pursuit during which two women stragglers were taken prisoner and one or two wounded males may have been killed. But, against all odds, Titokowaru had saved his people. Despite the usual colonist claims to the contrary, Otautu was by no means the least of his victories.

On the other hand, he had saved little else. The lack of a few minutes' warning from Te Wareo meant the loss of tents, baggage, and 'tools of every description', clothing, blankets, 'and even a very great many commonly used pipes', 'fresh meat, potted meat, fruit and potatoes'. Whitmore found Von Tempsky's journal and sent it to Haultain as a personal gift. According to Booth, it had comments written in it in Titokowaru's own hand, but the document itself cannot be located. The colonists also claimed 'many arms', but most of these seem to have been trophies, heirlooms, and surplus weapons – captured revolvers and pistols, and 'Maori spears'. Most warriors kept their first-line guns, though the last of the rearguard may have abandoned some of them before swimming the Patea. But the reserves of ammunition had been captured. And, though the warriors kept their bandoliers many, like Hakopa, had exhausted the contents in the battle. 'I do not suppose,' wrote Booth, that 'they have more than from 100 to 200 rounds' between them – as much as a constabulary sub-division would use in a minute. Titokowaru had lost his power of resistance.

Chapter Fourteen

THE HUNT

The final and most desperate phase of the hunt for Titokowaru now began. From Otautu, the Maori fled to Whakamara, a two-day journey through trackless bush with only a couple of potatoes each for men, women, and children alike. At Whakamara, Wharematangi's village with its great niu pole, they found food and rest, but not for long. After the battle at Otautu and the abortive pursuit, Whitmore encamped part of his force first at Kakaramea, then at Manutahi, parallel to what he rightly guessed was the line of Titokowaru's retreat. The colonel himself went to Patea to check on the rest of his command, leaving Lyon and Kepa to lead the pursuit force. From Manutahi, light columns harked back and forth like bloodhounds, searching for Titokowaru's trail. Late on 17 March, a column under Kepa discovered he was at Whakamara and quietly closed in on the village.

Kepa had been reinforced by 150 more Whanganui kupapa in addition to his own followers, the Arawa, and sixty Europeans who had volunteered to serve under him. This made 350 men, quite enough to take Whakamara by assault from a foe without ammunition. But Kepa feared Titokowaru would escape again, and he decided to trap him between two fires. He sent to Lyon at Manutahi, requesting him to come up. Meanwhile he and his men lay silently in the bush near Whakamara, talking in whispers and lighting no fires. Kepa's advanced scouts could actually hear Titokowaru speaking in the night, 'advising his people to use very great precautions, not to forget that this was the day of the white man and of the [kupapa?] Maori and that they were to place the women and children in front, and the men were to bring up the rear'. But 'there seemed to be a good deal of dissension in the Hauhau camp'. Kepa's messenger reached Manutahi at 10 pm, and Lyon immediately marched through the night for Whakamara with 300 constabulary. He sent his own messenger to Patea to tell Whitmore.

At Patea, Whitmore was delighted to hear that 115 Ngati Porou, optimistically designated 'No. 9 AC,' were on their way to him, despite an attempt to prevent the move by Donald McLean. Lyon's messenger aroused Whitmore's desire to be in at the kill. The tough

little colonel rode hard for the edge of the bush near Mokoia, left
his horse there, and force-marched inland with James Booth and a
small escort, arriving before Whakamara at the same time as Lyon.
Lyon had the more difficult route, 'much enhanced . . . by the steep
chasms he was compelled to pass in the dark'. These the column
crossed with 'a sort of rough ladder . . . by which they scrambled
down or up the worst of these perpendicular banks'. For Lyon, lacking
an arm, this must have been a personal nightmare. As dawn broke,
he and his men, with Whitmore, concealed themselves near the enemy
position while Kepa and his column circled round to the rear to
close the trap. All three colonist commanders had performed prodigies
of endurance. Now they closed in on Whakamara for their reward.

The colonists had not been spotted, but they were dealing with
a man of great caution and foresight. Titokowaru's words, overheard
by Kepa's scout in the night, may indicate that he planned to leave
Whakamara on 18 March anyway. Certainly everything was packed
ready for instant departure, and as the colonists waited concealed
in the bush two scouts rode out of the village towards them on the
last of the Maori horses. They were the best men available, Tutange
Waionui and Katene Tuwhakaruru. Katene was in the lead, and he
rode past Lyon's advance guard either not seeing them, or pretending
not to. But he 'unfortunately discovered the main body', wrote
Whitmore, then 'stopped, turned, and fired . . . his revolver, not
so much caring to hurt us, for he took no aim, as to give the alarm
to his friends'. Katene galloped off, unhurt by the fire of the enraged
colonists whose trap he had sprung.

Titokowaru's people now fled with the greatest possible speed,
but not in disorganised panic. They split into small parties, according
to a prearranged plan, and headed in the direction of Te Ngaere,
via Rimatoto, near the Upper Tangahoe River. There was a small
rearguard, with only a couple of rounds per man. The Europeans
of Lyon's column poured into Whakamara, only to find it empty.
Exhausted by their night march, they themselves could not pursue.
Apart from Katene's warning, 'there was not a single shot fired at
us', but all were 'disappointed', in Whitmore's understatement and
they somehow blamed him. 'Whitmore came up,' wrote Stuart Newall
laconically, 'spoiled everything'. The troops vented their ire by burning
Whakamara and cutting down the magnificent niu pole, then sat
down and dined on the remains of Titokowaru's breakfast.

Lyon's column did not pursue, but Kepa's did. They had had at
least some rest in the night and were determined the enemy would

not evade their vengeance this time. 'I do not see how they are to escape from us,' wrote James Booth, 'hampered as they . . . are with women, children, and wounded.' Titokowaru's rearguard tried to hold its pursuers on the afternoon of the 18th, not far from Whakamara, from a position half-way up a cliff which may have been prepared in advance. But Kepa's men saw them, took cover, and the rearguard's few rounds were spent harmlessly. Kepa's vanguard outflanked them and they fled across a steep gorge, 200 yards across and nearly as deep, with little foliage on its faces. The kupapa killed one and wounded another as they clambered up the far side. The wounded man was carried off by his comrades, and the dead warrior's head was taken for Whitmore's reward. It, and other heads taken next day, were smoke-cured according to the traditional method by a tohunga named Teoti who accompanied the column.

For forty-eight hours from the morning of 18 March, Kepa and his hardy Europeans, Arawa, and Whanganui pressed the retreating enemy hard. It was this pursuit which must have been etched most deeply in the memory of Ngati Ruanui, though such horrors are rarely talked about. For fit adults with few burdens, like Kimble Bent, it was bad enough: 'We travelled for all we were worth half-naked and foodless, tumbling over logs, scrambling in and out of creeks . . . just like wild pigs before the hunter.' Most forest foods took time to render edible and, apart from occasional huhu grubs, food was a dream. For the old people, children, and wounded, and the devoted men and women who supported and carried them, the flight must have been a nightmare.

There were at least half a dozen badly wounded warriors – one from the rearguard skirmish, two or three from Otautu, and one or more with slow-healing injuries from earlier engagements. Their lives were preserved with incredible determination by their kin and comrades. They were carried on stretchers, one of which was found by the colonists, through the worst of the pursuit. One man was later found far to the north, having died of exposure, despite a good greatcoat and blanket, after his back wound was nearly healed. Others may also have died, but at least two were carried all the way to Ngaere. When an injured person died, or one of the party succumbed to illness, exhaustion or starvation, his or her body was buried or hidden when possible. The skeleton of one, a woman, was found years later in a hollow tree trunk. It is hard to understand how children and babes-in-arms survived the retreat from Whakamara, but some did. Others, no doubt, had been fostered with neutral kin and deserting

allies in an emergency version of the traditional Maori practice. Of
those who marched with their parents, many must have died, but
they were not abandoned when they became exhausted.

On 19 March, Kepa's vanguard, including Tom Adamson, a dozen
Whanganui, and a dozen Arawa, the warrior Pirika Hohepa among
them, came upon one such group of 'two or three' children. With
them were two women, their mothers, and a Ngaruahine chief,
probably Matangi Orupe, a 'grey-haired middle-aged' kinsman of
Titokowaru's. He may have been the father of one or more of the
children, though he had another son named Kuku. Matangi carried
his gun and his tomahawk, but of course had no ammunition. The
group 'had not been able to travel so fast as their friends, on account
of the tired children, and so had been left behind'. When Matangi
saw the enemy, he ran to draw their fire and was shot and badly
wounded by one of the Arawa. Matangi fell beside a pukatea tree,
remembered Pirika Hohepa, but 'struggled up to a squatting position,
with his empty gun across his knees'. The Arawa warrior drew his
tomahawk and rushed in to take his head. Matangi 'sprang up with
a great effort,' holding his own tomahawk, but was too badly injured
to strike. The Arawa seized him, but was suddenly pushed aside by
Tom Adamson. Adamson grabbed Matangi by the hair, 'stretched
the neck across one of the root-flanges of the tree, and snatching
out a short-handled tomahawk from just behind his right hip he
chopped the Hauhau's head off'. The Arawa was furious, but Adamson
kept the head. Since Matangi was known to be a chief, it was worth
ten pounds.

Constable Thomas Adamson, New Zealand Cross, then turned to
Matangi's family. 'He rushed at the weeping *wahiné* and her children,
and their heads would have come off also had not Captain Porter,
fortunately for them, just come up.' The two women were taken
prisoner, and James Cowan maintained that the children were saved
too. But no contemporary account mentions this; reports of the total
number of heads vary suspiciously, and hasty smoke-curing might
disguise both sex and age. Captain Porter could not be everywhere
at once.

At Whakamara, or during the pursuit, the Pakakohe under Taurua
and Wharematangi finally abandoned Titokowaru. On 19 or 20 March,
the rump of his army gathered at Rimatoto, arriving in exhausted
dribs and drabs. Rimatoto, in rough country near the Upper Tanganoe
River, was a tiny and isolated place, and the enemy might take weeks
to find it. But Titokowaru stuck to his plan to go to Te Ngaere,

from where he hoped to reach Ngati Maru country, on the Upper Waitara north of the mountain. Here he hoped he might get some ammunition. Next day, he set off. Most of the remaining Tangahoe decided to stay at Rimatoto. They included Kimble Bent, who now said his farewells to his leader and friend. On 21 March, Titokowaru and his own Ngaruahine, with a few Ngati Maru and Tangahoe – fewer than 200 people in all – reached Te Ngaere.

On 20 March, Kepa and his men left off their pursuit and rejoined the rest of the field force, now camped at Taiporohenui. Some of his warriors went immediately to Whitmore's tent and dumped grizzly trophies before the colonel: 'There, Whitmore, your heads!' One rolled under his camp bed, and Whitmore was said to have been shocked and disgusted. In fact, he paid up, and was privately pleased with 'my £5 proposal': 'As yet only 4 have been killed [under the scheme] but of these one would have escaped but for it.' He and others interrogated the captured women, 'who appeared worn out with fatigue', and learned that Titokowaru was making for Te Ngaere. 'It is curious,' wrote Whitmore with false innocence, 'how willing prisoners so taken, of either sex, are to recount all they know.' Another observer wrote: 'The women said Titoko was short of food, and that his men were all leaving him. Under threats, they told Colonel Whitmore where Titoko was.'

Te Ngaere was a vast swamp about twenty miles inland of Taiporohenui over the roughest terrain, with an island of solid ground at its heart on which stood three villages. It was a legendary fastness of the Ngati Tupaea hapu of Tangahoe, said to have 'engulfed' a taua of 500 Waikato warriors generations before. None of Whitmore's men, Maori or European, had been there, but despite all warnings from students of legend, the colonel determined to make the attempt. He moved the field force to Keteonata on 21 March. Even pack horses could go no further, and four days' rations were isued to the men to carry themselves. At 7am on the 22nd, leaving Lyon at Keteonata with most of the Europeans, Whitmore himself, with Kepa's kupapa light column, set off for Te Ngaere. His scouts reached the edge of Te Ngaere swamp that afternoon, having found signs of Titokowaru's retreat along the way. Convinced his foe was before him, Whitmore ordered up Lyon from Keteonata and prepared to enter the swamp.

For the colonial troops, the march to Te Ngaere was another in the series which made this the most difficult campaign yet in the New Zealand Wars. 'Frightful precipices, the yawning abysses beneath

Example of the terrain
traversed in the pursuit of
Titokowaru
Wanganui Museum

which are concealed by the rank luxuriance of the vegetation –
impenetrable thickets – above all, the danger of being attacked by
a concealed enemy – these are some of the perils encountered by
Colonel Whitmore.' Tension and tiredness led to accidents and illness.
Constable Boyne drowned crossing a river; Constable Healey
accidentally wounded two comrades with his revolver. There was
real 'fever' – dysentery, high temperature, and acute headaches. On
21 March one soldier wrote: 'I think half the Force will be laid up
with the fever'. There was also feigned illness, the traditional refuge
of soldiers and schoolchildren, and Whitmore had his doctors crack
down on it. They swept up even Philip Putnam in their net, and
the 'bad cold and a swelled lip with playing the Cornet' that had
saved him from Otautu no longer sufficed. But Putnam was a match
for them. On 23 March he found himself leading twenty latecomers
across the 'frightful precipices' to join Lyon's column at Ngaere.
Putnam and his men got lost and returned to Keteonata camp, but
were forced out again next day with a kupapa guide. 'Guide left
us. Don't know the road and half my men in a funk . . . Never

had a wink of sleep all night.' But by the 26th Putnam was back at Keteonata and was soon telling his diary of a less fortunate kindred spirit. Caught feigning sick, Constable O'Donnell of No. 6 'went quietly into the Bush and shot himself with his own rifle through the mouth', the ultimate paradox of 'cowardice'.

Apart from Putnam, Lyon's column reached Whitmore at the edge of Te Ngaere by midday on 23 March. As he had done before Otautu and Whakamara, Whitmore laid careful plans to trap Titokowaru, determined that the third time would prove lucky. Whitmore knew that Titokowaru was ultimately headed for Ngati Maru country – he had received a report that they had offered him ammunition – and that Chute's Track would therefore be his route of retreat. The colonel sent a messenger to New Plymouth, ordering the local commander, Major Charles Brown, to take a column down from the north to block the track. Brown, 'the Crimea hero', was one of the few officers whom Whitmore liked and admired, and he was confident the job would be done properly. Meanwhile, he set his own force to work making hurdles or fascines to enable it to cross the treacherous swamp to the island villages. Throughout the rest of the 23rd and the 24th they were occupied with this task. The men had to work hard and quietly, and sleep rough, with only small, sheltered fires lit two hours after nightfall, but they were now used to this. Before dawn on 25 March, the fascines were ready, and the colonial troops quietly crossed the swamp to Te Ngaere island.

Their main prey had long gone. Above all, Titokowaru wanted ammunition to enable him to resist, and he had marched with great urgency, despite privations, for Ngati Maru country on the Upper Waitara. With about a hundred of his strongest men and women, he had left Te Ngaere on 22 March, after resting only a day, just as Whitmore arrived at the other edge of the swamp. Titokowaru reached the Upper Waitara before Brown could leave New Plymouth, received his ammunition, and began building a pa at Kawau, on the river bank near Totara, to await attack. But he had left seventy people at Te Ngaere – the small Araukuku section of Ngaruahine whose chief, Kaake, had fallen at Te Ngutu, a few Tangahoe and Ngati Maru, and the weaker women and children. Ten of the Tekau-ma-rua remained to guard them. On these would fall the vengeance of the frustrated colonists.

But the tribal politics that Whitmore had never understood now intervened to balk him even in this. Titokowaru's power and mana were in tatters, but still he had his sympathisers. The people of Te

Ngaere, Ngati Tupaea under Ahitana and his son, Takorangi, had never fought for him, and they feared sheltering him. A colonist scout overheard one say: 'Now this evil man will cause the Wanganuis to come down on us.' But they still gave him hospitality, and after he departed they intended to feed and protect the people he left with them. The same scout also heard a woman's ritual call: 'Come hither, come hither, ye brave. Come hither to the food.' Moreoever, Whanganui were related to Ngati Tupaea, and the chiefs Aperaniko and Kawana Paipai, if not Kepa, were extremely reluctant to fire on them. Whanganui's war aims had always been more moderate than the government's, and it is also said that they wished to repay Titokowaru's father, who once spared the life of a Whanganui chief after defeating him in battle. The principle of utu demands that good deeds, as well as bad, be repaid.

So when the colonists advanced on the Te Ngaere villages they found that Aperaniko and Kawana Paipai had preceded them, and that Ngati Tupaea ran towards them with a white flag, blocking the line of fire to Titokowaru's people who now fled into the bush. 'I was embarrassed what to do,' wrote Whitmore. He was less concerned with the taking of innocent lives than with the effect this might have both on the neutral Taranaki tribes and on his own Whanganui. Takorangi kept him talking for an hour, and when the pursuit finally began Whanganui stood aside. The Arawa set off but the fugitives, in Whitmore's words, 'ran away exceedingly fast'. 'Half an hour's start can never be regained completely, and the women and children go as fast as the men . . . the pursuit of the Arawa was fruitless.'

Whitmore could still hope that Brown's force would cut them off, but again tribal politics intervened. Some Te Atiawa chiefs told Robert Parris and Superintendent Henry Richmond that if troops marched from New Plymouth against Titokowaru, Atiawa and Taranaki would go to war on his behalf. They held that a tacit neutrality pact was in force in the region, and that it worked both ways. There were also renewed rumours of Kingite invasion. Parris and Richmond withdrew their permission for Brown's expedition, and it never left New Plymouth. The Te Ngaere fugitives, after another terrible march on which at least one wounded man died, rejoined Titokowaru at Kawau.

'Thwarted by the friendly or neutral Native nuisance', Whitmore withdrew from Te Ngaere and rested his troops at Keteonata and old Camp Waihi for a week. Ironically, he was at last joined by

115 Ngati Porou, seventy more Arawa, and even a few Ngapuhi from North Auckland – a plethora of good bushmen just too late to be of use. But Whitmore was not yet ready to give up. On 5 April he marched for New Plymouth. One column, with the baggage, went by the coast. The other went around the mountain by Chute's Track, crossing sixty-eight streams and rivers yet completing the march in three days – a third of the time it had taken Chute in 1866. Poor Fraser was 'struck down by an epileptic fit' on the first day: 'It must be caused by drink,' wrote Putnam unsympathetically. By 8 April, the field force was camped near New Plymouth.

Whitmore made the move to New Plymouth partly to meet the Ngati Maniapoto threat and partly to see what could be done against Titokowaru at Kawau. Indeed it seemed likely that the two might join forces, since Kawau was only a day's march from the Whitecliffs. At first Whitmore had few qualms about adding the King Movement to his enemies. His troops were now 'fit to go anywhere'. On 1 April, while Putnam and his mates indulged in 'plenty of fool-making', Whitmore wrote blithely to Haultain with plans for an invasion of Waikato. But in the ensuing week it transpired that this was a bad April Fool's joke. With ammunition, Titokowaru was again a formidable opponent, of whom even the new Ngati Porou contingent had 'a wholesome dread'. A large part of Atiawa and Taranaki might make common cause with him, and Tikaokao was said to have his 600 warriors at or near Mokau, still waiting for the reaction to the Whitecliffs massacre.

All this was clear to the kupapa, and they hastened to enlighten their commander. The Arawa told him: 'We fear if we fight Waikato, Waikato will take revenge on us. We are afraid for our kaingas and our families. We will take the risk of punishment but cannot go into a new war at Taranaki.' The Whanganui tribal chiefs said they would 'stand aside' – in fact they and their men went home rather than to New Plymouth. Ngati Porou and Ngapuhi 'refused to join in this thing'. Even Kepa, wrote Whitmore, 'seems startled at the idea of 600 Ngatimaniapoto being at Taranaki and alarmed that a new and useless war will commence for which we are unprepared and not strong enough.' Without the kupapa, Whitmore's field force shrank to 400 men, and on 8 April he bowed to their sound sense and decided to 'let sleeping dogs lie'. James Richmond, who had joined him at New Plymouth, confirmed this decision.

There was still the rumoured Ngati Maniapoto invasion, and Whitmore and Charles Brown massed their forces at Urenui and the Lower Waitara to meet it. But Tikaokao's thinking was probably not dissimilar to Whitmore's. His prospective ally, Titokowaru, no longer had an army, and Tikaokao planned no further aggression. On 9 April, Whitmore cruised up to Mokau in the *St Kilda*, a large steam ship chartered by the government, and fired four token shots at Ngati Maniapoto from a howitzer mounted on the deck. He then returned to New Plymouth, left a strong garrison, and on 10 and 11 April embarked his field force for the Bay of Plenty, where Te Kooti was again active. For George Whitmore, Titokowaru's War was over.

The war was also virtually over for Titokowaru himself, and he had clearly lost. From mighty Tauranga Ika and command of 1,000 people, to remote Kawau and command of a hundred, was a long way to fall. Yet his enemies can hardly be said to have won. They had not beaten him in battle, his downfall was due to no deed of theirs, and it was not complete. He remained uncaught and independent, and soon showed that the damage to his mana was not beyond repair. And the failure to catch or beat him was bitterly frustrating and humiliating for the colonists, as were the circumstances which forced them to leave him alone at Kawau. 'I am deeply sensible,' wrote Henry Richmond, 'of the humiliating position in which a Government is placed which has to consult the humours of savage tribes as to . . . their movements against a declared rebel. But it appears to me folly to ignore that such is our present position.' Officialdom put the best possible face on it, and Whitmore wrote: 'In everything but blood, our victory has been most complete.' But it was blood that the colonists wanted.

Many therefore considered Whitmore's whole pursuit of Titokowaru, from Tauranga Ika to Te Ngaere, to be yet another failed campaign. 'The Colonel writes highly coloured Reports,' wrote his interpreter, George Preece, very privately, 'saying that Titokowaru is utterly routed, which is not the case . . . [he] runs when he sees us, – not because he is beaten, as . . . Whitmore makes out . . . but because he has no powder.' 'The loss has been nearly all on our side, not theirs,' wrote a newspaper correspondent, 'the rebels have moved away and that is all. They have not been defeated.' In weak moments, Whitmore himself confessed to 'disappointment, almost grief' at Titokowaru's escape. 'My Dear Haultain,' he wrote after Te Ngaere, 'it is with the greatest regret and vexation that I have to report that after a bush campaign such as there has not yet been in this country for distance traversed and fatigue undergone,

I believe Titokowaru has slipped through my fingers under my nose.' Like McDonnell before him, Whitmore had been robbed of his revenge.

In the following generations, collective Pakeha memory gradually suppressed these facts. It was what should have happened that mattered, not what did. Titokowaru was 'completely beaten', 'utterly defeated', 'suffered a terrible defeat' at Otautu – or was it Tauranga Ika? The process of remolding history began almost immediately.

On 12 April, Whitmore and his men landed at Auckland en route for the Bay of Plenty. The men 'allowed themselves to fall into the temptation afforded by so many public houses' – such a drunken binge that fifty were left behind, dead to the world, when their ships sailed. Whitmore was uncharacteristically inclined to apologise for them, though of course he made the overstayers make good their passage from their own pockets. 'Some allowance is due to men who had worn their clothes to rags in the hard service they had undergone, and who had not for months seen any fare but their bare ration.' Whitmore did some celebrating of his own, which may explain his unusual tolerance. The gentlemen of Auckland gave the conquering hero a splendid dinner on 14 April at the Auckland Club. The bill of fare ran to thirty-three dishes, including mock-turtle soup, oyster patties, quenelles of rabbit, stewed pigeon, and braised ducks with olive sauce, followed by trifle, damson pie, and orange jelly. 'The wines were of the very finest quality', and the merchant princes of Auckland toasted the Little Tyrant frequently in them. In reply to the chairman's formal toast, he said:

Well, sir, I felt at first, and I believe it is capable of demonstration, that Englishmen have never yet taken the field but they have been defeated at the outset (cheers). It is a peculiarity of our race that the further they go and the more they are beaten the better they rise out of their difficulties (cheers).

The war was over for Whitmore and Titokowaru, but not for either of their subordinates. For another eight months colonial troops garrisoned and patrolled in Southern Taranaki, light columns pressed ever higher up into the river refuges, and Titokowaru's erstwhile allies fled in fear of their lives and sometimes lost them. Lyon was left in command at Patea, and Noake at Wanganui, the latter using Weraroa as his field base. There were also garrisons at Nukumaru, Wairoa, and Manawapou. Camp Waihi was reoccupied in October. In April 1869, the South Taranaki force exceeded 1,000 men, but

the number diminished as units were laid off and reinforcements sent
to the East Coast, where Whitmore conducted another awesomely
difficult campaign in the Urewera in May. But, later in the year,
Lyon and Noake still had 700 men, including a wide range of kupapa:
Arawa, with whom a few Ngapuhi served; Ngati Porou, accompanied
by some Whanau-a-Apanui and Ngai-te-Rangi, and, of course,
Whanganui. Counting Brown's 500 men at New Plymouth,
Titokowaru's War was still costing the government the pay, supply,
and support of 1,200 men as the year 1869 drew to its close. From
28 June, the government was no longer Stafford and Haultain, who
lost office partly because they had failed to catch Titokowaru, but
Fox and McLean. 'The principal charge against the Government was
its utter failure to deal with Native affairs – the doings of Titokowaru
in South Taranaki being specially selected to emphasise the need for
a change on the Treasury benches.' With McLean at the Defence
Office, Whitmore did not last long.

Between April and November, the colonial forces made many
expeditions into the interior, descending like vultures on the bones
of Titokowaru's following. Ngarauru, in their Upper Waitotara
refuges, were the target of the first, mounted by Noake and 156
picked men of the Kai Iwi Cavalry, Wairoa, Patea, and Wanganui
Veteran Volunteers. On 30 March, a Kai Iwi Cavalry patrol found
a Ngarauru man, woman, and child at Pakaraka, eking out an existence
hidden in the bush but betrayed by the smoke of their fire. The
man, the aged warrior Te Kerira, 'was spared on the condition that
he acted as guide'. On 1 April, the expedition set out, returning
nine days later. It caught only one Ngarauru, an old woman left
to receive them, according to the traditional practice, at the major
village of Piraunui. She had performed the same function at a village
occupied by Chute in 1866. She was the only human victim, but
the expedition penetrated sixty miles up the Waitotara, exposing
for ever the ancient refuges of the Ngarauru people. Noake's men
ate, carried off, burned or destroyed everything at a dozen villages
and cultivations, including Piraunui, 'leaving nothing behind but
devastated fields and smoking ruins'. Hunted and destitute, Ngarauru
fled to the middle Whanganui River, rejoining their traditional chiefs
and placing themselves under the protection of Whanganui.

Whanganui responded. 'Give the Ngarauru to me,' Kepa asked
the government, 'let them live on this river; I will be responsible
for their good conduct.' Couched as a polite request, that was in
fact non-negotiable. Noake had to call off his hunt for Ngarauru

for fear of an actual clash with Whanganui. The Wanganui settlers were furious, and Ballance published vitriolic editorials demanding that even Hare Tipene, Pehimana, and Aperahama be punished. Mete Kingi replied in kind:

[These chiefs] have taken no part whatever in Titoko Waru's proceedings . . . Are you better informed than we are on these matters? Have we not the better means of knowing who are with us and who against us? Was it you who lopped off the heads of Titoko Waru's men?

Noake mounted two other small expeditions in search of fugitives in late April, and Lyon did likewise from Patea. These found no one, but they did show Tangahoe that they were no longer secure in their hidden camps on the farthest reaches of the Patea River. Rupe, Bent, and their party had left Rimatoto and gone inland to Rukumoana, a still more isolated spot, but now they were warned by a visit from Tito Hanataua that Kepa was still hunting them. Still loyal to Titokowaru, they trekked off to join him in North Taranaki. Tukino and another party also left their Upper Patea hiding place, but in contrast to Rupe went to Parihaka, where Te Whiti took them in. Most Tangahoe, 117 people including Tito Hanataua, made their way to Hone Pihama at Oeo. Like Whanganui, Pihama had served the government well, and by calling in his debts he was able to protect his estranged tribespeople.

Thus the government's vengeance against Ngarauru and Tangahoe was blocked by its own allies, but Pakakohe were less lucky. Whanganui tried to protect them as well. 'Let those people be given up to me,' asked Kepa, 'to live on this river, and I will promise to keep them out of mischief.' But Ngarauru were living in Whanganui pa, whereas Pakakohe were still on the Upper Patea, vulnerable to Pakeha utu. On 3 May Lyon with 179 men including seventy Ngati Porou under the chief Hatiwhera, set out in search of them, his patrols having found fresh tracks. Leading Lyon's scouts, Hatiwhera came upon two Pakakohe a few miles up the Patea from Otautu. The Pakakohe approached Ngati Porou with guns reversed, thinking they were Whanganui and intending to surrender. Wrote Lyon:

On being disarmed – one of a breech-loading carbine and revolver, the other of a double-barrelled gun – they put the question, 'Where is Kemp?' The reply was, 'We have nothing to do with Kemp, we are Ngatiporous;' on hearing which one of them said, 'If this is so there is no chance for us;' and such was the case, for they were immediately shot.

Next day, Lyon's column, with Ngati Porou again in the van, saw forty more Pakakohe. These managed to escape them, except for two caught by the scouts. One, a chief named Te Iraia, was shot, and the other, a woman, was also killed. Lyon claimed that she died because she was 'dressed like a man', but another observer stated: 'Ngati Porou shot the woman as they said "she was too old to be bothered with".'

The travails of Pakakohe had only begun. The inland forest no longer held any fears for the colonists, and their patrols and expeditions ravaged the few remaining cultivations on the Upper Patea. On 10 June an expedition of 264 troops under Noake approached their last refuge of Paetata. Wharematangi and Taurua made preparations for defence but they had only forty warriors, little food, and less ammunition. They bowed to the inevitable, and sent an envoy to propose peace. James Booth, who was with the column, went ahead to Paetata and the people – 123 men, women and children – surrendered on the promise they would not be harmed. In the ensuing weeks, further Pakakohe came in, bringing the total to 233.

Though he papered it over in his official report, Noake found Booth's conduct 'ill-judged, and most discourteous to myself . . if Booth promised them anything, it was entirely without my knowledge'. The new government backed Noake, and Premier Fox handled the matter himself. The Pakakohe were at first imprisoned at Patea, but secret preparations were made to send them to penal servitude in Otago. In December ninety-four males were suddenly shipped to Wellington and tried. Despite the pleas of Whanganui and other government allies such as Wi Tako Ngatata, seventy-four, including many old men and youths, were sentenced to three to seven years' hard labour in Dunedin prison. For many, it was equivalent to a sentence of death. A desperate escape plan was discovered and came to nothing, and on 6 November 1869 the shipload of exiles steamed in to Port Chalmers.

They were a nine-days wonder in the gold-boom city of Dunedin, and some did not last much longer. The local newspapers reported that: 'Within a few minutes of the arrival of the prisoners inside the gaol, one of their number died.' Thereafter, cold, disease, and slave labour, combined with worry about their families left to the tender mercies of Ngati Porou and the likes of Tom Adamson, did their fatal work. 'It is my opinion,' wrote guard commander Charles Ferris, that 'if they were to have word from their women and children it would make a great deal of difference in them.' William Fox was

Pakakohe prisoners at Wanganui, en route to Otago   *Wanganui Museum*

responsible for the treacherous exile of Pakakohe, and he embodied
the colonist paradox. He was the same man who humanely adopted
young William Fox Omahura. Pakakohe unfairly blamed James Booth,
who had tried to save them from the war he started, but every other
line of bitter sarcasm in their lament was fully justified:

What are your thoughts, women?
We are thinking of returning home to Patea
The majority returned to Patea
A white flag was cunningly erected by Booth
Many were taken prisoner
And placed on the ship . . .
It sailed for Otago
There Christianity thrived for three years
The majority of the Ruanui died there
And peace was declared ever after

The silence of devastation descended again on South Taranaki. The
Pakeha settlers had lost at least £30,000 worth of property: Thomas
Eyton lost £150, James Dickie lost £800, Peyman the storekeeper £1,000,

and Moore and Currie £3,000. Many were permanently ruined, and a 'Reinstatement Fund' of £10,000, doled out in driblets as cheap loans, did them little good. The military settlement system failed in South Taranaki, less from inherent flaws than from Titokowaru's War. The settlers were still better off than the Maori, imprisoned, in hiding, or driven to live on the charity of kin while their fertile river valleys were laid waste. 'As regards Natives', wrote Premier Fox, 'they were entirely gone from the district . . . The entire destruction of the pas, cultivation, and stock, for a distance of 60 to 70 miles inland, has been effected.' But, north of the Waingongoro, Titokowaru remained at Kawau, determined to resist any government attack. 'Titoko says that if the Pakeha comes to attack him he will turn round and fight them,' wrote a Government spy, 'I told you before that Titoko won't give in.'

The spy was Lucy Takiora, reporting direct to Donald McLean. She had either regained the confidence of Titokowaru's followers or travelled among them incognito. 'I risk my life in giving information,' she told McLean, 'and you must be careful and not tell anyone of this.' He paid her a salary of ten pounds per month and later rewarded her with £400 worth of confiscated Ngati Ruanui land, but her motives were more complex than the merely mercenary. 'I have done more for the government in this district,' she wrote, 'than I ever did for anyone, or myself.' She may even have begun to wonder whether she was on the right side after all. But it was Takiora who, on 27 October 1869, caused the last deaths of Titokowaru's War.

Takiora was staying at Camp Waihi, her familiar haunt, now the headquarters of Ngati Porou. Ropata Wahawaha had come out to lead his tribe two or three months before, but the dreaded kupapa warleader was not at his best: 'Ropata has been drunk ever since he has been at Patea.' The command at Waihi was held by the chief Piniamino and Richard Blake, now a lieutenant. Takiora had heard that some Ngaruahine old people had returned to their homes near Araukuku, and she told Blake of this, making him promise to capture, not kill, them. He and Piniamino led out a strong patrol, with Takiora as guide. But when three of the old people were found, the two men, Wikiriwhi and Hami, were immediately shot dead and only a woman was taken alive. Grieving for her men, the woman recognised Takiora as her betrayer. 'When the old woman saw me she began to cry and beat me. I did not remonstrate, as I knew wrong had been done.'

Epilogue

THE LAST BATTLE

The £1,000 reward for Titokowaru was eventually collected, in part – by a nurse named Anne Evans, née Clive, one of Florence Nightingale's subordinates during the Crimean War. In 1863, she immigrated to New Zealand, married one Thomas Evans, and farmed for some years at Wanganui. In 1873, after her husband's death, she moved to Camp Waihi and set up as a storekeeper, midwife, and surgeon, becoming known as 'Anne the Doctor'. One day a party of Maori came to her home and asked her to go with them to treat a sick man. Unquestioningly, she went. North of the Waingongoro she was blindfolded to conceal the route from her, but ended up at a few huts in a small clearing near Te Ngutu o te Manu. Here, she found an old man with pneumonia – Titokowaru. She treated him, and others including Katene Tuwhakaruru, for six weeks. During this time 'the Maoris were kindness itself, each day sending a messenger to her family with a letter and gifts of pork and poultry'. When Titokowaru recovered 'he thanked her for what she had done and handed her a folded note. It was £100. "I don't want it", she said. "Take it" said the chief. "My life is worth more than that".' Titokowaru had recovered both his home and his sense of humour.

Titokowaru's revival seems to have begun as early as mid-April 1869, within a few days of Whitmore's departure for the Bay of Plenty and while Ngarauru, Tangahoe, and Pakakohe were still being hunted up the river valleys. Kawau was isolated, but it was not nearly as inaccessible as Te Ngaere. The enterprising Major Brown planned a sudden descent on it for 15 April, reasoning that news of Whitmore's departure might have put the Maori off their guard. But the expedition was called off. Two months later, knowing that the fall of the Stafford government meant his days as commander-in-chief were numbered, Whitmore decided to arrange one last attack on his arch-enemy. On 23 June, he ordered Brown and Lyon, each with 300 picked men, to mount a pincer movement on Kawau, set for 6 July. But this operation too was aborted.

The two expeditions were cancelled not solely because of the threat of Ngati Maniapoto and North Taranaki intervention, but because the colonist commanders had heard 'that Titokowaru had been reinforced and was 300 strong.' He had indeed been rejoined by some of his old followers, including Rupe's party of forty or fifty and some local Ngati Maru, and he was busy fortifying Kawau with his usual skill, determined to run no more. Equally important he had been ritually absolved of the sin of Tauranga Ika, whatever it was. According to Bent 'Titokowaru regained his *tapu* by means of incantations and ceremonies performed by another tohunga' about this time. And he was very active diplomatically. He was in close contact with Parihaka, though he had learned to expect no military help from there. The alliance with the King movement promised by Whitecliffs had failed of fruition, but his relations with the Kingites were now cordial. In August he sent his brother, Rapata Te Nuku, to Tokangamutu as an envoy and was invited to visit himself both by Rewi Maniapoto and the Kingite prophet, Hakaraia. He was also in touch with Te Kooti, who was then operating to the south and east of Lake Taupo, close to Upper Whanganui territory. 'Ten of Te Kooti's men came across from Upper Whanganui to Ngati Maru with an invitation for Titokowaru to go and join them'. Titokowaru declined to go himself, and vetoed Toi and Haowhenua's wish to do so, but he is said to have sent thirty men – the only known instance of co-operation between the two generals.

The restoration of such links meant Titokowaru was again able to accumulate ammunition, and in September 1869 he prepared to use it. He received word both of the removal of Pakakohe to Wellington and of Wharematangi's rumoured execution. He marched south 'to renew hostilities' but was intercepted by the Atiawa chief, Hapurona. After two days' debate, Hapurona persuaded him to give up his plan, probably helped by reports that Wharematangi had not been killed after all. In December, Titokowaru held another conference to discuss retaliation for the killing of Wikiriwhi and Hami on 27 October, but decided 'to remain quiet unless attacked'. So he remained in North Taranaki, a lurking power temporarily quiescent but quite strong enough to prevent the occupation of his old lands north of the Waingongoro by either colonists or other Maori. A year later, on 9 October 1870, there was a report from Camp Waihi, probably again derived from Takiora. 'Aroha' means love or goodwill.

Titoko told Honi Pihama and others to remain where they are, that they must not go on the land between Kapuni and Waingongoro, as that land was a matter between himself and the Government. If the Government was 'aroha' he would be 'aroha' . . . he and the Government were carrying their guns upright one watching the other – and when the Government bring their guns to the 'present' he would also bring his to the present.

In April 1871, a government minute referred to 'the uncomfortable attitude of Titokowaru', and from this time his people began drifting back to their homes around Te Ngutu o te Manu. A year later, Robert Parris wrote: 'Titokowaru's people . . . are now virtually in occupation of all their tribal territory from Waingongoro to Omutarangi.' Te Ngutu and Camp Waihi again shaped up to each other, and armed Ngaruahine and constabulary patrols observed each other warily across the Waingongoro frontier.

So Titokowaru emerged from his war not only uncaught and undefeated, but also unpunished in terms of land. Understandably this created resentment among Whanganui on behalf of Pakakohe and Ngarauru who lost most of their remaining territory. 'Titokowaru and his tribe have returned and all their land has been restored to them', wrote Kepa angrily to the government in 1872. 'If you do not punish the man that has done evil, then most certainly do not chastise me, the person who has committed no offence, or the person whose offence has been small.' But Donald McLean, realist *par excellence*, was at the helm. He knew that 'if Titokowaru were prevented from returning to his lands, there was every likelihood he would again resort to force'. McLean wrote: 'The lands north of the Waingongoro, as far as the Stoney river, although nominally confiscated . . . are quite unavailable for settlement.' Throughout the 1870s, Titokowaru's armed presence, and the memory of Moturoa and Te Ngutu, preserved the independence of central Taranaki.

It was during this period, however, that Titokowaru put aside the weapons of war and resumed his career as a prophet of peace. He himself resided not at Te Ngutu, deep in the forest, but at Okaiawa among the old fringe-villages of the Waimate Plains, where he renewed his friendship with his neighbour, Wiremu Hukanui. His new meeting house was Te Aroha Kainga, the House of Goodwill. He organised the mass production of cocksfoot grass seed which, sold to settlers south of the Waingongoro to sow their pastures, brought Titokowaru's people £3,000 a year. The Pakeha had taken the land by force and fraud, but they paid dearly for the grass.

From about 1875, Titokowaru allied himself closely with Te Whiti and gradually reconverted to that remarkable man's resolute pacifism. As Te Whiti put it, 'the lion shall lie down with the lamb.' Titokowaru acknowledged Te Whiti's leadership in some spheres, but was more partner than subordinate, and there were properly three 'prophets of Parihaka': Te Whiti, Tohu Kakahi, and Titokowaru. Under them, central Taranaki was an independent state whose history has still to be written: culturally and economically active, a place of peace and plenty. But in 1879 the old cancer burst out again. Creeping confiscation seeped at last across the Waingongoro.

Creeping confiscation had become subtle in its old age and at first the iron fist was concealed in a velvet glove – literally. Some Taranaki chiefs and their wives were feasted by the government and given 'ladies' side-saddles, habits, velvets, silks, French merino shawls . . . fancy biscuits, cocoa, salmon, sardines, jam, port wine, brandy . . . lobster, preserved peaches, and entertainments at the theatre'. These presents were charged to 'land acquisition', in the accounts, and there were still more explicit bribes in the form of takoha: secret payments to influential chiefs intended to sweeten them towards the government's land policy. Titokowaru accepted at least £900 of takoha, under his baptismal name Hohepa, the title 'Kohi Rangitira', and in the names Rangipokau and Pikirapu as well, for the government could officially sanction 'no expenditure of public money to that individual'. Behind takoha came the land surveyors, so often the harbingers of war. Initially, they made out that they were only marking out a road. They avoided Titokowaru's cultivations and had orders that he was 'to be treated with extra courtesy'. He was 'very friendly and hospitable', wrote Captain P. G. Wilson, the leader of one survey party, and 'if he had spirits, gave to all who came; he was, in fact, very sociable.' Wilson took friends to visit him, and Titokowaru 'used to "chaff" me about bringing these people up to look at the land, saying he knew very well they were people who wished to buy and possess the land.'

Wilson and Titokowaru were in fact accepting each others' whisky and takoha on the same basis. Charles Finnerty, a colleague of Wilson's wrote: 'Captain Wilson is very obstinate and assertive and at times not scrupulously correct in his relation of matters regarding Titokowaru's place . . . I know no one here so *afraid* of the Maoris as the Captain is.' The 'road surveys' crept closer and closer to the Okaiawa cultivations and settlers soon appeared on Ngaruahine land. Titokowaru met trickery with trickery. He accepted the bait of takoha, but spat out the hook with contempt, sent the money to Parihaka, and resisted the surveys. Weakened by age, hardship, asthma, and his bout of pneumonia he rode about in a buggy, directing polite but determined obstruction. 'The natives packed our things up,' wrote another surveyor, Harry Skeets, 'being very careful not to miss anything, putting what they could on the dray, saying they would bring the remainder afterward, which they did.' Titokowaru saw them off 'good humouredly though firmly.'

These were Te Ua's weapons, active but non-violent, and Te Whiti now added his famous refinement: not guns, but ploughs. His and Titokowaru's followers, progressively reinforced from other areas, ploughed up the survey lines and the settlers' fields. They were arrested and imprisoned in their hundreds, but more kept coming. The ploughing and arrests continued sporadically throughout 1879 and 1880, the former orchestrated by Titokowaru and the latter by John Bryce of the Kai Iwi Cavalry who was now native minister. But there was widespread support for the resisters from Maori across the whole country, including influential kupapa; humanitarians in Britain and New Zealand protested at the legally dubious imprisonment of the ploughmen, and the whole business was costing the government £5,000 a month. The surveys stopped, the ploughmen were released, and, in early 1881, John Bryce resigned.

It was only a respite. In October 1881, Bryce returned to power and mounted a great invasion of Central Taranaki, with constabulary and volunteers totalling over 2,000 men. A crowd of 4,000 watched the Wellington contingents depart and, on one side, the whole affair was reminiscent of 1868. But not on the other. When Bryce's army advanced on Parihaka on 5 November, the prophets opposed them with lines of singing children. They might have known this would not stop Bryce. One five-year-old, Maui Pomare, later a knight and cabinet minister, had his toe severed by a horse's sharp hoof. The children and their elders were cleared away, or forcibly carried off. Parihaka was destroyed and Te Whiti, Tohu, and Titokowaru were arrested and imprisoned in New Plymouth.

Bryce's army included other veterans of the war among its leaders – John Roberts, Stuart Newall, and Frederick Gascoyne to name a few. Holding Titokowaru prisoner must have been balm to their souls, though the £1,000 reward could no longer be collected owing to an act of general amnesty designed to conciliate the King Movement. A newspaper correspondent saw Titokowaru 'crouching handcuffed like a large dog in a low whare like a kennel' at the constabulary camp before being gaolled at New Plymouth. He responded with a hunger strike. 'But when after two days Dr O'Caroll produced a flexible tube to pump porridge into him,' wrote Fred Gascoyne

Parihaka in 1881, immediately before its destruction   *Taranaki Museum*

Armed constabulary camped outside Parihaka   *Taranaki Museum*

with satisfaction, 'the threatened indignity broke down his resolve
to starve himself.' This was humiliation perhaps, yet Te Whiti had
produced a movement in which all the prisoners, from Titokowaru
downwards, bore their chains patiently and with pride. And
Titokowaru was not above reminding his gaolers of who he was,
though he did so half-jokingly.

'Do you consider the Europeans a noble race?', he asked. 'Do you think my people will run away? Have the Europeans forgotten Te-Ngutu-o-te-Manu and Moturoa? This is your day but I have a day to come hereafter.'

The Europeans had not forgotten – yet. It was the memory of these defeats that induced John Bryce to take the biggest colonist army yet raised against a group of confirmed pacifists, so opening himself to a wave of liberal mockery. It was this memory that created tension and fear in the troops before Parihaka, and set hundreds of men, 'all looking so serious about it', to writing last letters to their loved ones. 'It is rumoured that Titokowaru has got 500 armed men behind Parihaka,' wrote Corporal William Parker,

so there is great excitement in camp. We do not undress when we go to sleep but sleep in our clothes with arms by our sides, ready. We have double sentrys and guards posted. In the night we got a scare on account of the sentrys challenging someone and doubling up. We thought the Maoris were on us.

So at least the memory of Titokowaru the general cost the invaders some sleepless nights.

Titokowaru was tried at New Plymouth on 8 May 1882. Judge Thomas Gillies rubbished the charges, which caused the government hastily to pass special legislation which would permit the imprisonment of Te Whiti and Tohu without trial. Despite Gillies' judgment, Titokowaru was held on the grounds that two sureties for £250 each could not be found. On 14 July, one J. Winks and old Wiremu Hukanui came forward with the money, and Titokowaru was released. He had spent his eight months in prison studying English.

Maori Central Taranaki had fallen. Backed by constabulary garrisons, the surveyors did their work, and the settlers moved in. Most of the Waimate Plain was occupied and the great forest was gradually cleared. Pakeha farms sprang up like mushrooms around Te Ngutu and Ruaruru. New road names told the tale: Palmer, Hastings, and Tempsky Roads – a dubious immortality for Ngaruahine's victims. Te Ngutu o te Manu is now a reserve and picnic spot. Its stone memorial, marking Von Tempsky's fall and other Pakeha deaths, is simple and tasteful enough. Its flaw is not so much that it is in the wrong place, but that it does not list Kaake, Reweti, and Paramena, or the crippled son of Katene.

Te Whiti and Titokowaru, of course, did not give up. Parihaka was no longer the capital of an independent state, safe behind the invisible shield of Titokowaru's name, but it was rebuilt; Te Whiti and Tohu returned, and it remained a focus of culture and protest. From 1882, Titokowaru renewed his 1867 policy of combining non-violent resistance with ceremonial visits of reconciliation. Prior to this, he avoided Pakeha settlements because 'he said he was afraid of drunken people and tutuas [commoners] insulting him'. Between March and June 1885, Titokowaru toured North Taranaki with a huge following of 1,200 people, visiting Maori and Pakeha settlements alike and preaching his message of peace anew. 'I will shower peace upon the people until the end of time,' he said. His proximity made the townsfolk of New Plymouth 'just a bit uneasy', and to allay their fears he invited some to eat with him on Sunday 22 March. 'He was genial in the extreme; but that pakeha who sought to pump him on subjects on native policy had . . . trouble for his reward.' Young W. F. Gordon was one of his guests, and wrote about the event fifty years later under the title 'Titokowaru's Tea Party'. Gordon approved of the waiter service, but was initially less impressed with his host. 'On being introduced to Titokowaru I must confess to have been taken aback as I failed to see in the thin careworn man, the fierce-looking savage he was said by some to be.' That evening, 'thinking the opportunity might never come again', Gordon sketched Titokowaru from memory, 'sitting at ease' at the 'tea party' and 'joining in the conversation'. Apart from a still-cruder courtroom drawing, it is the only portrait of Titokowaru that has so far been found.

Titokowaru also twice visited Patea, the town he had almost destroyed. Some settlers found it hard that this 'murderer' should be allowed to 'beard us in our very den', but most found more generosity of spirit. On his first visit, early in 1885, he and 800 followers marched around Patea, as they had done around Camp Waihi and other places in 1867. The townspeople accommodated their visitors in the immigration barracks and feasted them on two tons of bread and several bullocks – some compensation for listening to the speeches of the civic dignitaries. The visit went well; the settlers crowded to shake Titokowaru's hand, though they too were somewhat disappointed in their arch-villain: 'What a disappointment for the huge crowd who had visions of a giant in stature, a commanding "Wellingtonian" figure of manhood. Instead Titokowaru was a frail, one-eyed rather diminutive and aged thin man; a mere pigmy in comparison with Tutangi [Waionui], his lieutenant.'

On 14 July 1886, Titokowaru again came, in his buggy, with 200 followers to return the settlers' hospitality. The night before the feast

Gordon's sketch of Titokowaru   *Taranaki Museum*

some young Pakeha boys, greatly daring, peered into his tent. 'The pains and aches of acute rheumatism, the result of many campaigns, refused to let him rest, and he tossed from side to side, not noticing those who wanted to get a look at him.' Next day, his people cooked hundreds of turkeys, geese, and chickens to feast the townspeople, 'carefully cleaned and stuffed' to suit Pakeha palates. Before eating, Titokowaru made one of his last recorded public speeches.

He told them that when the Pakehas fed him on the Domain at the great feast, when many bullocks were consumed, it was in the middle of summer, he had felt strong then, even though he was old, and he could have overwhelmed the town, but the great Atua had withheld his hand. It was the same Deity which had prompted him to come back in the winter time, which was a symbol of his old age and his weakness, to show the people that he was past fighting and revenge now . . . When he awoke in the dark hours of the night and tossed on his bed he thought that after all peace was better than warfare. He had come back, not with a great crowd, but with a select few, to show that on [this] his last visit his thoughts were of a peaceful nature, and that he was a warrior no more.

It would be pleasant to end on this note of forgiveness, to mouth platitudes about 'mutual respect forged in war' as was customary until recently in books on this subject. But the harsh facts do not permit it. Three days after his speech at Patea, Titokowaru was in

the midst of his last battle, a battle without bullets but with its share
of blows and blood: the bitter riot of 18 July 1886, known as 'The
Battle of Hastie's Farm'.

The Taranaki Maori were still resisting creeping confiscation by
occasionally ploughing or digging up the fields of Pakeha farmers
on disputed land. A.J. Hastie's farm, two miles south of Manaia,
was one such, and at 10 am on Sunday 18 July a group of Maori
occupied one of his paddocks in a form of protest that a century
later was to be known as a 'sit-in'. Four policemen tried to arrest
the leaders; 'they anticipated no resistance' but 'after some rough
tussling the prisoners were torn from the hands of the police, Constable
McIvor being injured'. The Maori struck no blows: McIvor's injury
came from 'being squeezed in the gateway'. The Maori then began
digging up the paddock and building a large whare. During the next
hour reinforcements arrived, bringing their number to between 200
and 300 men, women, and children, including Titokowaru and
Natanahira Ngahina, once enemies, now allies.

Courtesy of the new telegraph, the Pakeha also received rapid
reinforcements – scores of settler volunteers. Around noon, the Maori
prepared food and invited the Pakeha to join them, but were refused.
At 3 pm twenty settler horsemen tried to drive off the Maori's horses
and cattle. To local historian C.J. Roberts, 'A most exciting scene
was now enacted.' The police and settlers struck at the Maori with
waddies, makeshift baton clubs and riding whips, and

*a great tug of war for the gate was going on . . . After a really hot melee
at the gate . . . nearly all the cattle and horses were seen to be galloping off
down the lower paddock and several natives on foot were being chased by pakehas
on horseback. Fred Bayley put one native to flight by the dexterous use of
a stock-whip; J.D. Mitchell charged another, striking him with a whip handle;
another native, seeing the fight, made a sharp blow at Mr Mitchell with a
pole . . . making him fall from the saddle; Mr Hendy was also very active,
and he also received a severe blow. He was seen riding down a native whose
head was bleeding.*

For half an hour, James Livingston, now a justice of the peace,
restrained his fellow settlers on the grounds that Maori deaths might
see 'families butchered for "utu" '. But it became evident that, though
some Maori had struck blows in the heat of the moment, their basic
policy was non-violent. By 3.30 pm 'it was clear that the able-bodied
Europeans on the ground greatly outnumbered the natives', and thirty
'special constables' were sworn in to assist Livingston and the four

police to seize the leaders. One by one, nine men were dragged from the tight-packed crowd, including Titokowaru. Livingston and his men were obstructed but not struck. 'The fact that none of the pakehas were injured showed that the Maoris were desirous not to shed blood.'

Titokowaru was taken off in a buggy, 'too weak to walk'. He was tried in Wellington in November for 'malicious trespass', and spent another month in a colonist gaol. Eighteen months later, on 18 August 1888, he died, with Te Kahupokoro and Kimble Bent at his bedside. Some 2,000 Maori attended his funeral, and he was buried secretly. Titokowaru's last known public act was to recover Von Tempsky's sword from its hiding place and break it, with the words: 'I will break this sword, and I will bury it. Let war be returned to the great nations of the earth.'

Katene Tuwhakaruru preceded him to the grave by about a year, after living near Mawhitiwhiti with his young wife and a pleasant garden. He gave E. S. Brookes a guided tour of Te Ngutu o te Manu before he died, omitting only to mention which side he was on. Big Kereopa lived at Waitotara during the 1870s, 'inciting quarrels and disturbing the peace'. He was sentenced to six months' hard labour for petty larceny in 1877, but 'resisted arrest so violently that bystanders were called upon to help Constable Hynes'. In the 1880s he supported his old leader, and was one of the few Maori who did fight at Hastie's Farm: 'It was reported that Kereopa, a Waitotara native, had made a most vicious blow at a pakeha.' When he died about the turn of the century, he left orders that he too be buried secretly 'as he was afraid the Pakeha were going to cut him up to see why he grew so big'.

The boy warriors Tutange Waionui, Tu-Patea Te Rongo, and Te Kahupokoro all lived on into the twentieth century to become leaders of their people, which is why their stories have survived in the books and papers of James Cowan. Ngawaka Taurua, that honourable man, returned from his Dunedin exile in 1873 with the remnants of Pakakohe. He led their struggle to retain a vestige of their land until his death in 1894. In 1880 he told William Fox, then leader of a Royal Commission on Taranaki Maori lands: 'As fast as one Commissioner succeeded another I repeated the same thing to him, and kept on with it, and will keep on until there are no more Commissioners left.' William Fox Omahura, despite his adoption and training as a lawyer, sided with his birth-people at Parihaka, which 'greatly displeased Sir William and Lady Fox'. He died as 'the well-known native interpreter' at Hawera in 1918. Kimble Bent lived with

Kimble Bent, in old age
*From J. Cowan, The
Adventures of Kimble Bent,
Alexander Turnbull Library*

the Maori until the end of the century, becoming a trained tohunga specialising in medicine, but eventually he moved to Blenheim. He died at Wairau Hospital on 22 May 1916. 'Of Tito-Kowaru, the great rebel chief . . . he always spoke in kindly terms.'

As for Titokowaru's enemies, Thomas McDonnell lived out his life to 1899 in poverty and bitterness. His appeals for medals, honours, pensions, and well-salaried posts make a thick file, but his only triumph was the New Zealand Cross, awarded in 1886 after eighteen years of intensive lobbying – and he and Von Tempsky had lobbied for the Victoria Cross for four years before that. Takiora married a surveyor named Dalton, lived on her own land at Normanby, and died in 1893. In her obituary's understatement, 'she was an intelligent woman', and she no doubt remembered the old woman at Araukuku until the end of her days. John Ballance died the same year, after a term as premier. His reputation as a humane liberal would have been hard to predict from his Wanganui days. Bryce's career was less august but truer to form. He died in 1913, leaving as his contribution to literature a 'valuable series of articles on Maori fanaticism which clearly illuminates his own native policy'. Tom Adamson also died in 1913, a renowned old war hero. His New Zealand Cross was auctioned in London in July 1988, and fetched a high price despite the blood on it. Philip Putnam's fate is unknown, but he is likely to have lived a long time.

Mete Kingi died in 1883, an immensely influential man, though the Pakeha he manipulated did not appreciate it. Gudgeon wrote: 'But O that mine enemy commanded a native contingent containing four Mete Kingis!' Kepa Te Rangiwhinui also had great mana and power, but it was he who became disillusioned with his Pakeha allies rather than vice versa. In 1880, he turned his government guns against their givers to block the sale of land. The government temporarily backed down, but Kepa, like his enemies, spent the rest of his life struggling to retain the land. He died, still widely honoured, in 1898. Theodore Haultain, one of the few Pakeha to emerge from the war with much credit, died in 1902 in straitened financial circumstances. He believed that Ballance had engineered his dismissal from the sinecures of his old age in revenge for that cornet's commission. George Whitmore died that same year. He had been knighted in 1882 and was made the colony's first major-general in 1887 to meet an expected Russian invasion. He also had something of a political career as a member of two liberal ministries, though his nearest approach to liberalism was to propose that a bill against Asian immigration be amended to 'Chinese immigration'. Indians made good servants. But his fame did not last. At a large gathering of volunteers in 1897, he was not recognised and was refused admittance. He 'felt his rejection keenly'. 'I am a stranger to the young men, and my services are forgotten.' The legend of his decisive victory over Titokowaru had never been very convincing, and his fellow Pakeha had to resort to historical amnesia which blanked out 'victors' as well as 'vanquished'. Forgotten in his own lifetime, Whitmore became a victim of the myth he had helped to create.

Titokowaru too was largely forgotten by the Pakeha. If you look hard enough, you can find a pale and distorted reflection of his deeds in the histories of James Cowan or the novels of Errol Braithwaite. But history almost falsified his prophecy: 'I shall not die, I shall not die; When death itself is dead, I shall be alive.' In this sense, this book is his instrument. Yet it is not a biography but the history of a war involving thousands, mostly Pakeha. We must be wary of allowing his name to subsume their story. The lives and deaths of the 'lesser' are too often conveniently packaged under the labels of the 'great'.

But the fact remains that he strides these pages like a giant, one of those rare leaders who seized fate and, for a time, shaped it in his hands. Fate won in the end, of course – not at Okaiawa in 1888, when Titokowaru died, but at Tauranga Ika in 1869, when he was tempted and fell. The hero had feet of clay. His weakness cost Maoridom a real chance of limited victory in the New Zealand Wars and a return to the situation of 1860, when the two peoples were equal. Yet it was his strengths which created that chance against impossible odds, and perhaps strength and weakness, vice and virtue, were inextricably linked. It would have surprised me if Titokowaru had not left the lines to end this book, and indeed he did. Rangiatea was Turi's house, in Hawaiki, on 'the mountain which could not be overlooked', and also one of the houses built in South Taranaki in the 1850s to symbolise Maori determination to defend their land and independence:

> *I am of the seed broadcast within the house Rangiatea.*
> *And though I may be insignificant,*
> *I have shaken the foundations of the earth.*

GLOSSARY

Some of the words listed below have multiple meanings. The ones given are those used in text.

ariki	high chief
aroha	love, goodwill
haka	dance, often war dance
hapu	clan, subtribe, or component of a subtribe
hikoi	march
hui	meeting
kainga	(unfortified) village
kumara	sweet potato
kupapa	pro-government Maori
mana	prestige, influence, spiritual capital
marae	sacred village square or assembly place
Mata Ika	'First Fish', first enemy slain in battle
mere	short, sharp-edged club
moko	tattoo
muru	customary plundering, exacting compensation for an offence, in which blood is seldom shed
pa	virtually any kind of Maori fortification
Pakeha	foreigner, especially European
poi	light ball on a string, twirled rhythmically in dancing
rangatira	chief
taiaha	spearlike fighting or ceremonial staff
tangi	funeral
tapu	holy, holiness
taro	a food plant
taua	war party
taumaihi	squat tower, part of a pa
toetoe	rush-like plant
tohunga	(religious) expert, priest
tupara	double-barrelled gun
whare	house
Whangai Hau	ceremony in which an enemy heart is singed in sacrifice to the god Tu
utu	payment, vengeance

SOURCES

Major sources are listed in shortened form below, by chapter. Full details of each source are listed alphabetically in the bibliography.

Abbreviations

A.D	Army Department
ADM	Admiralty (British)
AJHR	*Appendices to the Journals of the House of Representatives*
APL	Auckland Public Library
ATL	Alexander Turnbull Library, Wellington
BPP	*British Parliamentary Papers*
CMS	Church Missionary Society
CO	Colonial Office (British)
NA	National Archives, Wellington
NZPD	*New Zealand Parliamentary Debates*
PRO	Public Record Office, London
TM	Taranaki Museum, New Plymouth
WM	Wanganui Regional Museum

Chapter One: Titokowaru's Peace
AD, 1/1867: 690-1312, 2040, 2158, 2368
AD, 31/13 Patea Survey Papers
AJHR, 1864, A-7, E-3
AJHR, 1865, A-4, A-5, A-7, E-4
AJHR, 1866 A-1
AJHR, 1867, A1A, A-16, A-21, A-22
AJHR, 1868, A-8
AJHR, 1880, G-2
Anon., *Campaign on the West Coast*
Atkinson, Diary, Feb-April 1867
BPP, Vol.15, pp. 184-7, 321-2
Bremer, 'The Patea-Waverley District', pp. 18-39
Buick, *New Zealand's First War*, pp. 89, 215
Church, 'Heartland of Aotea'
Clark, *Hauhau*
Cowan, *Kimble Bent*, esp. pp. 102-6, 333-5
Cowan, *Wars*, esp. Vol.2, pp.46-71, 143-52
Dillon, *Letters*, p.69
Gordon, 'Titokowaru's Tea Party'
Grey Collection – Stafford Letters; Hauhau War Correspondence
Houston, *Maori Life in Old Taranaki*
Howitt, *A Pioneer Looks Back*, pp.61-3
'Juvenis', 'Pages from the Past'
Leslie et. al, *Patea: A Centennial History*

McDonnell, Family Papers
McDonnell, 'General Chute's Campaign'
McDonnell, Papers, APL, 4-6
McDonnell, Papers, ATL, 22
McDonnell, *Explanation,* pp. 31-4
McLean, Papers (TSS), Vol.28
McLean, Papers, 20
Newland, 'Campaign on the West Coast'
NZPD, 13 Aug. 1868
Parris, Papers
Power, *Sketches in New Zealand*, pp. 3-4
Skinner, *Reminiscences* pp. 44-6
Smith, *History and Traditions*
Smith, Letterbook, 1866-7
Stafford, Papers, 42
Taranaki Herald, 18 Aug, 1866; 22 June, 6, 13, 20 July 1867
Titokowaru Papers
Vale, *Some Interesting Occurrences* pp. 6, 20
W.B., Taupo Notes
Waldergrave, Notes

Chapter Two: The Year of the Daughters
AD, Registers, 1867-8
AD, 1/1866: 3497-8, 3523-4, 3528, 3664, 4102
AJHR, 1867, A-21, A-22
AJHR, 1868, A-8, A-3 (Proceedings of Pokaikai Commission)
AJHR, 1870, A-4
Atkinson, Diary, 1866-7
BPP Vol.15, pp. 149-157 (1867 Census); pp. 126-9 (List of Tribes)
Booth, Letters
Bremer, The Patea-Waverley District
Caines, Diary Extracts
Chapple and Veitch, *Wanganui*
Christchurch Star, 18 Sept. 1916
Cowan, *Kimble Bent*
Cowan, *Wars*, Vol. 2
Cyclopaedia, Vol. 1
Downes, *Old Whanganui*
Evening Post, 11 Aug. 1866
'Extract Books', Vols. A, B, C
Fildes Collection, 629, 631
Ginger, Record Book
Gorton, *Some Home Truths*, p. 55
Greaves, *Memoirs*, pp.105-9
Gudgeon, *Defenders* (esp. pp. 153-4)
Ingram, *New Zealand Shipwrecks*, p. 111
Leslie, Social History
Lomax, Letters
McDonnell, 'Survey of the Confiscated Lands'

McLean, Papers, 14
'Maori Troubles' File
Maxwell, Diary
O'Halloran, Autobiography
Patea Mail 14 Dec. 1878.
Pihama, List of Payments
Rawson, 'Evolutiuon of Rural Settlement'
Scholefield, *Richmond-Atkinson Papers,* Vol. 2, pp. 206, 227, 228
Roberts, *Hawera*
Roberts, *Patea*
Skinner, Diary
Smart and Bates, *Wanganui*
Smith, Letterbook
Sole, *Waverley*
Stafford, Papers, 38B
Stronge, 'Egmont County'
Taranaki Almanack
Taranaki Herald 1866-8 (misc. issues)
Taranaki Provincial Council, Hotel Licences
Taylor, *Past and Present*
Waitotara School and District History
Wanganui Times, 13 Aug. 1864
Warrington, 'Pakeha Agriculture'
Wellington Almanack

Chapter Three: 'I Shall Not Die'
AD, 1/1868: 996-1758
AD, 8/1:47
AJHR, 1868, A-8
BPP, Vol. 15, pp. 158-9, 196-8, 200-18
Bremer, 'The Patea-Waverley District', pp. 37-41
Cowan, Papers, 41E
Cowan *Kimble Bent*, pp. 116-18
Cowan *Wars,* Vol. 2, pp. 180-82
Gledhill, Journal, 16 June 1868
Gudgeon, *Reminiscences*, pp. 165-9
Justice Dept., J1/1868: 1903 (Inquest Proceedings into the killing of Cahill, Clarke and Squires)
'Juvenis', 'Pages from the Past'
Livingston, Diary, 9-26 June, 1868
Maxwell, Diary
McDonnell, *Explanation*, pp. 33-4
Newland, 'Campaign on the West Coast'
Sydney Morning Herald, 11 Sept, 1868
Taranaki Herald, 18 April, 20 June 1868

Chapter Four: The Patea Field Force
AD, 1/1868: 1719-1998, 3063
AJHR, 1868, A-8, D17, D21

AJHR, 1880, G-2
Cameron, Papers
Cowan, Papers, 41E
Cowan, *Kimble Bent*, p. 106
Downes, Papers
'Extract Books', Vol. B.
Ginger, Record Book
Gorton, *Some Home Truths*, pp. 63-84
Grey Collection – Stafford Letters
-Gudgeon, *Defenders*
Gudgeon, *Reminiscences,* pp. 175-6
Hooper, 'Military Tradition', pp. 51-60
Houston, Papers. 27
Livingston, Diary, June-Aug. 1868
Lomax, Letters
'Maori Troubles' Folder
McDonnell, Papers, ATL 19, 22, 23
McDonnell, *Explanation*, pp. 34-8
McLean, Papers, 45
New Zealand Advertiser, June-Aug, 1868
New Zealand Gazette, 12 Aug, 2 Oct, 1868
Newland, 'Campaign on the West Coast'
NZPD, July-Sept, 1868
O'Halloran, Autobiography
Owen, *After Shipwreck*
Parham, *Roberts*, pp 32-4
Parham, *Von Tempsky*
Paymaster's Order Book
Scholefield, *Richmond-Atkinson Papers,* Vol. 2, p. 278
Sole, *Waverley*, pp. 66-7, 269
Sydney Morning Herald, July 1868
Takiora, MS
Takiora, 'Notes'
Taranaki Herald, 20 June, 16 July, 8 and 18 Aug. 1868
Taranaki Provincial Gazette, 21 Sept., 23 Oct. 1868
Von Tempsky, Memoranda
Von Tempsky, Papers
Wanganui Chronicle, July-Aug. 1868
Wanganui Evening Herald, June-Aug. 1868
Wanganui Times, July-Aug. 1868
Wellington Independent, June-Aug. 1868
Whitmore, Papers, A.
Wright, 'Account of a Skirmish'

Chapter Five: The Death of Kane

AD, 1/1868: 2385
AD, 32/5013
AJHR, 1868, A-8
AJHR, 1868, D-9 ('Proceedings of the Board of Inquiry into charges against Inspector

Hunter'), A-8
BPP, Vol. 15, pp. 198-200
Cowan, Hero Stories, pp. 131-9
Cowan, Kimble Bent, pp. 119-38
Cowan, Wars, Vol. 2, pp. 187-201
Fildes Collection, 625, 628
Gudgeon, Reminiscences, pp. 170-4, 190-1
Houston, Papers, 27, 24, 31
Livingston, Diary, 12 July 1868
New Zealand Advertiser, 7 Aug. 1868
Prickett, 'Archaeology of Military Frontier'
Wanganui Times, 14 July 1868
Wellington Independent, 21 July 1868
Wells, Taranaki, pp. 273-4

Chapter Six: McDonnell's Revenge
AD, 1/1868: 2658-3108, 5284 (Inquiry into Conduct of Patrick Ready)
AJHR, 1868, A-8
BPP, Vol. 15, pp. 240-3
Cowan, Papers, 41E
Cowan, Kimble Bent, pp. 143-4
Cowan, Wars, Vol. 2, pp. 202-5
Fildes Collection, 625
Gudgeon, Reminiscences, pp. 176-80
Livingston, Diary, 20-3
McDonnell, Papers, ATL, 23
McDonnell, Explanation, pp. 36-8
McDonnell, NZ Medal File
Newland, 'Campaign on the West Coast'
Parham, Von Tempsky, pp. 196-9
Takiora, MS
Takiora, 'Notes'
Taranaki Herald, 8, 25, 29 Aug., 5 Sept 1868
Waldegrave, Notes
Wanganui Chronicle, 25 Aug., 1 Sept. 1868
Wanganui Evening Herald, 22 Aug., 10 Sept. 1868
Wanganui Times, 12 and 22 Aug. 1868
Wellington Independent, Aug-Sept. 1868
Wells, Taranaki, pp. 274-5
[Whitmore] 'West Coast Campaign'

Chapter Seven: The Beak
AD, 1/1868: 2886, 2997-8, 3106
AJHR, 1868, A-8
BPP, Vol. 15, pp. 267-76, 348-9
Brookes, Frontier Life, pp. 48-55, 193-4
Cowan, Kimble Bent, pp. 143-79
Cowan, Wars, Vol. 2. pp. 202-21
Fildes Collection, 625

Gordon, Papers.
Gudgeon, *Defenders*, 118, 185, 161-2, 215, 361-2, 375, 391-2
Gudgeon, *Reminiscences,* pp. 175-88, 191-2
Hamilton-Browne, *With the Lost Legion*, pp. 223-38
'Juvenis', 'Pages from the Past'
Livingston, Diary, 6-12 Sept. 1868.
McDonnell, Papers, ATL, 17, 23
McDonnell, *Explanation*, pp. 37-9
McDonnell, NZ Medal File
Newland, 'Campaign on the West Coast'
O'Halloran, Autobiography
Parham, *Roberts*, pp 36-42
Parham, *Von Tempsky*, pp 200-5
Takiora, MS
Takiora, 'Notes'
Taranaki Herald, 12, 14 Sept., 5 Oct 1868.
Waldegrave, Notes
Wanganui Chronicle, 9, 11, 12, 14 Sept. 1868
Wanganui Evening Herald, 9, 10, 14 Sept. 1868
Weekly News, 30 Jan. 1869
Weekly Press, 18 June 1902
Wellington Independent, 10, 12, 15, 17 Sept. 1868
Wells *Taranaki*, pp. 275-80
[Whitmore] 'West Coast Campaign'

Chapter Eight: The Little Tyrant
AD, 8/1
AD,32/5004 (Return of Men Courtmartialled, 1864-8)
AD, 1/1868: 3175-3920, 4182, 5285
AD, 32/5011 (Papers on the Mutiny of No. 5 A.C.)
AJHR, 1869, A-3, A-10
B. Taylor, Letters
BPP, Vol. 15, pp. 270-83
Bremer, pp. 41-54, 77
CO, 209/209
Cowan, *Hero Stories*, pp. 214-20
Cowan, *Kimble Bent*, pp. 180-99
Cowan, *Wars*, Vol. 2, pp. 244-7
'Extract Books', Vol. A, B
Fildes Collection, 625
Gorton, *Some Home Truths*, pp. 68, 85-90
Grey Collection — J. E. Fitzgerald Letters
Gudgeon, *Reminiscences,* pp. 192-7
Hamilton-Browne, *Campfire Yarns,* p. 161
Harrop, *England and the Maori Wars*, p. 330
Hawke's Bay Herald, 8, 22 Dec. 1869
[Hawthorne], *A Dark Chapter*
Hooper, 'Military Tradition', pp. 61-4, 53
Livingston, Diary, 8 Sept.-6 Nov. 1868

Lomax, Letters
Lovegrove, 'When Wanganui Stood to Arms', pp. 114-20
Mantell, Papers, 402
'Maori Troubles' file
McDonnell, Papers, ATL, 17, 22, 23
McDonnell, *Explanation*, pp. 29-32
McDonnell, NZ Medal File
McLean Papers (TSS), Vol. 29, 28
McLean, Papers, 45, 635
Moorsom, Papers, 60
New Zealand Advertiser, 14 Sept.-9 Nov. 1868
New Zealand Gazette, 17 Oct. 1868
New Zealand Mission Letterbook
Newland, 'Campaign on the West Coast'
NZPD, Sept. 1868
O'Halloran, Autobiography
Parham, *Roberts.* p. 55
Punch, (Auckland) Vol. 1, p. 107
Putnam, Diary, Oct. 1868
Scholefield, *Richmond-Atkinson Papers*, Vol. 2, p. 280
Stafford, Papers, 38 B, 48, 38
Takiora, MS
Takiora, 'Notes'
Taranaki Herald, 14, 16 Sept., 17 Oct. 1868
The Times, 27, 28 Nov. 1868
Waitotara School and District History, pp. 26-7
Wanganui Chronicle 12 Sept.-5 Nov. 1868
Wanganui Evening Herald, 14 Sept., 9, 10, 12 Oct., 6 Nov. 1868
Wellington Independent Sept.-Oct. 1868
Whitmore, Collection, 1, 2
Whitmore, Papers, A. B.
Whitmore, *Last Maori War,* pp. 28-43
[Whitmore] 'West Coast Campaign'

Chapter Nine: The Battle of Moturoa
AD, 1/1868: 3646, 3801, 3919, 4051-4254, 4371
AD, 8/1
AJHR, 1869, A-3
Booth, Letters
BPP, Vol. 15, pp. 283-91
CO, 209/208
Cameron, Papers
Cowan, Papers, 41 E
Cowan, *Kimble Bent,* pp. 198-225
Cowan, *Wars,* Vol. 2, pp. 248-62
Fildes Collection, 625
Gibson, Letters
Gudgeon, *Defenders,* pp. 162, 249, 260, 358, 383-5
Gudgeon, *Reminiscences,* pp. 197-201

Hamilton-Browne, *With the Lost Legion,* pp ?4?-9
Hawes, Papers
Livingston, Diary, 4-8 Nov. 1868
Lovegrove, 'When Wanganui Stood To Arms', pp. 119-21
McLean, Papers (TSS), Vol. 29
New Zealand Advertiser, Nov. 1868
Newland, 'Campaign on the West Coast'
O'Halloran, Autobiography
Punch (Auckland), Vol. 1, p. 51
Putnam, Diary, Oct.-Nov.1868.
Sole, *Waverley,* p. 63
Sydney Morning Herald, 25 Nov. 1868
Taranaki Herald, 21 Nov. 1868
Waitotara School and District History, p. 27
Wanganui Chronicle, 10, 12, 17 Nov 1868.
Wanganui Evening Herald, 9 Nov. 1868
Wanganui Times, 7 Nov. 1868
Weekly News, 19 Dec. 1868
Whitmore, Collection, 2
Whitmore, Papers, A.
Whitmore, *Last Maori War,* pp. 46-7
[Whitmore], 'West Coast Campaign'

Chapter Ten: Handley's Woolshed
AD, 1/1868: 4370, 4412, 4337
AJHR, 1869, A-3, A-10
BPP, Vol. 15, pp. 54-7
Bushranging Volunteers, Terms of Service
E. Maxwell, *Recollections,* p. 64
'Extract Books', Vol A.
Gibson, Letters
Gorton, *Some Home Truths,* pp 90-3
Grey Collection – Hauhau War Correspondence
Gudgeon, *Defenders,* pp. 312-13
Gudgeon, *Reminiscences,* p. 202
Harrop, 'Notes to Maxwell Diary'
Hunter, Diary
Livingston, Diary, Nov.-Dec. 1868
Lovegrove, Articles
Maxwell, Diary
McDonnell, Papers, (ATL), 23
New Zealand Advertiser. 27 Nov.-2 Dec. 1868
Newland, 'Campaign on the West Coast'
O'Halloran, Autobiography
Rusden, *History of New Zealand,* Vol. 2, p. 504
Rusden, *Tragedies in New Zealand* (including eyewitness accounts in full)
Smart and Bates, *Wanganui,* pp. 223-6
Stafford, Papers, 48
Waitotara School and District History, pp. 27-8

Wanganui Evening Herald, Nov.-Dec. 1868
Whitmore, *Last Maori War,* pp. 69-74
[Whitmore], 'West Coast Campaign'
Wright, 'Skirmish at Tauranga Ika'

Chapter Eleven: The Brink
AD, 8/1
AJHR, 1869, A-10, A1A, A-3F
AJHR, 1870, A-21
Bowen, Confidential report
BPP, Vol. 15, pp. 283-6, 292-5, 305-21, 378-80
CO, 209/210
Carrington, Diary, 16-24 Feb. 1869
Cowan *Wars,* Vol. 2, pp. 302-10
Cyclopaedia, Vol. 6, p. 125
'Extract Books', Vol. B
Fildes Collection, 631
Gledhill, Journal, 13 Feb. 1869
Grey Collection — Munro Letters
Gudgeon, *Defenders,* pp. 90-2
Hooker, Diary, 16-25 Feb. 1869
'Inquest Proceedings on those murdered at the Whitecliffs'
Jupp, Diary, Feb. 1869
McDonnell, Papers, ATL, 17
McLean, Papers (TSS), Vol. 29, 30, 31
McLean, Papers, 21, 22, 23, 45
Moorsom, Papers, 60
Nelson Evening Mail, 2 June 1931 (David Cockburn)
New Zealand Advertiser, Nov. 1868-Jan. 1869
New Zealand Mission Letterbook
Parris, Papers
Petersen, *Monrad,* pp. 109-15
Scholefield, *Richmond-Atkinson Papers,* Vol. 2, pp. 276, 282
Stafford, Papers, 38B, 42
Wanganui Chronicle, Nov.-Dec. 1868
Wanganui Evening Herald, 9 Nov. 1868, 1 Jan. 1869
Wanganui Times, 21 Jan., 25 Feb. 1869
Weekly News, Dec. 1868-Jan. 1869
Wells, *Taranaki,* pp. 281-7
Whitmore, Collection, 2
Whitmore, Papers, A
[Whitmore], 'West Coast Campaign'
Williams, Transcripts, 3
Young, *Hints on House Defence*

Chapter Twelve: Tauranga Ika
AD, 1/1868: 4161
AD, 1/1869: 69-722
AD, 8/1

AJHR, 1869, A-12, A-10
BPP, Vol. 15, p. 356-7
CO, 209/210
Cowan, Papers, 41 C
Cowan, *Kimble Bent,* pp. 226-61
'Extract Books', Vols. A, B, C.
Fildes Collection, 638, 629, 625
Gascoyne, *Soldiering in New Zealand,* p. 88
Gorton, *Some Home Truths,* pp. 98-107
Gudgeon, *Defenders,* p. 262
Gudgeon, *Reminiscences,* pp. 256-7
Hooper, 'Military Tradition', pp. 64-6
Hunter, Diary, Jan.-Feb. 1869
'Juvenis','Pages from the Past'
Lovegrove, Articles
'Maori Troubles' File
McDonnell, Papers, 17
McLean, Papers (TSS), Vol 30
McLean, Papers, 48, 278
Putnam, Diary, Jan.-Feb. 1869.
Rusden, *Tragedies in New Zealand,* pp. 567-9
Smart and Bates, *Wanganui,* p. 117
Southern Cross, 25 Dec. 1868
Stafford, Papers, 48, 38 B
Waitotara School and District History, pp. 28-9
Wanganui Chronicle, Jan.-Feb. 1869
Wanganui Evening Herald, Jan.-Mar. 1869
Wanganui Times, Jan.-Feb. 1869
Weekly News, Jan.-Feb., 8 May 1869
Whitmore, Collection, 2
Whitmore, Papers, A
Whitmore, *Last Maori War,* pp. 89-94
[Whitmore], 'West Coast Campaign'

Chapter Thirteen: The Lion at Bay
AD, 1/1869: 723-1584
ADM, 1/6096
ADM, 53/9888
AJHR, A-10, A-12
Austin, Diary, 3 Feb. 1869
BPP, Vol. 15. pp. 362-4, 382-6, 391-6
Cowan, Papers, 41 B, 41 D, 18
Cowan, *Kimble Bent,* pp. 262-76
Cowan, *Wars,* Vol. 2, pp. 292-6
Cyclopaedia, Vol. 1, p. 1346
'Extract Books, B
Gascoyne, *Soldiering in New Zealand,* pp. 88-93
Gorton, *Some Home Truths,* pp. 114-22
Gudgeon, *Defenders,* pp. 83, 150-1

Gudgeon, *Reminiscences*, pp. 255-61
Hooper, 'Military Tradition', p. 67
McDonnell, Papers, ATL (Featherston Letters)
McLean, Papers (TSS), Vol. 31
Moorsom, Papers, 60
Newall, Diary, Feb.-March 1869
Putnam, Diary, Feb.-March 1869
Stafford, Papers, 48, 38, B
Wanganui Chronicle, 16 Feb. 1869
Wanganui Times, Feb.-March 1869
Weekly News, Feb.-March 1869
Whitmore, Collection, 2
Whitmore, Papers, A, B
Whitmore, *Last Maori War*, pp. 94-124
[Whitmore], 'West Coast Campaign'

Chapter Fourteen: The Hunt

AD 1/1868: 4932
AJHR, 1869, A-3, A-3A, A-3B, A-3F, A-10, A-12, D-12
AJHR, 1870, A-4, A-13, A-16, A-21
AJHR, 1880, G-2
Austin, Diary
Bremer, 'The Patea-Waverley District', pp. 60-81
Buist, 'The Maori', pp. 11-13
Cowan, Papers, 41 D, 18
Cowan, *Kimble Bent*, pp. 277-97
Cowan, *Wars*, Vol.2, pp. 296-304, 310-13
'Extract Books', Vol. C
Fildes Collection, 638
Ginger, Record Book
Gudgeon, *Reminiscences*, pp. 261-9
Hunter, Diary, March, 1869
McLean, Papers, 278, 48, 38
McLean, Papers, (TSS), Vol. 31
Newall, Diary, March, 1869
Police Department, 1/1: 1868-9
Putnam, Diary, March-April 1869
Roberts, *Patea*, pp. 56-60
Scholefield, *Richmond-Atkinson Papers*, Vol. 2, pp. 281-8
Smart and Bates, *Wanganui*, pp. 127-31
Southern Cross, 7 June 1869
Takiora, 'Notes'
The Times, 12 July, 30 Nov. 1869
Waitotara School and District History, pp. 29-31
Wanganui Weekly Herald, Aug-Sept. 1869
Weekly News, April-May 1869
Whitmore, Collection, 2
Whitmore, *Last Maori War*, pp. 124-50
[Whitmore], 'West Coast Campaign'

Epilogue
AJHR, 1870, A–4
AJHR, 1880, G–2
Bremer, 'The Patea-Waverley District', pp. 79-82
Brookes, *Frontier Life*, p.49
Cowan, Papers, 41B, 18
Cowan, *Kimble Bent*, pp. 293-305
Evans, MS File
Fildes Collection, 629, 631
Finn, *Datus,* p. 168
Finnerty, Letters
Gapes, Letters
Gascoyne, *Soldiering in New Zealand*, p.116
Gordon, Papers
Gordon, 'Titokowaru's Tea Party'
Grey Collection – Rusden, McDonnell, Whitmore Letters
Houston, *Maori Life*, pp. 205-7
Howitt, *Pioneer Looks Back*, pp. 61-73
'Juvenis', 'Pages From the Past'
'Kapuni' series
Leslie et. al, *Patea: A Centennial History*, pp. 133-4
McDonnell, Papers, APL, 5
McDonnell Papers, ATL, 10, 46
McDonnell, NZ Medal File
McLean, Papers, 48, 605
NZPD, 27 Aug. 1894
Roberts, *Hawera*, pp. 334-45
Roberts, *Patea*, pp. 37-8, 84-5
Scholefield, *Dictionary of New Zealand Biography*
Scott, *Ask That Mountain*
Skeets, Letters
Skinner, Collection
Skinner, Diary
Slater, *Fifty Years of Volunteering*, pp. 93-4
Smart and Bates, *Wanganui*, pp. 219-23
Stafford, Papers, 38 B
Titokowaru, Papers
Waitotara School and District History, p. 45
Waldegrave, Notes
Whitmore, Papers, C

BIBLIOGRAPHY

Admiralty Archives, PRO
  ADM 1/6054   Despatches from the Australian Station, 1868-9
  ADM 1/6096   Despatches from the Australian Station, 1868-9
  ADM 53/9888 Log of HMS *Blanche*
Alexander, J.E., *Bush Fighting. Illustrated by Remarkable Actions and Incidents of the Maori War in New Zealand*, London 1873
Anon., *A Campaign on the West Coast . . . under the command of Major General Chute*, Wanganui 1866
Appendices to the Journals of the House of Representatives, 1864-72, 1880
Army Department Archives, NA
  AD 1/1866-9   Inwards Correspondence, 1866-9
  AD Registers   Registers of Inwards Correspondence, 1866-9
  AD 8/1   Outwards Telegrams, 1864-8
  AD 31/13   Papers Relating to the Survey of Confiscated Lands in the Patea District, 1866-7
  AD 32/5004   Return of Men Courtmartialled, 1864-8
  AD 32/5011   Papers Relating to the Mutiny of No. 5 A.C.
  AD 32/5013   Turuturu Mokai Reports
  AD 32/0-4999   New Zealand War Medal Files
Atkinson, Arthur S., Diary, 1866-7 (Richmond-Atkinson Papers), ATL
Austin, Samuel, Diary, 1844-70, WM

Babbage, S.B., *Hauhauism. An Episode in the Maori Wars, 1863-6*, Wellington 1937
Belich, James, 'Titokowaru's War and its Place in New Zealand History', Victoria University of Wellington MA Thesis, 1979
Belich, James, *The New Zealand Wars and the Victorian Interpretation of Racial Conflict*, Penguin edn, Auckland 1988
Booth, William, Letters, WM
Bowen, G.F., Confidential Report to Lord Lyttelton on the Maori War, 1869, ATL
Bowen, G.F., Letters 1868-9, ATL
Bremer, Ione Margaret, 'The Early Development of the Patea-Waverley District: A Study of the Problems of Settling Confiscated Land', Victoria University of Wellington MA Thesis, 1962
British Parliamentary Papers, Irish University Press Series, New Zealand, Vols. 3, 14, 15
Brookes, E.S., *Frontier Life, Taranaki*, Auckland 1892
Broughton, Ruka, 'The Origins of Ngaarauru Kiitahi', Victoria University of Wellington MA Thesis, 1979
Buick, T. Lindsay, *New Zealand's First War*, Wellington 1926
Buist, A.G., 'The Maori' in K.W. Thompson (ed.), *The Legacy of Turi*
Bushranging Volunteers, Terms of Enrolment, 23 November 1868, WM

Caines, William, Diary Extracts, WM
Cameron, John, Papers 1868-9, WM
Carrington, Wellington, Diary, 1865-9, TM

Chapple, L.J.B. and Veitch, H.C., *Wanganui*, Hawera 1939
Church, Ian, 'Heartland of Aotea. Maori and European in South Taranaki Before the Maori Wars', unpublished TS, WM
Clampitt, G., MS File, TM
Clark, Paul, *Hauhau: The Pai Marire Search for a Maori Identity*, Auckland 1975
Colonial Office Archives
    209/179-186   Inward Correspondence, 1864
    209/208-210   Inward Correspondence, 1868-9
Cooper, Barbara, 'George Hamilton-Browne: An Investigation into his Career in New Zealand', *Bay of Plenty Journal of History*, Vol.33, No.2, Nov 1985 (copy kindly supplied by the author)
Cowan, James, *The Adventures of Kimble Bent*, London, Wellington and Christchurch 1911
Cowan, James, *Hero Stories of New Zealand*, Wellington 1935
Cowan, James, *The New Zealand Wars and the Pioneering Period* (2 vols.), Wellington 1922-3
Cowan, James, Papers, ATL
Cox, Alfred, *Men of Mark in New Zealand*, Christchurch 1886
Christchurch Star, 'Orakau' articles, 1916
'Cyclopaedia of New Zealand (6 vols), Wellington and Christchurch 1897-1908

Dalton, B.J., 'The Military Reputation of Sir George Grey: The Case of Weraroa', *New Zealand Journal of History*, Vol.9, No.2, 1975
Davidson, Janet, *The Prehistory of New Zealand*, Auckland 1984
Dictionary of National Biography, Vol.15, London 1908
Dillon, Constantine, *The Dillon Letters/The Letters of the Hon. Constantine Dillon 1842-53* (ed. C.A. Sharp), Wellington 1954
Downes, W.T., *Old Whanganui*, Hawera 1915
Downes, W.T., Papers, ATL. (Reference to Titokowaru's horse, 'Niu Tirene', kindly supplied by Mr David Young)

Evans, Ann, MS File, TM
Evening Post, Wellington, 1866
'Extract Books', WM

Fildes, Horace, Collection, Victoria University of Wellington Library
Finn, George, *Datus: A Chronology of New Zealand from the Time of the Moa*, Auckland 1931
Finnerty, Charles, Letters, TM
Fox, William, *The War in New Zealand*, London 1866

Gascoyne, F.J.W., *Soldiering in New Zealand, being the Reminiscences of a Veteran*, London 1916
Gibson, John, Letters, 1868, ATL
Ginger, Diston, Record Book, ATL
Gledhill, U.F., Journal, TM
Gordon, W.F., Papers, ATL
Gordon, W.F., 'Titokowaru's Tea Party', *Taranaki Herald*, 1935, Fildes Collection, 625

Gorton, Edward, *Some Home Truths re. the Maori War 1863-9 on the West Coast of New Zealand*, London 1901

Grace, Morgan, S., *A Sketch of the New Zealand War*, London 1899

Greaves, George, *Memoirs of General Sir George Richard Greaves*, London 1924

Gretton, G. le M., *Campaigns and History of the Royal Irish Regiment 1684-1902*, n.p. 1911

Grey, George, Collection, APL

Gudgeon, T.W., *The Defenders of New Zealand*, Auckland 1887

Gudgeon, T.W., *Reminiscences of the War in New Zealand*, London 1879

Gudgeon, W.E., 'Whakamomore', *Journal of the Polynesian Society*, No.59, Sept. 1906

Hamilton-Browne, G., *Campfire Yarns of the Lost Legion*, London n.d.

Hamilton-Browne, G., *With the Lost Legion in New Zealand*, London n.d.

Hammond, Thomas Godfrey, *In the Beginning: The History of a Mission*, Hawera 1915

Hammond, Thomas Godfrey, *The Story of Aotea*, Christchurch 1924

Harrop, A.J., *England and the Maori Wars*, London 1937

Harrop, David, 'Notes to the Diary of George Maxwell' (copy kindly provided by Mr John Macdonald)

Hawes, Robert N., Papers, ATL

Hawke's Bay Herald, Dec. 1868

[Hawthorne, James], *A Dark Chapter from New Zealand History*, Napier 1869; Capper Reprint 1974

Hooker, Nathaniel, Diary, 1869, TM

Hooper, Keith Charles, 'The Rise of New Zealand's Military Tradition: The Wellington West Coast and Taranaki Regiment (5 Battalion NZIR) 1855-1964', Massey University MA Thesis, 1979

Houston, John, *Maori Life in Old Taranaki*, Wellington 1965

Houston, John, Papers, ATL

Houston, John, *Turuturu Mokai: An Historic Survey*, Hawera 1958

Howitt, W.K., *A Pioneer Looks Back*, Auckland 1945

Hunter, Moore, Diary, [1869]-1873, ATL

Ingram, C.W.N., *New Zealand Shipwrecks 1795-1975* (5th edn), Wellington 1977

'Inquest Proceedings on those murdered at the Whitecliffs', 18 Feb. 1869, TM

Jupp, George, Diary, Vol.2, 1860-69, TM

Justice Department Archives J1/1868:1903

'Juvenis', 'Pages from the Past' (*Taranaki Daily News* series, 1921), Fildes Collection, 638

'Kapuni' series, *Hawera Star*, 1959

Leslie, Margaret, 'Social History' in Thompson, K.W. (ed), *The Legacy of Turi*

Leslie, Margaret, Baker, Livingston and Church, Ian (eds), *Patea: A Centennial History*, Palmerston North 1981

Livingston, James, Diary, 1868-9, WM

Lomax, H.A., Letters, 1868-9 (in Robert Pharazyn Papers), WM

Lovegrove, C.L., Articles on the military history of Wanganui, *Wanganui Herald*, 1963

Lovegrove, C.L., 'When Wanganui Stood to Arms', unpublished TS, ATL

McDonnell Family Papers, WM
McDonnell, Thomas, 'Account of a Reconnaissance at Paparata', Grey Collection, ATL
[McDonnell, Thomas], *An Explanation of the principal causes which led to the present war on the West Coast . . .,* Wanganui 1869
McDonnell, Thomas, 'General Chute's Campaign on the West Coast', *Monthly Review* 2, 1890
McDonnell, Thomas, 'Incidents of the War: Tales of Maori Character and Customs', in Gudgeon, *The Defenders of New Zealand*
[McDonnell, Thomas], 'A Maori History of the Pakeha-Maori Wars in New Zealand' in Gudgeon, *The Defenders of New Zealand*
McDonnell, Thomas, New Zealand Medal File, AD, 32/3653
McDonnell, Thomas, Papers, APL
McDonnell, Thomas, Papers, ATL
McDonnell, Thomas, 'The Survey of the Confiscated Lands Campaign on the West Coast, 1866-1869', *Monthly Review* 2, 1890
McLean, Donald, Papers, ATL
McLean, Donald, Papers TS Volumes, ATL
McLintock, A.H. (ed), *The Encyclopaedia of New Zealand* (3 vols), Wellington 1966
Mantell, W.B.D., Papers, ATL
'Maori Troubles' Folder, WM
Maxwell, E., *Recollections and Reflections of an Old New Zealander*, Dunedin and Wellington 1937
Maxwell, George, Diary, 1868 (copy kindly provided by Mr John Macdonald)
Moorsom Papers, India Office Library, London

Nelson Evening Mail, 2 June 1931
Newall, Stuart, Diary, 1869, ATL
Newland, John, *Diary of John Newland 1841-73*, New Plymouth 1959
Newland, William, 'The Campaign on the West Coast, North Island against Titoko Waru June 1866 to the end of 1869', TS, TM
New Zealand Advertiser, 1868-9
New Zealand Gazette, 1868-9
New Zealand Mission Letterbook, 1868-70, CMS Archives, London
New Zealand Parliamentary Debates, 1868-9

O'Donnell, H. (ed), *Historical Records of the 14th Regt.,* Devonport 1894
O'Halloran, George Stuart, MS Autobiography, ATL
Owen, J.A, *After Shipwreck*, London 1889

Parham, W.T., *John Roberts, NZ.C. A Man in His Time. A Life of Lt. Col. John Mackintosh Roberts (1840-1928)*, Whakatane 1983
Parham, W.T., *Von Tempsky — Adventurer*, London and Auckland
Parris, Robert, Papers, TM
Patea Mail, 14 Dec. 1878
Paymaster's Order Book, Patea Field Force, July-Aug. 1868, WM
Petersen, G.C., *D.G. Monrad: Scholar, Statesman, Priest and New Zealand Pioneer*, Levin 1965

Phillips, Henry, Confession, 7 Sept. 1882, in W.E. Gudgeon Papers, TM
Pihama, Hone, List of Payments to, TM
Police Department Archives, NA 1/1 1868-9
Porter, T.W.R., *Major Ropata Wahawa. The Story of His Life and Times*, Gisborne 1897
Power, W. Tyrone, *Sketches in New Zealand/ With Pen and Pencil*, London 1849
Prickett, Nigel, 'The Archaeology of a Military Frontier: Taranaki, New Zealand, 1860-1881', Auckland University PhD Thesis, 1981
Punch, or the Auckland Charivari, 1868-9
Punch, or the Wellington Charivari, 1868
Putnam, Philip, Diary, 1868-9, ATL

Rawson, G.I., 'The Evolution of the Rural Settlement Pattern of Lowland South Taranaki 1860-1920', Canterbury University MA Thesis, 1967
Roberts, C.J., *Centennial History of Hawera and the Waimate Plains*, Hawera 1939
Roberts, C.J., *Official History of the County of Patea*, Hawera 1937
Rusden, G.W., *Auretanga; Groans of the Maoris*, London 1888
Rusden, G.W., *History of New Zealand* (3 vols), Melbourne 1889
[Rusden, G.W.], *Tragedies in New Zealand in 1868 and 1881, Discussed in England in 1886 and 1887*, London 1888

Scholefield, G.H. (ed), *Dictionary of New Zealand Biography* (2 vols), Wellington 1940
Scholefield, G.H. (ed), *Richmond-Atkinson Papers* (2 vols), Wellington 1960
Scott, Dick, *Ask That Mountain. The Story of Parihaka*, Auckland 1975
Sinclair, Keith, *The Origins of the Maori Wars*, Wellington 1957
Skeets, Harry M., Sketchbooks and Letters, TM
Skinner, W.H., Collection, TM
Skinner, W.H., Diary, 1880, New Plymouth Public Library
Skinner, W.H., *Reminiscences of a Taranaki Surveyor*, New Plymouth 1946
Slater, H., *Fifty Years of Volunteering*, Christchurch 1910
Smart, M.J.G. and Bates, A.P., *The Wanganui Story*, Wanganui 1972
Smith, S. Percy, Letterbook, 1866-8, ATL
Smith, S. Percy, *History and Traditions of the Maoris of the West Coast, North Island of New Zealand, Prior to 1840*, New Plymouth 1910
Smith, S. Percy, *Maori Wars of the Nineteenth Century* (2nd edn), Christchurch 1910
Sole, Laraine, *Waverley 1860-1920*, n.p., n.d.
Southern Cross (or *Daily Southern Cross*), 1861, 1868-9
Stafford, E.W., Papers, ATL
Stronge, J.S., 'The History of Egmont County', unpub MS, 1973, TM
Sydney Morning Herald, 1868

Takiora, Lucy, MS, TM
Takiora, Lucy, 'Notes Taken During Troublous Times', in W.F. Gordon Papers, ATL
Taranaki Almanac, 1869, New Plymouth 1869
Taranaki Herald, New Plymouth 1861, 1866-8
Taranaki Provincial Council, Hotel Licences, TM
Taranaki Provincial Gazette, 1868
Taylor, Basil K., Letters to CMS, 1861-78, CN/0 86, CMS Archives, London
Taylor, R., *Te Ika A Maui, or New Zealand and Its Inhabitants*, London 1855

Taylor, Richard, *The Past and Present of New Zealand With Its Prospects for the Future*, London and Wanganui 1868
Thompson, K.W., *The Legacy of Turi: An Historical Geography of Patea County*, Palmerston North 1976
Times, The, London 1868-9
Titokowaru Papers, WM

Vale, E. Earle, *Some Interesting Occurrences in Early Auckland City and Province*, n.p., n.d.
Von Tempsky, G.F., 'Memoranda of the New Zealand Campaign', Auckland Institute and Museum
Von Tempsky, G.F., Papers Relating to, Auckland Institute and Museum.

'W.B.', 'Taupo Notes', WM
Waitotara School Centennial 1876-1976: School and District History, Wanganui 1976
Waldegrave, Dorothy, Notes, TM
Wanganui Chronicle, 1868-9
Wanganui Evening Herald, 1868-70
Wanganui Herald, 1923, 1963
Wanganui Times, 1868-9
Wanganui Weekly Herald, 1869
War Office Archives, PRO
    WO 33/16 'Journals of the Deputy Quartermaster General in New Zealand from 24 Dec 1861 to 13 Oct. 1865'
    WO 33/16 'Selections from Despatches and Letters Relative to the Conduct of Military Operations in New Zealand, 1861-5'
Warre, H.J. (ed), *Historical Records of the 57th Regiment*, London 1878
Warrington, E.C.R., 'Pakeha Agriculture', in K.W. Thompson, *The Legacy of Turi*
Weekly News, Auckland 1869
Weekly Press, 1902
Wellington Almanack 1869, Wellington 1869
Wellington Independent, 1868-9
Wells, B., *History of Taranaki*, New Plymouth 1878
Wesleyan Aotea Mission, Report of the New Plymouth Circuit, 1863, TM
Whitmore, G.S., Collection, ATL
Whitmore, G.S., Papers, Hawke's Bay Museum, Napier
Whitmore, G.S., *The Last Maori War in New Zealand Under the Self-Reliant Policy*, London 1902
[Whitmore, G.S.], 'West Coast Campaign, from the outbreak of rebellion in June 1868 to the appointment of Col. Whitmore to the Command' (mainly newspaper clippings), ATL
Williams, E.T., Transcripts from various New Zealand Archives, Rhodes House Library, Oxford
Wilson, Owen, 'Reminiscences of the Kapuni District', TS, TM
Winks, Robin, 'The Doctrine of Hau-hauism', *Journal of the Polynesian Society*, Vol.62, No.3, Sept. 1953
Wright, John D., 'Account of a Skirmish at Tauranga Ika', WM

Young, H.W., *Hints on House Defence, Blockhouses and Redoubts*, Wellington 1869

INDEX